THE SARUM MISSAL

Alcuin Club Collections

XI

THE

SARUM MISSAL

IN ENGLISH

NEWLY TRANSLATED BY

FREDERICK E. WARREN, B.D., F.S.A.

*Rector of Bardwell, Hon. Canon of Ely, Late Fellow of
St. John's College, Oxford*

PART I

*Alcuin Club Edition. Printed by Alexander Moring Ltd. at
The De La More Press, 32 George Street, Hanover Square, W.*

A. R. MOWBRAY & CO. LTD.

LONDON: 28 Margaret Street, Oxford Circus, W.
OXFORD: 9 High Street
MILWAUKEE, U.S.A.: YOUNG CHURCHMAN CO.

1913

CONTENTS OF PART I.

CONTENTS OF PART II.

FOR PART I.

48557

CONTENTS OF PART II.—*continued.*

INTRODUCTION.

The Sarum Missal selected for translation in these volumes is the folio printed edition of 1526.

A perfect copy of it may be seen in two of our largest public libraries, under the following (present) press-marks:

Oxford, Bodleian Library, Gough Missals, 23;

Cambridge, University Library, Vel. A. 52. 3.

There are three other copies known, one in the Chapter Library at York; one at Maynooth College; and one (imperfect) the property of the late F. H. Dickinson, Esq. There is not a copy in the British Museum, where, however, there is a nearly perfect copy of the very similar folio edition of the Sarum Missal printed by Regnault at Paris in 1531.

The only modern reprint of the Sarum Missal (Burnt-island, 1861-83) is a reprint of the 1526 edition.[1] It was therefore, obviously, the most convenient edition to take from which to make the present translation.

It is desirable to give a description of its arrangement, and an outline of its contents, especially as its scheme of signatures and foliation (not pagination) is complicated, and not at all clear for purposes of reference. References to pages in the present reprint cannot be given here, because this Introduction is being prefixed to the first volume before the whole of the text of both volumes has been set up; but such pages will for the most part be easily found by reference to Indexes 2 and 3.

[1] With the exception of the Kalendar, which for some unexplained reason was printed from the 1497 edition. There are some, though not many, variations. The Kalendar in this volume is from the 1526 edition.

COLLATION.—Foll. [8] + clvi. (but cxxix.-cxxxviii. are omitted in the foliation) + [16] + lxxii. + lx. + [12]. Signatures a⁸, a-r⁸, A⁶, B⁴, C⁶, A-G⁸, H⁴, H-I⁶.

CONTENTS.

---

[1] *Incipit dictamen beati Augustini de regimine sacerdotum. Viri venerabiles, sacerdotes dei*, etc.

[2] Commencing, *Presbyter in mensa Christi quid agis bene pensa*, etc.

[3] *Cautele misse.*

SIGNATURES.	FOLIATION.	
A i—vi	None.	Ordinary and Canon of the Mass, includ-
B i—iv	None.	ing Prayers in prostration, and Mass end-
C i—vi	None.	ings. B ii and B iii are vellum. A full picture of the crucifixion occupies B ii *v*. The Canon begins on B iii *r*. The three signatures are red.
A i *r*—I viii *v*	i *r*—lxxii *v*	Proper of Saints: Vigil of St. Andrew (Nov. 29),—St. Linus (Nov. 26).
A i *r*—C ii *r*	i *r*—xviii *r*	Common of Saints.
C ii *r*—H iii *r*	xviii *v*—lix *r*	Votive Masses.
H iii *r*—H iv *r*	lix *r*—lx *r*	Farsed forms of Kyrie eleyson.
H iv *r*—H iv *v*	lx *r*—lx *v*	Short Index of Contents, and fuller Index of Common of Saints and of Votive Masses.
H i *r*—I vi *r*	None.	Prologue to *accentuarium*, and *accentuarium*, *i.e.*, a list of words, marking their long and short syllables or vowels, to save the priest from making false quantities when saying mass.
I vi *r*	None.	Colophon. "Explicit missale ad usum ecclesie *Sarum* optimis formulis (vt res ipsa indicat) diligentissime : reuisum ac correctum cum multis annotatiunculis ac litteris alphabeticis euangeliorum atque epistolarum originem indicantibus. *Impressum* impensis et sumptibus honesti viri *Francisci Regnault* librarij iurati alme vniuersitatis *Parisiensis* commorantis *Parisius* in vico sancti *Iacobi:* in intersignio elephantis. Anno domini M.CCCCC.XXVI. die penultima mensis Octobris." [1]
I vi *v*	None.	Blank.

It has not been found possible to preserve the above order of contents in the present translation. For purposes of pagination and cross-reference it was found necessary to re-arrange the order in the following way:

1. Kalendar
2. Ordinary and Canon of the Mass
3. Proper of Seasons
4. Common of Saints
5. Votive Masses
6. Proper of Saints.

[1] The words in italics are printed in red.

INTRODUCTION.

Votive Masses differ so much in different editions of the Sarum Missal, and of other early missals, that it may be useful to append a complete list of them as they occur in the 1526 edition of the Sarum Missal.

VOTIVE MASSES.

SIGNATURE.	FOLIATION.	TITLE.
c ii r	xviii r	Mass of the most holy Trinity [Sunday].
c ii v	xviii v	Mass of the angels [Monday].
c iii r	xix r	Mass entitled "The salvation of the people" [Tuesday].
c iii v	xix v	Mass in commemoration of the Holy Ghost [Wednesday].
c iiii v	xx v	Mass in commemoration of corpus Christi [Thursday].
c v r	xxi r	Mass of the holy Cross [Friday].
c v v	xxi v	Mass of the five wounds of our Lord Jesus Christ.
c vi v	xxii v	Mass on the feast of our Lord's crown.
c vii v	xxiii v	Mass of the B. V. M.[1] [Saturday].
		Daily Masses of the B. V. M., *viz.*:
		Mass of the B. V. M. in Advent.
		Mass of the B. V. M. from Christmas Day to the Purification.
		Mass of the B. V. M. from the Purification to Advent.
D iiii r	xxviii r	Mass for peace.
D iiii v	xxviii v	Mass for the king.
D v r	xxix r	Mass for invoking the grace of the Holy Ghost.
D v v	xxix v	Mass for oneself.
D vi r	xxx r	Mass of request for the gift of the Holy Ghost.
D vi r	xxx r	Mass for sinners.
D vi v	xxx v	Mass for penitents.
D vii r	xxxi r	Mass for the inspiration of divine wisdom.
D vii v	xxxi v	Mass for trouble of heart.
D vii v	xxxi v	Mass for a sick person.
D viii r	xxxii r	Mass for the welfare of a friend.
D viii v	xxxii v	Mass for fair weather.
E i r	xxxiii r	Mass for rain.

[1] This is the third of the three daily Masses of the B. V. M., *viz.*, that from the Purification to Advent.

[1] *i.e.* an Office for the Churching of Women.

SIGNATURE.	FOLIATION.	TITLE.
F iii *r*	xliii *r*	Blessing of bread on Sundays.[1]
F iii *r*	xliii *r*	Order of service for pilgrims.
F iiii *v*	xliv *v*	Mass for travellers.
F v *v*	lxv *v*	Mass for the dead.
		Mass for the dead, on the day of burial.
		Mass for the dead, on the thirtieth day.
		Mass for the dead, on anniversaries.
		Mass for the dead, for bishops.
		Mass for the dead, for brethren and sisters.
		Mass for the dead, for benefactors [1].
		Mass for the dead, for an abbot.
		Mass for the dead, for a priest.
		Mass for the dead, for a father and mother.
		Mass for the dead, for any deceased person.
		Mass for the dead, for a deceased friend.
		Mass for the dead, for one overtaken by sudden death.
		Mass for the dead, for male relations.
		Mass for the dead, for female relations.
		Mass for the dead, for a deceased woman.
		Mass for the dead, for trentals.
		Mass for the dead, for benefactors [2]
		Mass for the dead, for those at rest in a cemetery.
		Mass for the dead, for those for whom we are bound to pray.
		Mass for the dead, for all the faithful dead.
G ii *r*	l *r*	General prayers.
G iii *r*	li *r*	Trental of St. Gregory. [death.
G iiii *r*	lii *r*	Mass of Pope Clement Ifor escaping sudden
G v *r*	liii *r*	Gospel composed by Pope John XXII.
G v *r*	liii *r*	Mass of St. Sebastian in time of pestilence.
G v *v*		Mass of St. Erasmus.
G vi *r*	liiii *r*	Mass of St. Roch.
G vi *v*	liiii *v*	Mass of St. Christopher.
G vii *r*	lv *r*	Mass of St. Anthony.
G vii *v*	lv *v*	Mass of St. Raphael, Archangel.
G viii *v*	lvi *v*	Mass of St. Gabriel.
H i *r*	lvii *r*	Mass of the Compassion or Lamentation of the B. V. M.
H ii v	lviii *v*	Mass of St. Barbara.
H ii v	lviii *v*	Three prayers of the Passion of the Lord composed and indulgenced by Pope Innocent III.

[1] This is a duplicate. The form has already been given on Signature a viii *v*; no fol. See Part I., p. 17.

The Psalm after the Office, the Gradual and its Verses, the Offertory, the Communion and the Tracts, are printed in smaller type. This feature has been preserved except in the case of the Tracts which are printed in the larger type like the Sequences. The rubrics printed in red are represented by italics. The titles and head-lines also printed in red are represented by capitals.

The following portions of the 1526 edition have been omitted:

1. Tables for finding common and bisextile years, Sunday letters, etc. (sig. a i *v*).

2. Three lines at the top of each month in the Kalendar, with two additional lines at the top of January, and four lines or more at the bottom of each month, giving the lengths of months, days, and nights, the two unlucky days in each month, directions for feeding, bleeding, bathing etc. These are of astronomical and antiquarian, rather than of liturgical, interest or importance. Also hexameter lines at the bottom of each page from June to November, inclusive, giving the order in which the books of Holy Scripture are to be read.

3. The *Cautelæ missæ*, or directions of a minute character for the preparation of the celebrant, and for all possible accidents and contingencies at mass (foll. cliv *v*—clvi *v*).[1]

4. A short table of contents, and an index of the Common of Saints and Votive Masses only (fol. H iiii *v*). Fuller and more modern indexes have been substituted for these, partly in this Introduction, partly at the conclusion of these volumes.

5. An *accentuarium*. For explanation see table of Contents in Introduction, p. iii.

6. The introductions frequently prefixed to Epistles and Gospels, *e.g.*, "Thus saith the Lord," or "At that time, Jesus said unto the multitude" or "to his disciples," have been generally omitted, for the purpose of making

---

[1] These have been translated and printed by Dr. F. G. Lee in the "Directorium Anglicanum," 4th edit., London, 1879, pp. 106-118.

the identification of passages of Holy Scripture more easy at first sight; and for the same reason the similar class of sentences or words sometimes, but less frequently, introduced at the end of Epistles and Gospels, has been omitted also.

7. The poem entitled *Dictamen beati Augustini*, see list of Contents in Introduction on p. ii. A translation of this poem by A. H. Pearson has been printed in his "Sarum Missal," 2nd edit., London, 1884, p. 274.

On the other hand, the Sarum Processional and the Sarum Gradual have been utilized in order to present a more complete picture of the elaborate services on Maundy Thursday, Good Friday, Easter Even, and Easter Day.

Quotations and references have, throughout, been taken from and made to the Authorized Version of Holy Scripture, except in the case of the Psalms, which are quoted from the Version in the Book of Common Prayer.

Anglican nomenclature has been used in titles, in the text, and in the running titles at the heads of pages, except in the case of Palm Sunday, and the first of the three last days of Holy Week. Here "Maundy Thursday," "Good Friday," and "Easter Even" have been used instead öf "The Supper of the Lord" (*Cæna Domini*), "The Day of Preparation" (*Dies Parasceues*), and Holy Saturday (*Sabbatum Sanctum*).

The English form of a name has sometimes been used in the case of well-known saints, as in the case of St. Jerome (September 30th); and a more correct Latin form has sometimes been substituted for a less correct form as in the case of St. Chrysogonus (November 24th), but in such cases the Latin form, or the less correct Latin form, has generally been indicated below in a footnote.

The original, even though erroneous, orthography has been retained in the case of some words, *e.g.*, Kyrie eleyson, Alleluya, Osanna, Paraclyte.

The Prayer Book orthography, and form or use of words, although now antiquated, has been retained in some cases, *e.g.*, "quire," "even," "prevent," "memory."

As the last-named word has been used throughout, as it is used in the Anglican Eucharistic Prayer cf Consecration, instead of the more usual and modern word "memorial," it may be worth while to quote one or two examples of this usage.

In the "Injunctions of King Edward VI." in 1547 it is ordered that:

"At evensong-time the responds with all the memories shall be left off for that purpose." [1]

In the "Device for Alteration of Religion" in 1558 it is directed that:

"Where there be more chaplains at the Mass, that they do always communicate with the executor in both kinds. And for her highness' conscience, till then, if there be some other devout sort of prayer or memory, and the seldomer mass." [2]

In the use of capital letters the English Bible and Prayer Book have been followed, in the case of quotations from those books; but in the bulk of the text the 1526 edition has been followed, even where the text is capricious. Thus, both "Altar" and "altar" will be found in a rubric preceding the Nicene Creed. The only exceptions are in the case of such words as "Christus" and "Ecclesia," which are almost invariably so printed, and which we have always presented as "Christ" and almost always as "Church," though occasionally a small initial "c" or "e" makes its appearance, obviously through printers' inadvertence, or failure of fount of type.

In the *Offertory* for the Twelfth Sunday after Trinity the first ten Latin words are repeated. This has been concluded to be a printer's error, and the repetition has not been reproduced in the English translation. In the *Offertory* in the "Mass for the inspiration of divine wisdom" a similar repetition has been retained. [3]

[1] § 21. Cardwell (E.), "Documentary Annals," Oxford, 1844, vol. i., p 14.
[2] Burnet (G.), "History of the Reformation," Oxford, 1865, vol. v., p. 503.
[3] Part II., page 110.

In addition to the usual abbreviations used in kalendars, which need not be set out at length, or explained here, the following abbreviations have been made use of in the text or the notes :

A.V. for Authorised Version
H.S. for Holy Scripture
P. or p. for page
Ps. for Psalm
R. for Roman Missal or Use
℟. for Response
S. for Sarum Missal or Use
℣. for Verse
Vulg. for Vulgate.

℟. and ℣. have sometimes been printed before a Verse and Response for the sake of clearness, although they do not appear in the printed Sarum Missal.

It would be impossible within the limits of an Introduction to describe the origin and growth of the Sarum Use and its gradual spread throughout the greater part of England, Ireland, and Scotland ; or to discuss the many solved and unsolved problems which exist in connection with its text and ritual.

Those who wish to pursue these points are referred to the Introduction to W. H. Frere's "Use of Sarum," Cambridge, 1898, vol. i., pp. xi.-lxxi., and to J. Wickham Legg's "Introduction to the Westminster Missal," London, 1897, in vol. xii. of the publications of the Henry Bradshaw Society; *Fasciculus* iii., pp. 1404-1441.

Information about services and ceremonial will be found in Index III. to the present volumes. We append here, as being too long for insertion in that Index, the classification of Festivals, Sundays, and Ferias (*i.e.*, non-festal weekdays) according to the Use of Sarum. It is very elaborate, and the rules to be observed in the case of the occurrence or concurrence of any two days were contained in an *Ordinale* or *Directorium Sacerdotum*, commonly called the Pie, which the treatise " Concerning the Service of the Church" at the beginning of the Book of Common Prayer describes thus :

"The number and hardness of the Rules called the Pie, and the manifold changings of the Service, was the cause, that to turn the Book only was so hard and intricate a matter, that many times there was more business to find out what should be read, than to read it when it was found out."

The Pie has been reprinted with Introduction and Notes, under the auspices of the Henry Bradshaw Society, vol. i., London, 1901, vol. ii., 1902. Persons interested can examine it for themselves, and decide whether Archbishop Cranmer's description of it in the Book of Common Prayer is justifiable or not.

Festivals were divided into two classes, Doubles and Simples. Doubles were divided into four classes :

i. *Principal Doubles.*

1. Christmas Day (Dec. 25).
2. Epiphany (Jan. 6).
3. Easter Day.
4. Ascension Day.
5. Whitsunday.
6. Assumption of B.V.M. (Aug. 15).
7. Patron Saint.
8. Dedication Festival.

ii. *Greater Doubles.*

1. Purification of B.V.M. (Feb. 2).
2. Trinity Sunday.
3. Corpus Christi.
4. Visitation of B.V.M. (July 2).
5. Name of Jesus (Aug. 7).
6. Nativity of B. V. M. (Sept. 8).
7. All Saints' Day (Nov. 1).
8. Feast of Relics.

iii. *Lesser Doubles.*

1. Conception of B.V.M. (Dec. 8).
2. St. Stephen (Dec. 26).
3. St. John Evangelist (Dec. 27).
4. Holy Innocents (Dec. 28).
5. St. Thomas of Canterbury (Dec. 29).
6. Circumcision (Jan. 1).
7. Annunciation of our Lord (Mar. 25).
8. Monday in Easter-Week.
9. Tuesday in Easter-Week.
10. Wednesday in Easter-Week.
11. Low Sunday.
12. Monday in Whitsun-Week.
13. Tuesday in Whitsun-Week.
14. Wednesday in Whitsun-Week.
15. Invention of the Holy Cross (May 3).
16. Nativity of St. John Baptist (June 24).
17. SS. Peter and Paul (June 29).
18. St. James (July 25).
19. Exaltation of the Holy Cross (Sept. 14).

Also, though not so marked in the 1526 Kalendar:

   20. Translation of St. Thomas of Canterbury (July 7).
   21. Transfiguration (Aug. 6).

iv. *Inferior Doubles.*

1. St. Andrew (Nov. 30).
2. St. Thomas (Dec. 21).
3. St. Gregory (Mar. 12).
4. St. Ambrose (Apr. 4).
5. St. George (Apr. 23).
6. St. Mark (Apr. 25).
7. SS. Philip and James (May 1).
8. St. Augustine of Canterbury (May 26).
9. St. Bartholomew (Aug. 24).
10. St. Matthew (Sept. 21).
11. St. Michael (Sept. 29).
12. St. Jerome (Sept. 30).
13. Translation of St. Edward (Oct. 13).
14. St. Calixtus (Oct. 14).
15. St. Luke (Oct. 18).
16. SS. Simon and Jude (Oct. 28).

Also, though not so marked in the 1526 Kalendar:

St. Peter's Chair (Feb. 22).   St. Erkenwald (Apr.. 30).
St. Augustine of Hippo (Aug. 28).   All Souls (Nov. 2).[1]

Simple Feasts, though of nine varieties, form three classes:

   1. Simple Feasts with nine lessons, or three lessons with rulers, and triple invitatory.
   2. Simple Feasts with nine lessons, or three lessons with rulers, and double invitatory.
   3. Simple Feasts with three lessons, no rulers, and double or simple invitatory.

Long lists of these are given in Procter (F.) and Wordsworth (Chr.), "Breviarium ad Usum Sarum," fasciculus iii., Cambridge, 1886, index ii., pp. xl.-xliii., and another list of simples of nine lessons and simples of three lessons. *Ib.*, p. xliv.

These distinctions and others, such as "With Nocturn," affect the Breviary more than the Missal, and therefore are not more fully described here.

---

[1] There are variations among the Sarum Kalendars, some of which appear to be merely due to the carelessness of the scribe or the printer; for this remark applies to the Kalendars prefixed both to the earlier MS. and the later printed Sarum Missals.

A useful list of dates of the institution of Festivals from 1008-1457 is given in Wordsworth (Chr.) and Littlehales (H.), "The Old Service Books of the English Church," London, *n.d.*, pp. 190-2 ; also in W. H. Frere's "Sarum Gradual," London, 1895, pp. xxiii.-xxix.

Sundays were divided into four classes. This is in addition to those Sundays which rank as Doubles in the list of Feasts.

1. *Principal Sundays.*

First Sunday in Advent; fifth Sunday in Lent; Palm Sunday.

2. *Greater Sundays.*

Second, third, and fourth Sundays in Advent; all Sundays from Septuagesima to the fourth Sunday in Lent inclusive.

3. *Lesser Sunday.*

Fifth Sunday after Easter, or Rogation Sunday.

4. *Inferior Sundays.*

All other Sundays throughout the year.

Ferial days, *i.e.*, week days, were divided into four classes :

1. *Principal Ferias.*

Ash Wednesday ; Maundy Thursday ; Good Friday ; Holy Saturday ; Vigil of Pentecost.

2. *Greater Ferias.*

All week days from Monday after fifth Sunday in Lent to Wednesday in Holy Week inclusive.

3. *Lesser Ferias.*

All weekdays from Thursday after Ash Wednesday to Saturday after fourth Sunday in Lent inclusive ; Rogation Monday and Wednesday ; the third week in Advent.

4. *Inferior Ferias.*

All other weekdays in Advent.

There were also Vigils and Unoccupied Ferias, at other times of the year, which were few in number, and are not placed among the above four classes.

In conclusion the editor has to thank J. T. Bennett-Poë, Esq., the owner of the copyright, for permission to use the English translation of the Sequences which were printed in the Rev. C. B. Pearson's " Sequences from the Sarum Missal," London, 1871, and in Mr. A. H. Pearson's translation of the " Sarum Missal," 2nd edit., London, 1884. The labour, and in many cases the difficulty, of making a fresh translation would have been great. Some of them are written in rugged and almost untranslatable Latin.

Also the Rev. W. C. Green, Rector of Hepworth, Suffolk, and late Fellow of King's College, Cambridge, who has been the translator in the five following cases:

Easter Even: " Thou leader kind, whose word called forth," etc.

Easter Even: " Thou the holy angels' king," etc. (a Litany).

St. Sebastian: " Let us all with voiceful ring," etc.

St. Roch: " Let us to the Saviour's glory," etc.

St. Anthony: " This our day of holy joy," etc.

Also the proprietors of Hymns Ancient and Modern for permission to use two translations in their collection:

Good Friday: " Sing, my tongue, the glorious battle " (eight verses).

Easter Day: " Hail, festal day," etc.

He has also to thank the Very Rev. Provost Vernon Staley, the General Editor of " The Library of Ecclesiology and Liturgiology for English Readers," of which these volumes form a part, for looking through the proof sheets, and for many useful suggestions.

F. E. WARREN.

Bardwell Rectory,
    Bury St. Edmunds.
        Whitsuntide, 1911.

ERRATA.

PART I.

DAY OF MONTH.	GOLDEN NUMBER.	SUNDAY LETTER.	JANUARY.	RANK.	LESSONS.	INVITATORY.
1	III	A	**Circumcision of Our Lord.**	Lesser double.	9	
2		b	Oct. S. Stephen, Protomartyr.		3	
3	XI	c	Oct. S. John, Ap. and Evan.		3	
4		d	Oct. Holy Innocents, Martt.		3	
5	XIX	e	Oct. S. Thomas, Mart., and S. Edward, K. and Conf.			
6	VIII	f	**Epiphany of Our Lord.**	Principal double.	9	
7		g	Keys of Septuagesima.			
8	XVI	A	Mem. of Lucian, Presb. and his [Compp.			
9	V	b				
10		c				
11	XIII	d	Sun in Aquarius.			
12	II	e				
13		f	Oct. of Epiphany. Middle lessons of S. Hilary.		9	triple.
14	X	g	Felix, Presb. and Mart.		3	simple.
15		A	Maurus, Ab.		3	simple.
16	XVIII	b	Marcellus, Pope and Mart.		3	simple.
17	VII	c	Sulpicius, Bp. and Conf. S. Antony Conf.			
18		d	Prisca, V. and Mart. First day for LXX.		3	simple.
19	XV	e	**Wulstan, Bp. Conf.**		9	
20	IV	f	**SS. Fabian and Sebastian, Martt.**		9	
21		g	**Agnes, V. and Mart.**		9	
22	XII	A	**Vincent, Mart.**		9	
23	I	b				
24		c				
25	IX	d	**Conversion of S. Paul.** Mem. of S. Prejectus. Double.		9	triple.
26		e				
27	XVII	f	Julian, Bp. and Conf.		3	double.
28	VI	g	Agnes II. Keys of Lent.		3	double.
29		A				
30	XIV	b	Batildis, Q. V., not Mart.		3	simple.
31	III	c				

DAY OF MONTH.	GOLDEN NUMBER.	SUNDAY LETTER.	FEBRUARY.	RANK.	LESSONS.	INVITATORY.
1		d	Bridget, V. and Mart.		3	simple.
2	XI	e	Purification of Blessed Mary.	Greater double.	9	
3	XIX	f	Blase, Bp. and Mart.		3	double.
4	VIII	g				
5		A	Agatha, V. and Mart.		9	double.
6	XVI	b	SS. Vedast and Amandus, Bpp.		3	simple.
			[The Sunday next to the first moon after S. Agatha's Day will be XL Sunday.]			
7	VI	c				
8		d				
9	XIII	e	Sun in Pisces.			
10	II	f	Scholastica, V.		3	simple.
11		g	Translation of S. Fredeswide, V.			
12	X	A				
13		b				
14	XVIII	c	Valentine, Bp. and Mart.		3	simple.
15	VII	d				
16		e	Juliana, V. and Mart.		3	simple.
17	XV	f				
18	IV	g				
19		A				
20	XII	b				
21	I	c	Last day for LXX.			
22		d	S. Peter's Chair.		9	triple.
23	IX	e				
24		f	Mathias Ap.		9	double.
			[If it be leap year, the fourth day after S. Peter's Chair will be the Feast of S. Mathias, and the letter f will be counted twice.]			
25	XVII	g				
26	VI	A				
27		b				
28	XIV	c				

DAY OF MONTH.	GOLDEN NUMBER.	SUNDAY LETTER.	MARCH.	RANK.	LESSONS.	INVITATORY.
1	III	d	𝔇𝔞𝔳𝔦𝔡, 𝔅𝔭. 𝔞𝔫𝔡 𝔠𝔬𝔫𝔣.		9	
2		e	𝔠𝔥𝔞𝔡, 𝔅𝔭. 𝔞𝔫𝔡 𝔠𝔬𝔫𝔣.		9	
3	XI	f				
4		g				
5	XIX	A				
6	VIII	b				
7		c	SS. Perpetua and Felicitas, VV. and Martt.		3	
8	XVI	d				
9	V	e				
10		f				
11	XIII	g	Keys of Easter. Sun in Aries. Vernal Equinox.			
12	II	A	𝔊𝔯𝔢𝔤𝔬𝔯𝔶, 𝔓𝔬𝔭𝔢 𝔞𝔫𝔡 𝔠𝔬𝔫𝔣.	Inferior double.	9	
13		b	Last day for Lent to begin.			
14	X	c				
15		d				
16	XVIII	e	Entry of Noah into the Ark.			
17	VII	f	Patrick, Bp. and Conf.		9	
18		g	𝔈𝔡𝔴𝔞𝔯𝔡, 𝔎𝔦𝔫𝔤 𝔞𝔫𝔡 𝔐𝔞𝔯𝔱.		9	
19	XV	A				
20	IV	b	𝔠𝔲𝔱𝔥𝔟𝔢𝔯𝔱, 𝔅𝔭. 𝔞𝔫𝔡 𝔠𝔬𝔫𝔣.		9	
21		c	𝔅𝔢𝔫𝔢𝔡𝔦𝔠𝔱, 𝔄𝔟.		9	
22	XII	d	First day on which Easter can fall.			
23	I	e	Creation of Adam.			
24		f				
25	IX	g	𝔄𝔫𝔫𝔲𝔫𝔠𝔦𝔞𝔱𝔦𝔬𝔫 𝔬𝔣 𝔒𝔲𝔯 𝔏𝔬𝔯𝔡.	Lesser double.	9	
26		A				
27	XVII	b	𝔎𝔢𝔰𝔲𝔯𝔯𝔢𝔠𝔱𝔦𝔬𝔫 𝔬𝔣 𝔒𝔲𝔯 𝔏𝔬𝔯𝔡.	Principal double.		
28	VI	c				
29		d				
30	XIV	e				
31	III	f				

DAY OF MONTH.	GOLDEN NUMBER.	SUNDAY LETTER.	APRIL.	RANK.	LESSONS.	INVITATORY.
1		g				
2	XI	A				
3		b	𝕽𝖎𝖈𝖍𝖆𝖗𝖉, 𝕭𝖕. 𝖆𝖓𝖉 𝕮𝖔𝖓𝖋.		9	
4	XIX	c	𝕬𝖒𝖇𝖗𝖔𝖘𝖊, 𝕭𝖕. 𝖆𝖓𝖉 𝕯𝖔𝖈𝖙.	Inferior double.	9	
5	VIII	d				
6	XVI	e				
7	V	f				
8		g				
9	XIII	A				
10	II	b				
11		c	Sun in Taurus.			
12	X	d				
13		e				
14	XVIII	f	SS. Tyburcius, Valerianus, and Maximus, Martt.		3	
15	VII	g	Keys of the Rogation Days.			
16		A				
17	XV	b				
18	IV	c				
19		d	Alphege, Bp. and Mart.		3	
20	II	e				
21	I	f				
22		g				
23	IX	A	𝕲𝖊𝖔𝖗𝖌𝖊, 𝕸𝖆𝖗𝖙. With ruling of quire.	Inferior double.	3	
24		b				
25	XVII	c	𝕸𝖆𝖗𝖐, 𝕰𝖛𝖆𝖓. Greater Litany. Last day on which Easter can fall.	Inferior double.	3	
26	VI	d				
27		e				
28	XIV	f	𝖁𝖎𝖙𝖆𝖑𝖎𝖘, 𝕸𝖆𝖗𝖙. With ruling of quire.		3	
29	III	g	Departure of Noah from the Ark.			
30		A	𝕯𝖊𝖕𝖔𝖘𝖎𝖙𝖎𝖔𝖓 𝖔𝖋 𝕾. 𝕰𝖗𝖐𝖊𝖓𝖜𝖆𝖑𝖉, 𝕭𝖕. 𝖔𝖋 𝕷𝖔𝖓𝖉𝖔𝖓 𝖉𝖎𝖔𝖈𝖊𝖘𝖊.			

DAY OF MONTH.	GOLDEN NUMBER.	SUNDAY LETTER.	MAY.	RANK.	LESSONS.	INVITATORY.
1	XI	b	**Philip and James, App.**	Inferior double.	3	
2		c				
3	XIX	d	**Invention of the Holy Cross.** Mem. of Alexander and Eventius, [Martt.	Lesser double.	3	
4	VIII	e				
5		f				
6	XVI	g	**John before Port Latin.**		3	triple.
7	V	A	**John of Beverley, Bp. and Conf.** With ruling of quire.		3	
8		b				
9	XIII	c	Translation of S. Nicholas. With ruling of quire.			
10	II	d	SS. Gordian and Epimachus, Martt.		3	
11		e				
12	X	f	SS. Nereus, Achilleus, and Pancras. Sun in Gemini.		3	
13		g				
14	XVIII	A	Note that the Feast of the Transla-			
15	VII	b	tion of S. Chad, Bp., ought always			
16		c	to be celebrated on the Sunday			
17	XV	d	next before Ascension Day with			
18	IV	e	ruling of the quire.			
19		f	**Dunstan, Bp. and Conf.** Mem. of S. Potentiana.		9	
20	XII	g				
21	I	A				
22		b				
23	IX	c				
24		d	**Feast of S. Saviour.**			
25	XVII	e	**Aldhelm, Bp. and Conf.** Middle Lessons of S. Urban.		9	
26	VI	f	**Augustine, Apostle of the English.**	Inferior double.	9	
27		g				
28	XIV	A	Germanus, Bp. and Conf.		3	
29	III	b				
30		c				
31	XI	d	Petronilla, V. not Mart. When it falls outside the Oct. of Holy Trinity, three lessons.		3	

DAY OF MONTH.	GOLDEN NUMBER.	SUNDAY LETTER.	JUNE.	RANK.	LESSONS.	INVITATORY.
1		e	Nicomede, Mart.		3	
2	XIX	f	SS. Marcellinus and Peter, Martt.		3	triple.
3	VIII	g				
4	XVI	A				
5	V	b	Boniface and Compp.		3	double.
6		c				
7	XIII	d				
8	II	e	SS. Medardus and Gildardus, Conff.		3	
9		f	𝕿𝖗𝖆𝖓𝖘. of 𝕾. 𝕰𝖉𝖒𝖚𝖓𝖉, 𝕸𝖆𝖗𝖙. Mem. and Middle Lessons of Primus and Felicianus, Martt.		9	triple.
10	X	g				
11		A	𝕭𝖆𝖗𝖓𝖆𝖇𝖆𝖘, 𝕬𝖕.		9	triple.
12	XVIII	b	SS. Basilides, Cyrinus, and Nabor.		3	
13	VII	c	Sun in Cancer. Solstice.			
14		d	Basil, Bp. and Conf.		3	
15	XV	e	SS. Vitus, Modestus, and Crescentia.		3	
16	IV	f	Trans. of S. Richard. Middle Lessons of Ciricus and Julit[t]a.		9	
17		g				
18	XII	A	SS. Marcus and Marcellianus.		3	double.
19	I	b	SS. Gervasius and Protasius.		3	double.
20		c	𝕿𝖗𝖆𝖓𝖘. of 𝕾. 𝕰𝖉𝖜𝖆𝖗𝖉, 𝕶. 𝖆𝖓𝖉 𝕸𝖆𝖗𝖙. Unless it shall have been kept in Lent.		9	
21	IX	d				
22		e	𝕬𝖑𝖇𝖆𝖓, 𝕻𝖗𝖔𝖙𝖔𝖒𝖆𝖗𝖙𝖞𝖗.		9	
23	XVII	f	Etheldreda, V. With Nocturn. Vigil.		3	
24	VI	g	𝕹𝖆𝖙. of 𝕾. 𝕵𝖔𝖍𝖓 𝕭𝖆𝖕𝖙𝖎𝖘𝖙.	Lesser double.	9	
25		A				
26	XIV	b	SS. John and Paul.		3	double.
27	III	c				
28		d	Leo, Pope and Conf. With Nocturn. Vigil.		3	
29	XI	e	𝕻𝖊𝖙𝖊𝖗 𝖆𝖓𝖉 𝕻𝖆𝖚𝖑, 𝕬𝖕𝖕.	Lesser double.	9	
30		f	𝕮𝖔𝖒. of 𝕾. 𝕻𝖆𝖚𝖑.		9	triple.

DAY OF MONTH.	GOLDEN NUMBER.	SUNDAY LETTER.	JULY.	RANK.	LESSONS.	INVITATORY.
1	XIX	g	Oct. of S. John Baptist.		3	double.
2	VIII	A	𝕍isitation of 𝔹lessed 𝕄ary. Mem. of the Martyrs. Sub-silentio [Processus, Martinianus, and Swithin, Conff.]	[Greater] double.		
3		b				
4	XVI	c	Trans. and Ordination of S. Martin.		9	
5	V	d				
6		e	Oct. of Peter and Paul, App.		9	double.
7	XIII	f	Trans. of S. Thomas, Mart. The Feast of Relics is celebrated on the first Sunday after the Feast of the Trans. of S. Thomas.		9	
8	II	g				
9		A				
10	X	b	Seven Holy Brethren, Martt.		3	double.
11		c	Trans. of S. Benedict, Ab. Unless 9 Lessons have been kept in Lent, then 3 Lessons and double Inv.		9	
12	XVIII	d				
13	VII	e				
14		f	Sun in Leo. Dog days.			
15	XV	g	Trans. of S. Swithin & Compp.		9	
16	IV	A	Trans. of S. Osmund.		9	
17		b	Kenelm, K. and Mart.		3	double.
18	XII	c	Arnulph, Bp. and Mart.		3	
19	I	d				
20		e	Margaret, V. and Mart.		9	
21	IX	f	Praxedes, V., not Mart.		3	
22		g	Mary Magdalen.		9	triple.
23	XVII	A	Apollinaris, Bp. and Mart.		3	
24	VI	b	Christina V. and Mart. With Noc-	Lesser double.	3	
25		c	James, Ap. [turn. Vigil.		9	
26	XIV	d	Anne, Mother of Mary.		9	triple.
27	III	e	SS. Seven Sleepers, Martt.		3	double.
28		f	Samson, Bp.		3	double.
29	XI	g	SS. Felix and Faustus.		3	double.
30	XIX	A	SS. Abdon and Sennes, Martt.		3	double.
31		b	Germanus, Bp. and Conf.		3	

DAY OF MONTH.	GOLDEN NUMBER.	SUNDAY LETTER.	AUGUST.	RANK.	LESSONS.	INVITATORY.
1	VIII	c	**S. Peter's Chains.**		9	triple.
2	XVI	d	Stephen, Pope and Mart.		3	double.
3	V	e	**Invention of S. Stephen, Proto=**		9	
4		f	[martyr.			
5	XIII	g	Oswald, K. and Mart.		3	double.
6	II	A	**Transfiguration of Our Lord.**			
			Mem. of Martt.			
			[Sixtus, Felicissimus, and Agapitus.]			
7		b	**Feast of the Name of Jesus.**	Greater	9	
			Mem. of Donatus, Bp. and Mart.	double.		
8	X	c	Ciriacus and his Compp. Martt.			
			Mem. only.			
9		d	Romanus, Mart. Mem. only. Vigil.			
10	XVIII	e	**Laurence, Mart.**		9	triple.
11	VII	f	Tyburtius, Mart. Mem. only.			
12		g				
13	XV	A	Ipolitus and his Compp., Martt.		9	
14	IV	b	Oct. of [the Name of] Jesus.			
			Eusebius, Presb. and Conf. Vigil.			
15		c	**Assumption of Blessed Mary, V.**	Principal		
16	XII	d	Sun in Virgo. Equinox.	double.		
17	I	e	Oct. of S. Laurence. Mem. only.			
18		f	Agapitus, Mart. Mem. only.			
19	IX	g	Magnus, Mart. Mem. only.			
20		A				
21	XVII	b				
22	VI	c	Oct. of S. Mary. Mem. of SS.		9	
			[Timothy and Symphorian.]			
23		d	SS. Timotheus and Apollinaris.			
			With Nocturn. Vigil.			
24	XIV	e	**Bartholomew, Ap.**	Inferior	9	
25	III	f		double.		
26		g				
27	XI	A	Rufus, Mart.		3	double.
28	XIX	b	**Augustine, Bp. and Doct.**		9	double.
29		c	**Decollation of S. John Baptist.**		9	triple.
30	VIII	d	SS. Felix and Adauctus, Martt.		3	double.
31		e	Cuthberga, V., not Mart.		3	double.

DAY OF MONTH.	GOLDEN NUMBER.	SUNDAY LETTER.	SEPTEMBER.	RANK.	LESSONS.	INVITATORY.
1	XVI	f	**Giles, Ab.** Middle lessons of		9	
2	V	g	[S. Priscus.			
3		A				
4	XIII	b	**Trans. of S. Cuthbert, Bp. and Conf.** Nine lessons, unless read in Lent.		9	
5	II	c	Bertin, Ab. and Conf. With Noc-		3	
6		d	[turn.			
7	X	e				
8		f	**Natibity of Blessed Mary, V.**	Greater double.	9	
9	XVIII	g	Gorgonius, Mart. Mem. only.			
10	VII	A				
11		b	SS. Prothus and Hyacinth, Martt.			
12	XV	c	[Mem. only.			
13	IV	d	Sun in Libra.			
14		e	**Exaltation of Holy Cross.** Middle Lessons of SS. Cornelius and Cyprian. Autumnal Equinox. Dog Days end.	Lesser double.	9	
15	XII	f	Oct. of Blessed Mary.		9	triple.
16	I	g	Edith, V., not Mart. Middle lessons of [Euphemia, Lucia, Geminianus]		9	
17		A	Lambert, Bp. and Mart. [Martt.		3	simple.
			Keep the fast of the ninth month			
18	IX	b	[Ember] always on the Wednesday			
19		c	after the Exaltation of the Cross.			
20	XVII	d	Vigil. [of S. Laudus.	Inferior double.		
21	VI	e	**Matthew, Ap. and Evan.** Mem.		9	
22		f	Maurice and Compp. Martt.		9	
23	XIV	g	Thecla, V., not Mart. With Noc-		3	
24	III	A	[turn.			
25		b	Firminus, Bp. and Mart.		3	simple.
26	XI	c	Cyprian, Bp., and Justina, V.		3	double.
27	XIX	d	SS. Cosmas and Damian, Martt.		3	double.
28		e				
29	VIII	f	**Michael, Archangel.**	Inferior double.	9	
30		g	**Jerome, Presb. and Doct.**	Inferior double.	9	

DAY OF MONTH.	GOLDEN NUMBER.	SUNDAY LETTER.	OCTOBER.	RANK.	LESSONS.	INVITATORY.
1	XVI	A	𝕾𝕾. 𝕽𝖊𝖒𝖎𝖌𝖎𝖚𝖘, 𝕲𝖊𝖗𝖒𝖆𝖓, 𝖁𝖊𝖉𝖆𝖘𝖙, 𝖆𝖓𝖉 𝕭𝖆𝖇𝖔, 𝕭𝖕𝖕. Middle lessons of S. Melorus.		9	
2	V	b	Thomas of Hereford, Bp. and Conf. Middle lessons of S. Leger.		9	
3	XIII	c				
4	II	d				
5		e				
6	X	f	Faith, V. and Mart.		3	simple.
7		g	SS. Marcus and Marcellianus.		3	double.
8	XVIII	A				
9	VII	b	𝕯𝖊𝖓𝖞𝖘 𝖆𝖓𝖉 𝖍𝖎𝖘 𝕮𝖔𝖒𝖕𝖕.		9	
10		c	Gereon and his Compp.		3	simple.
11	XV	d	Nicasius and his Compp., Martt.		3	double.
12	IV	e				
13		f	𝕿𝖗𝖆𝖓𝖘. 𝖔𝖋 𝕾. 𝕰𝖉𝖜𝖆𝖗𝖉, 𝕶.	Inferior double.	3	
14	XII	g	Calixtus, Pope and Mart. Sun in Scorpio.	Inferior double.	3	
15	I	A	𝖂𝖚𝖑𝖋𝖗𝖆𝖓, 𝕭𝖕. 𝖆𝖓𝖉 𝕮𝖔𝖓𝖋.		9	
16		b	𝕸𝖎𝖈𝖍𝖆𝖊𝖑 𝖎𝖓 𝖙𝖍𝖊 𝕸𝖔𝖚𝖓𝖙𝖆𝖎𝖓 𝕿𝖔𝖒𝖇.		9	triple.
17	IX	c	𝕰𝖙𝖍𝖊𝖑𝖉𝖗𝖊𝖉𝖆, 𝖁., 𝖓𝖔𝖙 𝕸𝖆𝖗𝖙.		9	
18		d	𝕷𝖚𝖐𝖊, 𝕰𝖇𝖆𝖓.	Inferior double.	9	
19	XVII	e	𝕱𝖗𝖊𝖉𝖊𝖘𝖜𝖎𝖉𝖊, 𝖁., 𝖓𝖔𝖙 𝕸𝖆𝖗𝖙.		9	
20	VI	f				
21		g	Eleven thousand holy Virgins.		3	double.
22	XIV	A				
23	III	b	Romanus, Bp. and Conf., with Nocturn.		3	
24		c				
25	XI	d	𝕾𝕾. 𝕮𝖗𝖎𝖘𝖕𝖎𝖓 𝖆𝖓𝖉 𝕮𝖗𝖎𝖘𝖕𝖎𝖓𝖎𝖆𝖓. Middle lessons of S. John of Beverley, Bp. and Conf.		9	
26	XIX	e				
27		f	Vigil.			
28	VIII	g	𝕾𝖎𝖒𝖔𝖓 𝖆𝖓𝖉 𝕵𝖚𝖉𝖊, 𝕬𝖕𝖕.	Inferior double.	9	
29		A				
30	XVI	b	[Vigil.			
31	V	c	Quintinus, Mart., with Nocturn.		3	

DAY OF MONTH.	GOLDEN NUMBER.	SUNDAY LETTER.	NOVEMBER.	RANK.	LESSONS.	INVITATORY.
1		d	Feast of All Saints.	Greater double.	9	
2	XIII	e	Com. of All Souls. At Vespers, Mem. of S. Mary, Mem. of S. Eustachius and his Compp.		9	
3	II	f	Wenefred, V. and Mart.		9	
4		g				
5	X	A				
6		b	Leonard, Ab.		9	
7	XVIII	c				
8	VII	d	The Four Crowned Martyrs.		3	double.
9		e	Theodore, Mart.		3	simple.
10	XV	f				
11	IV	g	Martin, Bp. and Conf. Mem. of S. Menna, Mart.		9	triple.
12		A	Sun in Sagittarius. [S. Martin.			
13	XII	b	Bricius, Bp. and Conf. Mem. of		3	double.
14	I	c	Translation of S. Erkenwald, Bp.			
15		d	Machutus, Bp. and Conf. Middle lessons of S. Martin.		9	
16	IX	e	Deposition of S. Edmund, Archbp.		9	triple.
17		f	Hugh, Bp. and Conf. Middle lessons of S. Anianus.		9	
18	XVII	g	Oct. of S. Martin.		3	double.
19	VI	A				
20		b	Edmund, K. and Mart.		9	
21	XIV	c				
22	III	d	Cecilia, V. and Mart.		9	
23		e	Clement, Pope and Mart. Mem. of S. Felicitas, V.		9	
24	XI	f	Chrysogonus, Mart.		3	simple.
25	XIX	g	Katherine, V. and Mart.		9	
26		A	Linus, Pope and Mart.		3	simple.
27	VIII	b				
28		c	[Nocturn. Vigil.			
29	XVI	d	SS. Saturninus and Sisinnius. With		3	
30	V	e	Andrew, Ap.	Inferior double.	9	

DAY OF MONTH.	GOLDEN NUMBER.	SUNDAY LETTER.	DECEMBER.	RANK.	LESSONS.	INVITATORY.
1		f				
2	XIII	g				
3	II	A				
4	X	b	Osmund, Bp. and Conf.		9	
5		c				
6	XVIII	d	Nicholas, Bp. and Conf.		9	triple.
7	VII	e	Oct. of S. Andrew, Ap.		3	triple.
8		f	Conception of Blessed Mary.	Lesser double.	9	
9	XV	g				
10	IV	A				
11		b				
12	XII	c				
13	I	d	Lucy, V. and Mart.		9	
14		e	Sun in Capricornus. Winter [Solstice.			
15	IX	f				
16		g	O Sapientia.			
17	XVII	A	After this, there are to be no Preces			
18	VI	b	at Vespers.			
19		c				
20	XIV	d	Vigil.			
21	III	e	Thomas, Ap.	Inferior double.	9	
22		f				
23	XI	g				
24	XIX	A	Vigil.			
25		b	Nativity of Our Lord Jesus Christ.	Principal double.	9	
26	VIII	c	Stephen, Protomartyr.	Lesser double.	9	
27		d	John, Ap. and Evan.	Lesser double.	9	
28	XVI	e	Holy Innocents, Martt.	Lesser double.	9	
29	V	f	Thomas of Canterbury, Archbp. and Mart.	Lesser double.	9	
30		g				
31	XIII	A	Silvester, Bp. and Conf. Middle lessons of the Nativity of Our Lord.		9	

BLESSING OF SALT AND WATER.

Blessing of salt and water.—On all Sundays throughout the year, after prime and the chapter, the blessing of salt and water shall take place, at the step of the quire, by a priest, after the following manner.

I exorcize thee, O creature of salt by the living + God, by the true + God, by the holy + God, by the God who commanded thee to be cast into the water by Elisha the prophet that the barrenness of the water might be healed, that thou mayest become salt [*Here shall the priest look at the salt*] exorcized for the salvation of them that believe, and that thou mayest be salvation of soul and body to all that take thee ; and from that place where thou shalt have been sprinkled, let every delusion and wickedness, or craft of devilish cunning, when adjured, flee and depart. Through him who shall come to judge the quick and the dead and the world by fire. ℟. Amen.

The next collect follows without "The Lord be with you," and only with "Let us pray."

Collect.

Almighty everlasting God, we humbly implore thy boundless loving-kindness [*Here the priest shall look at the salt*] that of thy goodness thou wouldest deign to ble + ss and sancti + fy this creature of salt, which thou hast given for the use of mankind ; that it may be unto all who partake of it health of mind and body ; that whatsoever shall have been touched or sprinkled with it may be freed from all uncleanness, and from all assault of spiritual wickedness. Through our Lord Jesus Christ, thy Son, who liveth and reigneth with thee in the unity of the Holy Ghost, God, world without end. Amen.

Here follows the exorcism of the water.

I exorcize thee, O creature of water, in the name of God + the Father almighty, and in the name of Jesus + Christ his Son our Lord, and in the power of the Holy + Ghost ; that thou mayest become water exorcized for

c

putting to flight all power of the enemy ; that thou mayest have power to root out and transplant the enemy himself with his apostate angels, by the power of the same Jesus Christ our Lord ; who shall come to judge the quick and the dead and the world by fire.

℟.   Amen.

The next collect follows without " The Lord be with you," *but with* " Let us pray."

Collect.

O GOD, who for the salvation of mankind has hidden [one of thy] greatest sacraments[1] in the element of water, graciously hearken unto our invocations, and pour upon this element [*Here shall the priest look upon the water*] prepared for divers purifications the power of thy blessing, that this thy creature, serving in thy mysteries, may acquire the effectual power of divine grace for casting out devils, and for driving away diseases ; and that on whatsoever in the houses or dwelling places of the faithful this water shall have been sprinkled, it may be freed from all uncleanness, and may be delivered from hurt.   Let no pestilential spirit, no corrupting air, linger there.   Let all the insidious attacks of the lurking enemy be dissipated ; and if there be aught which threatens the safety or the peace of the inhabitants, let it be driven away by the sprinkling of this water, so that saved by the invocation of thy holy name they may be defended from all assaults.   Through our Lord Jesus Christ thy Son, who liveth and reigneth with thee in the unity of the Holy Ghost, God, world without end.

Here shall the priest cast salt into the water in the form of a cross, saying thus, without inflection :

Let this mixture of salt and water alike be made in the name of the Father, and of the Son, and of the Holy Ghost.   Amen.

---

[1]   Maxima quæque sacramenta.

℣. The Lord be with you.
℟. And with thy spirit.
Let us pray.

Collect.

O God, the author of unconquered might, and the king of unconquerable empire, who ever triumphest magnificently, who repressest the strength of adverse power, and overcomest the rage of the roaring adversary, and by thy might subduest the onslaughts of iniquity ; with fear and humility we entreat and beseech thee, O Lord, that thou wouldest deign to accept [*Here shall he look upon the salt mixed with water*] this creature of salt and water ; graciously illumine it, and by thy love and by thy pity sancti ✝ fy it ; that whenever it shall have been sprinkled, by the invocation of thy holy name, every attack of the unclean spirit may be parried, and dread of the venomous serpent may be driven far away ; and may the presence of the Holy Ghost be vouchsafed to be with us, as we ask thy mercy in every place, through our Lord Jesus Christ thy Son.

While the water is being sprinkled the following Anthem shall be sung :

Thou shalt purge me, O Lord, with hyssop, and I shall be clean ; thou shalt wash me, and I shall be whiter than snow.

Ps. Have mercy upon me, O God, after thy great goodness.[1]

Thou shalt purge me, etc.

℣. And according to the multitude of thy mercies, do away mine offences.

Thou shalt purge me, etc.

℣. Glory be to the Father, etc.   As it was, etc.

To be repeated. Thou shalt wash me, and I shall be whiter than snow.

---

[1] Ps. li. 7, 1.

This Anthem is said at the sprinkling of holy water on all Sundays throughout the year, except from Easter to the Feast of Trinity. It shall be said even on Palm Sunday and Passion Sunday with " Glory be to the Father," etc., *and* " As it was," etc.

From Easter to the Feast of Trinity the following Anthem should be said at the sprinkling of holy water, the precentor[1] commencing the Anthem.

I saw water issuing out of the temple on the right-hand side, alleluya. And all to whom that water came were made whole,[2] and shall say, alleluya, alleluya.[3]

Ps. O give thanks unto the Lord, for he is gracious : because his mercy endureth for ever.[4]

The Anthem shall be repeated : I saw water, etc. Glory be to the Father, etc. As it was, etc. And all, etc.

After the sprinkling of the water, the priest standing at the step of the quire shall say this Verse :

℣. Shew us thy mercy, O Lord.

℟. And grant us thy salvation.

Then shall the priest say thus :

Let us pray.

Hear us, O Lord, holy Father, almighty everlasting God, and vouchsafe to send thy holy angel from heaven to keep, cherish, protect, visit, and defend all who dwell in this habitation, through Christ our Lord.

℟. Amen.

If the bishop be the Officiant on any simple Sunday, then he himself, vested in a silk cope, with mitre and pastoral staff, together with all the above-mentioned Ministers, is wont to enter the quire for the blessing of salt and water ; and while the blessing of salt and water is being performed by a priest vested for that purpose, as described above, the bishop betakes himself to his episcopal throne. There, after the high altar has been sprinkled by the aforesaid priest, the bishop will sprinkle both the canons and the other clerks, approaching the throne

---

[1] Cantor.   [2] Salvi.   [3] Compare Ezek. xlvii. 12.
[4] Ps. cxviii. 1.

itself for that purpose, in the manner and order previously described; and in the same place he says both the Verse, ana the Collect after the Anthem : Thou shalt purge me, etc. *But if the bishop be not the Officiant, then vested in his quire habit, with only gloves and pastoral staff, he shall sprinkle the clerks, as above; the aforesaid priest always saying the Verse, and the Collect after the Anthem,* Thou shalt purge me, etc., *in the accustomed manner.*

BLESSING OF BREAD ON SUNDAYS.

First of all the priest shall say the Gospel following,
Gospel St. John, i., 1–14.
In the beginning . . . . . . grace and truth.

And afterwards he shall say this Verse :

℣. Blessed be the name of the Lord.
℟. From this time forth for evermore.
℣. Let us bless the Lord.
℟. Thanks be to God.

Then shall he say :

℣. The Lord be with you.
℟. And with thy spirit.

Let us pray.

Bless, O Lord, this creature of bread, as thou didst bless the five loaves in the wilderness, that all who partake thereof may receive health both of body and soul. In the name + of the Father, and + of the Son, and of the Holy + Ghost. Amen.

The holy water shall be sprinkled over the bread, and it shall be distributed.

PRAYER TO BE SAID BY THE PRIEST BEFORE MASS.[1]

O GOD, who makest worthy of the unworthy, just and holy of sinners, and clean of the unclean, cleanse my

---

[1] The following prayers before Mass are placed in the 1526 edition between Easter Even and Easter Day. It has been thought better to print them in this volume in their natural and appropriate position before the commencement of the Ordinary and the Canon of the Mass.

heart and body from all taint and defilement of sin, and make me a worthy and strenuous minister at thy holy altars ; and mercifully grant that on this altar, to which I unworthy make approach, I may offer a sacrifice acceptable and pleasing to thy lovingkindness, for my sins and offences, and for my innumerable daily transgressions, and likewise for washing away the sins of all Christian people. And may my desire be acceptable to thee, through him who offered himself a sacrifice for us to thee his God and Father. Who liveth, etc.

Prayer to be said by the priest before Mass.

LORD, I am not worthy that thou shouldest come under my roof, but trusting in thy lovingkindness I approach thine altar ; sick I come to the physician of life, blind to the light of eternal brightness, poor to the lord of heaven and earth, naked to the king of glory, a sheep to the shepherd, a thing formed to him that formed it, desolate to the kind comforter, miserable to the pitiful, guilty to the bestower of pardon, unholy to one that justifieth, hardened to the infuser of grace ; imploring the abundance of thy boundless mercy that thou wouldest vouchsafe to heal mine infirmity, to wash my foulness, to enlighten my blindness, to enrich my poverty, to clothe my nakedness, to bring back the wandering, to console the desolate, to reconcile the guilty, to give pardon to the sinner, forgiveness to the wretched, life to the accused, justification to the dead ; that I may be deemed worthy to receive thee, the bread of angels, the king of kings, and lord of lords, with such chastity of body and purity of mind, such contrition of heart and flow of tears, such spiritual happiness and heavenly joy, such fear and trembling, such reverence and honour, such faith and humility, such determination and love, such prayer and thanksgiving, as are becoming and thy due, so that I may profitably obtain eternal life, and the remission of all my sins. Amen.

A devout prayer concerning the sacrament of the altar.

Almighty and merciful God, behold I approach the sacrament of the body and blood of thy only-begotten Son, our Lord Jesus Christ. I approach, I say, sick to the physician of life, unclean to the fount of pity. I implore, therefore, the abundance of thy boundless majesty, that thou wouldest vouchsafe to heal my infirmity, to enrich my poverty, so that I may receive the bread of angels, the king of kings, with such reverence and trembling, such contrition and love, as is expedient for the welfare of my soul. Grant unto me, I beseech thee, not only to receive the sacrament of the Lord's body and blood, but also the virtue of the sacrament. O sweetest God, grant unto me so to receive the body of thy only-begotten one, our Lord Jesus Christ, which he took of the virgin Mary, that I may be found worthy to be incorporated into his mystical body, and to be numbered among its members. O most loving Father, grant that I may one day see thy beloved Son with open face, whom now I prepare to receive beneath a veil. Who liveth, etc.[1]

---

[1] Here follows in the 1526 edition a long poem in seventeen stanzas of four lines each, describing the character and duties of the priesthood. It is entitled "Dictamen beati Augustini de regimine sacerdotum," fol. lxxxvii. *verso*, and 1861 Reprint, Coll. 569–574.

ORDINARY OF THE MASS.

At the saying of Mass, while the priest is putting on the sacred vestments, he shall say the Hymn following:

Hymn.

Come, Holy Ghost, our souls inspire,
And lighten with celestial fire.
Thou the anointing Spirit art,
Who dost thy sevenfold gifts impart.

Thy blessed unction from above,
Is comfort, life, and fire of love.
Enable with perpetual light
The dulness of our blinded sight.

Anoint and cheer our soiled face
With the abundance of thy grace.
Keep far our foes, give peace at home :
Where thou art guide, no ill can come.

Teach us to know the Father, Son,
And thee, of both, to be but One.
That through the ages all along,
This may be our endless song ;

Praise to thy eternal merit,
Father, Son, and Holy Spirit.[1]

℣. Send forth thy Spirit, and they shall be made.
℟. And thou shalt renew the face of the earth.[2]

Collect.

O GOD, unto whom all hearts be open, all desires known, and from whom no secrets are hid ; cleanse the thoughts of our hearts by the inspiration of thy Holy Spirit, that we may perfectly love thee, and worthily magnify thee. Through, etc.

---

[1] This beautiful, but not very close, translation is taken from the service for the Ordering of Priests in the Book of Common Prayer.
[2] Ps. civ. 30.

Then shall follow the Anthem : I will go unto the altar of God.[1]

Ps. Give sentence with me, O God, and defend my cause, etc.[2]

The whole of the Psalm is said, together with Glory be to the Father, etc. *Then is said the Anthem :*

I will go unto the altar of God, even unto the God of my joy and gladness.

> Lord, have mercy.
> Christ, have mercy.
> Lord, have mercy.[3]

Our Father, etc.

Hail, Mary, etc.[4]

This done, and the Office of the Mass having been commenced, when at the conclusion of the Office, Glory be to the Father, etc., *is begun, the priest with his ministers is to approach to the step of the altar, and himself to say the confession, the deacon assisting on his right hand and the subdeacon on his left hand, beginning thus :*

℣. And lead us not into temptation,

℟. But deliver us from evil.

℣. O give thanks unto the Lord, for he is gracious,

℟. Because his mercy endureth for ever.[5]

Confession.

I confess to God, to blessed Mary, to all the saints, and to you, that I have sinned exceedingly in thought, word, and deed, by my fault : I pray holy Mary, all the saints of God, and you, to pray for me.

---

[1] Ps. xliii. 4.   [2] Ps. xliii.

[3] Here, as elsewhere, represented by the transliterated Greek words, Kyrie eleyson, Christe eleyson, Kyrie eleyson.

[4] The full form in 1526 would be : "Hail, Mary, thou that art highly favoured, the Lord is with thee. Blessed art thou among women and blessed is the fruit of thy womb, Jesus," with possibly the addition, dated by Gavantus in 1508, "Holy Mary, mother of God, pray for us sinners," and the Franciscan addition of 1525, "Now and in the hour of our death," *Thesaur. Sacr. Rit.*, edit. 1738, tom. ii., part 1, p. 235.

[5] Ps. cxviii. 1.

The ministers shall reply.

May almighty God have mercy upon you, and forgive you all your sins ; deliver you from all evil ; preserve and strengthen you in goodness, and bring you to everlasting life.

Priest. Amen.

Afterwards the ministers shall say the Confession, and the priest shall say, May almighty God have mercy, etc., *as above. Then shall the priest say :*

The almighty and merciful God grant unto you absolution and remission of all your sins, time for true repentance, and amendment of life, and the grace and consolation of the Holy Ghost.

The ministers shall reply, Amen.

And be it known, that whatever priest is the Officiant, if the bishop be present, the bishop shall always say, standing at the step of the altar, the Confession, May almighty God have mercy upon you, etc., *and the Absolution.*

Then shall the Priest say :

℣. Our help is in the name of the Lord,
℟. Who hath made heaven and earth.
℣. Blessed be the name of the Lord,
℟. From this time forth, now, and for evermore.

Let us pray.

Then, having finished his prayers, the priest shall kiss the deacon, and afterwards the subdeacon, saying thus : [1]

Receive the kiss of peace and love, that ye may be fit for the holy altar for the performance of divine offices.

This shall be observed always, throughout the whole year, except in masses for the dead, and on the three days next before Easter.

This done, the candlebearers shall set down their candlesticks with candles at the step of the altar; then the priest shall approach the altar, and say in the midst of the altar, silently, and with inclined body and joined hands :

Let us pray.

[1] This preliminary kiss of peace is not in R.

Take away from us, we beseech thee, O Lord, all our iniquities, that we may be found worthy to enter into the holy of holies with pure minds.　Through, etc.

Then shall the priest raise himself, and kiss the altar in the midst, and sign himself on his face, saying thus:

In the name of the Father, and of the Son, and of the Holy Ghost.　Amen.

Then shall the deacon place incense in the censer, and say first to the priest:

Bless.

And the priest shall say:

The Lord.　May this incense be blessed by him in whose honour it shall be burned.　In the name of the Father, and of the Son, and of the Holy Ghost.

Then the deacon, handing the thurible to the priest, shall kiss his hand, and the priest himself shall cense the midst of the Altar and either side[1] of the Altar, first on the right hand, then on the left hand, and in the meanwhile in the midst.

Then shall the priest himself be censed by the deacon, and afterwards the priest shall kiss the Text,[2] brought to him by the subdeacon.

These things having been thus done, with deacon and sub-deacon on the right side of the Altar, the priest shall proceed with the Office of the mass as far as the Collect, or as far as Gloria in Excelsis, *when it is said.*

After the Office and the Psalm, the Office is to be repeated; after which Glory be to the Father, *etc., and* As it was, *etc., are said.　Then the Office is to be repeated a third time.　And this is to be observed throughout the whole year, on Sundays, and on the feasts of saints, and on Octaves, and within [Octaves] when the quire is ruled, and at all masses of saint Mary; except from Passion Sunday and after, until Maundy Thursday, that is to say, at the Mass of the season only; for then the Office is to be recommenced directly after the Psalm which is said after the Office, without* Glory be to the Father, *etc., after the repetition of the Office.*

The principal ruler of the quire ought to ask for the Office of

---

[1] Cornu.　　[2] Textus, *i.e.* the Book of the Gospels.

*the mass from the precentor, and then intimate it to his com-
panion, and afterwards they shall begin it together. In the
same way the Kyrie, the Sequence, the Offertory, the Sanctus,
the Agnus, and the Communion should be asked for, intimated,
and begun.*

*This done, and the Office of the Mass having been com-
menced, when* Glory *be to the* Father, *etc., is begun at the
conclusion of the Office, then the ministers should approach the
Altar in order: first, the candlebearers walking two and two,
then the thurifers, after them the subdeacon, then the deacon,
after him the priest. The deacon and subdeacon are to be
vested in chasubles, that is to say, daily throughout Advent,
and from Septuagesima till Maundy Thursday, when the
mass of the season is said, except on vigils and on Ember days,
but they are not to hold their hands in the same way as the
priest. The other ministers, that is to say, the candlebearers, the
thurifers, and the acolytes, are to be vested in albs with amices.*

*At all other times of the year, when the mass of the season is
said, and on feasts of saints throughout the whole year, the
deacon and subdeacon shall use dalmatics and tunicles, except
on vigils and Ember days, and on the vigils of Easter,
Whitsunday, and Christmas Day, if it fall on a Sunday, and
except at the Ember fast which is celebrated in Whitsun-week;
then they should be vested in dalmatics and tunicles. On Good
Friday and on Rogation days, at the mass of the fast, and at
the procession, and at Sunday masses, and at the masses of the
saints which are said in chapter, then they should use albs with
amices.*

*In Easter-tide,[1] whatever the mass may be, except on the
Invention of the holy Cross, the ministers of the altar should
use white vestments at Mass, as likewise on the feasts of the
Annunciation of the blessed Mary, and of her Conception, and
on both feasts of St. Michael; and on the feast of St. John the*

---

[1] Tempus Paschale; for the probable duration of this period, see
Index. The omission of directions for Christmas Day is curious and
unexplained. The Christmas colour must be established by other
evidence, see "Essays on Ceremonial," De la More Press, London,
1904, pp. 114, 119.

Apostle in Christmas week, and throughout the octaves, and on the octaves of the Assumption and the Nativity of blessed Mary, ana in commemoration of her throughout the whole year, and throughout octaves, and on the octave of the Dedication of a church.

But they are to use red vestments on all Sundays throughout the year, outside Easter-tide, when the Mass is of the Sunday, and on Ash Wednesday, and on Maundy Thursday, and on both feasts of the holy Cross, and on all feasts of martyrs, apostles, and evangelists outside Easter-tide.

On all feasts of one or many confessors they are to use vestments of a yellow colour.

This being done, the priest and his ministers shall betake themselves to the seats prepared for them until Gloria in excelsis, *which is always to be begun in the midst of the Altar, whenever it is said.*

Here follow varieties of intonations for the four opening words of Gloria in excelsis Deo, *viz. :*

Three[1]; for all Sundays in the year when Gloria in excelsis *is said, one of them to be always selected by the precentor.*

Two ; for all feasts which are greater doubles.

Two ; for all other double feasts.

One ; for both feasts of St. Michael, and for the feast of St. Dunstan.

Two ; for all feasts and on octaves when the Invitatory is sung by three persons.

Two ; for all other simple feasts, whether of three or of nine lessons, when the quire is ruled.

Two ; for all feasts of three lessons, and on octaves when the quire is not ruled.

One ; in commemoration of blessed Mary throughout the whole year, when " Gloria in excelsis *" is said.*

Except when the service of saint Mary occurs for the last time before Advent, and before Septuagesima, and on the octaves of

---

[1] We have omitted the music for all these openings, which is printed in the original text. The translated text is slightly altered in consequence.

the Assumption and the Nativity of blessed Mary; for then the following chant is said both by the quire, and by the Priest and his ministers at the altar, together with its farsings, that is to say, in the quire : it is also said, with its prose,[1] in the daily masses in the chapel of blessed Mary on every Saturday.

Glory be to God on high, and in earth peace, good-will towards men. We praise thee. We bless thee. We worship thee. We glorify thee. We give thanks to thee for thy great glory, O Lord God, heavenly King, God the Father almighty.

O Lord, the only-begotten Son, Jesu Christ, *Spirit, and kind comforter of orphans;* O Lord God, Lamb of God, Son of the Father, *First born of Mary virgin mother,* Thou that takest away the sins of the world, have mercy upon us. Thou that takest away the sins of the world, receive our prayer, *To the glory of Mary.* Thou that sittest at the right hand of the Father, have mercy upon us.

For thou only art holy, *sanctifying Mary,* Thou only art the Lord, *governing Mary,* Thou only art most high, *crowning Mary,* Jesu Christ, with the Holy Ghost, in the glory of God the Father. Amen.

At all other masses, when Gloria in excelsis *is to be said, it is said without the prose.[1] After it has been commenced, the priest should turn himself to the right side of the altar, the ministers also following with him, the deacon on his right, and the subdeacon on his left, and they should repeat the same in a low tone. On double feasts, when* Gloria in excelsis *ought to be said, the principal rulers of the quire should ask for it from the precentor, and enjoin it to the priest.*

Be it noted that all clerks are bound to stand at Mass, except when the Epistle is read, and the Gradual, and Alleluya, or Tract is sung. But on double feasts they are bound to stand while Alleluya is sung by the quire. Boys are always to be standing at Mass while the quire is singing. The rulers of the quire, when there are only two of them, should

---

[1] Prose. The word evidently refers here to the farsings.

follow in all points the regulations as to clerks of the second grade, at Vespers, Matins, and at Mass; except that they are always bound to stand while the quire is singing Alleluya; and at the commencement of chants at Mass they should turn to the Altar. On double feasts all rulers of the quire should follow the above directions in all points.

It is also to be noted that all clerks, turning to the Altar, are bound to stand while Gloria in excelsis *is begun at Mass until the quire commence singing; and, in the course of the same hymn, at the words,* We worship thee, *and at the words,* Receive our prayer, *and at the end of the same hymn, when the words occur,* Jesu Christ, with the Holy Ghost, in the glory of God [the Father] *as far as the Epistle or Lesson.*

When the Gradual, Alleluya, or Sequence, or Tract, has been said privately by the priest and his ministers, the sub-deacon shall receive the bread and wine and water with the chalice, and shall prepare them for the administration of the Eucharist; a blessing of the water having first been demanded from the Priest in this form, Bless, *the priest to answer thus:* The Lord. May [this water] be blessed by him out of whose side flowed forth blood and water. In the name of the Father, etc.

In the meanwhile the priest will be seated in his own seat.

At the end of the Gradual, or Tract, or Alleluya, or Sequence, the quire shall bow[1] towards the Altar before they turn towards the reader of the Gospel; and at Glory be to thee, O Lord, *the reader of the Gospel shall always turn to the Altar, and, likewise, all the clerks shall sign themselves with the sign of the cross. This sign is to be made publicly thrice during Mass, namely, at the* Gloria in excelsis, *when the words,* In the glory of God the Father, Amen, *are said; and at* Glory be to thee, O Lord; *and after the Sanctus, when the words,* Blessed is he that cometh, *are said.[2] The quire is to bow towards the altar at the beginning of* I believe in one, etc., *until the quire*

---

[1] Se inclinet.   [2] The 1526 punctuation is defective here.

sing ; and again thrice ; firstly, while this clause is said, and was incarnate by the Holy Ghost of the Virgin Mary ; *secondly, at the words,* and was made man ; *thirdly, at the words,* and was crucified also for us under Pontius Pilate ; *and at the end* [*of the Creed*] *at the words,* and the life of the world to come. Amen. *From this point until the Offertory is begun, and after the Offertory until the whole office of the mass is finished, the quire should adopt the above gesture*[1] *on every feast throughout the year.* But Gloria in excelsis *is not said through the whole of Advent, whatever the mass may be, nor from Septuagesima up to the vigil of Easter.*

This done, and having made the sign of the cross upon his face, the priest shall turn to the people and, slightly elevating his arms and joining his hands, shall say thus :

The Lord be with you.[2]

And the quire shall respond,

And with thy spirit.

in the same tone.   And the priest shall turn again to the Altar, and shall say thus :

Let us pray.

As often as The Lord be with you *is said at Mass, it is always said with the same intonation, and likewise,* Let us pray ; *except in the case of Prefaces, and in the Nuptial Mass, when the blessing is given over the bridegroom and bride, before the* Peace of the Lord. *Then a different intonation is provided for it, as well as for the concluding phrase of the Collect.*

If any Memory is to be introduced the priest shall again say, Let us pray, *as above.   And when there are several Collects to be said, then all those which follow the first are said with one termination, and under one* Let us pray, *provided that the number of Collects is never to exceed seven, according to the use of the Church of Sarum.*

[1] *i.e.* of inclining, or bowing to the Altar.
[2] The musical intonations for the Salutation, etc., and for the Creed and Prefaces following, printed in the original text, are not reproduced here.

While the priest is standing for the office of the Mass, the deacon shall always stand directly behind him on the next step, and the subdeacon, in the same way, on the second step, directly behind the deacon. As often as the priest turns to the people, the deacon shall turn in a similar direction. The subdeacon in the meantime shall genuflect, and occupy himself in handling the priest's chasuble. If a bishop be celebrant all the deacons shall stand on the deacon's step, the principal deacon occupying the middle position among them. The subdeacons are to be ranged in the same way on their step, and all the rest of the deacons and of the subdeacons are to imitate the gestures of the principal deacon and the principal subdeacon; except that the principal subdeacon is to attend alone upon the priest[1] when he turns to the people.

It is to be observed that whatever is said by the priest before the Epistle is to be said at the right-hand side of the altar, except the commencement of Gloria in excelsis. *The same rule is to be observed after the reception of the sacrament. Everything else is to be done in the midst of the* Altar, *unless perchance there should be no deacon present. In that case the Gospel should be read at the left-hand side of the* Altar. *After the Introit[2] of the Mass one of the candlebearers shall bring the bread, and the wine, and the water, which are arranged for the administration of the Eucharist, another [candlebearer] shall carry a basin with water and a towel.*

The quire may be entered up to the end of the first Collect.

The rest of the service as far as the Creed is said in accordance with the directions laid down for the first Sunday in Advent.

Nicene Creed.

I believe in one God, the Father almighty, Maker of heaven and earth, and of all things visible, and invisible.

And in one Lord Jesus Christ, the only-begotten Son of God, And begotten of his Father before all worlds: God of God, Light of Light, very God of very God, Begotten not made, being of one substance with the

---

[1] "Sacerdoti," but apparently it should be "episcopo."
[2] Introitus. In almost every other case the word used is Officium.

Father, by whom all things were made. Who for us men and for our salvation came down from heaven,

Here the quire shall incline while they say,

And was incarnate by the Holy Ghost of the virgin Mary,

The quire shall again incline while they say:

And was made man.

The quire shall incline a third time while they say:

He was crucified also for us under Pontius Pilate, he suffered and was buried. And the third day he rose again according to the scriptures, and ascended into heaven, he sitteth on the right hand of the Father, And he shall come again with glory to judge the quick and the dead, Whose kingdom shall have no end.

And in the Holy Ghost the Lord and giver of life, Who proceedeth from the Father and the Son, Who with the Father and the Son together is worshipped and glorified, Who spake by the prophets. And in one holy Catholic and Apostolick Church. I acknowledge one baptism for the remission of sins, and I look for the resurrection of the dead,

The quire shall incline at the end, while they say:

And the life of the world to come. Amen.

After the commencement of the Creed, the ministers having returned from the pulpit to the altar, the deacon shall present the book of the Gospel to the priest to kiss ; or, otherwise, receiving the Text from the hand of the subdeacon, he shall present it to the priest, on his right hand, to kiss ; the acolyte then waiting on the subdeacon, and the subdeacon on the deacon himself.

Afterwards there shall follow, The Lord be with you, *and,* Let us pray. *Then shall be said the Offertory.*

After the Offertory the deacon shall present the chalice with the paten and the sacrifice, to the priest, kissing his hand each time. And the priest receiving the chalice from him, shall carefully place it in its proper place in the midst of the altar, and with an inclination shall raise it slightly with both hands, offering the sacrifice to the Lord, and saying this Prayer.

Receive, O Holy Trinity, this oblation, which I an unworthy sinner offer in thy honour, and in that of blessed Mary and all thy saints, for my sins and offences, and for the salvation of the living, and for the repose of all the faithful departed.

May this new sacrifice be acceptable to almighty God, in the name of the Father, and of the Son, and of the Holy Ghost.

When this prayer has been said, the priest shall replace the chalice, and cover it with the corporals, and shall place the bread upon the corporals, decently, before the chalice containing wine and water; and he shall kiss the paten, and replace it on the right of the sacrifice on the Altar, covering it somewhat under the corporals. This done, he shall take the censer from the deacon, and shall cense the sacrifice, that is to say, thrice in the form of a cross over [the paten], and [thrice] in a circle, and on both sides of the paten and sacrifice, and thrice the space between himself and the altar. And while he is censing, he shall say this verse following:

Let my prayer be set forth, O Lord, in thy sight as the incense.[1]

After this the priest himself shall be censed by the deacon, and the subdeacon shall bring to him the Text to be kissed. Then the acolyte shall cense the quire, beginning with the rulers of the quire; next the upper grade on the decani side, beginning with the dean himself, or, in the dean's absence, with the stall nearest to him; next, the upper grade on the cantoris side; then the second grades, then the lowest grades, in the same order. The boy is to bow to the clerks, one by one, as he censes them, the subdeacon following him with the Text for all to kiss.

If a bishop be celebrant, and if it be a double feast, two boys shall come with censers, and two subdeacons with two Texts, or with relics. But if it be a double feast, and a bishop be not celebrant, one acolyte shall carry the Text on the cantoris side.

The precentor is to be censed first, who stands in the midst

[1] Ps. cxli. 2.

D 2

*of the quire with the other rulers of the quire, that is to say,
on greater double feasts only ; then the principal rulers of the
quire on each side of him ; then the two secondary rulers ;
afterwards the quire in the usual manner ; and the Texts shall
follow in the same order.*

*When, however, the Creed is not said, then immediately
after "Let us pray" and the Offertory the deacon shall advance,
and offer the chalice with the paten to the priest. The rest
shall be done in the accustomed manner, and the priest shall
cense the sacrifice as usual ; but the quire shall not be censed.
For the quire is never censed after the Gospel at mass except
when the Creed is said, and then always.*

*This done, the priest shall go to the right side of the Altar,
and wash his hands, saying :*

Cleanse me, O Lord, from all pollution of mind and
body, that being cleansed I may be able to perform the
holy work of the Lord.

*The deacon in the meantime will cense the Altar itself on the
left side, and the relics, round about them, in the accustomed
manner.*

*After he has washed his hands the priest shall return to the
Altar to execute the divine office, and the deacon and subdeacon
shall dispose themselves in order on their own steps, in the
manner previously described.*

*Then having returned, and standing before the Altar, with
head and body inclined, and with joined hands the priest shall
say this Prayer :*

In the spirit of humility and with a contrite heart
may we be accepted, O Lord, of thee ; and may our
sacrifice be in such wise in thy sight, that it may be
accepted of thee this day, and be pleasing unto thee, O
Lord my God.

*Then raising himself he shall kiss the Altar on the right of
the sacrifice ; and giving the blessing over the sacrifice he shall
afterwards sign himself, saying :*

In the name of the Father, etc.

Then shall the priest turn to the people, and say in a low voice :

Brethren and sisters, pray for me, that my and your sacrifice may be alike acceptable to the Lord our God.

Response to be made by a clerk privately :

May the grace of the Holy Ghost illuminate thy heart and thy lips, that the Lord may deign to accept this sacrifice of praise at thy hands, for our sins and offences.

In masses for the dead, after he has washed his hands, the priest with hands joined in the midst of the Altar and facing the Altar, shall begin to say :

We offer to thee, O Lord, sacrifices and prayers.

And the quire shall chant in reply :

Do thou receive them for those souls whose memory we keep this day ; make them, O Lord, to pass from death unto life.

And meanwhile the priest shall say :

In the spirit of humility.

Then shall he say forthwith, turning to the people, in a low voice :

Brethren and sisters, pray for the faithful departed.

Response to be sung by a clerk :

Grant them, O Lord, eternal rest, and let perpetual light shine upon them, which thou didst promise to Abraham and to his seed of old.[1]

It is to be noted that the words "We offer to thee, O Lord," etc., with the verse "Grant them eternal rest," etc., and "Which thou didst promise . . . of old," etc. are to be said in all masses for the dead when the body is present, and in all anniversaries and trentals ; but at other masses for the dead they are not to be said, nor on All Souls' day.

Then returning to the Altar, the priest shall say the Secrets,

---

[1] 4 Esdras (A. V. 2 Esdras) ii., 34, 35.

in number and order corresponding to the Collects said before the Epistle, commencing thus :

Let us pray.

This done, the priest shall say with a loud voice [at the end], " World without end " ; *not raising his hands till he come to the words "* Lift up your hearts." *Then shall the subdeacon take the offertory-veil[1] and the paten from the hand of the deacon, and give the paten covered with the offertory-veil to the acolyte to hold until* Our Father, etc., *is said, the acolyte standing the while on the step behind the deacon. This order is to be observed at every mass which is celebrated at the high altar[2] throughout the whole year, except only in masses for the dead. Nevertheless it shall be observed on All Souls' day. Here follow the Prefaces. First of all, the Preface for Christmas Day. This Preface is said at all masses on Christmas Day, and daily throughout the week, and on the day of the Circumcision ; and at all masses of St. Mary, from this day until the Purification, and also on the day of the Purification itself. It is also to be said at masses of Corpus Christi, and on the feast of Corpus Christi, and on its octave, and within the octave, when the service is of that feast, and in commemorations of the same. But "* In communion with," *etc., is said only up to the Circumcision, and on the day of the Circumcision.*

[1] CHRISTMAS DAY.

. . . everlasting God. Because by the mystery of the incarnate Word the new light of thy brightness hath shone upon the eyes of our mind, so that while we acknowledge him to be God visibly, we may by him be caught up into the love of things invisible. And therefore with Angels, etc.

Note, that within the Canon, at the first mass in the night of Christmas Day, the words to be used are " In communion with and celebrating the most holy night," *etc., whereas at all other masses the words are "* the most holy day," *etc.*

---

[1] Offertorium.   [2] Autenticum altare.

Within the Canon.

In communion with and celebrating the most holy day on which the immaculate virginity of the blessed Mary, brought forth a Saviour for this world; and reverencing etc.

The following Preface is said on the day of the Epiphany, and throughout its octave, and on the octave day thereof; and "In communion with" etc., is said in a similar way.

[2] THE EPIPHANY.

. . . everlasting God. Because when thy only-begotten One appeared in substance of our flesh, he restored us into the new light of his immortality. And therefore with angels etc.

Within the Canon.

In communion with and celebrating the most holy day, on which thy only-begotten One, co-eternal with thee in thy glory, was visibly made manifest in the body in the verity of our flesh; and reverencing etc.

The following Preface is said on Ash Wednesday, and at every mass of the fast from that day till Maundy Thursday, Sundays excepted.

[3] ASH WEDNESDAY.

. . . everlasting God. Who by the fasting of the body restrainest vice, liftest up the understanding, bestowest virtue and its rewards, Through Christ our Lord, By whom etc.

Note, that on Sundays throughout Lent, and on Maundy Thursday the ferial Preface is said.
On Maundy Thursday the following are also said:

Within the Canon.

In communion with and celebrating the most holy day, in which our Lord Jesus Christ was betrayed for us; and reverencing etc.

Also,

This oblation, therefore, of our service, and that of thy whole family, which we offer unto thee because of the day on which our Lord Jesus Christ delivered unto his disciples the celebration of the mystery of his body and blood, We beseech thee, O Lord, etc.

Also,

Who the day before he suffered for our salvation, and for that of all men, that is, to-day took bread into his holy and adorable hands, and lifting up his eyes to heaven unto thee his God and Father, etc.

The following Preface is said on [Easter Even] Easter Day, and throughout the whole week, up to Ascension Day, whenever the mass is of the Sunday or of Easter. On Easter Even only, the words in the Preface are " But most chiefly on this night " ; *at every other time* " But most chiefly on this day " ; *but* " In communion with," etc., *and* " This oblation, therefore," etc., *are only said throughout Easter week, and on the octave of Easter. In the former, the expression* " the most holy night " *will be employed on Easter Even only; on Easter Day, and at other times the expression will be* " the most holy day."

[4] Easter Day.

. . . everlasting God. And thee indeed at all seasons, but most chiefly on this day ought we to praise more gloriously, since Christ our Passover is sacrificed for us. For he is the very lamb which hath taken away the sins of the world, who by his death hath destroyed death, and by his rising again hath restored life [to us]. And therefore with angels, etc.

Within the Canon.

In communion with and celebrating the most holy day (*or* most holy night) of the resurrection of our Lord Jesus Christ according to the flesh ; and reverencing etc.

Also,

This oblation, therefore, of our service, and that of thy whole family which we offer unto thee, on behalf of those also whom thou hast deigned to regenerate by water and the Holy Ghost, granting unto them the remission of all their sins, We beseech thee, O Lord, etc.

The following Preface is said on Ascension Day, and throughout the octave, and on the octave, and on the Sunday within the octave, when the mass is of the Sunday; also the "In communion with" etc.

[5] ASCENSION DAY.

. . . everlasting God. Through Christ our Lord Who after his resurrection manifestly appeared to all his disciples, and in their sight was taken up into heaven that he might make us partakers of his divinity. And therefore with angels, etc.

Within the Canon.

In communion with and celebrating the most holy day, on which our Lord Jesus Christ, thy only begotten Son, set upon the right hand of thy glory our frail substance, which he had united unto himself, and reverencing etc.

The following Preface is said on Whitsunday and throughout the week and at all masses of the Holy Ghost. "In communion with" etc., and "This oblation, therefore," etc., are saia only on Whitsunday, and from that day onward till Trinity Sunday.

[6] WHITSUNDAY.

. . . everlasting God. Through Christ our Lord, Who ascending above all heavens, and sitting at thy right hand, shed forth to-day the promised Holy Ghost on the children of adoption. Wherefore the whole world rejoiceth with exceeding joy and both the heavenly hosts and the angelic powers unite in hymning thy glory, evermore saying,

Within the Canon.

In communion with and celebrating the most holy day of Pentecost, on which the Holy Ghost appeared to the apostles in likeness of fiery tongues, and reverencing etc.

Also,

This oblation, therefore, of our service and that of thy whole family, which we offer unto thee on behalf of those also, whom thou hast deigned to regenerate by water and the Holy Ghost, granting unto them forgiveness of all their sins, We beseech thee, O Lord, etc.

[7] TRINITY SUNDAY.

The following Preface is said on Trinity Sunday, and on all the Sundays following up to Advent, when the mass is of the Sunday, although it is said in chapter,[1] and on all commemorations of the Holy Trinity throughout the year, and at every nuptial mass.

. . . everlasting God. Who with thy only-begotten Son and the Holy Ghost art one God, art one Lord, not one only Person, but three Persons in one substance. For that which we believe of thy glory, which thou hast revealed, the same do we think of thy Son, and of the Holy Ghost, without any difference or inequality ; that in the confession of a true and everlasting Godhead, both distinction in Persons, and unity in essence, and equality in majesty might be adored. Which Angels and Archangels praise, Cherubin also and Seraphin, who cease not to cry with one voice, saying :

[8] APOSTLES AND EVANGELISTS.

The following Preface is said on all feasts of apostles and evangelists and through the octaves of the apostles Peter and Paul, and Andrew, when the mass is of the octave ; except on the feast of saint John, apostle and evangelist, in Christmas week. It shall be said however on the octave of that feast, and on his feast in Easter-tide.[2]

---

[1] In capitulo.   [2] *i.e.,* May 6, St. John before Port Latin.

. . . everlasting God ; and humbly to beseech thee, that thou wouldest not desert thy flock, O Lord, eternal Shepherd, but that through thy blessed Apostles, thou wouldest keep it under thy continual protection ; that it may be governed by the same rulers, whom thou hast made to preside over it as vicars and pastors of thy work. And therefore with angels, etc.

[9] FEASTS OF THE HOLY CROSS.

The following Preface is said on both feasts of the Holy Cross,[1] and on commemorations thereof throughout the whole year.

. . . everlasting God. Who hast established the salvation of mankind by the wood of the cross, that so whence death arose, from thence life might arise again, and that he who by a tree had gained a victory might by a tree be also overcome. Through Christ our Lord. By whom, etc.

[10] FEASTS OF THE BLESSED VIRGIN MARY.

The following Preface is said on every feast of the blessed Virgin Mary, except on her Purification. It is also to be said throughout the octaves of the Assumption and Nativity of blessed Mary, and on Commemorations of her throughout the whole year, except from Christmas Day to the feast of the Purification.

. . . everlasting God. And thee on the
Conception[2]
Annunciation[3]
Assumption[4]
Nativity[5]
Visitation[6]
or in Veneration[7]
of the blessed and glorious ever Virgin Mary ought we with exulting souls to praise, to bless, and to proclaim.

---

[1] *i.e.*, May 3, the Invention, and Sep. 14, the Exaltation.
[2] Dec. 8.   [3] March 25.   [4] Aug. 15.   [5] Sept. 8.
[6] July 2.   [7] For use in daily Masses of the B. V. M.

Who by the overshadowing of the Holy Ghost did both conceive thy only-begotten One, and in the abiding glory of virginity did shed upon this world the eternal light, Jesus Christ our Lord. By whom, etc.

All Prefaces at Mass, throughout the whole year, both on ferial and festal days, shall be begun in the following manner:

. . . world without end. Amen.

Then the priest shall raise his hands, saying:

℣. The Lord be with you.
℟. And with thy spirit.
℣. Lift up your hearts.
℟. We lift them up unto the Lord.
℣. Let us give thanks unto our Lord God.
℟. It is meet and right so to do.

The following is the ferial Preface, and it is said daily, except on feasts, and throughout the octaves of feasts, for which proper Prefaces are assigned; provided that all Prefaces throughout the whole year, whether proper or otherwise, both on ferial days and feasts, are said under this one tone according to the use of the Church of Sarum.

[11] FERIAL PREFACE.

It is very meet and just, right and available for our salvation,[1] that we should at all times and in all places give thanks unto thee, O Lord, holy Father, almighty everlasting God.

Through Christ our Lord. By whom angels praise thy majesty, dominions adore, powers tremble, the heavens, and the heavenly hosts, and the blessed Seraphin unite in one glad voice in extolling thee. Together with whom, we pray thee, that thou wouldest command that our voices should have entrance, humbly confessing thee and saying:

Here followeth the Sanctus.

While the priest is saying the Sanctus he shall raise his

[1] Salutare.

arms slightly, and join his hands as far as the words " In the name of the Lord." *At that point he shall always sign himself on his face.*

Holy, Holy, Holy, Lord God of Hosts; heaven and earth are full of thy glory. Osanna in the highest. Blessed is he that cometh in the name of the Lord. Osanna in the highest.

When the service of St. Mary is said for the last time before Advent, and before Septuagesima, and on the octaves of the Visitation, Assumption, and Nativity of blessed Mary, then the words shall run thus :

Blessed be the son of Mary that cometh etc.

Then immediately, with hands joined and eyes raised, the priest shall begin "Therefore, O most merciful Father," *etc., inclining his body until he come to the words* " and entreat."

Canon of the Mass.

Here followeth the Canon.

Therefore, O most merciful Father, we humbly pray thee, through Jesus Christ thy Son our Lord,

The priest shall incline his body until he say,
and entreat thee

Here the priest shall raise himself and shall kiss the altar on the right of the sacrifice, saying :
to accept and bless

Here shall the priest make three crosses over the chalice ana bread, saying :
these gi + fts, these pre + sents, these ho + ly unspotted sacrifices,

Having made the signs over the chalice he shall raise his hands, saying thus :
which we offer to thee, in the first place, on behalf of thy holy Catholic Church, which do thou vouchsafe to keep in peace, to guard, to unite, and to govern, throughout the whole world ; together with thy servants our Pope *N.* and our Bishop *N.*

That is to say, the bishop of the diocese only,
and our King *N.*

The above persons are mentioned by name. Then shall follow :
and all who are orthodox, and who hold the catholic and apostolic faith.

Remember, O Lord, thy servants and thy hand-maidens *N.* and *N.*

in praying for whom a due order dictated by charity ought to be observed. The priest prays five times : firstly, for himself; secondly, for his father and mother, that is to say both carnal and spiritual, and for his other relations ; [1] *thirdly, for his special friends, parishioners and otherwise ; fourthly, for all persons present ; fifthly, for all Christian people ; and here the priest may commend all his own friends to God. I counsel,* [2] *however, that no one should pause at this point too long, both on account of possible distractions of mind, and also on account of suggestions which may be made by evil angels, as well as on account of other dangers.*

and all here present, whose faith is approved, and whose devotion is known to thee ; on behalf of whom we offer unto thee, or [3] who offer unto thee this sacrifice of praise, for themselves and for all pertaining to them, for the redemption of their souls, for the hope of their own salvation and security, and who are paying their vows unto thee, the eternal, living, and true God.

In communion with and reverencing the memory, in the first place, of the glorious and ever virgin

inclining a little as he says,

Mary, mother of our God and Lord Jesus Christ ; As also of thy blessed apostles and martyrs—Peter, Paul, Andrew, James, John, Thomas, James, Philip, Bartholomew, Matthew, Simon, and Thaddæus, [4] Linus, Cletus, Clement, Sixtus, Cornelius, Cyprian.

---

[1] Parentibus. A late Latin word in this sense.
[2] An addition not found in many editions.
[3] "Vel," originally a rubric which has crept into the text.
[4] It will be noticed that while Judas Iscariot is naturally omitted from this list of the twelve Apostles; St. Paul, and not St. Matthias, takes his place, and is named next to St. Peter.

Laurence, Chrysogonus, John and Paul, Cosmas and Damian, and of all thy saints ; through whose merits and prayers do thou grant that in all things we may be defended by the aid of thy protection. Through the same Christ our Lord. Amen.

Here the priest shall regard the host with great veneration, saying :

We beseech thee, therefore, O Lord, graciously to accept this oblation of our service, and of thy whole family, and to dispose our days in thy peace, bidding us to be delivered from eternal damnation, and to be numbered among the flock of thine elect. Through Christ our Lord. Amen.

Here let him regard the host again, saying :

Which oblation, we beseech thee, O almighty God, that thou wouldest vouchsafe in all respects

Here he shall make three crosses over each [oblation], while he says,

to ble + ss, ap + prove, rati + fy, and make reasonable and acceptable, that it may become to us

Here he shall make a cross over the bread, saying,

the bo + dy

And here over the chalice,

and the blo + od

And joining his hands he shall say,

of thy most dearly beloved Son our Lord Jesus Christ.

Here shall the priest raise and join his hands, and afterwards wipe his fingers, and elevate the host,[1] saying,

---

[1] This elevation of the host before consecration is a peculiarity of the Anglican ritual (Sarum, York, and Hereford Uses,)—see Simmons, T. F., *Lay Folks Mass Book*, London, 1879, p. 283.

Who on the day before he suffered took bread into his holy and adorable hands, and lifting up his eyes to heaven,

Here shall he raise his eyes,

to thee, O God, his almighty Father,

Here shall he incline, and afterwards raise himself a little, saying,

gave thanks to thee, bles + sed it, brake it,

Here shall he touch the host, saying,

and gave it to his disciples, saying, Take, and eat ye all of this.   For this is my body.

These words ought to be said in one breath, and one utterance, without the interposition of any pause.   After these words the priest should incline to the host, and afterwards elevate it above his forehead, so that it can be seen by the people, and then reverently replace it before the chalice, making the form of a cross therewith.   Then he shall uncover the chalice, and hold it between his hands, not disjoining the thumb from the forefinger, except only when he makes the benedictions, saying thus :

Likewise, after supper, taking this most excellent chalice into his holy and adorable hands, and giving thanks to thee,

Here he shall incline, saying,

he bles + sed it, and gave it to his disciples, saying, Take and drink ye all of this,

Here shall the priest elevate the chalice a little, saying thus :

For this is the cup of my blood of the new and everlasting testament, the mystery of faith, which shall be shed[1] for you and for many for the remission of sins.

[1] effundetur.   The present tense "is shed" in the Anglican rite corresponds to the old Gallican "effunditur" in the Sacramentarium

E

Here he shall elevate the chalice as high as his chest, or above his head, saying,

As oft as ye shall do these things, ye shall do them in remembrance of me.[1]

Here he shall replace the chalice, and rub his fingers over it, in case of any crumbs, and cover the chalice. Then he shall raise his arms in the form of a cross, with his fingers joined until the words " of thy gifts and bounties."

Wherefore also, O Lord, we thy servants, together with thy holy people, calling to mind both the blessed passion of the same Christ, thy Son, our Lord God, and also his resurrection from the dead, together with his glorious ascension into heaven, offer to thy most excellent majesty of thy gifts and bounties,

Here five crosses shall be made, the first three crosses over the host and chalice, at the words

a pu + re offering, a ho + ly offering, a spot + less offering,[2]

The fourth cross over the bread, at the words

the holy br + ead of eternal life,

The fifth cross over the chalice, at the words

and the cha + lice of everlasting salvation. Upon which do thou vouchsafe to look with a favourable and gracious countenance, and to accept them as thou didst vouchsafe to accept the gifts of thy righteous[3] servant Abel, the sacrifice of our

Gallicanum. Mabillon, *Museum Italicum*, Tom. 1, p. 280; and to the present tense used here in the Byzantine Rite, and in other Eastern Liturgies. Brightman (F. E.) *Eastern Liturgies*, pp. 328, 52, 133, etc.

[1] "in mei memoriam," *or* "for a memorial of me."

[2] "hostia," which might also be translated "host" or "sacrifice."

[3] "justi." The justi are among the classes of saints sometimes commemorated or invoked in Western Liturgies and Litanies.

patriarch Abraham, and the holy sacrifice, the pure oblation, which thy high priest Melchisedech offered unto thee.

Here shall the priest incline his body and cross his hands,[1] while he says, "We humbly beseech thee" as far as the words, "by partaking at this Altar." And then he shall raise himself, kissing the Altar on the right of the sacrifice, and shall make the sign of the cross over the host, and over the chalice, and on his face, while he says the words "all heavenly benediction."

We humbly beseech thee, almighty God, command these [gifts] to be borne by the hands of thy holy angel to thy altar on high, in the presence of thy divine majesty, that as many of us

Here he shall raise himself, and kiss the altar on the right of the sacrifice, saying :

as shall by partaking at this Altar receive the most sacred

Here he shall make the sign of the cross over the host, saying,

bo + dy

and over the chalice,

and bl + ood of thy Son, may be fulfilled

Here he shall sign himself on his face, saying :

with all heavenly bene + diction and grace, through the same Christ our Lord. Amen.

Here shall he pray for the dead.

Remember also, O Lord, [the souls of] thy servants and handmaidens *N.* and *N.*, who have gone before us with the sign of faith, and sleep the sleep of peace ; to them, O Lord, and to all who

---

[1] "Cancellatis manibus," *i.e.* lattice-wise.

rest in Christ, we pray thee that thou wouldest grant a place of refreshment, light and peace. Through the same Christ our Lord. Amen.

Here shall he strike his breast once, saying,

To us, also, thy sinful servants, who hope in the multitude of thy mercies, vouchsafe to grant some part and fellowship with thy holy apostles and martyrs, with John, Stephen, Matthias, Barnabas, Ignatius, Alexander, Marcellinus, Peter, Felicitas, Perpetua, Agatha, Lucy, Agnes, Cæcilia, Anastasia, and with all thy saints, into whose company do thou admit us, we beseech thee, not weighing our merits, but pardoning our offences. Through Christ our Lord.

"Amen" is not said here.

By whom, O Lord, thou ever createst,

Here the priest shall make the sign of the cross over the chalice thrice, saying,

sancti + fiest, quick + enest, bles + sest, and bestowest upon us all these good things.

Here let the priest uncover the chalice, and make the sign of the cross [over it] five times with the host: firstly, beyond the chalice, on either side; secondly, level with the chalice; thirdly, below the chalice; fourthly, as firstly; fifthly, before the chalice.

Through + him, and with + him, and in + him, all honour and glory are unto thee, God the Father al + mighty, in the unity of the Holy + Ghost.

Here the priest shall cover the chalice, and keep his hands upon the Altar until "Our Father" etc., is said, saying thus,

For ever and ever. Amen.
Let us pray.

Admonished by saving precepts, and directed by divine institution, we are bold to say,

Here shall the deacon receive the paten, and hold it up uncovered, with his arm extended on high, on the right-hand side of the priest; until the words " Graciously give peace in our days " etc. Then shall the priest raise his hands, and say,

Our Father, which art in heaven, hallowed be thy name. Thy kingdom come. Thy will be done in earth as it is in heaven. Give us this day our daily bread ; and forgive us our trespasses, as we forgive them that trespass against us. And lead us not into temptation,

The quire shall say,

But deliver us from evil.

The priest adding privately,

Amen.

Deliver[1] us, we beseech thee, O Lord, from all evils, past, present, and future, and at the intercession of the blessed, and glorious, and ever-virgin Mary, mother of God, and of thy blessed apostles, Peter, and Paul, and Andrew, with all saints,

Here the deacon shall give the paten to the priest, kissing his hand ; and the priest shall kiss the paten ; afterwards he shall place it before his left eye, and then before his right eye ; after which he shall make the sign of the cross with the paten over his head, and then he shall replace it in position, saying :

Graciously give peace in our days, that aided by the help of thy lovingkindness, we may both be ever free from sin, and secure from all disquietude.

Here he shall uncover the chalice, and take the body with an

---

[1] This expansion of the last petition in the Pater Noster is known as the Embolismus.

inclination, placing it over the bowl of the chalice, holding it between his thumbs and forefingers, and breaking it into three portions, saying at the first fraction,

Through the same our Lord Jesus Christ thy Son,

At the second fraction,

Who liveth and reigneth with thee in the unity of the Holy Ghost, God,

Here he shall hold the two broken portions in his left hand, and the third broken portion in his right hand on the top of the chalice, and shall say in a loud voice,

For ever and ever.

The quire answering,

Amen.

Here he shall make three crosses inside the chalice with the third portion of the host, saying,[1]

The peace of the Lord + be with y + ou al + ways.

The quire replying,

And with thy spirit.

At the saying of "Agnus Dei," the deacon and the subdeacon shall approach the priest, both of them on his right side, the deacon being the nearer, and the subdeacon the more remote, and shall say privately,

O Lamb of God, that takest away the sins of the world :

have mercy upon us.

O Lamb of God, that takest away the sins of the world :

have mercy upon us.

O Lamb of God, that takest away the sins of the world :

grant us thy peace.

[1] The episcopal form of blessing, with its ritual, at Mass is not referred to here.   It is described by Maskell (W.) *Mon. Rit. Eccles. Anglic.,* 2nd edit., Oxford, 1882, vol. i., pp. cxlv-vii.

In masses for the dead it is said thus,

O Lamb of God, that takest away the sins of the world :

> grant them rest.

with the addition of " eternal *" [before "* rest *"] in the third repetition thereof.*

Here, making the sign of the cross, he shall place the aforesaid third portion of the host in the sacrament of the blood, saying thus :

Let this most + holy commixture of the body and blood of our Lord Jesus Christ be to me and to all who receive it health of mind and body, and a salutary preparation for worthily attaining unto eternal life. Through the same Christ our Lord. Amen.

Before the pax is given, the priest shall say :

O Lord, holy Father, almighty everlasting God, grant me so worthily to receive this most holy body and blood of thy Son our Lord Jesus Christ, that I may thereby be found fit to obtain remission of all my sins, and to be filled with thy Holy Spirit, and to have thy peace ; because thou art God alone, and there is none other beside thee, whose kingdom and glorious dominion abideth for ever, world without end.[1] Amen.

Here the priest shall kiss the corporals on the right side, and the top of the chalice, and afterwards the deacon, saying :

℣. Peace be to thee and to the Church of God.

℞. And with thy spirit.

The deacon on the right side of the priest shall receive the

---

[1] This seems to be a Mozarabic prayer, see Hammond (C. E.) Litt. E. and W., Oxford, 1878, p. 351.

pax from him, and shall hand it to the subdeacon. Then the deacon himself shall carry the pax to the rulers of the quire at the step of the quire, and they shall carry the pax to the quire, each to his own side, beginning with the seniors. But on feasts and week-days, when the quire is not ruled, the pax shall be carried from the deacon to the quire, by the two end members of the second rank; the rest as before.

After the pax has been given, the priest shall say the following prayers privately, before he communicates himself, holding the host in both hands:

O God the Father, fount and source of all goodness, who, moved by thy lovingkindness, hast willed that thine Only-begotten One should descend to this lower world for our sakes, and take flesh, which I unworthy here hold in my hands,

Here the priest shall incline towards the host, saying:

I adore thee, I glorify thee, I laud thee with the whole intention of my mind and heart, and I beseech thee that thou wouldest not forsake us thy servants, but that thou wouldest forgive our sins; that so we may be enabled to serve thee, the only living and true God, through the same Christ our Lord. Amen.

O Lord Jesu Christ, Son of the living God, who by the will of the Father and the co-operation of the Holy Ghost, hast given life to the world by thy death; deliver me, I beseech thee, by this thy most holy body and blood, from all my iniquities, and from every ill; and make me ever obedient to thy commandments, and suffer me not to be for ever separated from thee, O Saviour of the world.[1] Who with God the Father, and the

---

[1] Salvator mundi. This is a Hispano-Gallican phrase. It has been dropped in R. The fact of a prayer being addressed to the second

same Holy Ghost livest and reignest God world without end. Amen.

Let not the sacrament of thy body and blood, O Lord Jesu Christ, which I although unworthy receive, be unto me for judgment and condemnation, but may it through thy goodness be profitable to my salvation both in body and soul. Amen.

Then shall he humbly[1] say to the body before he receives it:

Hail for evermore, most holy flesh of Christ, to me before all things and above all things the greatest sweetness.[2]

May the body of our Lord Jesus Christ be to me a sinner the way and the life.

In the na + me of the Father, and of the Son, and of the Holy Ghost. Amen.

Here he shall receive the body, having first made a cross with the body before his mouth.

Then let him [look] at the blood with great devotion, saying,

Hail for evermore, heavenly drink, to me before all things and above all things the greatest sweetness.[3]

May the body and blood of our Lord Jesus Christ be profitable to me a sinner for an eternal remedy unto everlasting life. Amen.

In the na + me of the Father, and of the Son, and of the Holy Ghost. Amen.

Here he shall receive the blood, and after receiving it the priest shall incline, and say with devotion the following prayer.

person in the Trinity is likewise almost a certain sign of Gallican or Mozarabic origin.

[1] cum humiliatione. Perhaps, with an act of prostration.

[2] This is a Mozarabic salutation. Hammond (C. E.), Litt. E. and W., Oxford, 1878, p. 351.

[3] *Ibid.*, p. 353.

I give thanks unto thee, O Lord, holy Father,
almighty everlasting God, who hast refreshed me
with the most holy body and blood of thy Son our
Lord Jesus Christ ; and I pray that this sacrament
of our salvation, which I, an unworthy sinner,
have received, may not turn to my judgment or
condemnation, according to my deserts ; but to the
preservation of my body and soul unto eternal life.
Amen.

*After this has been said, the priest shall go to the right side
of the altar with the chalice between his hands, and his fingers
still joined as before ; and the subdeacon shall approach and
pour wine and water into the chalice ; and the priest shall
rinse his hands, lest any relics of the body or blood remain on
his fingers, or in the chalice.*

*When, however, any priest has to celebrate twice on one day,
then at the first mass he ought not to take any ablution, but to
place it in the aumbry, or in a clean vessel until the end of the
second mass, when both ablutions should be taken together.*

After the first ablution this prayer is said :

What we have partaken of with our mouth, O
Lord, may we receive with a pure heart, and from
a temporal gift may it be made to us an everlasting
remedy.

*Here he shall wash his fingers in the bowl of the chalice
with wine poured in by the subdeacon, and after it has been
drunk this prayer shall follow.*

Let this communion, O Lord, cleanse us from
sin, and make us to be partakers of heavenly
healing.

*After receiving the ablution, the priest shall place the chalice
on the paten, so that if anything remain [in the former] it may
drain off [on to the latter]. And afterwards, inclining himself,
he shall say,*

Let us adore the sign of the cross : whereby we have received the sacrament of salvation.

Then the priest shall wash his hands, the deacon in the meanwhile folding the corporals. After the priest has washed his hands, and returned to the right side of the Altar, the deacon shall hold the chalice to the mouth of the priest, for him to drink, if there remain anything therein to be consumed. Afterwards the priest shall say the Communion with his ministers; then making the sign of the cross on his face, he shall turn to the people, and slightly raising his arms, and joining his hands, he shall say :

The Lord be with you.

And again returning to the altar, he shall say,

Let us pray.

Then he shall say the Postcommunion, after the same number and order as the Collects said before the Epistle. When he has finished the last Postcommunion, and has made the sign of the cross upon his forehead, the priest shall turn himself again to the people, and shall say :

The Lord be with you.

Then shall the deacon say,

Let us bless the Lord.

But at other times the words used are,

Depart, the mass is finished.[1]

Whenever "Depart, the mass is finished" is said, it is always said turning to the people, and whenever "Let us bless the Lord" or "May they rest in peace" is to be said, it is said turning to the altar. When these have been said, the priest, inclining his body and joining his hands, standing in the midst before the altar, shall say this Collect, silently.

[1] "Ite, missa est." The exact translation is uncertain. It may be, "Depart, the congregation is dismissed."

Let the obedient performance of my bounden duty be pleasing unto thee, O Holy Trinity, and grant that this sacrifice, which I unworthy have offered in the presence of thy majesty, may be acceptable unto thee, and through thy mercy may be a propitiation for myself, and for all for whom I have offered it. Who livest and reignest God world without end. Amen.

This [Collect] ended, the priest shall raise himself, and, making the sign of the cross on his face, shall say :

In the name of the Father etc.

And so, after making an inclination [the clergy] shall retire, with the candlebearer[s] and the other ministers, in the same order, and so vested, as they approached the altar at the beginning of mass.

And immediately after "Thanks be to God," None shall be said in the quire, when it is said after mass.

While returning [from the altar], the priest shall say the Gospel, In the beginning[1] etc.

[THANKSGIVING AFTER MASS.]

When the priest has put off his chasuble and his other sacerdotal vestments, he shall say the following Psalms, with the Anthem "Let us sing" etc.

Psalm. O ye priests of the Lord, etc.

As far as to the end of the Canticle.[2]

Psalm. O praise God in his holiness, etc.[3]

Psalm. Lord, now lettest thou [thy servant] etc.[4] *with* Glory be to the Father, etc. *and* As it was in the beginning, etc.

---

[1] St. John, i. 1–14.   [2] Song of the Three Children, 62–66.
[3] Ps. cl.   [4] St. Luke, ii. 29–32.

Then the whole anthem is repeated.

Let us sing the song of the three children, which they sang in the furnace of fire as a thanksgiving unto the Lord.

Lord, have mercy.
Christ, have mercy.
Lord, have mercy.
Our Father etc.

℣. And lead us not into temptation
℟. But deliver [us from evil].
℣. Let us praise the Father, and the Son, with the Holy Ghost.
℟. Let us praise and magnify him for ever.
℣. Blessed art thou, O Lord, in the firmament of heaven ; and to be praised and glorified for ever.
℟. May the Holy Trinity bless and keep us.   Amen
℣. Enter not into judgment with thy servant, O Lord :[1]
℟. For in thy sight shall no man living be justified.[1]
℣. Turn us, O Lord God of hosts ;
℟. And shew the light of thy countenance, and we shall be whole.
℣. Lord, hear my prayer.
℟. And let my crying come unto thee.
℣. The Lord be with you.
℟. And with thy spirit.

Let us pray.

Collect.

O God, who for the three children didst assuage the flames of fire, mercifully grant that we thy servants may not be consumed by the flame of our sins.

Collect.

Kindle our reins and our hearts, O Lord, with the fire of the Holy Ghost, that we may serve thee with a chaste body, and please thee with a clean heart.

---

[1] This ℣. and ℟. are not separated in the Latin text ; but their non-separation is probably accidental.

Collect.

Prevent us, O Lord, we beseech thee, in all our doings with thy favour, and further us with thy help, that all our works may be begun, continued, and ended in thee.

These three Collects are all to be concluded thus :
Through Christ our Lord. Amen.

PRAYERS IN PROSTRATION.

Be it known that at every ferial mass, prostration is to be made by the whole quire directly after the " Sanctus " *up to* " The peace of the Lord," *throughout the whole year except from Easter to the first Sunday after Trinity.*[1]

Note, that from the second Sunday after the Epiphany[2] *up to Maundy Thursday, and from the first Sunday after Trinity to Christmas Eve the following prayers are said at mass only on ferial days and on feasts of three lessons without ruling of the quire, and on octaves, and within octaves when the quire is not ruled. And they are said after* "For ever and ever " *and* " Our Father etc." *between* " For ever and ever " *and* " The peace of the Lord etc." *After the priest has said* "For ever and ever " *and the quire has responded* "Amen," *the Prayers in prostration shall be immediately begun by the quire in this manner.*

Psalm.

O God, the heathen are come into thy inheritance,[3] *with* Glory be to the Father, etc.

Psalm.

God be merciful unto us, and bless us,[4] *with* Glory be to the Father, etc.

---

[1] Called "Deus Omnium" from the opening words of the first Respond after the first Lesson in the first Nocturn at Matins. This rubric may throw light upon the duration of Easter-tide.

[2] Called "Domine ne in ira" for the same reason.

[3] Ps. lxxix.   [4] Ps. lxvii.

Psalm.

The king shall rejoice in thy strength, O Lord, etc.,[1]
with Glory be to the Father, etc.

Anthem.

Thine is the power, thine the kingdom, O Lord ; thou
art above all nations ; give peace, O Lord, in our time.
Lord, have mercy.
Christ, have mercy.
Lord, have mercy.
Our Father, etc.

*All the above are said without inflection of voice both by the
clerks in the quire, and by the priest with his ministers.*

Then shall the priest say with inflection :

℣. And lead us not into temptation,
℟. But deliver [us from evil].
℣. Let God arise and let his enemies be scattered.
℟. Let them also that hate him flee before him.[2]
℣. Not unto us, O Lord, not unto us.
℟. But unto thy name give the praise.[3]
℣. Let us pray for those in affliction and captivity.[4]
℟. Deliver Israel, O God, out of all his troubles.[5]
℣. Send unto them, O Lord, help from the holy
place,
℟. And defend them out of Sion.[6]
℣. Be unto them, O Lord, a strong tower.
℟. From the face of their enemy.[7]
℣. O Lord, save the king.
℟. And hear us in the day in which we call upon
thee.[8]
℣. Lord, hear my prayer,
℟. And let my crying come unto thee.[9]

[1] Ps. xxi. [2] Ps. lxviii. 1. [3] Ps. cxv. 1.
[4] So in the Deacons' Litany is the Lit. of St. Chrysostom, δεηθῶμεν
ὑπὲρ . . . καμνόντον αἰχμαλώτων. Brightman (F. E.), *Eastern Liturgies,*
pp. 362, 363. [5] Ps. xxv. 21.
[6] Ps. xx. 2. Ps. lxi. 3. [8] Ps. xx. 9. (Vulg.)
[9] Ps. cii. 1.

℣. The Lord be with you.
℟. And with thy spirit.

Let us pray.

Collect.

O God, who in thy wonderful providence orderest all things, we humbly beseech thee that thou wouldest restore back to Christian worship, out of the hands of the enemies of the cross of Christ, the land which thy Only-begotten Son consecrated with his own blood ; mercifully directing the prayers of the faithful who plead for its liberation into the way of eternal peace. [Through etc.]

Collect.

Guide, we beseech thee, O Lord, thy servant our bishop,[1] and through the intercession of the blessed mother of God, the ever virgin Mary, and that of all thy saints, multiply the gifts of thy grace in him, that he may be delivered from all offences, and that being not without thy help in this world, he may rejoice in the ordinances of life everlasting. [Through etc.]

Collect.

Grant, we beseech thee, Almighty God, unto thy servant our king health both of mind and body ; that by ministering in good works he may ever deserve to be defended by thy strong protection. Through the same Christ our Lord. Amen.

Then shall follow :

The peace of the Lord be with you always.[2]

---

[1] "Pontificem nostrum," evidently the bishop of the diocese.

[2] Here follow 27 various ways of intoning "Ite missa est" or "Benedicamus Domino"; and one way of intoning "Requiescant in pace. Amen." in masses for the dead, with musical notes, which have not been reproduced here.

PRAYERS TO BE SAID AFTER MASS.

Prayer to be said by the priest after mass.

Almighty and everlasting God, saviour of souls, and redeemer of the world, most graciously look upon me thy servant prostrate before thy majesty ; and of thy great lovingkindness behold this sacrifice, which in honour of thy name I have offered for the salvation of the faithful both quick and dead, and also for our sins and offences. Put away thine anger from me, grant me thy grace and mercy, open unto me the door of paradise, and deliver me by thy might from all evils ; whatsoever guilt I have personally committed do thou pardon ; and make me so to persevere in thy commandments in this world, that I may be found worthy to be joined to the flock of thine elect. Grant this, O my God, whose blessed name, and honour, and dominion, abideth for ever and ever. Amen.[1]

Prayer to be said by the priest after mass.

Almighty and everlasting God, Jesu Christ [our] Lord, be merciful unto my sins through the partaking of thy body and blood; for thou hast spoken, saying, Whoso eateth my flesh and drinketh my blood, dwelleth in me and I in him. Wherefore, I humbly beseech thee, to create a clean heart in me, and to renew a right spirit within me ; deign to stablish me with thy free spirit, and cleanse me from all the snares and vices of the devil, that I may be worthy to be a partaker of heavenly joys. Who livest etc.[2]

Prayer to be said by the priest after mass.

I give thanks unto thee, O Lord God, Father almighty, who hast vouchsafed to feed me with the body and blood of thy beloved Son, Jesus Christ our Lord. I beseech

---

[1] In the 1526 edit. this prayer is printed on fol. lxxxvii. *r.*
[2] *Ib.*

F

thy boundless goodness, almighty and merciful Lord, that this holy communion may not be unto me for judgment or condemnation, but that it may be unto me an earnest of faith and a shield of good will, to cast out of my mind all the frauds of the enemy, to root out the plague of pride, the lust of appetite, and the wantonness of tongue ; and that I may enter into that banquet where are the true light and the everlasting joys of the just. Also I beseech thee, O Lord, that this holy communion may be my guide and viaticum to the haven of eternal salvation. Let it be consolation unto me when I am troubled in my thoughts ; most sweet delight in [every] good purpose ; patience in tribulation and difficulties ; medicine in sickness. Through these most holy mysteries which I have received, grant unto me a right faith, a firm hope, and a perfect charity ; renunciation of the world, purification of desire, sweet contentment of mind, ardent love of thee, remembrance of the passing of thy dear Son, and bowels of compassion ; let it fulfil my life with virtue, and preserve it in thy praise and faith unfeigned ; and grant that in the hour of my departure I may receive the grace of so great a mystery with true faith, firm hope, and sincere charity, so that I may behold thee for ever. Amen.[1]

> What thou doest at Christ's table,
> Presbyter, think well ;
> Life eternal is prepared
> There for thee, or hell.

> As the sacred taper burning
> Dwindles in its size,
> So the presbyter, if guilty,
> Celebrating, dies.

> Think of these—the death of Jesus,
> Thine own death as well,
> Earth's deceptions, heaven's glories,
> And the pains of hell.[2]

---

[1] *Ib.*, fol. lxxxvii. *v.*   [2] *Ib.*, fol. lxxxviii. *r.*

MASS IN REMEMBRANCE OF THE FEASTS OF THE BLESSED VIRGIN MARY.

Office.

Let us all rejoice in the Lord, celebrating this festal day in honour of the virgin Mary; in whose festivals angels rejoice, and together praise the Son of God.

Ps. My heart is inditing of a good matter : I speak of the things which I have made unto the King.[1]

Glory be to the Father, etc.

Collect.

O God, who causest us to rejoice in recalling the joys of the conception, the nativity, the annunciation, the visitation, the purification, and the assumption of the blessed and glorious virgin Mary ; grant to us so worthily to devote ourselves to her praise and service, that we may be conscious of her presence and assistance in all our necessities and straits, and especially in the hour of death, and that after death we may be found worthy, through her and in her, to rejoice in heaven with thee. Through etc.

Lesson. Song of Sol. ii. 13, 14 ; iv. 1, 2, 7, 8, 9, 11. Arise my love . . . . . . smell of Lebanon.

Gradual.

Thou shalt shine in glorious light, and all the ends of the world shall worship thee.

℟. The nations from afar shall come to thee bearing gifts, and shall in thee adore the Lord, and shall account thy land holiness.

Alleluya. ℟. Blessed are all they that love thee, O virgin, and who rejoice in thy peace ; blessed be the Lord who hath exalted thee, and hath set his dominion upon thee for ever and ever.

[1] Ps. xlv. 1.

Sequence.

No messenger mean
to the barren is sent,
but an angel of might
most refulgent in light
from the lover of men.

She wonders, believes,
and in joy she conceives,
the blest mother of God,
whom exulting she bore,
most beloved of all.

The most excellent maid
in seclusion abides,
serving God in her heart,
sweetly singing apart,
born a blessing to man.

Her mind's pious intent
with a vow she confirmed,
angels associate
best befit her estate
who came us to restore.

From the city above
the archangel he sends ;
to the message of love
the Maid meekly attends,
believes and conceives.

Then the virgin with child
rises up in her haste ;
he whom none can declare
doth the barren who bare
his forerunner salute.

Undefiled she brought forth
the redeemer of earth ;
vast advantage to men,
angel-heralded birth—
to the vanquished a palm.

In her meekness the babe
unto God she presents,
and the gift offers there
which the law bade prepare,
  while Symeon stood by.

Mistress she of the world
in assumption is seen
beyond angels to shine—
of the heavens the queen,
  favoured mother of God.

There the Son sets her down
with himself on his throne,
and the virginal crown
to the glory of God
  Deigns to put on her head.

These most marvellous acts
we thy people recite;
to thee sing in our hearts
in thy praises unite,
  whom the fatherless love.

O then for us obtain
pardon, mother benign!
let our guilt melt away,
let that city divine
  be our dwelling for aye.   Amen.

Gospel.   St. Luke i. 39–47.

And Mary arose . . . . . . God my Saviour.

Offertory.

All generations shall call thee blessed, for the Lord that is
mighty hath done to thee great things; and holy is his name.[1]

---

[1] St. Luke i. 48, 49.

Secret.

O Lord Jesu Christ, from whom all holy thoughts do come; who hast taught thy servants to honour thy glorious mother; mercifully grant us so to celebrate her[1] on earth with the solemn sacrifice of praise and with due devotion, that by her intercession we may be found worthy to reign in joy in heaven. Who livest etc.

Preface of the blessed Virgin Mary.[2]

Communion.

Bless the God of heaven with fear, and rejoice before him with trembling; for he hath shewed his mercy upon us, since he hath willed that his mother should be an advocate for us in heaven.

Postcommunion.

Grant, we beseech thee, almighty God, that we may keep with an immaculate heart the sacrament which we have received in honour of the blessed virgin mother Mary; so that we who celebrate her feast now, may be found worthy when we have left this life to pass into her company. Through etc.[3]

---

[1] Ipsius apparently a misprint for "ipsam."

[2] No. [10] p. 39.

[3] Here follow lengthy "cautelæ missæ" or directions for the priest, referring to his preparation and conduct; and to various possible emergencies and accidents at Mass. They are not translated and reproduced here.

[The Proper of Seasons.]

FIRST SUNDAY IN ADVENT.

At Mass :   *Office.*

Unto thee, O Lord, will I lift up my soul ; my God,
I have put my trust in thee : O let me not be confounded, neither let mine enemies triumph over me.[1]

Ps. Shew me thy ways, O Lord : and teach me thy paths.[2]

The Office shall be repeated, that is to say, Unto thee, O
Lord, will I lift up etc. *and afterwards there shall be said,*
Glory be to the Father, etc. *and* As it was etc. *After
this has been said, the Office shall be repeated again as before.
And thus shall it be done throughout the whole year, as well
on Sundays as on holy-days with ruling of the quire, and in
all masses of saint Mary ; except on Passion Sunday, and
from that day till Maundy Thursday, at the mass of the
season only. Then, after the Psalm the Office shall be repeated
without* Glory be to the Father etc.

" Kyrie eleison " *shall follow.*

" Gloria in excelsis " *is not said throughout the whole of
Advent, whatever the mass may be ; nor from Septuagesima
to the vigil of Easter.*

*When this has been done, and when the priest has made
the sign of the cross on his face, he shall turn to the people,
and slightly elevating his arms, and joining his hands, shall
say thus,* The Lord be with you. *And the Quire shall
answer,* And with thy spirit, *under the same tone, and the
priest shall again turn to the altar, and say,* Let us pray.

And whensoever "The Lord be with you" *is said at mass,
it is always said under the same tone, as likewise* " Let us
pray," *except in Prefaces, and except in a Nuptial mass,
when the blessing is given over the bridegroom and bride before*

[1] Ps. xxv. I.   [2] *Ib.* 3.

"The peace of the Lord." *For then the words are said thus* "The Lord be with you." "Let us pray" "For ever and ever". *The reply is made* "Amen," *and in similar cases with a like ending.*

Then the following Collect shall be said:

Stir up, we beseech thee, O Lord thy power, and come; that we may be found worthy to be rescued by thy protection from the threatening dangers of our sins, and to be set free by thy deliverance. Who livest and reignest with God the Father in the unity of the Holy Spirit, God for ever and ever. Amen.

Again the priest shall say "Let us pray" *as above.*

Memory of saint Mary. Collect.

O God, who wast pleased that thy Word etc. *as below.*[1]

And whatever mass is said there shall always be a memory of saint Mary till the vigil of Christmas Day. But when the mass is of any saint, even if it be a double feast, or when the mass "I am the salvation of the people etc."[2] *is said, then there shall be a memory both of Advent and of saint Mary.*

Note, that on all Sundays, and on feasts with ruling of the quire throughout the whole year this direction is to be generally observed, that as many Collects should be said at mass as were said at matins; except on Christmas Day; yet in such wise that an uneven number of Collects should always be preserved at mass save only in Christmas week. For if two or four Collects are for use, then a third or fifth Collect of all saints shall be introduced, to wit: Grant we beseech thee, almighty God, that the intercession of the holy mother of God etc.[3] *and this throughout the whole year, throughout Advent as well as in the Paschal season. Nevertheless, when*

---

[1] See Collect for the Annunciation of the B. V. M., March 25, in the Proper of Saints.

[2] The votive mass generally known by the opening words of its Office "Salus populi," assigned to Tuesday.

[3] This Collect will be found among the Common Memories near the end of the Votive Masses, under the heading, "Of all Saints throughout the Year."

mass is said on a feast day in chapter, if there is a memory of any saint appointed for use, memories also of other saints are said at the same mass at discretion. But if it be a Sunday mass which is said in chapter, then there shall be at the same mass of the Sunday a memory of the Trinity; but the other memories are to be said at high mass.[1] But on Sundays, and on feasts with ruling of the quire from Easter to our Lord's Ascension, when Sundays occur on them, there should be no memory at the Sunday mass.

Besides, on all feasts of nine lessons, which occur on Ember Days, or on vigils, or throughout the whole of Lent, there shall be no memory of the fast at the mass of the feast. For after the mass of the feast, there should be a solemn mass of the fast, both of them at the high altar.[2]

But on ferial days, and on feasts without ruling of the quire, and from the second Sunday after the Epiphany to the first Sunday in Lent, and from the first Sunday after Trinity to Advent, five Collects are wont to be said at mass; namely, the first the Collect of the day; the second the Collect of saint Mary; the third the Collect of all saints (viz., Grant, we beseech thee, almighty God, *etc., and this same Collect of all saints is said throughout Advent as well as in Easter-tide, and also generally throughout the whole year); the fourth the Collect for the Church universal, viz.,* Mercifully receive, O Lord, the prayers of thy Church, *etc.; the fifth, the Collect for peace, viz.,* O God, from whom all holy desires, *etc.*

On the octave of saint Andrew, or when the mass I am the salvation of the people *is said, then the second Collect will be that of Advent; the third that of saint Mary; the fourth that of all saints; the fifth that for the Church universal.*

Also on ferial days, and on feasts without ruling of the quire, and when the mass I am the salvation of the people *is said, from the octave of the Epiphany to Ash Wednesday, five Collects are said, of which the first is that of the day; the second is that of saint Mary (viz.,* O God who by the

---

[1] Ad magnam missam.   [2] Ad principale altare.

fruitful virginity, etc., *up to the Purification; but after the Purification the Collect,* Grant, we beseech thee, O Lord God, that we, etc.); *the third is that of all saints, as above; the fourth is for the Church universal ; the fifth is for peace.*

On *Ash Wednesday, and on the three days following, these five Collects are said at the Mass of the fast : the first, of the day; the second, for penitents, viz.,* O Lord, we beseech thee, hear the prayers, etc. ; *the third, of saint Mary, namely,* Grant, we beseech thee, etc. ; *the fourth, of all saints, namely,* Grant, we beseech thee, almighty God, etc. ; *the fifth, for the Church universal, namely,* Mercifully receive, O Lord, etc. *No general Collect is said till Lent.*

On *the Monday of the first week in Lent, and thereafter until Maundy Thursday, seven Collects are said at the mass of the fast, of which the first is of the day ; the second, for penitents ; the third, of saint Mary ; the fourth, of all saints ; the fifth, for the Church universal; the sixth, for peace ; the seventh, one of the general Collects taken in order, namely, the Collect,* Of thy lovingkindness, etc., *or the Collect,* We beseech thee, almighty God, by the merits, etc., *or the Collect,* We beseech thee, O Lord, through the intercessions, etc., *or the Collect,* Almighty, everlasting God, who rulest, etc.

Note *that according to the use of Sarum more than seven Collects are never said at mass, because God only appointed seven petitions in the Lord's prayer. But on Sundays in Lent only one Collect is said, a custom which should be observed through the whole of Lent.*

On *ferial days, and on feasts when the quire is not ruled, and when the mass,* I am the salvation of the people *is said, from the octave of Easter until Ascension Day, three Collects only are said; of which the first is that of the day ; the second is that of the Resurrection, namely,* O God, who through thy only-begotten Son, etc. ; *the third being that of all saints, as above. But on Sundays, when the Sunday mass is said, there should be no memory except only when the feast of some saint occurs. Yet in summer when there is a memory of any saint on any festival of three lessons (as within an octave, or on the feast of St. Sampson, when there is a memory of*

*St. Pantaleon, and in similar cases), then let the third Collect
be that of saint Mary, the fourth Collect that of all saints, and
the fifth Collect for the Church universal. Also from the First
Sunday after Trinity to Advent Sunday, on ferial days, and
on feasts of three lessons without ruling of the quire, and on
octaves, and within octaves, when the quire is not ruled, five
Collects are said, of which the first is of the day; the second,
of saint Mary; the third, of all saints; the fourth, for the
state of the Church; and the fifth, for peace. On the feasts
of SS. Processus and Martinianus, there should be, firstly, the
memory of saint Swithin; next, of the Apostles; and afterwards of saint Mary, and then of all saints. But when the*
mass, I am the salvation of the people, etc., *is said, then
the second Collect will be of saint Mary; the third, of all
saints; the fourth, for the Church universal; the fifth, for
peace.*

*On the commencement of the last Collect before the Epistle,
the subdeacon shall advance through the middle of the quire to
the Pulpit, to read the Epistle. And the Epistle shall be read
in the Pulpit on every Sunday, and whenever the quire is ruled,
throughout the whole year, and on Maundy Thursday, and on
the vigils of Easter and Pentecost, and on All Souls' Day. On
all other feasts and ferial days, and on vigils and on Ember
Days outside the week of Pentecost, it should be read at the
Step of the quire, both in Lent and out of Lent.*

The Epistle. Rom. xiii. 11—14.

And that knowing the time . . . the Lord Jesus Christ.

*While the Epistle is being read, two boys in surplices, having
bowed to the Altar before the Step of the quire, shall go into
the Pulpit through the midst of the Quire, and make themselves ready to begin the gradual and to sing their Verse.*

Gradual. For all they, etc.

*The quire is to follow up the same through the whole of
it up to its conclusion; and this shall be done throughout the
whole year at the mass of the day, except when it is begun by
the Precentor, and in masses which are said in Chapter; and
in Procession, only when a Station takes place.*

Gradual.

For all they that hope in thee shall not be ashamed, O Lord.
℣. Shew me thy ways, O Lord, and teach me thy paths.[1]

After this verse the quire shall repeat the Gradual.

*Note, that the Gradual is to be repeated after its verse at
the mass of the day throughout the whole year, except on double
feasts, and except on the fifth and sixth days of Easter Week,
and at the Ember Seasons after the Lesson, when the Gradual
occupies a position after the* [Old Testament] *Lesson, and when
a Tract is said. It shall also be repeated at the second mass on
Christmas Day; and in a similar way on Commemorations,
namely, of the Trinity, of the Holy Spirit, and in the mass of
the Cross, and in the mass* I am the salvation *of the people,
and in that of Peace, and in other Commemorations, that is to
say, between Septuagesima and Easter only; and in masses of
saint Mary, when a Sequence cannot be used, nor a Chant in
place of a Sequence. But in daily masses of saint Mary it is
sufficient that the Chant be used in the place of a Sequence,
that is to say, in her Chapel.*

*While the Verse of the Gradual is being sung, two clerks of
superior rank shall put on silk copes, and advance through the
midst of the Quire to the Pulpit for the purpose of singing the
Alleluya. When the Verse of the Gradual has been said, the
boys shall begin the Gradual again, and it shall be sung
through by the quire, as has been directed above. Then shall
follow Alleluya, the quire repeating it, and following it up
with the pneuma.*

Clerks. ℣. Shew us thy mercy, O Lord: and grant us thy
salvation.[2]

*And it is to be finished by the quire. Then shall the clerks
begin the Alleluya without the pneuma, which order shall be
observed through the whole year, when the Sequence is said
only. But when there is no Sequence, then the pneuma is
performed by the whole quire after the repetition of Alleluya.
When Alleluya is finished, the Sequence shall follow.*

[1] Ps. xxv. 2, 3.   [2] Ps. lxxxv. 7.

Sequence.

Thou for ever our salvation,
thou the life of all creation,
thou our hope of restoration,
    thou the never-failing light ;
Grieving for man's loss impending,
by the tempter's wiles pretending,
camest down thine aid extending,
    leaving not the starry height.
In our flesh thy glory veiling,
all on earth, in ruin failing,
thou didst save by might prevailing,
    bringing joy to all our race.
Grant, O Christ, thine expiation,
unto us thine own creation,
take us for an habitation
    cleansed for thyself to grace.
By thy first humiliation
grant us, Lord, justification ;
when again in exaltation
    thou shalt come, O set us free.
When in glory manifested
thou the secret heart hast tested,
in unsullied robes invested
    may we closely follow thee !

On no Sunday throughout the year is a Sequence said at mass, when the service is of the sunday, except throughout Advent and in Easter-tide and on the sixth day after Christmas Day. A sequence is said on saints' days when the quire is ruled, throughout the whole year, except from Septuagesima Sunday to Easter Day, and except on feasts of many confessors, and on the feast of St. Michael in the Mountain Tomb. But from Septuagesima up to Maundy Thursday, on Sundays and on feasts of nine lessons, a Tract is sung by four Clerks of superior rank, in red silk copes, at the step of the quire, except on the feasts of the Purification and of the Annunciation of blessed Mary. But on the first sunday in Lent and on Palm

*sunday the Tract shall be sung in the quire by alternate verses
from side to side.*

At the end of Alleluya *or of the Sequence, or of the Tract,
before the deacon advances to announce the Gospel, he shall
cense the midst of the altar only; for the lectern should never
be censed either at mass or at matins before the Gospel is
announced. Then he shall take the Text, that is to say the
book of the Gospels, and bowing to the priest standing before
the altar, and facing east, he shall say thus without note :*
Bid, Sir, a blessing. *The priest shall reply :* The Lord
be in thy heart and in thy mouth, that thou mayest
announce the holy Gospel of God. In the name of the
Father, etc. *But if the priest is celebrating by himself, he
shall say privately :* Bid, Sir, a blessing, *and afterwards
shall say to himself :* The Lord be in my heart and in
my mouth, that I may announce the holy Gospel of God.
In the name of the Father, etc.

*And thus the deacon shall advance through the midst of the
Quire, solemnly carrying the Text itself in his left hand, with
thurifer and taper-bearers preceding him, to the Pulpit.
And if it be a double feast the cross shall precede him, which
should be on the right hand opposite to, that is facing the
reader of the Gospel, the face of the figure on the Crucifix being
turned toward the reader. For whenever the Epistle is read
in the Pulpit, the Gospel should be read in the same place also.
And when they have arrived at the place for reading, the
subdeacon shall take the Text itself, and hold it in the left hand
of the deacon himself, being, as it were, opposite to him, while
the gospel is being read, the taper-bearers standing by the
deacon, the one on his right hand, the other on his left, and
turning toward him. But the thurifer shall stand behind the
deacon, turning towards him. And the gospel shall always be
read by a reader facing north. And if a Bishop be the
Officiant, all the ministers in the quire shall come forward to
sing the Sequence, when there is a Sequence, except the principal
deacon and the principal subdeacon. And the deacons and
subdeacons, together with the rulers of the quire, shall remain
in the middle of the quire until the principal deacon returns*

*from the pulpit through the quire, after reading the Gospel.
But when he begins the Gospel, after* The Lord be with you,
*he shall make the sign of the cross over the book, then on his
forehead, and afterwards on his breast with his thumb.*

The Gospel. St. Mat., xxi. 1—9.

And when Jesus drew nigh . . . . Hosanna in the highest.

*When the Gospel has been read he shall kiss the book;
and the subdeacon shall immediately approach and hand the
Text to the Deacon, which the latter shall carry upright on
his breast. When the Gospel is finished, the priest standing
in the midst of the altar shall begin,* I believe in one God.
*Then the Creed shall be sung by the quire, not in alternate
fashion, but by the whole quire. See below.*

*These are the feasts on which the Creed is to be said, according
to the use of Sarum. On all sundays throughout the whole
year at high mass, whether the mass is of the sunday or not.
But it is not said in masses of vigils and of saints of three lessons,
and in masses for the dead which are said in chapter on
sundays. But if the sunday mass is said in chapter, then the
Creed is said. The Creed shall also be said throughout the
octaves of Christmas Day, Easter, and Pentecost, and on every
double feast throughout the year, and on all feasts of Apostles
and Evangelists, and on both feasts of the Holy Cross, and on
the feast of saint Mary Magdalene, and on both feasts of saint
Michael, and at a nuptial mass. It shall also be said at the
mass of saint Mary, throughout the whole year (whenever it is
to be said at the mass of the day), and at the mass of any saint
in whose honour the church or the altar has been dedicated, but
at the altar of that same saint only.*

After the Creed the Priest shall say, The Lord be with
you *and* Let us pray.

Offertory.

Unto thee, O Lord, will I lift up my soul; my God, I have
put my trust in thee : O let me not be confounded, neither let
mine enemies triumph over me, for all they that hope in thee
shall not be ashamed.

℣. Lead me forth in thy truth and learn me ; for thou art the God of my salvation ; in thee hath been my hope all the day long.

℣. Look upon me and have mercy upon me ; O Lord, keep my soul and deliver me, because I have put my trust in thee.[1]

These two Verses are said alternately throughout the week, when the service is of the week-day and not of the sunday. This custom is to be observed through the whole year, whenever there are Verses attached to the Offertory. Two Verses are never said with the offertory on one week-day ; nor are they said after the offertory, except on week-days in Advent, and from Septuagesima to Maundy Thursday only.

Secret.

May these sacred gifts, O Lord, cleanse us by their powerful virtue, and make to us come with more purity to him who gave them.   Through.

Another Secret, of blessed Mary.

Strengthen we beseech Thee, O Lord, etc.[2]

Throughout the whole of Advent only the daily Preface is used, when the mass is of the season.

Communion.

The Lord shall shew lovingkindness, and our land shall give her increase.[3]

Postcommunion.

May we receive, O Lord, thy mercy in the midst of thy temple, and anticipate with due honours the approaching solemnity of our restoration.   Through.

Another Postcommunion, of blessed Mary.[2]

Pour down, we beseech thee, O Lord, etc.

And the mass shall be finished with

Let us bless the Lord.

[1] Ps. xxv. 1, 2 (part), 4, 19.
[2] From the Advent Mass of the B. V. M.
[3] Ps. lxxxv. 12.

MONDAY.

When the mass is ferial.

At Mass.   *Office.*

Unto thee, O Lord etc.

Ps. Shew me thy ways etc.

Glory be to the Father, etc.

The Office Unto thee, O Lord, *is to be repeated.*

The Office is always said in this way at mass, when the quire is not ruled, except in Passion-tide. This mass is said through the whole week, unless a feast of nine lessons, or the octave of St. Andrew intervene; and except when the mass I am the salvation of the people *is said, or any commemoration shall have to be made of a holy place, or of saint Mary. And the sunday mass is always said with its own* Alleluya, *a rule to be observed throughout the whole year when* Alleluya *is said.* Alleluya *shall also be said at every mass of the day throughout the year, except from Septuagesima to the vigil of Easter, and except on vigils which fall not on a sunday, and not in Easter-tide; except also in the ember seasons which fall outside Whitsun week.*

WEDNESDAY.

Epistle. St. James v. 7—10.

Be patient, therefore . . . of patience.

Gospel. St. Mark i. 1—8.

The beginning . . . the Holy Ghost.

If any feast, the service of which ought to be used, should fall on this wednesday, the above epistle and gospel should be used on thursday, if that day is vacant; otherwise, they shall be altogether omitted in that year.

FRIDAY.

Lesson. Is. li. 1—8.

Hearken to me . . . to generation.

Gospel. St. Mat. iii. 1—6.

In those days . . . confessing their sins.

G

If, however, friday should not be a vacant day, the above Epistle and Gospel are altogether omitted. This applies to the whole of Advent and from the first Sunday after the octave of the Epiphany to Quinquagesima, and from the octave of Easter to the sunday next before Ascension Day. But from the first sunday after Trinity to Advent, if wednesday or thursday be not vacant, then the wednesday Epistle and Gospel shall be read upon friday, if it be a vacant day. Otherwise they shall be altogether omitted. For the wednesday Epistle and Gospel should never be read on monday or tuesday, nor should the friday Epistle and Gospel be read on thursday; because a service ought never to be anticipated according to the use of Sarum.

Second Sunday in Advent.

At Mass.   *Office.*

O people of Sion, behold the Lord shall come to save the nations, and the Lord shall make his glorious voice to be heard in the gladness of your heart.[1]

Ps. Hear, O thou Shepherd of Israel, thou that leadest Joseph like a sheep.[2]

Let the Office be repeated, namely, O people of Sion. Glory be to the Father. O people.

Collect.

Stir up, O Lord, our hearts to prepare the way of thy only-begotten One, that through his coming we may be found worthy to serve thee with pure hearts, who liveth and reigneth with thee in the unity of the Holy Spirit, God for ever and ever.

Epistle. Rom. xv. 4—13.

Brethren, whatsoever things . . . of the Holy Ghost.

Gradual.

Out of Sion hath God appeared in perfect beauty. Our God shall come and shall not keep silence.[3]

℣. Gather my saints together unto me; those that have made a covenant with me with sacrifice.[4] Alleluya.

---

[1] Adapted from Is. xxx. 30.   [2] Ps. lxxx. 1.
[3] Ps. l. 2, 3.   [4] Ps. l. 5.

℣. The powers of heaven shall be shaken. And then shall they see the Son of man coming in the clouds of heaven with power and great glory.[1]

Sequence.

Let the choir devoutly bring
Welcome to th' eternal King,
And with one consent renew
The Creator's homage due.
Him angelic legions praise,
On his face enraptured gaze.
On him wait all earthly things
Till his nod their trial brings.
Awful he in judgements deep
Yet in might doth mercy keep;
By thine agony of woe
Pity, Lord, and save us now.
To the gleaming stars on high
Raise the world in purity:
Let thy saving health appear
Scattering perils far and near.
Bid the universe be clean,
Let us live in peace serene,
Till unto those realms we soar
Where thou reignest evermore.

Gospel. St. Luke xxi. 25—33.

There shall be signs . . . not pass away.

Offertory.

Wilt thou not turn again and quicken us that the people may rejoice in thee? Shew us thy mercy, O Lord, and grant us thy salvation.[2]

℣. Lord, thou art become gracious unto thy land: thou hast turned away the captivity of Jacob: thou hast forgiven the offence of thy people.[3]

℣. Mercy and truth are met together. Truth shall flourish out of the earth, and righteousness hath looked down from heaven.[4]

---

[1] St. Mat. xxiv. 29, 30.　　　　[2] Ps. lxxxv. 6, 7.
[3] *Ib.* 1, 2.　　　　　　　　　　[4] *Ib.* 10, 11.

Secret.

Be pleased, O Lord, we beseech to accept our humble prayers and oblations, and whereas our merits avail nothing, succour us with thy protection. Through etc.

Ferial Preface.

Communion.

Arise, O Jerusalem, and stand on high, and behold the joy that cometh unto thee from God.[1]

Postcommunion.

Refreshed and nourished with this spiritual food and drink we humbly beseech thee, O Lord, that by participation in this mystery thou wouldest teach us to despise earthly, and to love heavenly things. Through etc.

WEDNESDAY.

Epistle. Zech. viii. 3—8.
Thus saith the Lord . . . in righteousness.

Gospel. St. Mat. xi. 11—15.
Verily I say . . . let him hear.

FRIDAY.

Epistle. Is. lxii. 6—12.
I have set watchmen . . . not forsaken.

Gospel. St. John i. 15—18.
John bare witness . . . declared him.

THIRD SUNDAY IN ADVENT.

At Mass.   *Office.*

Rejoice in the Lord alway : and again I say, Rejoice. Let your moderation be known unto all men. The Lord is at hand. Be careful for nothing ; but in everything by prayer and supplication let your requests be made known unto God.[2]

---

[1] Baruch iv. 36 ; v. 5.   [2] Phil. iv. 4–6.

Ps. And the peace of God, which passeth all understanding, shall keep your hearts and minds.[1]

Collect.

Incline thine ear, we beseech thee, O Lord, to our prayers, and lighten the darkness of our minds by the grace of thy visitation. Who livest etc.

Epistle. 1. Cor. iv. 1—5.

Let a man so account . . . praise of God.

Gradual.

Thou, O Lord, that sittest upon the cherubims, stir up thy strength and come.

℣. Hear, O thou Shepherd of Israel, thou that leadest Joseph like a sheep. Alleluya.

℣. Stir up, O Lord, thy strength and come and help us.[2]

Sequence.

Thou who dost each earthly throne
Rule by thy right hand alone,
Raise up thy great power and shine,
Shew thy flock thy face divine.
Saving gifts on him bestow
Whom the prophets did foreshow.
From the palace of the sky,
Jesu, to our land draw nigh.

Gospel. St. Mat. xi. 2—10.

Now when John . . . way before thee.

Offertory.

Lord, thou art become gracious unto thy land : thou hast turned away the captivity of Jacob. Thou hast forgiven the offence of thy people.

℣. Thou hast covered all their sins. Thou hast taken away all thy displeasure.

℣. Shew us thy mercy, O Lord, and grant us thy salvation.[3]

---

[1] *Ib.* 7.   [2] Ps. lxxx. 1, 2.   [3] Ps. lxxxv. 1, 2, 3, 7.

Secret.

We beseech thee, O Lord, that the sacrifice of our devotion may be continually offered unto thee, and that it may both fulfil the institution of thy sacred mystery, and wonderfully work in us thy salvation. Through etc.

Ferial Preface.

Communion.

Say to them that are of a fearful heart, Be strong, fear not; behold our God will come and save us.[1]

Postcommunion.

We implore thy mercy, O Lord, that being cleansed from sin by this thy divine assistance, we may be found prepared for the approaching feast. Through etc.

WEDNESDAY IN EMBER WEEK.

At Mass.   *Office.*

Drop down ye heavens from above, and let the skies pour down righteousness; let the earth open, and bring forth a Saviour.[2]

Ps. And let righteousness spring up together; I the Lord have created it.[3]

The Collect shall follow without The Lord be with you, *and only with* Let us pray.

Collect.

Grant, we beseech thee, Almighty God, that the approaching solemnity of our redemption may both afford us succour in this present life, and bestow on us abundantly the rewards of eternal happiness. Through the same etc.

Lesson. Is. ii. 2—5.

And it shall come to pass . . . light of the Lord our God.

---

[1] Is. xxxv. 4.   [2] Is. xlv. 8.   [3] *Ib.*

Gradual.

Lift up your heads, O ye gates, and be ye lift up, ye everlasting doors ; and the King of Glory shall come in.[1]

℣. Who shall ascend into the hill of the Lord? or who shall rise up in his holy place? Even he that hath clean hands and a pure heart.[2]

The gradual shall not be repeated, but there shall immediately follow The Lord be with you *and* Let us pray.

Collect.

Hasten we beseech thee, O Lord, and tarry not ; and grant us the assistance of thy strength from above ; that they who trust in thy goodness may be sustained by the consolations of thy coming. Who livest etc.

The accustomed memories are said here.

Lesson. Is. vii. 10—15.

Gradual.

The Lord is nigh unto all them that call upon him : yea, all such as call upon him faithfully.

℣. My mouth shall speak the praise of the Lord : and let all flesh give thanks unto his holy name.[3]

The gradual is to be repeated.

Gospel. St. Luke i. 26—38.

The angel Gabriel . . . according to thy word.

Offertory.

Hail, Mary, full of grace ; the Lord is with thee : blessed art thou among women, and blessed is the fruit of thy womb.[4]

℣. Therefore also that holy thing which shall be born of thee shall be called the Son of God.[5]

Secret.

We present offerings, O Lord, befitting this health-giving fast : grant that by these offices we may be prepared for the nativity of the eternal Bread. Through etc.

---

[1] Ps. xxiv. 7.   [2] *Ib.* 3, 4.   [3] Ps. cxlv. 18, 21.
[4] Adapted from St. Luke i. 28.   [5] St. Luke i. 35.

Ferial Preface.

Communion.

Behold, a virgin shall conceive, and bear a son, and shall call his name Emmanuel.[1]

Postcommunion.

Being filled, O Lord, with the gift of thy salvation, we humbly pray thee, that rejoicing in the taste thereof we may by it be effectually renewed. Through etc.

FRIDAY IN EMBER WEEK.

At Mass.   *Office.*

Be thou nigh at hand, O Lord; for all thy commandments are true. As concerning thy testimonies I have known long since: that thou hast grounded them for ever.[2]

Ps. Blessed are those that are undefiled in the way: and walk in the law of the Lord.[3]

Collect.

Stir up, we beseech thee, O Lord, thy power and come, that they who do trust in thy lovingkindness may be speedily delivered from all adversity. Who livest etc.

Lesson. Is. xi. 1—5.

There shall come forth a rod . . . of his reins.

Gradual.

Shew us thy mercy, O Lord, and grant us thy salvation.[4]
℣. Lord, thou art become gracious unto thy land: thou hast turned away the captivity of Jacob.[5]

The gradual is to be repeated.

Gospel. St. Luke i. 39—47.

And Mary arose . . . God my Saviour.

Offertory.

Wilt thou not turn again, and quicken us, O God, that thy

---

[1] Is. vii. 14.   [2] Ps. cxix. 151, 152.   [3] *Ib.* 1.
[4] Ps. lxxxv. 7.   [5] *Ib.* 1.

people may rejoice in thee ? Shew us thy mercy, O Lord, and grant us thy salvation.[1]

℣. Lord, thou art become gracious unto thy land : thou hast turned away the captivity of Jacob. Thou hast forgiven the offence of thy people.[2]

℣. Mercy and truth are met together. Truth shall flourish out of the earth : and righteousness hath looked down from heaven.[3]

Secret.

We beseech thee, O Lord, that by the saving sacrifice we may be more readily prepared for those days, in which that mystery is to be celebrated, on which all the fulfilment of thy commands doth wait. Through etc.

Ferial Preface.

Communion.

Behold, the Lord shall come, and all his saints with him ; and there shall be a great light in that day.[4]

Postcommunion.

Fulfil, O Lord, we beseech thee, thy mercy to thy people that prayeth ; and grant that being refreshed with the abundance of thy gifts they may both more earnestly ask for a greater measure of thy grace, and also may more confidently hope to obtain the same. Through etc.

SATURDAY IN EMBER WEEK.

At Mass.   *Office.*

Come, O Lord, thou that sittest upon the cherubims ; shew us the light of thy countenance, and we shall be whole.[5]

Ps. Hear, O thou Shepherd of Israel, thou that leadest Joseph like a sheep.[6]

All Collects are said without The Lord be with you, *except the last Collect before the Epistle, and with* Let us

---

[1] *Ib.* 6, 7.   [2] *Ib.* 1, 2.
[3] *Ib.* 10, 11.   [4] Adapted from Zech. xiv. 5, 6, 7.
[5] Ps. lxxx. 1, 3.   [6] *Ib.* 1.

pray *only*. *And all Lessons are to be announced with their titles.*

. Let us pray.

Collect.

O God, who seest that we are afflicted through our own wickedness, mercifully grant that we may be consoled by thy visitation. Who livest etc.

Lesson. Is. xix. 20—22.

They shall cry . . . shall heal them.

Gradual.

It goeth forth from the uttermost part of the heaven, and runneth about unto the end of it again.[1]

℣. The heavens declare the glory of God : and the firmament sheweth his handiwork.[2]

The gradual is not to be repeated, but there shall immediately be said :

Let us pray.

Collect.

Grant, we beseech thee, Almighty God, that we who from long bondage are bowed down under the yoke of sin may by the expected new birth of thy Only-begotten Son be set free. Who liveth etc.

Lesson. Is. xxxv. 1—7.

The wilderness . . . springs of water.

Gradual.

In them hath he set a tabernacle for the sun : which cometh forth as a bridegroom out of his chamber.[3]

℣. It goeth forth from the uttermost part of heaven, and runneth about unto the end of it again.[4]

Collect.

Grant, we beseech thee, O Lord, to us thy unworthy servants, that we who are saddened by the guilt of our own deeds may be gladdened by the advent of thy only-begotten Son. Who liveth etc.

---

[1] Ps. xix. 6.   [2] *Ib.* 1.
[3] Ps. xix. 5.   [4] *Ib.* 6.

Lesson. Is. xl. 9—11.
O Zion . . . in his bosom.

Gradual.

Turn us again, O Lord God of hosts : shew the light of thy countenance, and we shall be whole.[1]

℣. Stir up thy strength, and come and help us.[2]

Collect.

Grant, we beseech thee, almighty God, that the approaching solemnity of thy Son may both bring us healing in the present life, and win for us reward everlasting. Through etc.

Lesson. Is. xlv. 1—8.
Thus saith the Lord . . . have created it.

Gradual.

Stir up thy strength, O Lord, and come and help us.[3]

℣. O thou Shepherd of Israel, thou that leadest Joseph like a sheep ; shew thyself thou that sittest upon the Cherubims, before Ephraim, Benjamin and Manasses.[4]

Let us pray.

Collect.

O Lord, we beseech thee, favourably to hear the prayers of thy people ; that we who are justly punished for our offences may be comforted by the visitation of thy lovingkindness. Who livest etc.

Lesson. Song of the Three Holy Children, 26—28.
The angel of the Lord . . . in the furnace saying,

Two clerks of the second rank in surplices at the step of the quire shall sing the Tract, the clerks singing each verse, and the quire singing each refrain.

Tract.

Clerks. ℣. Blessed art thou, O Lord God of our fathers.

---

[1] Ps. lxxx, 19.   [2] *Ib.* 2.
[3] *Ib.*   [4] *Ib.* 1, 2.

Quire. And to be praised and exalted above all for ever.

Clerks. 𝒱. And blessed is thy glorious and holy name.

Quire. And to be praised and exalted above all for ever.

Clerks. 𝒱. Blessed art thou in the temple of thine holy glory.

Quire. And to be praised and exalted above all for ever.

Clerks. 𝒱. Blessed art thou on the glorious throne of thy kingdom.

Quire. And to be praised and exalted above all for ever.

Clerks. 𝒱. Blessed art thou in the sceptre of the kingdom of thy divinity.

Quire. And to be praised and exalted above all for ever.

Clerks. 𝒱. Blessed art thou that beholdest the depths, and sittest upon the cherubims.

Quire. And to be praised and exalted above all for ever.

Clerks. 𝒱. Blessed art thou who walkest upon the wings of the winds.

Quire. And to be praised and exalted for ever.

Clerks. 𝒱. Let all thy angels and saints bless thee.

Quire. And praise and exalt thee for ever.

Clerks. 𝒱. Let the heavens, and the earth, and the sea, and all things that are therein bless thee.

Quire. And praise and exalt thee for ever.

Clerks. 𝒱. Glory be to the Father, and to the Son, and to the Holy Ghost,

Quire. And praise and honour, power and dominion.

Clerks. 𝒱. As it was in the beginning, is now, and ever shall be, world without end. Amen.

Quire. And praise and honour, power and dominion.[1]

---

[1] This Tract is taken from the Song of the Three Holy Children, 29–34, with certain interpolations and additions.

Then shall the clerks recommence the first verse of the Tract, which will be sung through by the quire. And afterwards the priest shall say The Lord be with you, *and* Let us pray.

Collect.

O God, who for the three children didst quench the flames of fire, mercifully grant that we thy servants may not be consumed by the flame of our sins. Through etc.

The usual memories are to be said here.

Epistle. 2 Thess. ii. 1—8.

Now we beseech . . . of his coming.

Two clerks of the second rank, in black copes, that is to say, in their ferial habit, standing at the step of the quire, shall say together the following Tract wholly and entirely.

Tract.

Hear, O thou Shepherd of Israel, thou that leadeth Joseph like a sheep.[1]

℣. Shew thyself also thou that sittest upon the cherubims, before Ephraim, Benjamin, and Manasses.[2]

℣. Stir up thy strength, O Lord, and come and help us.[3]

Gospel. St. Luke iii. 1—6.

Now in the fifteenth year . . . salvation of God.

Offertory.

Rejoice greatly, O daughter of Zion; shout, O daughter of Jerusalem : behold thy King cometh unto thee : he is holy, and having salvation.[4]

℣. He shall speak peace unto the heathen ; and his dominion shall be from sea even to sea, and from the river even to the end of the earth.[5]

---

[1] Ps. lxxx. 1.   [2] *Ib.* 1, 2.   [3] *Ib.* 2.
[4] Zech. ix. 9.   [5] *Ib.* 10.

Secret.

Look down, we beseech thee, O Lord, with the eye of favour upon these offerings of the faithful; and because we have no strength of our own merits, may we rather by these gifts be made acceptable to thee at thy coming. Who livest etc.

Ferial Preface.

Communion.

He rejoiceth as a giant to run his course. It goeth forth from the uttermost part of the heaven, and runneth about unto the end of it again.[1]

Postcommunion.

We beseech thee, O Lord our God, that these holy mysteries, which thou hast given unto us for our restoration and defence, may be made to us a source of healing both now and for evermore. Through etc.

On whatever day of the week Christmas Day shall fall, the Ember fasts shall always be kept in the third week of Advent.

FOURTH SUNDAY IN ADVENT.

At Mass.   *Office.*

Remember us, O Lord, according to the favour that thou bearest unto thy people; O visit us with thy salvation; that we may see the felicity of thy chosen: and rejoice in the gladness of thy people, and give thanks with thine inheritance.[2]

Ps. We have sinned with our fathers, we have done amiss, and dealt wickedly.[3]

Lord have mercy upon us.

Collect.

O Lord, raise up, we pray thee, thy power and come, and with great might succour us, that whereas through

---

[1] Ps. xix. 5, 6.   [2] Ps. cvi. 4, 5.   [3] *Ib.* 6.

our sins we are sore let and hindered, thy bountiful grace
and mercy may speedily help and deliver us. Who
livest etc.

Epistle. Phil. iv. 4—7.
Rejoice in the Lord . . . in Christ Jesus.

Gradual.

The Lord is nigh unto all them that call upon him : yea, all
such as call upon him faithfully.[1]

℣. My mouth shall speak the praise of the Lord : and let all
flesh give thanks unto his holy name. Alleluya.[2]

℣. Come, Lord, and tarry not; forgive the sins of thy
people.[3]

Sequence.

Before the all-creating Lord
Let us rejoice with one accord,
Who made the worlds, the beaming sky,
The stars that glitter variously ;
The sun, creation's central light,
The moon which softly decks the night,
All other orbs that gleam around,
Sea, land, hills, plains, and deeps profound ;
The air, where fly the feather'd tribes,
The winds go forth, the tempest rides ;
All, now and ever, thee alone,
Ceaselessly praising, Father own ;
Who to this lower earth hast sent
Thine only Son, all innocent,
Bringing salvation from on high,
For our transgressions here to die.
To thee, blest Trinity, we pray,
Guide all our goings in thy way,
Control our wills, our hearts revive,
To our offences pardon give.

Gospel. St. John i. 19—28.
The Jews sent . . . John was baptizing.

---

[1] Ps. cxlv. 18.   [2] *Ib.* 21.   [3] Source unknown.

Offertory.

Be strong, fear not ; behold our God will come with vengeance,
even God with a recompense ; he will come and save us.[1]

℣. Then the eyes of the blind shall be opened, and the ears
of the deaf shall be unstopped. Then shall the lame man leap as
an hart, and the tongue of the dumb sing.[2]

Secret.

We beseech thee, O Lord, look graciously upon this
present sacrifice, and grant that by it we may be purified
to take part in the nativity of thy Son. Through etc.

Ferial Preface.

Communion.

Behold, a virgin shall conceive, and bear a son, and shall call
his name Emmanuel.[3]

Postcommunion.

Accompany thy people, we beseech thee, O Lord, with
the plenteousness of thy gifts, that they being defended
from all evil by the virtue of thy sacraments, may be
prepared both in mind and body to celebrate the ineffable
mystery. Through etc.

WEDNESDAY.

Lesson.   Joel ii. 23, 24 ; iii. 17—21.
Be glad then . . . dwelleth in Zion.

Gospel.   St. Luke vii. 17—28.
And this rumour . . . greater than he.

FRIDAY.

Lesson.   Zech. ii. 10—13.
Sing and rejoice . . . holy habitation.

Gospel.   St. Mark viii. 15—26.
And he charged . . . in the town.

---

[1] Is. xxxv. 4.   [2] *Ib.* 5, 6.   [3] Is. vii. 14.

CHRISTMAS EVE.[1]

At Mass.   *Office.*

To-day ye shall know that the Lord will come and save you, and in the morning, then shall ye see his glory.[2]

Ps. The earth is the Lord's, and all that therein is: the compass of the world, and they that dwell therein.[3]

If this vigil occur on a Sunday the chant of the Kyrie, Sanctus, *and* Agnus *is the same as on a simple feast of nine lessons: otherwise the ferial chant is used.*

Collect.

O God, who makest us glad with the yearly expectation of our redemption, grant that as we joyfully receive thy only begotten Son for our redeemer, so we may also with sure confidence behold him when he shall come to be our judge, even Jesus Christ, thy Son, our Lord. Who with thee etc.

There shall be no memory.

One boy, an acolyte, shall read the lesson, vested in an alb, at the step of the quire. But if it be a Sunday, it should be read in the pulpit, and always with its title.

Lesson. Is. lxii. 1—4.
For Zion's sake . . . shall be married.

Then the Epistle shall be read without any pause.

Epistle. Rom. i. 1—6.
Paul a servant . . . of Jesus Christ.

Gradual.

To-day ye shall know that the Lord will come and save you, and in the morning, then shall ye see his glory.[2]

℣. Hear, O thou Shepherd of Israel, thou that leadest Joseph like a sheep. Shew thyself also thou that sittest upon the cherubims, before Ephraim, Benjamin, and Manasses.[4]

---

[1] In vigilia Nativitatis Domini.   [2] Exod. xvi. 6, 7.
[3] Ps. xxiv. 1.   [4] Ps. lxxx. 1, 2.

H

If this Vigil occur on a Sunday, the mass of the Sunday is said in chapter; and then there shall be a memory of saint Mary, and of All Saints only. But the mass of the Vigil is to be said at the high altar without any memory, with this Alleluya.

℣. To-morrow the iniquity of the earth shall be blotted out, and the Saviour of the world shall reign over us.[1]

Sequence.

Before the all-creating Lord etc.[2]

But if it be not a Sunday, then the Alleluya *and the Sequence shall be omitted.*

Gospel. St. Matt. i. 18—21.
When as his mother . . . from their sins.

Offertory.

Lift up your heads, O ye gates, and be ye lift up, ye everlasting doors; and the King of glory shall come in.[3]

℣. The earth is the Lord's, and all that therein is: the compass of the world, and they that dwell therein.[4]

This Verse, if it be a Sunday, shall be omitted for that year.

Secret.

Grant to us, we beseech thee, almighty God, that like as we do anticipate the adorable birth of thy Son, so we may receive with joy his everlasting gifts. Through the same etc.

Ferial Preface.

Communion.

The glory of the Lord shall be revealed, and all flesh shall see the salvation of our God.[5]

Postcommunion.

Grant to us, we beseech thee, O Lord, that we may be refreshed by the rehearsal of the birth of thy Only-begotten

---

[1] From an unknown (probably Gallican) source, the phrase 'Salvator mundi' is specially if not exclusively Gallican.

[2] As on Fourth Sunday in Advent, p. 91.

[3] Ps. xxiv. 7.   [4] *Ib.* 1.   [5] Is. xl. 5.

Son, whose heavenly mysteries form our food and drink. Through the same etc.

IN THE NIGHT OF CHRISTMAS.

After the ninth lesson [at Matins] this Gospel shall be chanted in the pulpit by the Deacon.

Gospel. St. Mat. i. 1—16.
The book of the generation . . . called Christ.

When the Gospel is finished, the priest shall begin the Psalm Te Deum ; *when that has been said the rulers of the quire shall begin mass.*

CHRISTMAS DAY.

AT THE MASS AT COCK-CROW.

Office.

The Lord hath said unto me: Thou art my Son, this day have I begotten thee.[1]

Ps. Why do the heathen so furiously rage together : and why do the people imagine a vain thing?[2]

The Kyrie with its verses. Then shall Gloria in Excelsis *follow, after the manner of a double feast.*

Note, that Gloria in Excelsis *is always said at mass, when* Te Deum *is said at Matins, except where there shall be chanted the mass* I am the Salvation of the people, *or the mass of the Cross, or the mass of a Sunday on some feast of three Lessons, or within an octave, without ruling of the quire. But when any mass of a vigil or of a feast of three Lessons, is said in chapter on Sunday, then also the chant is used for the* Kyrie *and* Gloria in Excelsis, *when the* Sanctus, Agnus Dei, *and* Ite Missa est *are said, as on a feast of three Lessons. The same rule shall be observed when the sunday mass is said in chapter on Sunday, when the Creed shall also be said.*

[1] Ps. ii. 7. [2] *Ib.* 1.

Collect.

O God, who hast caused this most holy night to shine with the illumination of the true light; grant, we beseech thee, that as we have known the mysteries of this light on earth, we may also attain to the full enjoyment of it in heaven, Who with thee etc.

Two clerks, of the second rank, in silk copes, shall chant the following lesson together in the pulpit.

I will sing praises to God for ever, who hath formed me in his right hand, and hath redeemed me on the cross with the purple blood of his Son.

Then shall there be sung in alternate sentences :

The lesson of Isaiah the prophet,[1]
In which the glorious birth of Christ is foretold.
Thus saith the Lord.
Father, Son, and Holy Ghost, by whom all things have been created in heaven and in earth.
The people that walked in darkness,
Whom thou hast created ; whom the enemy expelled from paradise by subtle fraud, and led captive with him to hell,
Have seen a great light,
And at midnight great light shone upon the shepherds,
On them that dwell in the region of the shadow of death, the light
Everlasting, and truly our redemption,
Hath shined on them.
O marvellous birth !
For unto us a child is born,
He shall be great, Jesus, the Son of God.
And a Son,
Of the Father in the highest,
Unto us is given.
So it had been foretold from the highest heaven.
And the government shall be upon his shoulder,

[1] Is. ix. 2, 6, 7, with numerous interpolations or farsings.

That he may rule over heaven and earth,
And his name shall be called,
Messias, Sother, Emmanuel, Sabaoth, Adonai,
Wonderful,
The Root of David,
Counsellor,
Of God the Father,
God,
Who created all things,
Mighty,
Overthrowing the most horrible gates of hell,
The everlasting Father,
King almighty, and Ruler over all,
The Prince of peace,
Now and for ever,
Of the increase of his government,
In Jerusalem, Judæa, and Samaria,
And of his peace there shall be no end,
For ever and ever.
He shall sit upon the throne of David and upon his
kingdom,
And there shall be no bound to his kingdom,
To order it,
With the pledge of faith,
And to establish it with judgment and with justice,
When he shall come as Judge to judge the world.
From henceforth
To him are due glory, laud, and shouts of joy,
Even for ever.

Here shall they chant together to the end,

From the rising of the sun to the going down of the
same let meet praise resound to the Creator, through all
climes to the ends of the whole world. Let everything
say Amen.

*Where there is no chanting this Lesson from Isaiah the
prophet shall be read.*

Lesson. Is. ix. 2, 6, 7.

The people that walked . . . even for ever.

The Epistle is to immediately follow.

Epistle. Titus ii. 11—15.

For the grace . . . speak and exhort.

Gradual.

In the day of the power shall the people offer thee free-will offerings with an holy worship: the dew of thy birth is of the womb of the morning.[1]

℣. The Lord said unto my Lord: Sit thou on my right hand, until I make thine enemies thy footstool.[2] Alleluya.

℣. The Lord hath said unto me: Thou art my Son, this day have I begotten thee.[3]

Sequence.

> All hosts, above, beneath,
>   Sing the incarnate Lord,
> With instruments and pious breath
>   Attune each measured word.
> This is the hallow'd morn
>   When on our fallen race
> In full effulgence rose the dawn
>   Of new-born joy and grace.
> Glory to God on high,
>   On this renownèd night
> Was thundered forth in harmony
>   By angel legions bright.
> Amazing splendours shone—
>   A strange unwonted sight—
> Upon the shepherds biding lone
>   Under the veil of night.
> Sudden, while peacefully
>   They watch'd their sheep-folds still,
> Good tidings wafted from on high
>   Their ears attentive fill.

[1] Ps. cx. 3.   [2] *Ib.* 1.   [3] Ps. ii. 7.

Who was before all time
  Is born of purest Maid ;
Glory to God in heights sublime,
  Peace comes the world to aid.
E'en thus the choir on high
  Sings praises jubilant,
From pole to pole their voices fly,
  Heaven echoes to their chant.
Let all with thrilling voice
  Give back the glorious lay,
Let the wide universe rejoice,
  That God is born this day.
Burst are the iron chains
  Which held the world in thrall ;
The cruel foe no longer reigns,
  Peace is restored to all.
For lo ! an order new
  Doth the glad world adorn ;
Let all things render praises due
  Unto the Virgin-born.
He all upholds alone,
  He all alone did frame ;
May he who hath such pity shown
  Blot out our sin and shame.

Gospel. St. Luke ii. 1—14.
And it came to pass . . . toward men.

Creed.

Offertory.

Let the heavens rejoice, and let the earth be glad, for he
cometh.[1]

Secret.

We beseech thee, O Lord, that the offering of this
day's festival may be acceptable to thee, that by the favour
of thy grace, through this holy communion, we may be
found in the likeness of him, in whom our nature is

[1] Ps. xcvi. 11, 13.

united to thine, Jesus Christ our Lord. Who with thee etc.

Preface. Because by the mystery etc.

This Preface is said on Christmas Day at all masses, and daily throughout the week, and on the day of the Circumcision of our Lord, and at all masses of saint Mary from this day up to the Purification. But In communion with *is only said* up to *the Circumcision, and on the day of the Circumcision.*

Communion.

The dew of thy birth is of the womb of the morning.[1]

Postcommunion.

Grant, we beseech thee, O Lord our God, that we who celebrate with joy the birth of our Lord Jesus Christ, may by a worthy course of life be found meet to attain to fellowship with him. Who with thee etc.

MASS AT DAYBREAK.

Office.

Light shall shine upon us to-day, because unto us the Lord is born, and he shall be called Wonderful, God the Prince of Peace, the everlasting Father, of whose kingdom there shall be no end.[2]

Ps. The Lord is King, and hath put on glorious apparel : the Lord hath put on his apparel, and girded himself with strength.[3]

At this mass, Kyrie, *without verses,* Gloria in Excelsis, Sanctus, *and* Agnus *are said as on a simple feast of nine lessons.*

Collect.

Grant, we beseech thee, Almighty God, unto us on whom is largely shed the new light of thy incarnate Word, that as by faith it enlightens the mind, so also it may shine forth in action. Through etc.

[1] Ps. cx 3.   [2] Adapted from Is. ix. 6, 7   [3] Ps. xciii. 1.

Memory of St. Anastasia with this Collect.

Grant, we beseech thee, almighty God, that we who celebrate the feast of thy blessed martyr Anastasia may be assured of her advocacy with thee. Through etc.

Neither more nor less Collects are said at this mass. The following Lesson shall be read in the pulpit by one clerk of the second rank.

Lesson. Is. lxi. 1—3 ; lxii. 11, 12.
The spirit of the Lord . . . not forsaken.

Then without any interval the

Epistle. Titus iii. 4—7.
But after that . . . eternal life.

Gradual.

Blessed is he that cometh in the name of the Lord. God is the Lord who hath shewed us light.[1]

℣. This is the Lord's doing: and it is marvellous in our eyes.[2] Alleluya.

℣. The Lord is King and hath put on glorious apparel : the Lord hath put on his apparel, and girded himself with strength.[3]

Sequence.

Unto the King new-born new praises sing,
Whose Father by his word did frame the worlds,
Whose mother a most hallow'd virgin is ;
Begotten of the Father, God of God,
Born of his mother without carnal stain,
Word of the Father ere the world was made,
In the full time forth from his mother's womb
He issues in a human body veil'd.
O wonderful, mysterious generation !
O most astonishing nativity !
O glorious child ! O Deity incarnate !
So had the prophets, by thy Spirit moved,
Declared thou should'st be born, thou Son of God !
So, at thy dawning, angels sing thee praises,
And to the earth glad tidings bring of peace.

[1] Ps. cxviii. 26, 27.　　[2] *Ib.* 23.　　[3] Ps. xciii. 1.

The face of all the elements is gladden'd,
And all the saints exultingly rejoice,
Crying, All hail! save us, we pray, O God,
In persons trine, one undivided substance.[1]

The Gospel shall be read in the pulpit as on Sunday.

Gospel.   St. Luke ii. 15—20.
The shepherds said . . . told unto them.

Creed.

Offertory.

He hath made the round world so sure that it cannot be moved.
Ever since the world began hath thy seat been prepared: thou
art from everlasting.[2]

Secret.

We beseech thee, O Lord, that the offerings which we
bring may be suitable to the mysteries of this day's
nativity; that like as he who was born as man shone forth
as God, so this earthly substance may impart to us that
which is divine.   Through etc.

Another Secret.

Receive, we beseech thee, O Lord, these gifts which
we offer worthily, and grant that by the merits of the
blessed Anastasia pleading for us they may avail to
further our salvation.   Through etc.

Preface and In communion with etc., *as above.*

Communion.

Rejoice greatly, O daughter of Zion: shout, O daughter of
Jerusalem, behold thy King cometh unto thee, holy, and the
Saviour of the world.[3]

Postcommunion.

Grant, we beseech thee, O Lord, that we may be evermore restored by the sacramental and commemorative

---

[1] Usia.   [2] Ps. xciii. 2, 3.
[3] Salvator mundi; adapted from Zech. ix. 9.

renewal of the marvellous birth of him whose nativity cast off the old man.   Through etc.

Another Postcommunion.

Thou hast fed thy family, O Lord, with sacred gifts ; evermore, we beseech thee, comfort us by the intercession of her [1] whose feast we celebrate.   Through etc.

AT THE THIRD MASS.

Office.

Unto us a Child is born, unto us a Son is given: and the government shall be upon his shoulder, and his name shall be called the angel of great counsel.[2]

Ps. O sing unto the Lord a new song, for he hath done marvellous things.[3]

Collect.

Grant, we beseech thee, almighty God, that we who are held in bondage by the old yoke of sin may be set free by the new birth in the flesh of thy only-begotten Son. Through the same etc.

The following lesson shall be read in the pulpit by some one of superior rank in a surplice.

Lesson.

Is. lii. 6—10.   Therefore my people . . . of our God.

Epistle.   Heb. i. 1—12.

God who at sundry . . . shall not fail.

Gradual.

All the ends of the world have seen the salvation of our God : shew yourselves joyful unto the Lord, all ye lands.[4]

℣.   The Lord declared his salvation : his righteousness hath he openly shewed in the sight of the heathen.[5]   Alleluya.

---

[1] *i.e.,* St. Anastasia.

[2] Magni consilii angelus, Is. ix. 6, the last three words coming from the LXX.

[3] Ps. xcviii. 1.   [4] Ps. xcviii. 4, 5.   [5] *Ib.* 3.

℣. The hallowed day hath shone upon us : come ye nations, and adore the Lord, for to-day a great light hath descended on the earth.[1]

Sequence.

This day celestial melody
    Resounded o'er the earth,
What time the virgin bare a Son,
    Seraphs proclaimed his birth.
What aileth thee, thou world below?
    Haste thee with them to sing ;
In pastoral charge the shepherds watch,
    Hark ! angel voices ring,
Chanting their strains of holy joy,
    With glory fraught and peace,
To Christ they render homage due,
    To us they sing of grace.
Not unto all such gifts are given,
    But to the good of heart,
Not irrespectively bestowed,
    But measured by desert.
Affections must be weaned from sin,
So shall we gain that peace within
    Reserved for pure in heart ;
Lo ! earth is join'd with things divine,
In this respect their lays combine,
    But fitly fall apart.
O man, rejoice, and ponder this accord ;
O flesh, rejoice, associate with the Word.
    This verse shall be repeated thrice.

His rising by the stars is told
    With indicating light ;
Lo ! star-lit chiefs to Bethlehem
    Follow that planet bright.
The King of heaven is cradled found
    Amid the beasts he made,
In a rude manger's narrow bed
    The Lord of all is laid.

[1] Source unknown.

Star of the sea! thy blessed Son
The holy Church adores,
That he our service will accept
Devoutly she implores.
Let each redeeméd thing the Redeemer's praises sing.

Gospel.   St. John i. 1—14.
In the beginning . . . grace and truth.

Offertory.

The heavens are thine, the earth also is thine: thou hast laid
the foundation of the round world, and all that therein is.
Righteousness and equity are the habitation of thy seat.[1]

Secret.

Sanctify, O Lord, the gifts we offer by the new Birth
of thy only-begotten Son; and mercifully cleanse us from
the stains of our sins.   Through the same etc.

Communion.

All the ends of the world have seen the salvation of our God.[2]

Postcommunion.

Grant, we beseech thee, almighty God, that as the
Saviour of the world,[3] who was born to-day, bestoweth
upon us a heavenly birth, so he may also himself bestow
on us the gift of immortality.   Who with thee etc.

ST. STEPHEN, PROTOMARTYR.

At Mass.   *Office.*

Princes also did sit and speak against me, and wicked
men did persecute me.   Help me, O Lord, my God, for
thy servant is occupied in thy statutes![4]

Ps.   Blessed are those that are undefiled in the way: and walk
in the law of the Lord.[5]

---

[1] Ps. lxxxix. 12, 15.   [2] Ps. xcviii. 4.
[3] Salvator mundi.   [4] From Ps. cxix. 23, 161.   [5] *Ib.* 1.

Collect.

Grant to us, Lord, we beseech thee, to imitate that
which we commemorate, that we may learn to love even
our enemies, forasmuch as we celebrate the feast of him
who knew how to pray even for his persecutors to our
Lord Jesus Christ, thy Son.   Who liveth etc.

Memory of Christmas only.

Lesson.   Acts vi. 8—10 ; vii. 54—60.
Stephen, full of faith . . . fell asleep.

Gradual.

Princes also did sit and speak against me ; and wicked men did
persecute me.[1]

Help me, O Lord my God : O save me according to thy
mercy.[2]   Alleluya.

Behold, I see the heavens opened : and Jesus standing on the
right hand of the power of God.[3]

Sequence.

Great is the Lord in all the earth,
Great are his works in heaven above,
And in the earth below.
He is the King of kings and Lord of all,
Before all worlds begotten of the Father.
He of his love and truth doth Stephen now
Exalt from earth to heaven,
And in eternal life adorn his brow
With glittering martyr crown.
For Stephen, full of grace and power Divine,
Did wonders great, and spake with faith and wisdom ;
But whilst he preached the new and joyful tidings
That our redemption doth no longer tarry,
Looking up steadfastly he saw heaven opened,
And cried aloud, full of the Holy Ghost,
Unto the multitude which stood around him,
Behold, I see God's glory wonderful
In bright effulgence, and the Son of Man

[1] Ps. cxix. 23, 161.   [2] Ib. 25.   [3] Acts vii. 56.

Stand at the right hand of the power of God,
Which when the impious Jewish people heard
With furious cries they violently ran
And stoned Stephen, crushing all his limbs;
Yet boldly, patiently, the martyr stands,
And prays, Lay not this sin unto their charge,
But now, Lord Jesus Christ, receive my spirit.
And when he had said this, he fell asleep
In peace eternal, resting in the Lord.
Pray for us too, O Stephen, holy martyr,
That we may have a part in joys eternal.

Gradual.

Princes also did sit and speak against me: and wicked men
have persecuted me.[1]

℣.   Help me, O Lord my God : O save me according to thy
mercy.[2]   Alleluya.

℣.   I see the heavens opened : and Jesus standing on the right
hand of the power of God.[3]

*This last verse is said thrice on this feast, and on the
feast of the Invention of St. Stephen.*[4]

Gospel.   St. Mat. xxiii. 34—39.
Wherefore, behold I send . . . name of the Lord.

Creed.

Offertory.

The Apostles chose Stephen, a Levite, a man full of faith and
of the Holy Ghost; whom the Jews stoned, praying and saying,
Lord Jesus, receive my spirit.[5]   Alleluya.

Secret.

Receive, O Lord, we beseech thee, these gifts in
commemoration of the holy martyr Stephen, and grant
that as his passion made him glorious, so our devotion
may make us blameless.   Through etc.

---

[1] Ps. cxix. 23, 161.   [2] Ps. cix. 25.   [3] Acts vii. 56.
      [4] August 3rd.   [5] Acts vi. 5 ; vii. 59.

Communion.

I see the heavens opened, and Jesus standing on the right hand of the power of God. Lord Jesus, receive my spirit: and lay not this sin to their charge, for they know not what they do.[1]

Postcommunion.

May the mysteries which we have received, O Lord, be our assistance, and by the intercession of thy blessed protomartyr Stephen, evermore strengthen and protect us. Through etc.

ST. JOHN THE EVANGELIST.

At Mass.   *Office.*

In the midst of the congregation he opened his mouth; and the Lord filled him with the spirit of wisdom and understanding, and clothed him with the robe of glory.[2]

In Easter-tide is added Alleluya, Alleluya.[3]

Ps. He shall find joy and a crown of gladness.[4]

Collect.

Merciful Lord, we beseech thee to cast thy bright beams of light upon thy church, that it being enlightened by the doctrine of thy blessed Apostle and Evangelist saint John may attain to the gift of everlasting life. Through etc.

Memories of Christmas and of St. Stephen only.

Lesson. Ecclus. xv. 1—6.

He that feareth . . . everlasting name.

Gradual.

Then went this saying abroad among the brethren, that that disciple should not die.[5]

℣. But, if I will that he tarry till I come, what is that to thee?[6] Alleluya.

℣. This is the disciple which testifieth of these things; and we know that his testimony is true.[7]

---

[1] Adapted from Acts vii. 56, 59, 60, and St. Luke xxiii. 34.
[2] Ecclus. xv. 5, Vulg.
[3] *i.e.*, on the Feast of St. John before the Latin Gate, May 6.
[4] Ecclus. xv. 6.   [5] St. John xxi. 23.   [6] *Ib.*   [7] *Ib.* 24.

Sequence.

O John! disciple chaste, whom Jesus lov'd,
Thou for the love which thou didst bear to him
Didst leave thy earthly parent in the ship ;
Unwedded didst Messiah follow, drinking
Pure streams of wisdom from his holy breast.
Thou saw'st the glory of the Son of God
Whilst yet alive on earth, whom to behold
The saints do look only in life eternal.
To thee, Christ, triumphing upon the cross,
In charge his [holy] Mother did commit,
That to the virgin thou, thyself a virgin,
With filial care should'st minister protection.
In prison cast, and torn with cruel scourges,
Thou didst rejoice to bear Christ's testimony.
Thou, too, didst raise the dead, and deadly poison
Didst drink, and take no harm, in Jesu's name.
To thee the most high Father doth reveal
His word of prophecy, denied to others.
Do thou, O John, belov'd of Jesus Christ,
Commend us all to God, in never-ceasing prayers!

The last line should be repeated thrice on this feast only.

Gospel. St. John xxi. 19—24.
Follow me . . . testimony is true.

Creed.

Offertory.

The righteous shall flourish like a palm-tree: and shall spread
abroad like a cedar in Libanus.[1]

In Easter tide, Alleluya.

Secret.

Receive, O Lord, we beseech thee, the gifts which we
offer to thee on his feast by whose patronage we trust to
be delivered. Through etc.

[1] Ps. xcii. 11.

I

Communion.

Then went this saying abroad among the brethren, that that disciple should not die : yet Jesus said not unto him, He shall not die ; but, If I will that he tarry till I come, what is that to thee? [1]

In Easter-tide, Alleluya.

Postcommunion.

We humbly beseech thee, O Lord, that having been refreshed with heavenly food and drink, we may be fortified by the prayers of him on whose commemoration day we have received them. Through etc.

DAY OF THE HOLY INNOCENTS, MARTYRS.

At Mass.   Office.

Out of the mouth of very babes and sucklings, O God, hast thou ordained strength, because of thine enemies. [2]

Ps. O Lord our Governor, how excellent is thy Name in all the world ! [3]

Collect.

O God, whose praise the martyred Innocents shewed forth this day not by their speech but by their death, mortify all evil vices in us, that our life may shew forth by its actions that faith which we profess with our lips. Who livest etc.

Memories of Christmas, of St. Stephen, and of St. John only.

Epistle. Rev. xiv. 1—5.
And I looked . . . throne of God.

Gradual.

Our soul is escaped even as a bird out of the snare of the fowler. [4]

℣. The snare is broken, and we are delivered. Our help standeth in the name of the Lord who hath made heaven and earth. [5] Alleluya.

℣. The noble army of martyrs praise thee, O Lord. [6]

---

[1] St. John xxi. 23.   [2] Ps. viii. 2.   [3] *Ib.* 1.
[4] Ps. cxxiv. 6.   [5] *Ib.* 6, 7.
[6] Te Deum laudamus, verse 9.

Sequence.

Let children sing high melodies,
The Innocents' triumphant lay,
Whom Christ, the holy child, did bear to heaven
      to-day.
These for no crime, in cruel fraud,
Herod in madness and in rage,
In Bethlehem and all its coasts,
From two years old and under slew.
Herod, unhappy king, alarmed
Lest Christ the new-born king should reign,
Is filled with wrath, and seizes arms
With haughty hand and troubled mind,
And seeks the King of light and heaven,
Bent to destroy with murderous dart
The life of him who giveth life.
Unable with his clouded mind
To look on that bright light he seeks,
Fierce Herod weaves his dark designs
To slay the band of infant saints.
The wicked king his troops prepares,
Pierces with sword the tender limbs ;
Babes at the breast he slays, ere yet
The milk can curdle into blood.
The murderous unnatural foe
Infants new-born in pieces tears ;
Ere their frail limbs have gathered strength
Under his feet he tramples them.
O blessed Innocents ! O blest
The little ones that Herod slew !
O blessed mothers ! ye who there
Such pledges of your love did bear.
O sweet array of children dear !
O holy fight of babes for Christ !
Thousands of tender age lie slain around ;
Their mother's milk flows from them in their
    throes.

Angelic hosts to welcome stand
The little white-robed martyr band.
A marvellous victory they win,
Gaining the prize of life, ere yet the strife begin.
O Christ, thee we devoutly pray,
Thou who didst come the world to mend,
Grant us, with those blest Innocents,
The glories which shall never end.

Gospel. St. Mat. ii. 13—18.

The angel of the Lord . . . they are not.

Creed.

Offertory.

Our soul is escaped even as a bird out of the snare of the fowler : the snare is broken and we are delivered.[1]

Secret.

Be present, O Lord, at the consecration of these gifts on the feast of the Innocents, and grant that as we venerate their infancy dedicated to thee, so we may be able to imitate their guilelessness.   Through etc.

Communion.

In Rama was there a voice heard, lamentation and great mourning, Rachel weeping for her children, and would not be comforted, because they are not.[2]

Postcommunion.

Grant, O Lord, that by the prayers of the holy Innocents, the votive offerings of which we have partaken may both support us in our present life, and bring us to the life eternal.   Through etc.

St. Thomas the Martyr.

At Mass.   *Office.*

Let us all rejoice in the Lord, and celebrate a feast in honour of Thomas the martyr ; over whose passion the angels rejoice, and praise the Son of God.

[1] Ps. cxxiv. 6.   [2] St. Mat. ii. 18.

Ps. Hear my voice, O God, in my prayer : preserve my life from fear of the enemy.[1]

Collect.

O God, in behalf of whose Church thy glorious bishop Thomas fell by the swords of wicked men ; grant, we beseech thee, that all who implore his help may effectually obtain their petitions.   Through etc.

Epistle.   Heb. v. 1—4, 6.

Every high priest . . . order of Melchisedech.

Gradual.

Thou shalt set, O Lord,[2] etc.   Alleluya.
℣. Thou shalt crown him etc.[3]

Sequence.

This day let solemn strains
Resound on earth below,
And o'er the martyr's palm
Triumph the heavenly host.
What do ye, joyous folk ?
Give thanks with them above.
Let every living soul rejoice,
And with free voice to Christ sing praise.
Let Canterbury at this feast
Devoutly homage pay.
The furious soldier band
Shouts forth the tyrant king's command,
Lawless will and fierce decree
Forced their way full haughtily.
Armed men with passion wild
Places dear to Christ defiled :
But Christ's footsteps following,
Thomas with unswerving tread
Stood unshaken, undismayed,
In obedience to his King

---

[1] Ps. lxiv. 1.   [2] Ps. xxi. 3, 4.
          [3] Ps. viii. 5, 6.

Meets the sword with steady eye,
Counting it all gain to die.
Thomas, rejoice, thy victory adds a lay
To swell the praise of Christ's own natal day.
The martyr's glory is proclaimed,
   By divers signs assured,
Within the fane the pastor chief
   A cruel death endured ;
Nor day nor place from murderous hand
   Awe or respect procured,
Star of the sea, who didst rejoice to feed
   Christ at thy holy breast,
Him do we humbly pray, that in the end we may
   With Thomas surely rest,
And through his prayer be blest.

Gospel. St. Luke xix. 12—28.
A certain nobleman . . . up to Jerusalem.

Creed.

Offertory.

Thou shalt set, O Lord,[1] etc.

Secret.

Grant, we beseech thee, O Lord, that blessed Thomas, Bishop and Martyr, may obtain for us, that the gift of the saving offering now to be consecrated may avail to our salvation ; so that we may both know the excellency of his conversation, and partake of the benefit of his intercession. Through etc.

Communion.

His honour is great etc.[2]

Postcommunion.

Almighty and merciful God, grant unto us, through these holy gifts which we have received, that the revered

[1] Ps. xxi. 3, 4.   [2] *Ib.* 5.

intercession of thy blessed Martyr and Bishop may assist
us, who for the honour of thy name was deemed worthy
to be crowned with a glorious martyrdom. Through etc.

SIXTH DAY FROM CHRISTMAS.

Whether it be a Sunday or not.

At Mass.   *Office.*

For while all things were in quiet silence, and that
night was in the midst of her swift course, thine Almighty
Word, O Lord, leaped down from heaven out of thy
royal throne.[1]

Ps. The Lord is King, and hath put on glorious apparel:
the Lord hath put on his apparel, and girded himself with
strength.[2]

The Office is to be repeated. Then shall be said, Glory
be to the Father etc., *and* As it was etc. *And then the
Office is to be repeated a third time.*

Kyrie eleison, Gloria in excelsis, Sanctus, *and Agnus,
are said on this day as on a simple feast of nine lessons, whether
it be a sunday or not.*

Collect.

Almighty everlasting God, direct our actions according
to thy good pleasure, that in the name of thy dear Son
we may be found worthy to abound in good works.
Who with thee etc.

*Memories of Christmas, of St. Stephen, of St. John, of the
Innocents, and of St. Thomas only.*

Epistle. Gal. iv. 1—7.

The heir as long as he is . . . heir through God.

Gradual.

Thou art fairer than the children of men : full of grace are thy
lips.[3]

---

[1] Wisdom xviii. 14, 15.   [2] Ps. xciii. 1.

[3] Ps. xlv. 3.

℣. My heart is inditing of a good matter: I speak of the things which I have made unto the King. My tongue is the pen of a ready writer.[1] Alleluya.

℣. The Lord is King and hath put on glorious apparel: the Lord hath put on his apparel and girded himself with strength.[2]

The following Sequence is always to be said on this day, whether it be a sunday or not.

Sequence.

Let us celebrate this day, Christ the Lord's nativity;
Let the heavenly army's cry ring in praise incessantly,
Giving thanks, and honouring the wedding banquet of
     their king.
Now new light illumes the land, darkness flees at its
     command,
Grace descending opens wide the courts long shut on
     every side,
O happy mother, undefiled virgin, who hast borne a Child!
Great with thy holy burden, lo! yet a man thou didst
     not know.
Lady, of thee a suppliant crowd doth crave,
Procure from us escape from bands of sin,
O virgin, blessed of all generations;
For thou alone wast worthy found to bear
Within thy womb him who bare all our sins,
Who ruleth things above and things beneath.
Him they above do magnify, rejoicing
In that good state of being which he gave them;
We, lowly multitude, give him due reverence,
Beseeching favour of his clemency,
That, granting quiet times and present peace,
He will be pleased to give us holy lives,
Bestowing on his servants meet endowments;
Heal our divisions left behind at death,
And lead us where no sin or death is known,
Where at the Father's own right hand he sitteth,
And reigneth co-eternal over all,

[1] Ps. xlv. 1, 2.　　　　　[2] Ps. xciii. 1.

The world disposing by his power, with him
In concert, present things and things to come ;
On all the just conferring blest rewards
Which shine in brightness, where the true light shineth,
Which is our health eternal and our glory.

Gospel. St. Luke ii. 33—40.
And Joseph and . . . was upon him.

Creed.

Offertory.

God hath made the round world so sure that it cannot be moved.
Ever since the world began hath thy seat been prepared : thou art
from everlasting.[1]

Secret.

Accept, we beseech thee, O Lord, the sacrifice of thy
people, and direct that they may have fellowship with
Jesus Christ thy Son our Lord who deigned to be a
partaker of our humanity.   Who with thee etc.

Communion.

Take the young child and his mother, and go into the land of
Judah : for they are dead which sought the young child's life.[2]

Postcommunion.

We beseech thee, O Lord, that the sacrifice having
been now received, thy whole Church may rejoice in him
who hath taken upon himself her infirmities, that she
might become herself a partaker of the divine substance.
Through etc.

St. Silvester.

Office.

Let thy priests be clothed etc.[3]

Collect.

Grant, we beseech thee, Almighty God, that the revered
feast of the blessed Silvester, thy confessor and bishop,

---

[1] Ps. xciii. 2, 3.   [2] St. Mat. ii. 20.
[3] Ps. cxxxii. 9, 10.

may both increase our devotion, and further our salvation. Through etc.

Memories of Christmas, of St. Stephen, of St. John, of the Innocents, and of St. Thomas.

Epistle. Ecclus. xliv. 16, 17, 19—23 ; xlv. 3, 7, 16.

Gradual.

Behold, a high priest . . . sweet savour.[1] Alleluya.

℣. I have found David etc.[2]

Sequence.[3]

Gospel. St. Mat. xxv. 14—23.

A certain man travelling . . . joy of thy Lord.

Creed.

Offertory.

I have found David etc.[2]

Secret.

Be present, we beseech thee, O Lord, at our oblations, and suffer not those who are fortified by the glorious confession of blessed Silvester, thy confessor and bishop, to be exposed to any perils of mind or body. Through etc.

Postcommunion.

We beseech thee, Almighty God, that through the intercession of blessed Silvester, thy confessor and bishop, the gift which we have received at this day's feast may impart salvation both to our bodies and souls.   Through etc.

CIRCUMCISION OF OUR LORD.

Office.

Unto us a Child is born etc.[4]

Collect.

O God, who permittest unto us to celebrate the octave of our Saviour's birth, grant, we beseech thee, that as we

---

[1] From Ecclus. xliv. 16, 19, 20.   [2] Ps. lxxxix. 20, 21.
[3] From Common of a Confessor.   [4] Is. ix. 6.

have been renewed by the communion of his flesh, so we may be defended by his perpetual Divinity. Who with thee etc.

There should be no memory at this mass.

Epistle. Titus ii. 11—15.

For the grace of God . . . speak and exhort.

Gradual.

All the ends etc.[1] Alleluya.

℣. God, who at sundry times and in divers manners spake in time past unto the fathers by the prophets, hath in these last days spoken unto us by his Son.[2]

Sequence.

Let us devoutly pay
  With joy and praises meet,
Our reverence to this holy day,
  Which dawns with radiance sweet.
Darkness hath passed away,
  The mist of night retires,
The day star of the sea to-day
  With health the world inspires.
He of her womb is born
  Before whom hell doth shake,
And conscious of his empire shorn
  Grim death himself doth quake.
Despoiled the serpent mourns,
  Who wrought the world's annoy;
Fall'n man, the erring sheep, returns,
  Restored to endless joy.
With songs the angelic host
  Make all the heaven resound,
That the tenth piece, which once was lost,
  This day is safely found.

[1] Ps. xcviii. 4, 5.   [2] Heb. i. 1, 2.

O offspring highly blest,
  Redeeming man forlorn,
God, maker of the world confest,
  Is of a woman born.
What marvel passing strange
  This nature doth enfold!
Taking the new without a change,
  Retaining still the old.
The very Godhead is
  In human flesh arrayed :
What ear of earthly witnesses
  Hath heard such things essayed?
To seek that which was lost
  The shepherd good came down ;
Like warrior armèd at his post
  A helm his head doth crown.
On his own darts the foe
  Himself doth headlong thrust;
Stripped of his arms he lieth low,
  Wherein he put his trust.
Divided is the spoil,
  The captor captive ta'en ;
Christ's valiant fight the foe doth foil,
  And sure salvation gain.
Then to his home on high
  Our champion led the way,
Triumphing in his victory,
  Where thou art praised for aye.

Gospel. St. Luke ii. 21.
And when eight days . . . in the womb.

Creed.

Offertory.
The heavens are thine etc.[1]

Secret.

Grant, we beseech thee, Almighty God, that by these
gifts which we bring in honour of the mystery of the

[1] Ps. lxxxix. 12, 15.

hidden birth of our Lord Jesus Christ, we may attain to the understanding of a cleansed soul.   Through etc.

Communion.

All the ends etc.[1]

Postcommunion.

Grant, we beseech thee, Almighty God, that this which we have received on the recurring commemoration of our Saviour's birth may procure for us the healing of salvation.   Through etc.

On the octaves of St. Stephen, St. John, and the Holy Innocents, whether it be a sunday or not, everything shall be done as on the original day, except as regards the Sequence, the Creed, and the Preface.   And the chant is used for the Kyrie, Gloria in excelsis, Sanctus, *and* Agnus, *as on a simple feast of nine lessons.   Nevertheless, if it be a sunday, the Creed is to be used, but no Sequence.   But there should be a memory of St. Mary on the octave of St. Stephen, and thenceforward up to the Purification, both on festivals, and on ferial days, and on sundays, except on the Vigil and Feast of the Epiphany, together with the Collect,* O God, who by the fruitful virginity of blessed Mary etc.

VIGIL OF THE EPIPHANY.

At Mass.   *Office.*

Light shall shine etc.[2]

On this day, if it be a sunday, Kyrie, Gloria in excelsis, Sanctus, *and* Agnus *are chanted as on a simple feast of nine lessons ; but if it be not a sunday they are chanted as on a feast of three lessons, without ruling of the quire, and neither* Gloria in excelsis *nor* Credo *nor* Ite Missa est *are said, because the day is treated as a vigil ; nevertheless the deacon and sub-deacon are to be vested in dalmatic and tunicle.*

Collect.

We beseech thee, O Lord, that the brightness of the coming festival may illuminate our hearts, that so we may

---

[1] Ps. xcviii. 4.   [2] From Is. ix. 6, 7.

be able to free ourselves from the darkness of this world, and may reach the land of eternal light.   Through etc.

Memory of St. Thomas.   Collect.

O God, on behalf of whose[1] etc.

Memory of St. Edward, King and Confessor.   Collect.

O God, who didst manifest thy only begotten Son Jesus Christ our Lord in visible form to the most glorious King Edward, grant, we beseech thee, that by his merits and prayers we may be found worthy to attain to the eternal vision of our Lord Jesus Christ himself. Who liveth etc.

Neither more nor fewer Collects are to be said at this mass, whether it be a sunday or not.

Epistle.   Titus iii. 4—7.

But after that the kindness . . . eternal life.

Gradual.

Blessed is he that cometh etc.[2]
℣.   This is the Lord's doing etc.[3]

Alleluya *is always said on this day, whether it be a sunday or not.*

℣.   The Lord is King etc.[4]

There is no Sequence.

Gospel.   St. Mat. ii. 19—23.

But when Herod was dead . . . a Nazarene.

Offertory.

He hath made the round world so sure etc.[5]

Secret.

Grant, we beseech thee, O Lord, that in this present sacrifice we may both offer and receive him whom the

---

[1] As on p. 113.   [2] Ps. cxviii. 26, 27.   [3] *Ib.* 23.
[4] Ps. xciii. 1.   [5] *Ib.* 2, 3.

devout gifts of the coming solemnity proclaim beforehand, Jesus Christ thy Son our Lord. Who with thee etc.

Secret of St. Thomas.

Grant, we beseech thee, O Lord etc.[1]

Secret of St. Edward.

Pour out, we beseech thee, O Lord, the light of thy Holy Spirit upon us now assisting at thy sacred altars, so that what we devoutly offer to thee in honour of blessed king Edward may by his intercession turn to our health and salvation. Through etc.

Ferial Preface.

Communion.

Take the young child etc.[2]

Postcommunion.

Grant to us, Lord, we beseech thee, worthily to celebrate the mystery, which in the infancy of our Saviour is declared by brilliant miracles, while his humanity is manifestly shewn by his bodily growth. Through etc.

Postcommunion of St. Thomas.

Almighty and merciful God etc.[1]

Post communion of St. Edward.

Having been replenished with this feast of living food, we beseech thee, O Lord our God, that by the pleading of the merits of the blessed king Edward thy confessor, we may be found worthy to be partakers of the heavenly banquet. Through etc.

IN THE NIGHT OF THE EPIPHANY.

After the ninth Responsory the following Gospel shall be chanted.

℣. The Lord be with you.
℟. And with thy spirit.

---

[1] As on p. 114.　　　　[2] St. Mat. ii. 20.

Gospel. St. Luke iii. 21—iv. 1.
Glory be to thee, O Lord.
Now when all the people . . . from Jordan.

When the Gospel is ended, the priest, in a silk cope, shall begin Te Deum laudamus.

THE EPIPHANY.

At Mass. *Office.*

Behold the Lord, the ruler, cometh ; and dominion power and empire are in his hand.

Ps. Give the king thy judgments, O God : and thy righteousness unto the king's son.[1]

Behold etc.
Glory be etc.
Behold etc.
Kyrie, fountain of goodness etc.[2]

Collect.

O God, who by the leading of a star didst to-day manifest thy only begotten Son to the gentiles; mercifully grant that we who know thee now by faith may be admitted to the vision of thy majesty. Through etc.

Lesson. Is. lx. 1—6.
Arise, shine . . . of the Lord.

Gradual.

All they from Sheba shall come : they shall bring gold and incense ; and they shall shew forth the praises of the Lord.[3]

℣. Arise and shine, O Jerusalem, for the glory of the Lord is risen upon thee.[4] Alleluya.

℣. We have seen his star in the east, and are come with gifts to adore the Lord.[5]

Sequence.

Let us duly magnify
This renowned Epiphany,

---

[1] Ps. lxxii. 1.   [2] No. 3.   [3] Is. lx. 6.
     [4] *Ib.* 1.   [5] St. Mat. ii. 2.

To the Child of God to-day
Wise men rightful homage pay.
Whom, immeasurably great,
Chaldee sages venerate,
To whose coming, man to save,
All the prophets witness gave:
His majestic throne on high,—
Such his great humility,—
He refused not to forsake,
And a servant's form to take;
God from all eternity,
Ere the world began to be,
He was man of Mary made:
Whom predicting Balaam said,—
Out of Jacob, seen from far,
There shall come a flaming star,
Which with power shall smite the host
Of Moab to his utmost coast.
Him their costly offering,
Gold, myrrh, incense, wise men bring.
God, sweet incense; precious gold
A king; myrrh doth a man unfold:
Angel-warned, no word they bring
Back to Herod, ruthless king,
Fearing much, in rage and hate,
He should lose his royal state.
Lo! the star before them went,
Homeward on their journey bent,
Glad they seek their native land,
Heeding not the king's command.
Maddened with exceeding ire
Forth he sends the mandate dire
Throughout Bethlehem's coasts to seek
And to slay the infants meek.
Now the choir their voice unite,
Organs swell with mystic rite,
Bringing to the King of kings,
Praise and costly offerings.

K

O'er all kingdoms, o'er all lands
May he spread his sheltering hands
Ever present to defend,
Unto worlds that never end.

Gospel. St. Mat. ii. 1—12.
When Jesus was born . . . another way.

Offertory.

The kings of Tharsis and of the isles shall give presents, the kings of Arabia and Saba bring gifts. All kings shall fall down before him: all nations shall do him service.[1]

Secret.

Regard, we beseech thee, O Lord, with favour the gifts of thy Church, whereby are now no longer offered gold, frankincense, and myrrh, but what is signified by the same gifts is sacrificed and received, Jesus Christ our Lord. Who with thee etc.

Preface.

Because when thy only-begotten etc.[2]

This Preface is said throughout the whole Octave and on the Octave, and the In communion *with* likewise.

Communion.

We have seen his star in the east, and are come with gifts to adore the Lord.[3]

Postcommunion.

Grant, we beseech thee, Almighty God, that what we celebrate in this solemn office we may apprehend with the intelligence of a purified mind. Through etc.

The same mass is said daily within the Octave, but without the Sequence and the Creed. But on Sunday the Creed is said, yet not the Sequence.

SUNDAY WITHIN THE OCTAVE.

At Mass. Kyrie, Gloria in excelsis, Sanctus, *and* Agnus *are chanted in order, as also throughout the Octave, with*

[1] Ps. lxxii. 10, 11.   [2] See p. 597.   [3] Based on St. Mat. ii. 2.

*ruling of the quire.   Other things are to be as on the day
itself, with the exception of the Sequence, and with this Gospel.*

Gospel.   St. John i. 29—34.
The next day John . . . is the Son of God.

*But if Sunday do not fall within the Octave, then the above
Gospel shall be read on the Wednesday within the Octave.*

THIRD DAY WITHIN THE OCTAVE.

*Memory shall be made of the martyrs Lucian and his com-
panions, with the Collect from the Common of many martyrs.*

OCTAVE OF THE EPIPHANY.

At Mass.   *Office.*
Behold the Lord, the ruler, cometh etc.[1]

Collect.
O God, whose only-begotten Son appeared in the
substance of our flesh, grant, we beseech thee, that we
may be found worthy to be inwardly renewed by him,
whom we have known to resemble ourselves in outward
appearance.   Who with thee etc.

Memory of St. Hilary, Confessor.
Be favourable, O Lord, to our prayers, and through
the intercession of the blessed Hilary, thy confessor and
bishop, whose deposition we commemorate, graciously
bestow upon us thy perpetual mercy.   Through etc.

Memory of St. Mary.
O God, who by the fruitful virginity etc.[2]

Lesson.   Is. xxv. 1—xii. 5.[3]
O Lord, thou art my God . . . in all the earth.

---

[1] As on the Epiphany, p. 124.   [2] See Index.
[3] Put together mainly from Is. xxv. 1 ; xli. 18 ; lii. 13 ; xii. 3—5.

Gradual.

All they from Sheba etc.[1]

Alleluya. ℣. We have seen his star etc.[1]
No Sequence is said even if it be a Sunday.

Gospel. St. Mat. iii. 13—17.
Then cometh Jesus . . . I am well pleased.

Offertory.

The kings of Tharsis etc.[2]

Secret.

We bring thee offerings, O Lord, in honour of the manifestation of the birth of thy Son ; humbly beseeching thee, that as the same our Lord Jesus Christ is the author of our gifts, so he may also himself mercifully receive the same. Who with thee etc.

Another secret [of St. Hilary].

We beseech thee, O Lord, that this offering may be rendered acceptable to thee through the prayers of St. Hilary, in memory of whose deposition it is presented. Through etc.

Preface and In communion with *as on the Epiphany.*

Communion.

We have seen his star etc.[3]

Postcommunion.

We beseech thee, O Lord, that thy heavenly light may always and everywhere prevent us; that we may contemplate with clear vision, and receive with due effect the mystery of which thou hast been pleased that we should be partakers. Through etc.

Another Postcommunion [of St. Hilary].

We beseech thee, O Lord, that through the intercession of blessed Hilary, thy confessor and bishop, the pledge of eternal redemption which we have received may be our aid both in this life and in the life to come. Through etc.

[1] As on p. 124.   [2] p. 126.   [3] *Ib.*

First Sunday after the Octave of Epiphany.

At Mass.   *Office.*

I saw seated on a high throne, a man whom a multitude of angels worshipped, chanting together; behold him, the name of whose kingdom is for everlasting.

Ps.   O be joyful in the Lord all ye lands; serve the Lord with gladness.[1]

Collect.

O Lord, we beseech thee, mercifully to receive the prayers of thy people which call upon thee, that they may both perceive what things they ought to do, and also may have power to fulfil the same.   Through etc.

Epistle.   Rom. xii. 1—5.

I beseech you therefore . . . one of another.

Gradual.

Blessed be the Lord God, the God of Israel; thou who alone from eternity doest great and wonderful things.[2]

℣.   The mountains also shall bring peace, and the little hills righteousness unto the people.[3]

Alleluya.   ℣.   O be joyful in the Lord, all ye lands; serve the Lord with gladness.[4]

On no Sunday throughout the year is a Sequence said at Mass when the Mass is of the Sunday, except in Advent, and in Easter-tide, and on the Sunday in the week after Christmas Day.

Gospel.   St. Luke ii. 42—52.

And when he was twelve . . . God and man.

Offertory.

O be joyful in the Lord all ye lands; be joyful in the Lord all ye lands: serve the Lord with gladness, and come before his presence with a song.   Be ye sure that the Lord he is God.[5]

---

[1] Ps. c. 1.   [2] Partly from Ps. lxxii. 18.   [3] *Ib.* 3.
[4] Ps. c. 1.   [5] *Ib.* c. 1, 2.

Secret.

We beseech thee, O Lord, that the sacrifice offered unto thee may ever quicken and defend us.   Through etc.

Ferial Preface.
Communion.

Son, why hast thou thus dealt with us ?   Behold, thy father and I have sought thee sorrowing.   And how is it that ye sought me ?   Wist ye not that I must be about my Father's business ?[1]

Postcommunion.

In partaking, O Lord, of thy holy gifts may we both receive the effect of perfect purification, and the continual help of divine protection.   Through etc.

If the time shall be so short between the octave of the Epiphany and Septuagesima that the three Sunday masses I saw seated etc.   Let all the world etc.   Worship him etc.[2] *cannot be sung in separate weeks, then two or three masses, if the shortness of the time demand it, may be sung in one and the same week.   And if any feast of three lessons shall occur, the whole service is to be of the feast until mass, and at that mass, which shall be of the season,*[3] *the second Collect shall be of the feast itself, the third of saint Mary, the fourth of All Saints, and the fifth for the Church universal.   But the other masses which follow shall be altogether omitted in that year. It is also to be carefully observed that the mass* I saw seated etc. *is never to be sung before the first Sunday after the Octave of the Epiphany except when no Sunday shall intervene between the Octave of the Epiphany and Septuagesima.   In that case it should be sung in the first place on some weekday after the Octave of the Epiphany, and the two masses* Let all the world etc., *and* Worship him etc. *should be sung on following weekdays in the same week, and no notice should be taken of any feasts of three lessons which may occur then. But when the season is prolonged the Office* Worship him

---

[1] St. Luke ii. 48, 49.

[2] *i.e.,* the masses for the 1st, 2nd, and 3rd Sundays after the Octave of the Epiphany.   Sundays were frequently designated from the opening words of their offices.

[3] *i.e.,* of the Sunday after Epiphany.

etc. *may be sung for three Sundays. If, however, there shall be* [*exactly*] *three Sundays between the Octave of the Epiphany and Septuagesima, so that the three previously mentioned Offices are sung, then the Epistles and Gospels of the fourth and fifth Sundays* [*after the Octave of the Epiphany*] *should be used at mass on weekdays after the third Sunday, if they are unoccupied.*

WEDNESDAY.

Epistle. Rom. x. 1—4.

Brethren, my heart's desire . . . that believeth.

Gospel. St. Mat. iv. 12—17.

Now when Jesus had heard . . . is at hand.

FRIDAY.

Epistle. Rom. xiii. 1—6.

Let every soul . . . this very thing.

Gospel. St. Luke iv. 14—22.

And Jesus returned . . . out of his mouth.

The Sunday mass is said throughout the whole week, unless a feast intervene, from which the service is taken, and except when the Mass I am the salvation *or the Mass of a local Feast, or the Mass of saint Mary is said.*

SECOND SUNDAY AFTER THE OCTAVE OF EPIPHANY.

Office.

Let all the world worship thee, O God ; let it sing of thee and praise thy name, O most highest.[1]

Ps. O be joyful in God all ye lands : sing praises unto the honour of his name, make his praise to be glorious.[2]

---

[1] From Ps. lxvi. 3.   [2] *Ib.* 1.

Collect.

Almighty and everlasting God, who dost govern all things in heaven and earth ; mercifully hear the supplications of thy people, and grant us thy peace all the days of our life. Through etc.

Gradual.

The Lord sent his word and healed them : and they were saved from their destruction.[1]

℟. O that men would therefore praise the Lord for his goodness, and declare the wonders that he doeth for the children of men.[2]

Alleluya. ℟. Praise him all ye angels of his : praise him all his host.[3]

Gospel. St. John ii. 1—11.

There was a marriage . . . believed on him.

Offertory.

O be joyful in God all ye lands ; be joyful in God all ye lands : sing praises unto the honour of his name. O come hither and hearken, all ye that fear God, and I will tell you what things the Lord hath done for my soul.[4]

Secret.

We beseech thee, O Lord, to cleanse thy people from all contamination of frowardness, that their offerings may be acceptable unto thee. Through etc.

Communion.

The Lord saith, Fill the water pots with water, and bear unto the governor of the feast. And when the ruler of the feast had tasted the water that was made wine, he saith unto the bridegroom, Thou hast kept the good wine until now. This was the first miracle that Jesus did in the presence of his disciples.[5]

Postcommunion.

Grant, we beseech thee, O Lord, that the efficacy of thy power may be increased in us, that being quickened by divine sacraments, we may through thy gifts be made ready evermore to receive what they promise. Through etc.

[1] Ps. cvii. 20. [2] *Ib.* 21. [3] Ps. xlviii. 2.
[4] From Ps. lxvi. 1, 14. [5] Adapted from St. John ii. 7, 9, 10, 11

WEDNESDAY.

Epistle. 1 Tim. i. 15—17.

This is a faithful saying . . . Amen.

Gospel. St. Mark vi. 1—6.

And he went out . . . their unbelief.

FRIDAY.

Epistle. Rom. xiv. 14—23.

I know and am persuaded . . . is sin.

Gospel. St. Luke iv. 31—37.

And he came down . . . country round about.

THIRD SUNDAY AFTER THE OCTAVE OF EPIPHANY.

At Mass.   *Office.*

Worship him, all ye gods. Sion heard of it, and rejoiced : and the daughters of Judah were glad.[1]

Ps. The Lord is King, the earth may be glad thereof : yea, the multitude of the isles may be glad thereof.[2]

Collect.

Almighty and everlasting God, mercifully look upon our infirmities, and stretch forth the right hand of thy majesty to defend us. Through etc.

Epistle. Rom. xii. 16—21.

Be not wise in . . . evil with good.

Gradual.

The heathen shall fear thy name, O Lord : and all the kings of the earth thy majesty.[3]

When the Lord shall build up Sion : and when his glory shall appear.[4]

Alleluya. ℣. The Lord is King, the earth may be glad thereof : yea, the multitude of the isles may be glad thereof.[5]

---

[1] Ps. xcvii. 7, 8.   [2] *Ib.* 1.   [3] Ps. cii. 15.
[4] *Ib.* 16.   [5] Ps. xcvii. 1.

Gospel. St. Mat. viii. 1—13.

When he was come down . . . selfsame hour.

Offertory.

The right hand of the Lord hath the pre-eminence: the right hand of the Lord bringeth mighty things to pass. I shall not die, but live: and declare the works of the Lord.[1]

Secret.

We celebrate the adorable mysteries of eternal life, beseeching thee that by devout sacrifices and by good works we may attain the same. Through etc.

Ferial Preface.

Communion.

They all wondered at the words which proceeded out of the mouth of God.[2]

Postcommunion.

Grant, we beseech thee, O Lord, that we to whom thou vouchsafest the use of so great mysteries, may be made truly worthy to receive the effects thereof. Through etc.

WEDNESDAY.

Epistle. Rom. xv. 30—33.

Now I beseech you . . . Amen.

Gospel. St. Mark iii. 1—5.

And he entered . . . as the other.

FRIDAY.

Epistle. 1 Cor. iii. 16—23.

Know ye not . . . Christ is God's.

Gospel. St. Mat. iv. 23—25.

And Jesus went . . . multitudes of people.

FOURTH SUNDAY AFTER THE OCTAVE OF EPIPHANY.

Office.

Worship him etc.[3]

---

[1] Ps. cxviii. 16, 17.   [2] St. Luke iv. 22.   [3] As on third Sunday.

Collect.

O God, who knowest us to be set in the midst of so many and great dangers that by reason of the frailty of our nature we cannot stand upright, grant to us such health of mind and body, that by thy aid we may overcome those things which we suffer for our sins. Through etc.

Epistle. Rom. xiii. 8—10.

Owe no man . . . fulfilling of the law.

Gradual.

The heathen shall fear etc.[1]

Gospel. St. Mat. viii. 23—27.

And when he was entered . . . obey him.

Offertory.

The right hand etc.[1]

Secret.

Grant, we beseech thee, Almighty God, that the offering of this sacrifice may cleanse and defend our frailty from all evil. Through etc.

Ferial Preface.

Communion.

They all wondered etc.[1]

Postcommunion.

May thy gifts, O God, both detach us from earthly delights, and ever strengthen us with heavenly food. Through etc.

WEDNESDAY.

Epistle. 1 Cor. vii. 1—5.

It is good for a man . . . your incontinency.

Gospel. St. Luke ix. 57—62.

And it came to pass . . . kingdom of God.

[1] As on third Sunday.

FRIDAY.

Epistle. 1 Cor. vii. 20—24.
Let every man . . . abide with God.

Gospel. St. Mark x. 13—16.
And they brought . . . and blessed them.

FIFTH SUNDAY AFTER THE OCTAVE OF EPIPHANY.

At Mass.   *Office.*
    Worship him etc.[1]

Collect.

O Lord, we beseech thee to keep thy houshold in
continual godliness, that they who do lean only upon the
hope of thy heavenly grace, may ever be defended by thy
protecting power.   Through etc.

Epistle.   Col. iii. 12—17.
Put on, therefore . . . Father by him.

Gradual.
The heathen shall fear etc.[1]

Gospel.   St. Mat. xiii. 24—30.
Another parable . . . into my barn.

Offertory.
The right hand etc.[1]

Secret.

Receive, we beseech thee, O Lord, the offerings and
prayers of thy servants, that by the help of thy protection,
they may not lose what they have obtained, and may get
those things which they desire.   Through etc.

Ferial Preface.

[1] As on third Sunday.

Communion.

They all wondered etc.[1]

Postcommunion.

O God who dost approach us in our participation of thy sacrament, work out in our hearts the effects of its power, that through the gift itself we may be made fit for the divine gift which we have received. Through etc.

WEDNESDAY.

Epistle. 1 Tim. ii. 1—7.
I exhort therefore . . . in faith and verity.

Gospel. St. Mat. xxi. 28—32 and xiii. 9.
A certain man . . . let him hear.

SEPTUAGESIMA SUNDAY.

At Mass.   *Office.*

The sorrows of death compassed me : the pains of hell came about me. In my trouble I will call upon the Lord, so shall he hear my voice out of his holy temple.[2]

Ps. I will love thee, O Lord my strength ; the Lord is my strong rock and my defence, and my Saviour.[3]

From this day till Easter Even Gloria in excelsis *is not said at any mass, except when a Bishop shall celebrate on Maundy Thursday.*

Collect.

O Lord, we beseech thee favourably to hear the prayers of thy people, that we who are justly punished for our offences may be mercifully delivered for the glory of thy name. Through etc.

Epistle. 1 Cor. ix. 24—27 ; x. 1—4.
Know ye not . . . Rock was Christ.

---

[1] As on third Sunday.   [2] Ps. xviii. 3, 4, 5, 6.   [3] *Ib.* 1.

Gradual.

A refuge in due time of trouble. And they that know thy Name will put their trust in thee; for thou, Lord, hast never failed them that seek thee.[1]

℞. For the poor shall not alway be forgotten : the patient abiding of the meek shall not perish for ever. Up, Lord, and let not man have the upper hand.[2]

The Gradual is not to be repeated when there is a Tract.

Tract.

Out of the deep have I called unto thee, O Lord : Lord, hear my voice.[3]

℣. O let thine ears consider well : the voice of my complaint.[4]

℣. If thou, Lord, wilt be extreme to mark what is done amiss ; O Lord, who may abide it.[5]

℣. For there is mercy with thee : therefore shalt thou be feared, O Lord.[6]

Gospel. St. Mat. xx. 1—16.

The kingdom of heaven . . . few chosen.

Offertory.

It is a good thing to give thanks unto the Lord : and to sing praises unto thy Name, O Most Highest.[7]

℞. O Lord, how glorious are thy works : thy thoughts are very deep.[8]

℞. For lo, thine enemies, O Lord, lo, thine enemies shall perish : and all the workers of wickedness shall be destroyed.[9]

Secret.

Having received, O Lord, we beseech thee, our gifts and prayers, both cleanse us by these heavenly mysteries, and mercifully hear us. Through etc.

Ferial Preface.

Communion.

Shew thy servant the light of thy countenance, and save me for thy mercy's sake. Let me not be confounded, O Lord, for I have called upon thee.[10]

[1] Ps. ix. 9, 10.   [2] *Ib.* 18, 19.   [3] Ps. cxxx. 1.   [4] *Ib.* 2.
[5] *Ib.* 3.   [6] *Ib.* 4.   [7] Ps. xcii. 1.   [8] *Ib.* 5.
[9] *Ib.* 8.   [10] Ps. xxxi. 18, 19.

Postcommunion.

May thy faithful people, O Lord, be strengthened by thy gifts, that both by receiving them they may seek them anew, and by seeking them may receive them evermore. Through etc.

Note, that the service of this day is not to be transferred on account of any feast, except when the Purification of blessed Mary or the dedication of the Church occurs on this day. Then it should be transferred to the third day of the week, and the Tract Out of the deep *should be omitted. Because no Tract is said on weekdays before Ash Wednesday, save only in masses for the Dead, and on feasts with ruling of the quire. Whatever other feast occurs on this Sunday, or on any Sunday up to Passion Sunday, should always be transferred even although it be a double feast : and the service should be the service of the Sunday, without any memory of the feast, unless it be a feast of three lessons, which is not to be transferred. In that case let a memory of it be made up to the beginning of Lent only. But from Ash Wednesday to the morrow of the octave of Easter, no notice should be taken of feasts of three lessons, not even a memory being made of them.*

WEDNESDAY.

Epistle. 2 Cor. iv. 3—12.
If our gospel be hid . . . life in you.

Gospel. St. Mark ix. 30—37, and iv. 23.
Jesus departed thence . . . let him hear.

FRIDAY.

Epistle. 2 Cor. iv. 13—18.
We having the same . . . are eternal.

Gospel. St. Mat. xii. 30—37.
He that is not with me . . . be condemned.

SEXAGESIMA SUNDAY.

At Mass.   *Office.*

Up, Lord, why sleepest thou? Awake and be not absent from us for ever. Wherefore hidest thou thy face, and forgettest our misery and trouble? Our belly cleaveth unto the ground. Arise, Lord, help us and deliver us.[1]

Ps. We have heard with our ears, O God, our fathers have told us.[2]

Collect.

O God who seest that we put not our trust in anything that we do, mercifully grant that by the protection of the teacher of the gentiles we may be defended against all adversities. Through etc.

The following Epistle is to be read wholly on this day only. When it is read on weekdays it shall always be begun with the verse In Damascus the governor *and read thence to the finish.*

Epistle. 2 Cor. xi. 19—33; xii. 1—9.
Ye suffer fools . . . rest upon me.

Gradual.

Let the nations know that thy name is Lord, and that thou only art the Most Highest over all the earth.[3]

℣. O my God, make them like unto a wheel: and as the stubble béfore the wind.[4]

Tract.

Thou hast moved the land, O Lord, and divided it.[5]

℣. Heal the sores thereof, for it shaketh.[6]

℣. That they may flee from the face of thy bow, that thy beloved may be delivered.[7]

Gospel. St. Luke viii. 4—15.
When much people . . . with patience.

---

[1] Ps. xliv. 23—26.   [2] *Ib.* 1.   [3] From Ps. lxxxiii. 18.   [4] *Ib.* 13.
[5] Ps. lx. 2.   [6] *Ib.*   [7] *Ib.* 5. (Vulg.)

Offertory.

O hold thou up my goings in thy paths, that my footsteps slip not. Incline thine ear unto me, and hearken unto my words. Shew thy marvellous lovingkindness, thou that art the Saviour of them which put their trust in thee.[1]

℣. Hear the right, O Lord, consider my complaint, and hearken unto my prayer.[2]

℣. Keep me, O Lord, as the apple of an eye: hide me under the shadow of thy wings: deliver me, O Lord, from the ungodly man.[3]

Secret.

Regard, we beseech thee, O Lord, the offering of thy family, and grant that those whom thou makest to be partakers of thy holy gifts, may attain unto the fulness of the same. Through etc.

Ferial Preface.

Communion.

I will go unto the altar of God, even unto the God of my joy and gladness.[4]

Postcommunion.

Almighty God, we humbly beseech thee to grant that those whom thou refreshest with thy sacrament may worthily serve thee in a life well pleasing unto thee. Through etc.

WEDNESDAY.

Epistle. 2 Cor. i. 23—24 ; ii. 1—11.
I call God . . . of his devices.

Gospel. St. Mark iv. 1—9.
Jesus began to teach . . . let him hear.

FRIDAY.

Epistle. 2 Cor. v. 11—15.
Knowing the terror of . . . and rose again.

Gospel. St. Luke xvii. 20—37.
When he was demanded . . . gathered together.

---

[1] From Ps. xvii. 5, 6, 7.   [2] *Ib.* 1.   [3] *Ib.* 8, 9.   [4] Ps. xliii. 4.

L

QUINQUAGESIMA SUNDAY.

At Mass.　　　　　　　　*Office.*

Be thou my strong rock, and house of defence, that thou mayest save me.　For thou art my strong rock and my castle : be thou also my guide and lead me for thy Name's sake.[1]

Ps.　In thee, O Lord, have I put my trust; let me never be put to confusion, deliver me in thy righteousness, and save me.[2]

Collect.

O Lord, we beseech thee, mercifully hear our prayers, and loose us from the chains of our sins, and keep us from all adversity.　Through etc.

Epistle.　1 Cor. xiii. 1—13.
Though I speak . . . is charity.

Gradual.
Thou art the God that doest wonders, and hast declared thy power among the people.[3]

℣.　Thou hast mightily delivered thy people, even the sons of Jacob and Joseph.[4]

Tract.

O be joyful in the Lord all ye lands ; serve the Lord with gladness.[5]

℣.　Come before his presence with a song.[6]

℣.　Be ye sure that the Lord he is God.[7]

℣.　It is he that hath made us, and not we ourselves ; we are his people, and the sheep of his pasture.[8]

Gospel.　St. Luke xviii. 31—43.
Then he took . . . praise unto God.

Offertory.
Blessed art thou, O Lord, O teach me thy statutes.　Blessed art thou, O Lord, O teach me thy statutes.　With my lips have I been telling of all the judgments of thy mouth.[9]

---

[1] Ps. xxxi. 3, 4.　　　[2] *Ib.* 1.　　　[3] Ps. lxxvii. 14.
[4] *Ib.* 15.　　　[5] Ps. c. 1.　　　[6] *Ib.*　　　[7] *Ib.* 2.
　　　[8] *Ib.*　　　　　　[9] Ps. cxix. 12, 13.

℣. Blessed are those that are undefiled in the way, and walk in the law of the Lord. Blessed are they that keep his testimonies, and seek him with their whole heart.[1]

℣. O turn from thy people shame and rebuke, because we have not forgotten thy law, O Lord.[2]

Secret.

We beseech thee, O Lord, that this offering may cleanse away our sins ; and sanctify the bodies and souls of thy servants for the celebration of this sacrifice. Through etc.

Communion.

They did eat, and were well filled ; for the Lord gave them their own desire ; they were not disappointed of their lust.[3]

Postcommunion.

We beseech thee, almighty God, that we who have received heavenly food, may be thereby defended against all adversities. Through etc.

Ash Wednesday.

After sext, first shall the sermon, if there be one, be addressed to the people. Then shall the clerks prostrate themselves in the quire, and say the seven penitential Psalms, with Glory be to the Father *etc., and* As it was *etc., and with the* Anthem Remember not *etc. The superior priest, having put on his priestly vestments, being in a red silk cope, with the deacon on his right hand, and the subdeacon on his left, and with the rest of the ministers of the altar vested in albs and amices, in prostration before the altar, shall say by themselves the seven penitential Psalms with the anthem* Remember not *etc.*

Pss. vi., xxxii., xxxviii., li., cii., cxxx., cxliii.[4]

---

[1] *Ib.* 1, 2.   [2] Adapted from *ib.* 22.   [3] Ps. lxxviii. 30.
[4] These are the proper Psalms for Ash Wednesday in the Book of Common Prayer, if the Commination Service is included.

Anthem.

Remember not, Lord, our offences, nor the offences of our forefathers, neither take thou vengeance of our sins.[1]

> Lord, have mercy.
> Christ, have mercy.
> Lord, have mercy.
> Our Father, etc.

All the above are said, without chanting, both by the priests and by the whole quire, a boy meanwhile holding a sackcloth banner near the left side of the altar. Then the priest shall rise, with the deacon and subdeacon, and turning himself to the east, and standing in front of the right side of the altar, shall say over the people as follows, alone :

> And lead us not into temptation.

The quire shall answer :

> But deliver us from evil.

O my God, save thy servants and thy handmaids : that put their trust in thee.

Send them, O Lord, help from thy holy place : and defend them out of Sion.

Turn thee again, O Lord, at the last : and be gracious unto thy servants.

Help us, O God of our salvation : and for the glory of thy name deliver us, O Lord, and be merciful unto our sins for thy name's sake.

> Lord, hear my prayer.
> And let my crying come unto thee.
> The Lord be with you.
> And with thy spirit.

Let us pray.

O Lord, we beseech thee, hear our prayers, and spare all those who confess their sins unto thee, that they whose consciences by sin are accused by thy merciful pardon may be absolved. Through etc. ℞. Amen.

---

[1] Opening portion of fifth petition in the Litany, *ib.*

All these Collects are said with Let us pray *and are to be concluded after the manner of a Lesson.* The Lord be with you *is said before the first Collect only.*

Collect.

Inspire, we beseech thee, O Lord, thy servants with thy saving grace, that their hearts being melted by plenteousness of tears may be so softened and subdued that the working of thy anger may be turned away by a fitting satisfaction. Through etc.

Collect.

Grant, we beseech thee, O Lord our God, unto these thy servants that by repentance they may continually work out the conditions of their purification ; and that to enable them more effectually to fulfil the same the grace of thy visitation may prevent and follow them. Through etc.

Collect.

Let thy merciful kindness, O Lord, we beseech thee, prevent these thy servants, that all their iniquities may be blotted out by thy speedy forgiveness. Through etc.

Collect.

Be favourable, O Lord, to our supplications, and let not the pitifulness of thy mercy be far from thy servants ; heal their wounds, and forgive their sins, that being separated from thee by no iniquities, they may ever hold fast to thee their Lord. Through etc.

Collect.

O Lord our God, who art not overcome by our transgression, but dost graciously accept satisfaction, look, we beseech thee, upon thy servants who confess that they have grievously sinned against thee ; to thee it appertaineth to give absolution from offences, and to grant pardon to sinners ; thou hast said that thou wouldest rather the repentance than the death of sinners ; grant, therefore, O Lord, to these thy servants, that they may keep unto thee the vigil of penitence, and amending their ways may rejoice that everlasting joys have been conferred on them by thee. Through etc.

Collect.

O God, whose pardon every man needeth, remember thy servants and thy handmaidens; and because through the uncertain frailty of their mortal bodies, they are despoiled of virtue, and in many things have done amiss, we beseech thee that thou wouldest give pardon to them as they confess their sins, and spare thy suppliants, that they who are accused by their own deserts may be saved by thy pity. Through etc.

At this point neither The Lord be with you *nor* Let us pray *are said; but the priest shall turn to the people, and extending his hand shall say over them, without chanting, but audibly, as follows:*

We absolve you in the place of blessed Peter, prince of the Apostles, to whom there hath been granted by the Lord the power of binding and loosing; and so far as self-accusation appertaineth to you and remission to us, may almighty God be unto you life and salvation, and the gracious pardoner of all your sins. Who liveth etc.

Here shall all rise from prostration, kissing the earth or the stalls, while the priest is saying Who liveth etc. *Then shall take place the blessing of ashes, without either* The Lord be with you *or* Let us pray, *the priest turning to the east.*

Collect.

Almighty and everlasting God, who hath compassion upon all men, and hateth nothing that thou hast made, passing over the sins of men because of their repentance; who also succourest them that labour in necessity, vouchsafe to bless and sanctify these ashes, which thou hast ordered that, after the manner of the Ninevites, we should bear upon our heads, for the sake of humility, and of our holy religion, and for the cleansing away of our offences; and grant that by calling on thy holy name, all those who have thus borne ashes on their heads may be thought worthy to receive from thee pardon of all their sins, and so to-day commence the observation of their holy fasts, that on the day of Resurrection they may be found worthy to approach the holy Paschal feast with minds purified, and hereafter to share in glory everlasting. Through etc.

Here holy water shall be sprinkled over the ashes. Then is said The Lord be with you *and* Let us pray.

Collect.

O God, who desirest not the death but the repentance of sinners, most graciously look upon the frailty of our human condition, and vouchsafe for thy lovingkindness to bless + and sanctify + these ashes which as a token of humility and for the obtaining of pardon, we have determined to have placed upon our heads ; that we whom thou hast warned that we are but ashes, and who know that we shall return to the dust as the recompense of our depravity, may be mercifully found worthy to receive the pardon of all our sins and the rewards which have been promised anew to them that repent. Through etc.

Afterwards the ashes shall be distributed on the heads of the clergy and laity by the higher dignitaries, making the sign of the cross with the ashes, and saying thus :

Remember, O man, that thou art ashes, and unto ashes shalt thou return. In the name of the Father, and of the Son, and of the Holy Ghost. Amen.

In the meanwhile the following anthems shall be sung :

Hear us, O Lord, for thy lovingkindness is comfortable : according to the multitude of thy mercies look thou upon us, O Lord.[1]

Ps. Save me, O God ; for the waters are come in, even unto my soul.[2]

Only the first verse of the Psalm is said ; then shall follow

---

[1] From Ps. lxix. 17.   [2] *Ib.* 1.

immediately Glory be to the Father etc., *after which the anthem* Hear us, O Lord etc., *shall be repeated.*

Another anthem.

Let the priests and Levites, ministers of the Lord, weep between the porch and the altar, saying, Spare thy people, O Lord, spare them, and turn not away the faces of them that call upon thee, O Lord.[1]

Another anthem.

Let us change our garments for sackcloth and ashes; let us fast and weep before the Lord, for our God is very merciful to put away our sins.

When this office is ended, the priest, standing at the step of the quire, shall say: The Lord be with you.   And with thy spirit.   Let us pray.

Collect.

O God, who art justly angry, and dost mercifully pardon, accept the tears of thy afflicted people and graciously turn away thy wrathful indignation, which they righteously deserve.   Through etc.

Another collect.

Let us pray.

Grant unto us, we beseech thee, O Lord, so to commence and protect our Christian warfare by holy fasts, that we who are about to fight against spiritual wickedness may be fortified by the aid of continence.   Through etc.

After the penitents have been ejected, in the way shewn by the office in the processionals, Mass shall be begun in the following manner.

Office.

Thou hast mercy upon all, O Lord, and hatest nothing that thou hast made; and winkest at the sins of men, because they should amend.   But thou sparest all, because thou art the Lord our God.[2]

---

[1] Partly from Joel ii. 17.   [2] Partly from Wisdom xi. 23, 24, 26.

Ps. Be merciful unto me, O Lord, be merciful unto me, for my soul trusteth in thee.[1]

The office is not to be repeated, but Glory be to the Father *is to follow immediately.* When Kyrie eleyson *is finished, the Priest shall say* The Lord be with you *and* Let us pray. *Afterwards the deacon shall say* Let us kneel, *whereupon all shall kneel. Then shall the deacon say* Rise, *and all shall rise, and kiss the stalls.*

Collect.

Grant, we beseech thee, O Lord, unto thy faithful people, that they may both enter upon the holy solemnities of the fast with befitting piety, and pass through them with undisturbed devotion. Through etc.

From this day till Maundy Thursday, at all masses of the fast, there shall be a memory for penitents, with this Collect, O Lord, we beseech thee, hear the prayers etc.[2] *On this day and on the three days following, five Collects are said, as has been laid down in the directions for the first Sunday in Advent.*

Lesson. Joel ii. 12—19.

Therefore also now . . . among the heathen.

Gradual.

Be merciful unto me, O God, be merciful unto me, for my soul trusteth in thee.[1]

℣. He shall send from heaven ; and save me from the reproof of him that would eat me up.[3]

The quire shall then say the Tract alternately.

O Lord, deal not with us, after the sins which we have committed, nor reward us according to our iniquities.[4]

℣. O Lord, remember not our old sins, but have mercy upon us, and that soon, for we are come to great misery.[5]

Here shall no genuflexion be made, while there is said :

---

[1] Ps. lvii. 1.   [2] Collect in the Mass for Sinners.
[3] Ps. lvii. 3.   [4] From Ps. ciii. 10.   [5] Ps. lxxix. 8.

℣. Help us, O God of our salvation for the glory of thy name : O deliver us, and be merciful unto our sins for thy name's sake.[1]

This Tract is said on every monday and friday,[2] at the mass of the fast, up to Maundy Thursday.

Gospel. St. Mat. vi. 16—21.

Moreover, when ye fast . . . heart be also.

Offertory.

I will magnify thee, O Lord, for thou hast set me up : and not made my foes to triumph over me. O Lord my God, I cried unto thee, and thou hast healed me.[3]

℣. Thou, Lord, hast brought my soul out of hell; thou hast kept my soul from them that go down into the pit.[4]

Secret.

Make us, we beseech thee, O Lord, to be duly fitted to present these offerings, by which we celebrate the beginning of this venerable fast. Through etc.

Preface. Who by the fasting of the body etc.[5]

This Preface is said at every mass of the fast up to Maundy Thursday; also Let us kneel, Rise, *and* Bow down your heads before God.

Communion.

In the law of the Lord will he exercise himself day and night : he will bring forth his fruit in due season.[6]

Postcommunion.

May the sacrament which we have received, O Lord, be our support, that our fast may both be acceptable to thee, and also avail to our healing. Through etc.

When the Postcommunions, with the exception of that said over the people, are finished, the priest shall say :

Let us pray.

Then shall the deacon say :

Bow down your heads before God.

[1] *Ib.* 9.   [2] Omni secunda feria et sexta feria.   [3] Ps. xxx. 1, 2.
[4] *Ib.* 3.   [5] Page 35.   [6] Ps. i. 2, 3.

Collect over the people.

Look mercifully, O Lord, upon those who bow themselves down before thy majesty, that they who have been refreshed with the divine gift, may ever be nourished by help from heaven. Through etc.

And thus shall the mass be concluded with

Let us bless the Lord.

THURSDAY AFTER ASH WEDNESDAY.

At Mass.   *Office.*

When I cried unto the Lord, he heard my voice from the battle that was against me; and he that endureth for ever shall bring them down. O cast thy burden upon the Lord, and he shall nourish thee.[1]

Ps. Hear my prayer, O God, and hide not thyself from my petition. Take heed unto me, and hear me.[2] Glory be to the Father etc. When I cried etc.

Let us pray. Let us kneel. Rise.

Collect.

O God, who art offended by sin and propitiated by repentance, mercifully regard the prayers of thy people which call upon thee, and graciously turn away the scourge of thine anger, which we deserve for our sins. Through etc.

Lesson. Is. xxxviii. 1—6.

In those days . . . defend this city.

Gradual.

O cast thy burden upon the Lord, and he shall nourish thee.[3]

℣. When I cried unto the Lord, he heard my voice from the battle that was against me.[4]

Gospel. St. Mat. viii. 5—13.

And when Jesus . . . selfsame hour.

[1] From Ps. lv. 19, 20, 23. [2] *Ib.* 1, 2. [3] *Ib.* 22. [4] *Ib.* 19.

Offertory.

Unto thee, O Lord, will I lift up my soul; my God, I have put my trust in thee : O let me not be confounded, neither let mine enemies triumph over me.   For all they that hope in thee shall not be ashamed.[1]

℣.   Lead me forth in thy truth and learn me ; for thou art the God of my salvation; in thee hath been my hope all the day long.[2]

Secret.

We offer to thee, O Lord, the gifts which thou hast given, that they may both help our mortal nature which thou hast created, and work in us an immortal cure. Through etc.

Preface.

Who by the fasting of the body etc.[3]

Communion.

Then shalt thou be pleased with thy sacrifice of righteousness, with the burnt-offerings and oblations upon thine altar, O Lord.[4]

Postcommunion.

Grant we beseech thee, O Lord, to thy faithful people, that they may both continually receive the paschal sacraments, and earnestly look forward to that which is approaching ; so that stedfastly abiding in the mysteries by which they have been renewed, they may by this means be brought to newness of life.   Through etc.

Over the people.

Let us pray.

Bow down your heads before God.

Collect.

Spare, O Lord, spare thy people, that having been justly chastised, they may be revived by thy mercy. Through etc.

---

[1] Ps. xxv. 1, 2.   [2] *Ib.* 4.   [3] Page 35.   [4] Ps. li. 19.

FRIDAY AFTER ASH WEDNESDAY.

At Mass. *Office.*

Hear, O Lord, and have mercy upon me : Lord, be thou my helper.[1]

Ps. I will magnify thee, O Lord, for thou hast set me up, and hast not made my foes to triumph over me.[2]

Glory be to the Father etc.
Hear, O Lord etc.
Lord have mercy etc. Let us pray. Let us kneel. Arise.

Collect.

Graciously favour us, O Lord, we beseech thee, in the fast which we have begun, that we may be enabled to fulfil with pure minds the duties which we outwardly perform. Through etc.

Lesson. Is. lviii. 1—9.
Cry aloud . . . Here I am.[3]

Gradual.

One thing have I desired of the Lord, which I will require, even that I may dwell in the house of the Lord.[4]

℣. That I may see the will of the Lord, and be protected by his holy temple.[5]

Tract.

O Lord, deal not with us etc.[6]

Gospel. St. Mat. v. 43—48, and vi. 1—6.
Ye have heard . . . shall reward thee openly.

Offertory.

Quicken me, O Lord, according to thy word, that I may know thy testimonies.[7]

℣. O deal with thy servant according unto thy lovingkindness : and take not the word of thy truth utterly out of my mouth.[8]

---

[1] Ps. xxx. 11.   [2] *Ib.* 1.
[3] To which the Sarum Missal adds : " For I the Lord thy God am merciful."
[4] Ps. xxvii. 4.   [5] Adapted from *ib.*   [6] As on Ash Wednesday.
[7] From Ps. cxix. 7.   [8] *Ib.* 124.

Secret.

We offer, O Lord, the sacrifice of Lenten observance ; grant, we beseech thee, that it may both render our minds acceptable unto thee, and dispose us more readily to continence.　Through etc.

Communion.

Serve the Lord in fear, and rejoice unto him with reverence; kiss the Son lest ye perish from the right way.[1]

Postcommunion.

Grant, we beseech thee, Almighty God, that the heavenly gifts which we ofttimes approach with due devotion may prove continually profitable to our salvation.　Through etc.

Over the people.

Let us pray.

Bow down your heads before God.

Collect.

Guard thy people, O Lord, and graciously cleanse them from all their sins ; for no adversity shall harm them, if no wickedness get the dominion over them.　Through etc.

SATURDAY AFTER ASH WEDNESDAY.

At Mass.　　　　　　　　　*Office.*

Hear me, O Lord, and have mercy upon me : Lord, be thou my helper.[2]

Ps.　I will magnify thee, O Lord, for thou hast set me up: and not made my foes to triumph over me.[3]

Hear me, O Lord etc.

Let us pray.　Let us kneel.　Rise.

Collect.

Hearken, O Lord, to our supplications, that we may observe with devout service this holy fast which was

---

[1] Ps. ii. 11, 12.　　　[2] Ps. xxx. 11.　　　[3] *Ib.* 1.

instituted to give health and salvation to our souls and bodies. Through etc.

Lesson. Is. lviii. 9—14.

If thou take away . . . hath spoken it.

Gradual.

One thing have I desired of the Lord which I will require, even that I may dwell in the house of the Lord.[1]

℣. To behold the will of the Lord and to be protected by his holy temple.[2]

Gospel. St. Mark vi. 47—56.

When even was come . . . were made whole.

Offertory.

Quicken me, O Lord, according to thy word, that I may know thy testimonies.[3]

℣. Give me understanding that I may know thy law, and let the free-will offerings of my mouth please thee, O Lord.[4]

Secret.

Prepare us, O Lord, we beseech thee, for the bounden duties of this fast, that we may ever celebrate this adorable sacrifice with sober minds. Through etc.

Preface.

Who by the fasting of the body etc.[5]

Communion.

Serve the Lord with fear, and rejoice unto him with reverence. Kiss the Son, lest ye perish from the right way.[6]

Postcommunion.

Grant, we beseech thee, Almighty God, that invigorated with the gift of heavenly life, we may find that what to us is a mystery in this present life may prove to be a help to life eternal. Through etc.

Over the people.

Let us pray.

Bow down your heads before God.

---

[1] Ps. xxvii. 4.   [2] *Ib.* with variations.   [3] Ps. cxix. 25.
[4] *Ib.* 34, 108.   [5] Page 35.   [6] Ps. ii. 11, 12.

Collect.

Make us, we beseech thee, O Lord, both at all times
to frequent with devout observance the means of our
salvation, and with still greater devotion to attend them
after their special commencement.   Through etc.

First Sunday in Lent.[1]

At Mass.   *Office.*

He shall call upon me, and I will hear him.   I will
deliver him, and bring him to honour.   With long life
will I satisfy him.[2]

Ps.   Whoso dwelleth under the defence of the most High shall
abide under the shadow of the Almighty.[3]

He shall call etc.   Glory be to the Father etc.   He
shall call etc.   Kyrie eleyson etc.

Collect.

O God, who purifiest thy church by the annual
observation of Lent, grant unto thy family that what they
endeavour to obtain of thee by fasting they may follow
up by good works.   Through etc.

Epistle.   2 Cor. vi. 1—10.
We beseech you . . . possessing all things.

Gradual.

He shall give his angels charge over thee to keep thee in all thy
ways.[4]
℣.   They shall bear thee in their hands, that thou hurt not thy
foot against a stone.[5]

Tract.

Whoso dwelleth under the defence of the most High:
shall abide under the shadow of the Almighty.[3]

---

[1] Called in Latin "Invocavit," from the first word of the Office.
[2] From Ps. xci. 15, 16.   [3] *Ib.* 1.   [4] *Ib.* 12.   [5] *Ib.* 13.

℣. I will say unto the Lord, Thou art my hope and my strong hold: my God, in him will I trust.

℣. For he shall deliver thee from the snare of the hunter: and from the noisome pestilence.

℣. He shall defend thee under his wings, and thou shalt be safe under his feathers.

℣. His faithfulness and truth shall be thy shield and buckler: thou shalt not be afraid for any terror by night.

℣. Nor for the arrow that flieth by day; for the pestilence that walketh in darkness: nor for the sickness that destroyeth in the noonday.

℣. A thousand shall fall beside thee, and ten thousand at thy right hand: but it shall not come nigh thee.

℣. For he shall give his angels charge over thee: to keep thee in all thy ways.

℣. They shall bear thee in their hands: that thou hurt not thy foot against a stone.

℣. Thou shalt go upon the lion and adder: the young lion and the dragon shalt thou tread under thy feet.

℣. Because he hath set his love upon me, therefore will I deliver him: I will set him up, because he hath known my name.

℣. He shall call upon me, and I will hear him: yea I am with him in trouble.

℣. I will deliver him and bring him to honour; with long life will I satisfy him: and shew him my salvation.[1]

Gospel.   St. Mat. iv. 1—11.
Then was Jesus led up . . . ministered unto him.

Offertory.
He shall defend thee under his wings, and thou shalt be safe under his feathers: his faithfulness and truth shall be thy shield and buckler.[2]

Secret.
Solemnly we offer our sacrifice at the beginning of Lent, beseeching thee, O Lord, that as we abstain from

---

[1] Ps. xci. 1—7, 11—16.   [2] Ps. xci. 4.

carnal feastings, so likewise we may be withheld from hurtful pleasures. Through etc.

Ferial preface.

Communion.

He shall defend thee under his wings, and thou shalt be safe under his feathers : his faithfulness and truth shall be thy shield and buckler.[1]

Postcommunion.

May the holy drink-offering of thy sacrament, O Lord, create us anew ; and through laying aside the old man may it make us partakers of this saving mystery. Through etc.

MONDAY AFTER FIRST SUNDAY IN LENT.

At Mass.   *Office.*

Behold, even as the eyes of servants look unto the hand of their masters : even so our eyes wait upon the Lord our God, until he have mercy upon us. Have mercy upon us, O Lord, have mercy upon us.[2]

Ps. Unto thee lift I up mine eyes, O thou that dwellest in the heavens.[3]

Let us pray. Let us kneel. Rise.

Collect.

Turn thou us, O God our Saviour, and that the Lenten fast may benefit us, instruct our minds with heavenly teaching. Through etc.

From this day until Maundy Thursday, at all masses of the fast, seven collects are said, as has been laid down above, in the first Sunday in Advent.[4]

Epistle. Ezek. xxxiv. 11—16.
Thus saith the Lord . . . with judgment.

Ps. xci. 4.   [2] Ps. cxxiii. 2, 3.   [3] *Ib.* 1.   [4] Page 70.

Gradual.

Behold, O Lord our defender, and look upon thy servants.[1]

℣. O Lord God of hosts, hear the prayers of thy servants.[2]

Tract.

O Lord, deal not with us etc.[3]

Gospel. St. Mat. xxv. 31—46.

When the Son of man . . . life eternal.

Offertory.

I will lift up mine eyes, that I may see the wondrous things of thy law; that thou mayest teach me thy righteousness. O grant me understanding that I may know thy testimonies.[4]

℣. Lay thy law upon me, O Lord, and let me learn the way of thy righteousness, and I will be exercised in thy precepts.[5]

Secret.

We beseech thee, O Lord, that the offerings of our devotion may be acceptable unto thee; that through thy operation they may both sanctify our fast, and obtain for us the favour of thy comfort. Through etc.

Preface.

Who by the fasting of the body etc.[6]

Communion.

I did call upon the Lord with my voice: and he heard me out of his holy hill. I will not be afraid for ten thousands of the people: that have set themselves against me round about.[7]

Postcommunion.

We beseech thee, O Lord, that the frequenting of thy mysteries may aid us, and both wean us from earthly desires, and train us to love heavenly things. Through etc.

Over the people.

Bow down your heads before God.

---

[1] Adapted from Ps. lxxxiii. 9. [2] *Ib.* 8.
[3] As on Ash Wednesday, p. 149. [4] From Ps. cxix. 18, 124, 125.
[5] From *ib.* 33, 27 (Vulg.). [6] Page 35. [7] Ps. iii. 4, 6.

Collect.

Loose us, we beseech thee, O Lord, from the chains of our sins, and mercifully turn away from us the punish· ment which we deserve for them. Through etc.

TUESDAY AFTER FIRST SUNDAY IN LENT.

At Mass.   *Office.*

Lord, thou hast been our refuge from one generation to another. Thou art God from everlasting, and world without end.[1]

Ps. Before the mountains were brought forth, or ever the earth and the world were made.[2]

No more of the Psalm is said.

Let us pray. Let us kneel. Rise.

Collect.

Look down, O Lord, upon this thy family, and grant that while we chastise ourselves by mortifying the flesh, our minds may be inflamed with desire of thee. Through etc.

Lesson. Is. lv. 6—11.

Seek ye the Lord . . . whereto I sent it.

Gradual.

Let my prayer be set forth in thy sight as the incense, O Lord.[3]

℣. Let the lifting up of my hands be an evening sacrifice.[4]

Gospel. St. Mat. xxi. 10—17.

When he was come . . . into Bethany.

Offertory.

My hope hath been in thee, O Lord : I have said, Thou art my God. My time is in thy hand.[5]

℣. Shew thy servant the light of thy countenance, and save me for thy mercy's sake, O Lord : let me not be confounded, for I have called upon thee.[6]

---

[1] Ps. xc. 1, 2.   [2] *Ib.* 2.   [3] Ps. cxli. 2.
[4] *Ib.*   [5] Ps. xxxi. 16, 17.   [6] *Ib.* 18, 19.

Secret.

Grant, we beseech thee, O Lord, that our devotion which we offer unto thee may be in accordance with the gift which we have dedicated to thee. Through etc.

Preface.

Who by the fasting of the body etc.[1]

Communion.

Hear me when I call, O God of my righteousness : thou hast set me at liberty when I was in trouble ; have mercy upon me, O Lord, and hearken unto my prayer.[2]

Postcommunion.

Almighty God, we beseech thee that we may effectually obtain that salvation, of which we have received the pledge in these mysteries. Through etc.

Over the people.

Bow down your heads before God.

Collect.

May our prayers ascend to thee, O Lord, and keep far all iniquity from thy church. Through etc.

WEDNESDAY IN EMBER WEEK IN LENT.

At Mass.   *Office.*

Call to remembrance, O Lord, thy tender mercies, and thy lovingkindnesses which have been ever of old. Neither let our enemies triumph over us. Deliver us, O God of Israel, out of all our troubles.[3]

Ps. Unto thee, O Lord, will I lift up my soul : my God, I have put my trust in thee : O let me not be confounded.[4]

The Collect follows without The Lord be with you, *but with* Let us pray *and* Let us kneel. Rise.

---

[1] Page 35.   [2] Ps. iv. 1.
[3] Ps. xxv. 5, 1, 21.   [4] *Ib.* 1.

Collect.

Mercifully hear our prayers, O Lord, we beseech thee ; and stretch forth the right hand of thy majesty to be our defence against all our enemies. Through etc.

Lesson. Exod. xxiv. 12—18.

The Lord said . . . and forty nights.

Gradual.

The sorrows of my heart are enlarged : O bring thou me out of my troubles, O Lord.[1]

℣. Look upon my adversity and misery : and forgive me all my sin.[2]

The gradual is not to be repeated, but there shall follow The Lord be with you. Let us kneel. Rise.

Collect.

Regard graciously, O Lord, we beseech thee the devotion of thy people, that they who are mortified in the body by abstinence, may be renewed in mind by the fruit of good works. Through etc.

The usual memories are said here.

Lesson. 1 Kings xix. 3—8.

He arose and went . . . the mount of God.

The Quire is to say the Tract in alternate verses.

Bring thou me out of my troubles, O Lord; look upon my adversity and misery : and forgive me all my sin.[3]

℣. Unto thee, O Lord, will I lift up my soul ; my God, I have put my trust in thee: O let me not be confounded, neither let mine enemies triumph over me.[4]

℣. For all they that hope in thee shall not be ashamed : but such as transgress without a cause shall be put to confusion.[5]

This Tract shall be said on every wednesday until Palm Sunday.

[1] Ps. xxv. 16.   [2] *Ib.* 17.   [3] *Ib.* 16, 17.
[4] *Ib.* 1.   [5] *Ib.* 2.

Gospel.   St. Mat. xii. 38—50.
Then certain . . . and sister and mother.

Offertory.

My delight shall be in thy commandments which I have loved.
My hands also will I lift up unto thy commandments which I
have loved.[1]

℣.   Thou art my portion, O Lord, I have promised to keep
thy law.   I made my humble petition in thy presence with my
whole heart.[2]

Secret.

Look we beseech thee, O Lord, upon this our only
sacrifice ; that we, who have waited for these things which
we believe and hope for in the reception of these mysteries,
may obtain the same.   Through etc.

Preface.

Who by the fasting of the body etc.[3]

Communion.

Consider my meditation.   O hearken thou unto the voice of
my calling, my king, and my God : for unto thee will I make my
prayer.[4]

Postcommunion.

Grant, we beseech thee, almighty God, that these holy
gifts may cleanse away our guilt, and work in us the
fruit of good living.   Through etc.

Over the people.

Let us pray.   Bow down your heads before God.

Collect.

We beseech thee, O Lord, to illuminate our minds
with the bright beams of thy light, that we may both
perceive what things we ought to do, and also may have
power rightly to fulfil the same.   Through etc.

THURSDAY AFTER FIRST SUNDAY IN LENT.

At Mass.   *Office.*

Glory and worship are before him : power and honour
are in his sanctuary.[5]

---

[1] Ps. cxix. 47, 48.   [2] *Ib.* 57, 58.   [3] Page 35.
          [4] Ps. v. 1, 2.   [5] Ps. xcvi. 6.

Ps. O sing unto the Lord a new song: sing unto the Lord, all the whole earth.[1]

Let us pray.   Let us kneel.   Rise.

Collect.

Almighty and everlasting God, who hast appointed the observances of fasting and almsgiving as remedies against sin, grant to us ever to be devoted to thee both in mind and body.   Through etc.

Epistle.   Ezek. xviii. 1—19.
The word of the Lord . . . shall surely live.

Gradual.
Keep me as the apple of an eye: hide me under the shadow of thy wings.[2]

℣. Let my sentence come forth from thy presence: and let thine eyes look upon the thing that is equal.[3]

Gospel.   St. John viii. 31—47.
Then said Jesus . . . heareth God's words.

Offertory.
The Angel of the Lord tarrieth round about them that fear him.   O taste and see how gracious the Lord is.[4]

℣. I will alway give thanks unto the Lord: his praise shall ever be in my mouth.[5]

Secret.

We beseech thee, O Lord, that those sacrifices which have been instituted to accompany this wholesome fast may favourably conduce to our salvation.   Through etc.

Preface.
Who by the fasting of the body etc.[6]

Communion.
The bread which I will give is my flesh, which I will give for the life of the world.[7]

Postcommunion.

By the free grant of these thy gifts, O Lord, increase

---

[1] Ps. xcvi. 1.   [2] Ps. xvii. 8.   [3] *Ib.* 2.   [4] Ps. xxxiv. 7, 8.
[5] *Ib.* 1.   [6] Page 35.   [7] St. John vi. 51.

our safety in things temporal, and renew it in things eternal. Through etc.

Over the people.
Bow down your heads before God.

Collect.

Grant, we beseech thee, O Lord, to all Christian people that they may acknowledge what they profess, and love the heavenly gift which they often approach. Through etc.

FRIDAY IN EMBER WEEK IN LENT.

At Mass. *Office.*

Bring thou me out of my troubles, O Lord. Look upon my adversity and misery: and forgive me all my sin.[1]

Ps. Unto thee, O Lord, will I lift up my soul; my God, I have put my trust in thee. Let me not be confounded.[2]

Let us pray. Let us kneel. Rise.

Collect.

Be favourable, O Lord, to thy people, and pitifully comfort again with thy gracious help those whom thou makest to be devout towards thee. Through etc.

Lesson. Ezek. xviii. 20—28.
The soul that sinneth . . . shall not die.

Gradual.

My God, save thy servant that putteth his trust in thee.[3]
℣. Give ear, Lord, unto my prayer.[4]

Tract.
O Lord, deal not with us etc.[5]

Gospel. St. John v. 1—15.
After this there was . . . made him whole.

---

[1] Ps. xxv. 16, 17.   [2] *Ib.* 1.   [3] Ps. lxxxvi. 2.
[4] *Ib.* 6.   [5] As on Ash Wednesday, p. 149.

Offertory.

Bless the Lord, O my soul, and forget not all his benefits; making thee young and lusty as an eagle.[1]

℣. Who forgiveth all thy sin, and saveth thy life from destruction: who crowneth thee with mercy and lovingkindness.[2]

Secret.

Receive, O Lord, we beseech thee, the offerings of our homage, and graciously sanctify thine own gifts. Through etc.

Preface.

Who by the fasting of the body etc.[3]

Communion.

All mine enemies shall be confounded and sore vexed: they shall be turned back, and put to shame suddenly.[4]

Postcommunion.

Grant, O Lord, that by the operation of this mystery our sins may both be washed away, and our just desires fulfilled. Through etc.

Over the people.

Bow down your heads [before God].

Collect.

Hear us, O merciful God, and shew the light of thy grace within our minds. Through etc.

SATURDAY IN EMBER WEEK IN LENT.

At Mass.   *Office.*

Let my prayer enter into thy presence, incline thine ear unto my calling, O Lord.[5]

Ps. O Lord God of my salvation, I have cried day and night before thee.[6]

All collects are said without The Lord be with you, *except*

---

[1] Ps. ciii. 2, 5.   [2] *Ib.* 3, 4.   [3] Page 35.
[4] Ps. vi. 10.   [5] Ps. lxxxviii. 1.   [6] *Ib.*

the last collect, preceding the Epistle. Let us pray *is said before all the Collects.* Similarly Let us kneel *is said before all the Collects except the last; and all lessons should be read with their titles.*

Collect.

We beseech thee, O Lord, look graciously upon thy people, and mercifully turn away from them the scourge of thine anger. Through etc.

Lesson. Deut. xxvi. 15—19.

Look down from thy . . . as he hath spoken.

Gradual.

Be merciful, O Lord, unto our sins. Wherefore do the heathen say, Where is now their God?[1]

℣. Help us, O Lord God of our salvation, and for the glory of thy name deliver us, O Lord.[2]

The Gradual is not to be repeated.

Let us pray. Let us kneel. Rise.

Collect.

O God, who leadest us through things temporal to things eternal, extend thy mercy to us who are striving after heavenly promises; and because it is wholly thy gift that we believe in thee, may it also be thy gift that we live in thee. Through etc.

Lesson. Deut. xi. 22—25.

If ye shall diligently . . . said unto you.

Gradual.

Behold, O God our defender, and look upon the face of thy servants.[3]

O Lord God of hosts, hearken unto the prayers of thy servants.[4]

Let us pray. Let us kneel. Rise.

Collect.

Behold, O Lord our protector, and grant that we who

[1] Ps. lxxix. 9, 10. [2] *Ib.* 9. [3] Ps. lxxxiv. 9. [4] *Ib.* 8.

are pressed down by the weight of our own evils, may receive thy pity, and serve thee with a quiet mind. Through etc.

Lesson.   2 Macc. i. 23, 2—5.

The priest made . . . time of trouble.

Gradual.

Turn thee again, O Lord, at the last, and be gracious unto thy servants.[1]

℟. Lord, thou hast been our refuge from one generation to another.[2]

Collect.

Hearken, we beseech thee, O Lord, unto our prayers, that through thy bountiful grace, we may be both humble in prosperity and safe in adversity.   Through etc.

Lesson.   Ecclus. xxxvi. 1—8.

Have mercy . . . thy wonderful works.

Gradual.

O Lord, save thy people, and bless thine heritage.[3]

℟. Unto thee will I cry, O Lord my strength : think no scorn of me, lest I become like them that go down into the pit.[4]

Let us pray.   Let us kneel.   Rise.

Collect.

Prevent us, O Lord, we beseech thee, in all our doings, and further us with thy continual help ; that all our works may be begun, continued, and ended in thee. Through etc.

Lesson.   Song of the Three Children 24—32.[5]

The angel . . . above all for ever.

Two clerks of the second rank, vested in surplices, shall say the Tract at the step of the quire.

Tract.

Blessed art thou in the firmament of heaven: and to be praised and exalted above all for ever.

---

[1] Ps. xc. 13.   [2] *Ib.* 1.   [3] Ps. xxviii. 10.
[4] *Ib.* 1.   [5] A cento with interpolations.

To be repeated by the quire.

℣. (*The clerks*) O all ye works of the Lord, bless ye the Lord: O ye heavens, bless ye the Lord: O ye Angels of the Lord, bless ye the Lord.

After each verse the quire respond,

℟. Praise him, and magnify him for ever.

℣. O all ye waters that be above the firmament, bless ye the Lord ; O all ye powers of the Lord, bless ye the Lord ; O ye sun and moon, bless ye the Lord.

℟. Praise him, and magnify him for ever.

℣. O ye stars of heaven, bless ye the Lord ; O ye showers and dew, bless ye the Lord ; O all ye winds of God, bless ye the Lord.

℟. Praise him, and magnify him for ever.

℣. O ye fire and heat, bless ye the Lord ; O ye nights and days, bless ye the Lord ; O ye darkness and light, bless ye the Lord.

℟. Praise him, and magnify him for ever.

℣. O ye cold and heat, bless ye the Lord ; O ye frost and snow, bless ye the Lord; O ye lightnings and clouds, bless ye the Lord.

℟. Praise him, and magnify him for ever.

℣. O let the earth bless the Lord ; O ye mountains and hills, bless ye the Lord ; O all ye things that grow upon the earth, bless ye the Lord.

℟. Praise him, and magnify him for ever.

℣. O ye seas and floods, bless ye the Lord ; O ye wells, bless ye the Lord ; O ye whales, and all that move in the waters, bless ye the Lord.

℟. Praise him, and magnify him for ever.

℣. O ye fowls of the air, bless ye the Lord ; O all ye beasts and cattle, bless ye the Lord ; O ye children of men, bless ye the Lord.

℟. Praise him, and magnify him for ever.

℣. O let Israel bless the Lord ; O ye priests of the Lord, bless ye the Lord ; O ye servants of the Lord, bless ye the Lord.

℟. Praise him, and magnify him for ever.

℣. O ye spirits and souls of the righteous, bless ye the Lord ; O ye holy and humble men of heart, bless ye the Lord.

℟. Praise him, and magnify him for ever.

℣. O Ananias, Azarias, and Misael, bless ye the Lord.

℟. Praise him, and magnify him for ever.

After this the clerks shall recommence the Tract.

Blessed art thou in the firmament of heaven etc.

and it shall be sung through by the quire.

Then shall follow The Lord be with you *and* Let us pray ; *but there shall not be said* Let us kneel *nor* Rise.

Collect.

O God, who for the three children didst quench the flames of fire, mercifully grant that we thy servants may not be consumed by the flame of our sins. Through etc.

The usual Memories are to be said here.

Epistle.   1 Thess. v. 14—23.
Now we exhort . . . our Lord Jesus Christ.

Two clerks of the second rank, vested in black copes, and standing at the step of the quire shall together sing, wholly and entirely, the following Tract :

Tract.

O praise the Lord, all ye heathen : praise him all ye nations.

For his merciful kindness is ever more and more towards us: and the truth of the Lord endureth for ever.[1]

Gospel.   St. Mat. xvii. 1—9.
After six days . . . again from the dead.

Offertory.

O Lord God of my salvation, I have cried day and night before thee : O let my prayer enter into thy presence, O Lord.[2]

[1] Ps. cxvii.   [2] Ps. lxxxviii. 1.

℣. Incline thine ear unto my calling, O Lord : thou hast put away mine acquaintance far from me. Lord, I have called daily upon thee, I have stretched forth my hands unto thee.[1]

Secret.

Sanctify, O Lord, we beseech thee, our fast by this present sacrifice, that what we outwardly profess by its observance, may be inwardly wrought in us. Through etc.

Preface.

Who by the fasting of the body etc.[2]

Communion.

O Lord my God, in thee have I put my trust : save me from all them that persecute me, and deliver me.[3]

Postcommunion.

Defend, O Lord, with thy perpetual protection those whom thou feedest with the divine mysteries ; and guide with thy saving consolations those whom thou hast filled with heavenly ordinances. Through etc.

If there be no Bishop present the following Collect is to be said over the people.

Bow down your heads before God.

Collect.

O Lord, let thy longed-for blessing strengthen thy faithful people, both making them never to swerve from thy will, and bestowing on them the continual joy of thy favour. Through etc.

But if a Bishop be present, and confer Orders, this Collect shall not be said.

SECOND SUNDAY IN LENT.[4]

At Mass.   *Office.*

Call to remembrance, O Lord, thy tender mercies : and thy lovingkindnesses which have been ever of old. Let

---

[1] Ps. lxxxviii. 1, 7, 9.   [2] Page 35.   [3] Ps. vii. 1.
[4] Called in Latin "Reminiscere" from the first words of the Office.

not our enemies triumph over us.　Deliver us, O God of Israel, out of all our troubles.[1]

Ps.　Unto thee, O Lord, will I lift up my soul; my God, I have put my trust in thee : let me not be confounded.[2]

Collect.

Almighty God, who seest that we have no power of ourselves to help ourselves, keep us both outwardly in our bodies, and inwardly in our souls ; that we may be defended from all adversities which may happen to the body, and from all evil thoughts which may assault and hurt the soul.　Through etc.

Epistle.　1 Thess. iv. 1—7.
We beseech . . . but unto holiness.

Gradual.

The sorrows of my heart are enlarged : O bring thou me out of my troubles, O Lord.[3]

℣.　Look upon my adversity and misery : and forgive me all my sin.[4]

Tract.

The Lord said to the woman of Canaan, It is not meet to take the children's bread, and to cast it to dogs.[5]

℣.　And she said, Truth, Lord, yet the dogs eat of the crumbs which fall from their masters' table.[6]

℣.　And Jesus answered and said unto her, O woman, great is thy faith ; be it unto thee even as thou wilt.[7]

Gospel.　St. Mat. xv. 21—28.
Then Jesus went . . . from that very hour.

Offertory.

And my delight shall be in thy commandments, which I have loved : my hands also will I lift up unto thy commandments, which I have loved.[8]

Secret.

Graciously receive, O Lord, the gifts of thy church, which thou in thy mercy hast ordained to be offered, and

---

[1] Ps. xxv. 5, 1, 21.　　[2] *Ib.* 1.　　[3] *Ib.* 16.　　[4] *Ib.* 17.
[5] St. Mat. xv. 26.　　[6] *Ib.* 27.　　[7] *Ib.* 28.　　[8] Ps. cxix. 47, 48.

which in thy power thou causest to pass into the mystery of our salvation. Through etc.

Ferial Preface.

Communion.

Consider my meditation; hearken thou unto the voice of my calling my King and my God; for unto thee will I make my prayer, O Lord.[1]

Postcommunion.

We beseech thee, O Lord, that the grace of the most sacred body and blood which we have received may quicken us, and that it may largely bestow in everlasting effect that which it doth promise in these mystic actions. Through etc.

MONDAY AFTER SECOND SUNDAY IN LENT.

At Mass.   *Office.*

Deliver me, O Lord, and be merciful unto me: my foot standeth right, I will praise the Lord in the congregations.[2]

Ps. Be thou my judge, O Lord, for I have walked innocently; my trust hath been also in the Lord, therefore shall I not fall.[3]

Let us kneel. Rise.

Collect.

Grant, we beseech thee, Almighty God, that thy family, which mortify their flesh by abstinence from meat, may likewise fast from sin, and follow righteousness. Through etc.

Lesson. Dan. ix. 15—19.

And now, O Lord our God . . . by thy name.

---

[1] Ps. v. 1, 2.   [2] Ps. xxvi. 11, 12.   [3] *Ib.* 1.

Gradual.

Thou art my helper and my redeemer, O Lord : make no long tarrying.[1]

℣. Let mine enemies be ashamed and confounded that seek after my soul.[2]

Tract.

O Lord, deal not with us etc.[3]

Gospel. St. John viii. 21—29.

Then said Jesus . . . that please him.

Offertory.

I will thank the Lord for giving me warning. I have set God always before me ; for he is on my right hand, therefore I shall not fall.[4]

℣. Preserve me O God, for in thee have I put my trust. O my soul, thou hast said unto the Lord, thou art my God. The Lord himself is the portion of mine inheritance.[5]

Secret.

Let this sacrifice of propitiation and praise, O Lord, make us worthy of thy reconciliation. Through etc.

Preface.

Who by the fasting of the body etc.[6]

Communion.

O Lord our Governor, how excellent is thy name in all the world.[7]

Postcommunion.

May this communion, O Lord, cleanse us from sin, and make us partakers of the heavenly remedy. Through etc.

Over the people.

Bow down your heads before God.

Collect.

Hearken unto our supplications, almighty God, and mercifully grant that they on whom thou bestowest boldness to hope for thy pity may experience the effect of thy wonted lovingkindness. Through etc.

[1] Ps. lxx. 6.   [2] *Ib.* 2.   [3] As on Ash Wednesday, p. 35.
[4] Ps. xvi. 8, 9.   [5] *Ib.* 1, 2, 6.   [6] Page 35.   [7] Ps. viii. 1.

TUESDAY AFTER SECOND SUNDAY IN LENT.

At Mass.   *Office.*

My heart hath talked of thee, seek ye my face: thy face, Lord, will I seek. O hide not thou thy face from me.[1]

Ps. The Lord is my light and my salvation: whom then shall I fear?[2]

Collect.

Graciously perfect in us, O Lord, we beseech thee, the help of this holy observance, that what through thy guidance we have known to be our duty, we may through thy working indeed fulfil. Through etc.

Lesson. 1 Kings xvii. 8—16.

The word of the Lord . . . spake by Elijah.

Gradual.

O cast thy burden upon the Lord, and he shall nourish thee.[3]

℣. As for me I will call upon God, and he shall hear my voice from the battle that was against me.[4]

Gospel. St. Mat. xxiii. 1—12.

Then spake Jesus . . . shall be exalted.

Offertory.

Have mercy upon me, O Lord, after thy great goodness: do away, O Lord, mine offences.[5]

℣. For I acknowledge my faults: and my sin is ever before me.[6]

Secret.

Be pleased, O Lord, to work out in us thy sanctification by these mysteries: that it may both cleanse us from earthly vices, and lead us onward to receive heavenly gifts. Through etc.

Preface.

Who by the fasting of the body etc.[7]

Communion.

I will speak of all thy marvellous works. I will be glad and rejoice in thee: yea, my songs will I make of thy name, O thou most Highest.[8]

[1] Ps. xxvii. 8, 9.   [2] *Ib.* 1.   [3] Ps. lv. 23.   [4] *Ib.* 17, 19.
[5] Ps. li. 1.   [6] *Ib.* 3.   [7] p. 35.   [8] Ps. ix. 1, 2.

N 2

Postcommunion.

We beseech thee, O Lord, that what we have received at thy holy altar, may be the medicine both of soul and body ; that we who are fortified by the participation of so great a remedy, may not be wearied out by any adversities. Through etc.

Over the people.

Bow down your heads before God.

Collect.

O Lord, graciously accept our prayers, and heal the infirmities of our souls, that having received the remission of our sins, we may ever rejoice in thy blessing. Through etc.

WEDNESDAY AFTER SECOND SUNDAY IN LENT.

At Mass.   *Office.*

Forsake me not, O Lord my God ; be not thou far from me. Haste thee to help me, O Lord God of my salvation.[1]

Ps. Put me not to rebuke, O Lord, in thine anger, neither chasten me in thy displeasure.[2]

Let us pray. Let us kneel. Rise.

Collect.

O Lord, we beseech thee graciously to behold thy people, and grant that those whom thou commandest to abstain from fleshly food, may also cease from hurtful vices. Through etc.

Epistle. Esther xiii. 11—17.

Thou art Lord . . . praise thee, O Lord.

Gradual.

O Lord, save thy people, and give thy blessing unto thine inheritance.[3]

℣. Unto thee will I cry, O Lord my strength : think no scorn of me, lest I become like them that go down into the pit.[4]

---

[1] Ps. xxxviii. 21, 22.   [2] *Ib.* 1.
[3] Ps. xxviii. 10.   [4] *Ib.* 1.

Tract.

Bring thou me out of my troubles etc.[1]

Gospel.   St. Mat. xx. 17—28.

And Jesus going up . . . ransom for many.

Offertory.

Unto thee, O Lord, will I lift up my soul; my God, I have put my trust in thee; O let me not be confounded, neither let my enemies triumph over me; for all they that hope in thee shall not be ashamed.[2]

℣. Lead me forth in thy truth and learn me: for thou art the God of my salvation; in thee hath been my hope all the day long.[3]

Secret.

Graciously look, O Lord, upon the offerings which we make unto thee, and by this most sacred intercourse absolve us from the bonds of our sins.   Through etc.

Preface.

Who by the fasting of the body etc.[4]

Communion.

The righteous Lord loveth righteousness: his countenance will behold the thing that is just.[5]

Postcommunion.

We beseech thee, O Lord, that the frequent reception of these mysteries may be profitable to us; so that being cleansed from the condition of the old man, we may progress and increase in newness of life.   Through etc.

Over the people.

Let us pray.   Bow down your heads before God.

Collect.

O God, the restorer and lover of innocence, draw to thyself the hearts of thy servants, that being inflamed with the fervour of thy spirit, they may be found steadfast in faith, and active in good works.   Through etc.

---

[1] As on Wednesday in Ember Week in Lent, p. 162.
[2] Ps. xxv. 1, 2.   [3] *Ib.* 4.   [4] P. 35.   [5] Ps. xi. 8.

THURSDAY AFTER SECOND SUNDAY IN LENT.

At Mass.   *Office.*

Haste thee, O Lord, to deliver me : make haste to help me, O Lord. Let mine enemies be ashamed and confounded that seek after my soul.[1]

Ps. Let them be turned backward and put to confusion that wish me evil.[2]

Let us pray. Let us kneel. Rise.

Collect.

Grant unto us we beseech thee, O Lord, the help of thy grace, that, duly giving ourselves up to fasting and prayer, we may be delivered from the enemies both of our souls and bodies. Through etc.

Lesson. Jer. xvii. 5—10.
Cursed is the man . . . fruit of his doings.

Gradual.

Be merciful to our sins, O Lord. Wherefore do the heathen say, Where is now their God ?[3]

℣. Help us, O God of our salvation ; and for the glory of thy name deliver us, O Lord.[4]

Gospel. St. John v. 30—47.
I can of mine own self . . . believe my words.

Offertory.

Moses prayed before the Lord his God and said ; Moses prayed before the Lord his God and said ; Lord, why doth thy wrath wax hot against thy people? Turn from thy fierce wrath ; remember Abraham, Isaac, and Jacob ; to whom thou swearest to give a land flowing with milk and honey. And the Lord repented of the evil which he thought to do unto his people.[5]

℣. The Lord said unto Moses, Thou hast found grace in my sight, and I know thee before all men. And Moses made haste, and bowed himself to the ground, and worshipped saying ; I know that thou keepest mercy for thousands, forgiving iniquity and sin.[6]

---

[1] Ps. lxx. 1, 2.   [2] *Ib.* 2.   [3] Ps. lxxix. 9, 10.
[4] *Ib.* 9.   [5] Adapted from Exod. xxxii. 11–14.
[6] From Exod. xxxiii. 17 and xxxiv. 7, 8.

Secret.

O God, to whom we now offer a single offering, the variety of all earlier sacrifices having passed away, hearken unto the prayers which have been conceived under thy inspiration, and bid the desires of them that hope in thee to be fulfilled, and their sins to be blotted out. Through etc.

Preface.

Who by the fasting of the body etc.[1]

Communion.

He that eateth my flesh, and drinketh my blood, dwelleth in me, and I in him, saith the Lord.[2]

Postcommunion.

We beseech thee, O Lord, that thy grace may never leave us, but that it may make us intent on thy holy service, and ever procure for us thy abundant help, and defend us from all adversities. Through etc.

Over the people.

Bow down your heads before God.

Collect.

Be favourable, O Lord, to thy servants, and bestow thy perpetual lovingkindness on them that ask thee; that they who glory in thee as their creator and governor may have all blessings restored and perpetuated to them. Through etc.

FRIDAY AFTER SECOND SUNDAY IN LENT.

At Mass.   *Office.*

But as for me, I will behold thy presence in righteousness: and when I awake up after thy likeness, I shall be satisfied with it.[3]

Ps. Hear the right, O Lord, and consider my complaint.

---

[1] P. 35.   [2] St. John vi. 56.   [3] Ps. xvii. 16.   [4] *Ib.* 1.

Let us kneel. Rise.

Collect.

Grant, we beseech thee, almighty God, that thou wouldest make us who have been purified with this holy fast, to come to the approaching feast with pure minds. Through etc.

Lesson. Gen. xxxvii. 6—22.
Here I pray you . . . his father again.

Gradual.

When I was in trouble, I called upon the Lord, and he heard me.[1]

℣. Deliver my soul, O Lord, from lying lips : and from a deceitful tongue.[2]

Tract.

O Lord, deal not with us etc.[3]

Gospel. St. Mat. xxi. 33—46.
There was a certain householder . . . for a prophet.

Offertory.

Make haste, O Lord, to help me. Let them be ashamed and confounded together, that seek after my soul to destroy it.[4]

℣. Let them be driven backward, and put to rebuke that wish me evil.[5]

Secret.

May these sacrifices, O Lord God, both actively abide with us, and by their effectual working be confirmed. Through etc.

Preface.

Who by the fasting of the body etc.[6]

Communion.

Thou shalt keep them, O Lord : thou shalt preserve him from this generation for ever.[7]

Postcommunion.

Make us, O Lord, we beseech thee, who have received the pledge of eternal salvation, so to direct our course

[1] Ps. cxx. 1.   [2] *Ib.* 2.   [3] As on Ash Wednesday, p. 149.
[4] Ps. xl. 16, 17.   [5] *Ib.* 17.   [6] P. 35.   [7] Ps. xii. 8.

agreeably thereto, that we may be able to attain unto the same. Through etc.

Over the people.

Bow down your heads before God.

Collect.

Grant unto thy people, we beseech thee, O Lord, health both of mind and body; that they, cleaving to good works, may ever be worthy to be defended by thy mighty protection. Through etc.

SATURDAY AFTER SECOND SUNDAY IN LENT.

At Mass.   *Office.*

The law of the Lord is an undefiled law, converting the soul: the testimony of the Lord is sure, and giveth wisdom unto the simple.[1]

Ps. The heavens declare the glory of God: and the firmament sheweth his handy-work.[2]

Let us kneel. Rise.

Collect.

Grant, we beseech thee, O Lord, a saving effect to our fasts, that the chastisement of our flesh which we have undertaken may redound to the quickening of our souls. Through etc.

Lesson.   Gen. xxvii. 6—39.

And Rebekah spake . . . heaven from above.

Gradual.

It is a good thing to give thanks unto the Lord: and to sing praises unto thy name, O most Highest.[3]

℣. To tell of thy lovingkindness early in the morning: and of thy truth in the night season.[4]

Gospel.   St. Luke xv. 11—32.

A certain man . . . lost and is found.

---

[1] Ps. xix. 7.   [2] *Ib.* 1.   [3] Ps. xcii. 1.   [4] *Ib.* 2.

Offertory.

Lighten mine eyes that I sleep not in death, lest mine enemy say, I have prevailed against him.[1]

℣. How long wilt thou forget me, O Lord, for ever? How long shall I seek counsel in my soul?[2]

Secret.

Mercifully grant, O Lord, by this holy sacrifice, that we who pray to be freed from our own sins may not be burdened by the sins of others. Through etc.

Preface.

Who by the fasting of the body etc.[3]

Communion.

Son, it was meet that thou shouldest be glad, for this thy brother was dead and is alive again; and was lost, and is found.[4]

Postcommunion.

May the taste of thy divine sacrament, O Lord, penetrate the innermost recesses of our hearts, and make us plentifully to partake of its effects. Through etc.

Over the people.

Bow down your heads before God.

Collect.

Keep, we beseech thee, O Lord, this thy family with thy continual goodness; that they who do lean only on the hope of thy heavenly grace, may also be defended by thy heavenly power. Through etc.

THIRD SUNDAY IN LENT.[5]

At Mass.   *Office.*

Mine eyes are ever looking unto the Lord: for he shall pluck my feet out of the net. Turn thee unto me

----

[1] Ps. xiii. 3, 4.   [2] *Ib.* 1, 2.   [3] P. 35.   [4] St. Luke xv. 32.
[5] Called in Latin "Oculi," from the first word of the Office.

and have mercy upon me: for I am desolate, and in misery.[1]

Ps. Unto thee, O Lord, will I lift up my soul; my God, I have put my trust in thee: let me not be confounded.[2]

Collect.

We beseech thee, Almighty God, look upon the hearty desires of thy humble servants, and stretch forth the right hand of thy majesty to be our defence. Through etc.

Epistle. Eph. v. 1—9.

Be ye therefore followers . . . righteousness and truth.

Gradual.

Up, Lord, and let not man have the upper hand: let the heathen be judged in thy sight.[3]

℣. While mine enemies are driven back: they shall fall and perish at thy presence.[4]

Tract.

Unto thee lift I up mine eyes, O thou that dwellest in the heavens.[5]

℣. Behold, even as the eyes of servants look unto the hand of their masters.[6]

℣. And as the eyes of a maiden unto the hand of her mistress.[7]

℣. Even so our eyes wait upon the Lord our God, until he have mercy upon us.[8]

℣. Have mercy upon us, O Lord, have mercy upon us.[9]

Gospel. St. Luke xi. 14—28.

Jesus was casting out . . . and keep it.

Offertory.

The statutes of the Lord are right and rejoice the heart: sweeter also than honey and the honey-comb. Moreover, by them is thy servant taught.[10]

---

[1] Ps. xxv. 14, 15. [2] *Ib.* 1. [3] Ps. ix. 19. [4] *Ib.* 3.
[5] Ps. cxxiii. 1. [6] *Ib.* 2. [7] *Ib.* [8] *Ib.*
[9] *Ib.* 3. [10] Ps. xix. 8, 10, 11.

Secret.

Receive, we beseech thee, O Lord, the gifts of thy devout servants ; and of thy lovingkindness cleanse them who serve the divine mysteries, by which thou dost also justify them that are in ignorance. Through etc.

Ferial Preface.

Communion.

Yea, the sparrow hath found her an house, and the swallow a nest where she may lay her young : even thy altar, O Lord of hosts, my King and my God. Blessed are they that dwell in thy house, they will be always praising thee.[1]

Postcommunion.

Mercifully deliver us, O Lord, from all guilt and danger, whom thou admittest to be partakers of this so great mystery. Through etc.

MONDAY AFTER THIRD SUNDAY IN LENT.

At Mass.　　　　　　　*Office.*

In God's word will I rejoice : in the Lord's word will I comfort me. Yea, in God have I put my trust : I will not fear what man can do unto me.[2]

Ps. Be merciful unto me, O God, for man goeth about to devour me : he is daily fighting, and troubling me.[3]

Let us kneel. Rise.

Collect.

O Lord, we beseech thee, mercifully to pour thy grace into our hearts, that like as we abstain from fleshly food, so also we may restrain our senses from hurtful excesses. Through etc.

Lesson. 2 Kings v. 1—15.
Now Naaman . . . but in Israel.

[1] Ps. lxxxiv. 3, 4.　　　[2] Ps. lvi. 10, 11.　　　[3] *Ib.* 1.

Gradual.

Thou tellest my flittings : put my tears into thy bottle.[1]

℣. Be merciful unto me, O Lord, for man goeth about to devour me : he is daily fighting and troubling me.[2]

Tract.

O Lord, deal not with us etc.[3]

Gospel. St. Luke iv. 23—30.

Whatsoever we have heard . . . went his way.

Offertory.

Hear my prayer, O God : and hide not thyself from my petition. Take heed unto me, and hear me :[4]

℣. How I am vexed. The enemy crieth so and the ungodly cometh on so fast. I would make haste to escape.[5]

Secret.

Grant, O Lord, that the offering which we make unto thee of our bounden duty, may be made to us a sacrament profitable to our salvation. Through etc.

Preface.

Who by the fasting of the body etc.[6]

Communion.

Who shall give salvation unto Israel out of Sion? When the Lord turneth the captivity of his people : then shall Jacob rejoice, and Israel shall be glad.[7]

Postcommunion.

Grant we beseech thee, almighty and merciful God, that what we touch with our lips we may receive with a pure mind. Through etc.

Over the people.

Bow down your heads before God.

Collect.

Let thy mercy, O Lord, we beseech thee, assist us, that we may be accounted worthy to be rescued from the threatening dangers of our sins by thy protection, and to be saved by thy deliverance. Through etc.

---

[1] Ps. lvi. 8.   [2] Ib. 1.   [3] As on Ash Wednesday, p. 149.
[4] Ps. lv. 1, 2.   [5] Ib. 2, 3, 8.   [6] P. 35.   [7] Ps. xiv. 11.

Tuesday after Third Sunday in Lent.

At Mass.　　　　　　　　*Office.*

I have called upon thee, O God, for thou shalt hear me: incline thine ear unto me, and hearken unto my words. Keep me as the apple of an eye: hide me under the shadow of thy wings.[1]

Ps. Hear the right, O Lord, consider my complaint.[2]

Let us kneel. Rise.

Collect.

Hear us, almighty and merciful God, and mercifully grant unto us the gift of saving continence. Through etc.

Lesson. 2 Kings iv. 1—7.
Now there cried . . . of the rest.

Gradual.

Cleanse me, O Lord, from my secret faults. Keep thy servant also from presumptuous sins.[3]

℣. Lest they get the dominion over me: so shall I be undefiled, and innocent from the great offence.[4]

Gospel. St. Matt. xviii. 15—22.
Moreover, if thy brother . . . seventy times seven.

Offertory.

The right hand of the Lord hath the pre-eminence: the right hand of the Lord bringeth mighty things to pass. I shall not die but live: and declare the works of the Lord.[5]

℣. I called upon the Lord in my trouble: and he heard me at large. The Lord is on my side.[6]

Secret.

We beseech thee, O Lord, that our redemption may be made effectual through this sacrament; that it may withdraw us ever from worldly excesses, and lead us to all things profitable to our salvation. Through etc.

---

[1] Ps. xvii. 6, 8.　　[2] Ib. 1.　　[3] Ps. xix. 12, 13.
[4] Ib. 13.　　[5] Ps. cxviii. 16, 17.　　[6] Ib. 5, 6.

Preface.

Who by the fasting of the body etc.[1]

Communion.

Lord who shall dwell in thy tabernacle: or who shall rest upon thy holy hill? Even he that leadeth an uncorrupt life, and doeth the thing which is right.[2]

Postcommunion.

Grant, we beseech thee, O Lord, that being cleansed by these holy mysteries, we may obtain both pardon and grace. Through etc.

Over the people.

Bow down your heads before God.

Collect.

Defend us, O Lord, by thy protection, and ever keep us from all iniquity. Through etc.

WEDNESDAY AFTER THIRD SUNDAY IN LENT.

At Mass. *Office.*

My trust hath been in the Lord. I will be glad, and rejoice in thy mercy: for thou hast considered my trouble.[3]

Ps. In thee, O Lord, have I put my trust: let me never be put to confusion, deliver me in thy righteousness.[4]

Let us kneel. Rise.

Collect.

Grant unto us, we beseech thee, O Lord, that being disciplined by this wholesome fast, and abstaining from hurtful vices, we may the more readily obtain thy mercy. Through etc.

[1] P. 35.   [2] Ps. xv. 1, 2.   [3] Ps. xxxi. 7, 8.   [4] *Ib.* 1.

Lesson. Exod. xx. 12—24.

Honour thy father . . . I will bless thee.

Gradual.

Have mercy upon me, O Lord, for I am weak. O Lord heal me.[1]

℣. For my bones are vexed. My soul also is sore troubled.[2]

Tract.

Bring thou me out of my troubles etc.[3]

Gospel. St. Matt. xv. 1—20.

Then came to Jesus . . . defileth not a man.

Offertory.

But deal thou with me, O Lord God, according unto thy name: for sweet is thy mercy.[4]

℣. Hold not thy tongue, O God of my praise: for the mouth of the deceitful is opened upon me.[5]

Secret.

Receive, we beseech thee, O Lord, the prayers of thy people together with the offerings of their oblations; and defend us, who celebrate thy mysteries, from all dangers. Through etc.

Preface.

Who by the fasting of the body etc.[6]

Communion.

Thou shalt shew me the path of life: in thy presence is the fulness of joy, O Lord.[7]

Postcommunion.

May the holy table from which we have been fed sanctify us, we beseech thee, O Lord, so that being freed from all errors we may be made worthy to attain thy heavenly promises. Through etc.

Over the people.

Bow down your heads before God.

---

[1] Ps. vi. 2.   [2] Ib. 2, 3.
[3] As on Wednesday in Ember Week in Lent, p. 162.   [4] Ps. cix. 20.
[5] Ib. 1.   [6] P. 35.   [7] Ps. xvi. 12.

Collect.

Grant, we beseech thee, Almighty God, that we, who seek the grace of thy protection, may be delivered from all evils, and serve thee with a quiet mind.   Through etc

THURSDAY AFTER THIRD SUNDAY IN LENT.

At Mass.   *Office.*

I am the salvation of the people, saith the Lord : in whatsoever distress they shall call upon me I will hear them, and I will be their Lord for ever.[1]

Ps.   Hear my law, O my people, incline your ears unto the words of my mouth.[2]

Let us kneel.   Rise.

Collect.

Grant, we beseech thee, almighty God, that the holy devotion of this fast, may both make us pure, and render us acceptable to thy majesty.   Through etc.

Lesson.   Jer. vii. 1—7.
The word that came . . . for ever and ever.

Gradual.

The eyes of all wait upon thee, O Lord : and thou givest them their meat in due season.[3]

℣.   Thou openest thine hand : and fillest all things living with plenteousness.[4]

Gospel.   St. John vi. 27—35.
Labour not for . . . shall never thirst.

Offertory.

Though I walk in the midst of trouble, yet shalt thou refresh me, O Lord : thou shalt stretch forth thy hand upon the furiousness of mine enemies, and thy right hand shall save me.[5]

℣.   When I called upon the Lord, thou heardest me : and enduedst my soul with much strength.[6]

---

[1] Source unknown.   [2] Ps. lxxviii. 1.   [3] Ps. cxlv. 15.
[4] *Ib.* 16.   [5] Ps. cxxxviii. 7.   [6] *Ib.* 3.

O

Secret.

O Lord, we beseech thee to make us approach thy holy mysteries with pure minds, that we may ever offer unto thee a suitable service. Through etc.

Preface.

Who by the fasting of the body etc.[1]

Communion.

Thou hast charged: that we shall diligently keep thy commandments. O that my ways were made so direct: that I might keep thy statutes![2]

Postcommunion.

May the reverent receiving of thy sacrament, O Lord, both cleanse us by its mystic working, and defend us by its abiding virtue. Through etc.

Over the people.

Bow down your heads before God.

Collect.

We beseech thee, O Lord, that thy heavenly favour may increase thy people that is under thee, and make them always to keep thy commandments. Through etc.

FRIDAY AFTER THIRD SUNDAY IN LENT.

At Mass. *Office.*

Shew some token upon me for good, that they who hate me may see it, and be ashamed: because thou Lord hast holpen me and comforted me.[3]

Ps. Bow down thine ear, O Lord, and hear me: for I am poor, and in misery.[4]

Collect.

We beseech thee, O Lord, that thy gracious favour may accompany our fast, that as we abstain from food in our

---

[1] P. 35.   [2] Ps. cxix. 4, 5.   [3] Ps. lxxxvi. 17.   [4] *Ib.* 1.

bodies, so we may fast from sin in our minds. Through etc.

Lesson. Num. xx. 6—13.[1]

In those days . . . sanctified in them.

Gradual.

My heart hath trusted in God, and I am helped : therefore my heart danceth for joy, and in my song will I praise him.[2]

℣. Unto thee will I cry, O Lord my strength, think no scorn of me, depart not from me.[3]

Tract.

O Lord, deal not with us etc.[4]

Gospel. St. John iv. 5—42.

Then cometh he . . . the Saviour of the world.

Offertory.

O hearken thou unto the voice of my calling, my King and my God : for unto thee will I make my prayer, O Lord.[5]

℣. Ponder my words, O Lord, consider my meditation, and hear me.[6]

Secret.

Regard, O Lord, with thy favour the offerings which we consecrate, that they may both be acceptable to thee, and always further our salvation. Through etc.

Preface.

Who by the fasting of the body etc.[7]

Communion.

Whosoever drinketh of the water that I shall give him, saith the Lord to the woman of Samaria, it shall be in him a well of water, springing up into everlasting life.[8]

Postcommunion.

May the receiving of this sacrament, O Lord, cleanse us from sin, and lead us to the heavenly kingdom. Through etc.

---

[1] With variation and additions.   [2] Ps. xxviii. 8.
[3] Ib. 1, with variation.   [4] As on Ash Wednesday, p. 149.
[5] Ps. v. 2.   [6] Ib. 1, with addition.   [7] P. 35.
[8] St. John iv. 14.

Over the people.

Bow down your heads before God.

Collect.

Grant, we beseech thee, Almighty God, that we who do trust in thy protection may by thy aid overcome all things that oppose us.   Through etc

SATURDAY AFTER THIRD SUNDAY IN LENT.

At Mass.   *Office.*

Ponder my words, O Lord : consider my meditation. O hearken thou unto the voice of my calling.[1]

Ps.   My King and my God.[2]

Let us kneel.   Rise.

Collect.

Grant, we beseech thee, almighty God, that they who for the mortification of the flesh abstain from food, may by following after righteousness fast from sin.   Through etc.

Lesson.   History of Susanna 1—9, 15—17, 19—30, 33—62.

There dwelt a man . . . the same day.

Gradual.

Yea, though I walk through the valley of the shadow of death, I will fear no evil : for thou art with me, O Lord.[3]

℣.   Thy rod and thy staff comfort me.[3]

Gospel.   St. John viii. 1—11.

Jesus went unto . . . sin no more.

Offertory.

Order my steps, O Lord, in thy word : and so shall no wicked-ness have dominion over me.[4]

℣.   When thy word goeth forth : it giveth light and under-standing unto the simple.[5]

[1] Ps. v. 1, 2.   [2] *Ib.* 2.   [3] Ps. xxiii. 4.
[4] Ps. cxix. 133.   [5] *Ib.* 130.

Secret.

May this offering, O Lord, we beseech thee, be made pleasing unto thee through our solemn fast; and that it may be the more acceptable, may it be presented unto thee from pure hearts.   Through etc.

Preface.

Who by the fasting of the body etc.[1]

Communion.

Woman, hath no man condemned thee?   Neither do I condemn thee: sin no more.[2]

Postcommunion.

We beseech thee, almighty God, that we may be reckoned among his members, of whose body and blood we have received communion, Jesus Christ, thy Son, our Lord.   Who with thee etc.

Over the people.

Bow down your heads before God.

Collect.

Stretch forth, O Lord, over thy faithful people the right hand of thy heavenly help, that they may seek thee with their whole heart, and that what they ask worthily they may obtain effectually.   Through etc.

FOURTH SUNDAY IN LENT.[3]

At Mass.   *Office.*

Rejoice, O Jerusalem, and gather together, all ye that love the Lord: rejoice with joy for her, all ye that mourn for her, that ye may rejoice and be satisfied with the breasts of her consolation.[4]

---

[1] P. 35.   [2] St. John viii. 10, 11.
[3] "Dominica media Quadragesimæ" or Midlent Sunday; also called in Latin "Laetare," from the first word of the Office.
[4] Is. lxvi. 10, 11, with variation.

Ps.   I was glad when they said unto me : we will go into the house of the Lord.[1]

Collect.

Grant, we beseech thee, almighty God, that we who for our evil deeds do worthily deserve to be punished, by the comfort of thy grace may be relieved.   Through etc.

Epistle.   Gal. iv. 22—31, v. 1.

It is written . . . made us free.

Gradual.

I was glad when they said unto me : we will go into the house of the Lord.[2]

℣.   Peace be within thy walls : and plenteousness within thy palaces.[3]

Tract.

They that put their trust in the Lord shall be even as the mount Sion : which may not be removed but standeth fast for ever.[4]

℣. The hills stand about Jerusalem : even so standeth the Lord round about his people, from this time forth for evermore.[5]

Gospel.   St. John vi. 1—14.

Jesus went over . . . into the world.

Offertory.

O praise the Lord, for the Lord is gracious : O sing praises unto his name, for it is lovely.[6]

℣.   Whatsoever the Lord pleased, that did he in heaven and in earth.[7]

Secret.

Grant to us, Lord, we beseech thee, ever to be occupied in divine service, and alike in mind and body to be made meet for these holy mysteries.   Through etc.

Ferial Preface.

Communion.

Jerusalem is built as a city : that is at unity in itself.   For

---

[1] Ps. cxxii. 1.   [2] *Ib.* 1.   [3] *Ib.* 7.   [4] Ps. cxxv. 1.
[5] *Ib.* 2.   [6] Ps. cxxxv. 3.   [7] *Ib.* 6.

thither the tribes go up, even the tribes of the Lord : to give
thanks unto the name of the Lord.[1]

Postcommunion.

Grant, we beseech thee, merciful God, that we may
both handle with true reverence, and ever receive with
faithful mind thy holy gifts with which we are fed unceasingly. Through etc.

MONDAY AFTER FOURTH SUNDAY IN LENT.

At Mass.   *Office.*

Save me, O God, for thy Name's sake : and avenge me
in thy strength. Hear my prayer, O God.[2]

Ps. For strangers are risen up against me, and tyrants seek
after my soul.[3]

Let us kneel. Rise.

Collect.

Grant, we beseech thee, almighty God, that we who
yearly celebrate these holy observances, may be well-
pleasing to thee both in body and mind. Through etc.

Lesson. 1 Kings iii. 16—28.

Then came there two women . . . to do judgment.

Gradual.

And be thou my strong rock, and house of my defence : that
thou mayest save me.[4]

℣. In thee, O Lord, have I put my trust : let me never be
put to confusion.[5]

Tract.

O Lord, deal not with us etc.[6]

Gospel. St. John ii. 13—25.

And the Jews' passover . . . what was in man.

---

[1] Ps. cxxii. 3, 4.   [2] Ps. liv. 1, 2.   [3] Ib. 3.
[4] Ps. xxxi. 3.   [5] Ib. 1.   [6] As on Ash Wednesday, p. 149.

Offertory.

O be joyful in the Lord, all ye lands : serve the Lord with gladness, and come before his presence with a song. Be ye sure that the Lord he is God.[1]

℣. It is he that hath made us and not we ourselves; we are his people, and the sheep of his pasture.[2]

Secret.

Work in us, O Lord, we beseech thee, by thy mysteries, that we may offer these gifts to thee with worthy feelings. Through etc.

Preface.

Who by the fasting of the body etc.[3]

Communion.

O cleanse thou me from my secret faults. Keep thy servant also from presumptuous sins.[4]

Postcommunion.

We beseech thee, O Lord, sustain with thine aid those whom thou refreshest with thy divine sacraments, that those whom thou cherishest by temporal may be fed by eternal blessings. Through etc.

Over the people.

Bow down your heads before God.

Collect.

Graciously hear our prayer, we beseech thee, O Lord, that we to whom thou givest a hearty desire to pray may obtain the help of thy defence. Through etc.

TUESDAY AFTER FOURTH SUNDAY IN LENT.

At Mass.   *Office.*

Hear my prayer, O God : and hide not thyself from my petition. Take heed unto me, and hear me.[5]

---

[1] Ps. c. 1, 2.   [2] *Ib.* 2.   [3] P. 35.   [4] Ps. xix. 12, 13.
[5] Ps. lv. 1, 2.

Ps. How I mourn in my prayer, and am vexed. The enemy crieth so.[1]

Let us kneel. Rise.

Collect.

We beseech thee, O Lord, that the sacred fast which we observe may be for our increase in holy conversation, and may draw down upon us the constant succour of thy mercy. Through etc.

Lesson. Exod. xxxii. 7—14.

And the Lord said . . . unto his people.

Gradual.

Arise, O Lord, and help us: and deliver us for thy mercy's sake.[2]

℣. We have heard with our ears, O God, our fathers have told us: what thou hast done in their time of old.[3]

Gospel. St. John vii. 14—31.

Now about the midst . . . believed on him.

Offertory.

I waited patiently for the Lord: and he inclined unto me and heard my calling. And he hath put a new song in my mouth: even a thanksgiving unto our God.[4]

℣. He set my feet upon the rock, and ordered my goings.[5]

Secret.

We beseech thee, O Lord, to look favourably upon the offerings of thy faithful people, that the oblation made by the reverent service of thy devout servants may be ratified by thy favour. Through etc.

Preface.

Who by the fasting of the body etc.[6]

Communion.

We will rejoice in thy salvation, and triumph in the name of the Lord our God.[7]

---

[1] Ps. lv. 2, 3.   [2] Ps. xliv. 26.   [3] *Ib.* 1.   [4] Ps. xl. 1, 3.
[5] *Ib.* 1.   [6] P. 35.   [7] Ps. xx. 5.

Postcommunion.

May this holy food and this cup of salvation be profitable to us, O Lord, and both protect us in this transitory life, and obtain for us life eternal. Through etc.

Over the people.

Bow down your heads before God.

Collect.

O Lord, we beseech thee to have compassion upon thy people, and mercifully to refresh those who are laden with continual tribulations. Through etc.

WEDNESDAY AFTER FOURTH SUNDAY IN LENT.

At Mass.   *Office.*

When I shall be sanctified in you I will gather you out of all countries, and I will sprinkle clean water upon you, and ye shall be clean from all your filthiness, and a new spirit will I put within you.[1]

Ps. I will alway give thanks unto the Lord : his praise shall ever be in my mouth.[2]

The Collect is to follow without The Lord be with you ; *but only with* Let us pray *and* Let us kneel. Rise.

Collect.

O God, who both givest to the just the rewards of their merits, and to sinners their pardon through fasting, have mercy upon thy suppliants, that the confession of our guilt may obtain the remission of our sins. Through etc.

Lesson. Ezek. xxxvi. 23—28.

And I will sanctify . . . will be your God.

---

[1] Adapted from Ezek. xxxvi. 23—26.   [2] Ps. xxxiv. 1.

Gradual.

Come, ye children, and hearken unto me : I will teach you the fear of the Lord.[1]

℣. They had an eye unto him and were lightened : and their faces were not ashamed.[2]

The gradual is not to be repeated, but there shall follow The Lord be with you *and* Let us kneel. Rise.

Collect.

Grant, we beseech thee, almighty God, that we who mortify ourselves in this appointed fast may also be gladdened by holy devotion, and that subduing all earthly affections we may the more readily receive heavenly gifts. Through etc.

Here the usual Memories are said.

Lesson. Is. i. 16—19.

Wash you . . . good of the land.

Gradual.

Blessed are the people, whose God is the Lord : blessed are the folk that he hath chosen to him to be his inheritance.[3]

℣. By the word of the Lord were the heavens made : and all the hosts of them by the breath of his mouth.[4]

Tract.

Bring thou me out of my troubles etc.[5]

Gospel. St. John ix. 1—38.

And as Jesus passed by . . . worshipped him.

Offertory.

O praise our Lord God, ye people, and make the voice of his praise to be heard ; who holdeth our soul in life, and suffereth not our feet to slip. Praised be the Lord, who hath not cast out my prayer : nor turned his mercy from me.[6]

℣. O be joyful in God all ye lands : sing praises unto the honour of his name, make his praise to be glorious.[7]

Secret.

We humbly beseech thee, almighty God, that our sins

---

[1] Ps. xxxiv. 11.   [2] *Ib.* 5.   [3] Ps. xxxiii. 12.   [4] *Ib.* 6.
[5] As on Wednesday in Ember Week in Lent, p. 162.
[6] Ps. lxvi. 7, 8, 18.   [7] *Ib.* 1.

may be cleansed away by this sacrifice ; forasmuch as then
thou dost bestow on us true health both of mind and
body.   Through etc.

Preface.

Who by the fasting of the body etc.[1]

Communion.

The Lord made clay of spittle, and anointed my eyes, and I
went and washed, and saw, and believed in God.[2]

Postcommunion.

May the sacrament, O Lord our God, which we have
received, both fortify us with spiritual food, and protect
us with bodily help.   Through etc.

Over the people.

Bow down your heads before God.

Collect.

Let thy merciful ears, O Lord, be open to the prayers
of thy humble servants ; and that they may obtain their
petitions, make them to ask such things as shall please
thee.   Through etc.

Thursday after Fourth Sunday in Lent.

At Mass.   *Office.*

Let the heart of them rejoice that seek the Lord.
Seek the Lord and his strength : seek his face evermore.[3]

Ps.   O give thanks unto the Lord, and call upon his name :
tell the people what things he hath done.[4]

Let us kneel.   Rise.

Collect.

Grant, we beseech thee, almighty God, that we who
mortify ourselves in this appointed fast may also be

---

[1] P. 35.   [2] From St. John ix. 11.
[3] Ps. cv. 3, 4.   [4] *Ib.* 1.

gladdened by holy devotion ; and that subduing all earthly
affections we may the more readily receive heavenly gifts.
Through etc.

Lesson.   2 Kings iv. 25—38.
So she came . . . again to Gilgal.

Gradual.

Look, O Lord, upon the covenant, and forget not the congregation of the poor for ever.[1]

℣.   Arise, O Lord, maintain thine own cause : remember the
reproach of thy servants.[2]

Gospel.   St. John v. 17—29.
But Jesus answered . . . of damnation.

Offertory.

Make haste, O Lord, to help me.   Let them be driven backward, and put to rebuke, that wish me evil.[3]

℣.   I waited patiently for the Lord, and he inclined unto me,
[and brought me] out of the horrible pit, out of the mire and
clay.[4]

Secret.

Purify us, O merciful God, that the prayers of thy
Church, which are pleasing to thee, being accompanied
with pious offerings, may through the purification of our
minds become more acceptable.   Through etc.

Preface.

Who through the fasting of the body etc.[5]

Communion.

O Lord, I will make mention of thy righteousness only.
Thou, O God, hast taught me from my youth up : forsake me
not, O God, in mine old age, when I am gray-headed.[6]

Postcommunion.

We beseech thee, O Lord, suffer not the heavenly gifts,
which thou hast provided for the saving health of thy
faithful people to turn to the condemnation of those that
receive them.   Through etc.

---

[1] Ps. lxxiv. 20, 21.   [2] From *Ib.* 23.   [3] Ps. xl. 16, 17.
[4] *Ib.* 1, 2.   [5] P. 35.   [6] Ps. lxxi. 14, 15, 16.

Over the people.

Bow down your heads before God.

Collect.

O God, the founder and governor of thy people, drive far away the sins by which they are beset, that they may always be well pleasing unto thee, and safe under thy protection. Through etc.

FRIDAY AFTER FOURTH SUNDAY IN LENT.

At Mass. *Office.*

Let the meditation of my heart be always acceptable in thy sight, O Lord, my strength, and my redeemer.[1]

Ps. The heavens declare the glory of God : and the firmament sheweth his handy-work.[2]

Let us kneel. Rise.

Collect.

O God, who renewest the world through thy ineffable sacraments, grant, we beseech thee, that thy Church may advance in the observance of thy eternal precepts, and not be left destitute of thy temporal assistance. Through etc.

Lesson. 1 Kings xvii. 17—24.

And it came to pass . . . mouth is truth.

Gradual.

It is better to trust in the Lord : than to put any confidence in man.[3]

℣. It is better to trust in the Lord : than to put any confidence in princes.[4]

Tract.

O Lord, deal not with us etc.[5]

----

[1] Ps. xix. 14, 15.   [2] *Ib.* 1.   [3] Ps. cxviii. 8.
[4] *Ib.* 9.   [5] As on Ash Wednesday, p. 149.

Gospel. St. John xi. 1—45.

Now a certain man . . . believed on him.

Offertory.

For thou shalt save the people that are in adversity, O Lord, and shalt bring down the high looks of the proud : for who is God, but thou, O Lord ? [1]

℣. My complaint shall come before him, it shall enter even into his ears.[2]

Secret.

We beseech thee, O Lord, that the gifts which we have offered may purify us, and make thee ever favourable to us. Through etc.

Preface.

Who by the fasting of the body etc.[3]

Communion.

The Lord, seeing the sisters of Lazarus weeping at the grave, wept in the presence of the Jews, and said : Lazarus, come forth ; and he came forth, bound hand and foot, who had been dead four days.[4]

Postcommunion.

We beseech thee, O Lord, that the partaking of this sacrament may both continually free us from our own guilt, and defend us from all adversities. Through etc.

Over the people.

Bow down your heads before God.

Collect.

Grant, we beseech thee, almighty God, that we who are conscious of our own infirmity, and trust in thy mercy, may ever rejoice under thy protection. Through etc.

---

[1] Ps. xviii. 27, 31.   [2] *Ib.* 6.   [3] P. 35.
[4] Adapted from St. John xi. 33, 35, 43, 44.

SATURDAY AFTER FOURTH SUNDAY IN LENT.

At Mass.   *Office.*

Ho, every one that thirsteth come ye to the waters saith the Lord, and he that hath no money ; come and drink with joy.[1]

Ps. Hear my law, O my people : incline your ears unto the words of my mouth.[2]

Let us kneel. Rise.

Collect.

We beseech thee, O Lord, that our devotion may bring forth fruit through thy grace ; for then will our fast profit us, if it be well-pleasing to thy goodness. Through etc.

Lesson. Is. xlix. 8—15.
Thus saith the Lord . . . not forget thee.

Gradual.
The poor committeth himself unto thee, O Lord : for thou art the helper of the friendless.[3]

℣. Why standest thou so far off, O Lord : and hidest thy face in the needful time of trouble ? The ungodly for his own lust doth persecute the poor.[4]

Gospel. St. John viii. 12—20.
Then spake Jesus . . . not yet come.

Offertory.
The Lord is my strong rock and my defence, my refuge, and my Saviour in whom I will trust.[5]

℣. I will follow upon mine enemies and overtake them : neither will I turn again till I have destroyed them.[6]

Secret.

We beseech thee, O Lord, favourably to receive our offerings, and mercifully to subdue unto thyself even our rebellious wills. Through etc.

---

[1] Adapted from Is. lv. 1.   [2] Ps. lxxviii. 1.   [3] Ps. x. 16.
[4] *Ib.* 1, 2.   [5] Ps. xviii. 1.   [6] *Ib.* 37.

Preface.

Who by the fasting of the body etc.[1]

Communion.

The Lord is my shepherd : therefore can I lack nothing.　He shall feed me in a green pasture : and lead me forth beside the waters of comfort.[2]

Postcommunion.

We beseech thee, O Lord, that thy holy gifts which we have received may purify us, and that by their healing operation they may make thee favourable to us. Through etc.

Over the people.

Bow down your heads before God.

Collect.

O God who choosest rather to shew mercy than to be angry with those that hope in thee, grant to us worthily to lament the evils which we have committed, that so we may find the favour of thy comfort.　Through etc.

FIFTH SUNDAY IN LENT.[3]

At Mass.　　　　　　*Office.*

Give sentence with me, O God, and defend my cause against the ungodly people : O deliver me from the deceitful and wicked man, for thou art the God of my strength.[4]

Ps.　O send out thy light and thy truth that they may lead me : and bring me unto thy holy hill and to thy dwelling.[5]

From this day till Easter Gloria Patri *is not said after the Office at ferial masses, except only on Maundy Thursday when a Bishop celebrates.*

[1] P. 35.　　　　　　　　　[2] Ps. xxiii. 1, 2.
[3] "Dominica in passione Domini," or "Passion Sunday."
[4] Ps. xliii. 1, 2.　　　　　　[5] *Ib.* 3.

Collect.

We beseech thee, almighty God, mercifully to look upon this thy family, that by thy great goodness they may be governed and preserved evermore both in body and soul. Through etc.

Epistle. Heb. ix. 11—15.

But Christ being come . . . inheritance.

Gradual.

Deliver me, O Lord, from mine enemies. Teach me to do the thing that pleaseth thee.[1]

℣. It is he that delivereth me from my cruel enemies, and setteth me up above my adversaries: thou shalt rid me from the wicked man.[2]

Tract.

Many a time have they fought against me from my youth up.[3]

℣. May Israel now say: yea, many a time have they vexed me from my youth up.[4]

℣. But they have not prevailed against me: the plowers plowed upon my back.[5]

℣. And made long furrows. But the righteous Lord hath hewn the snares of the ungodly in pieces.[6]

Gospel. St. John viii. 46—59.

Which of you convinceth . . . out of the temple.

Offertory.

I will thank thee, O Lord, with an unfeigned heart. O do well unto thy servant, that I may live and keep thy word. O quicken thou me according to thy word, O Lord.[7]

Secret.

Almighty God, graciously behold the offerings of thy faithful people; and grant that the chain of the world may not hold them captive whom by the passion of thy Son thou didst will to set free in all things. Who with thee etc.

---

[1] Ps. cxliii. 9, 10.   [2] Ps. xviii. 49.   [3] Ps. cxxix. 1.
[4] *Ib.* 1, 2.   [5] *Ib.* 2, 3.   [6] *Ib.* 3, 4.   [7] Ps. cxix. 7, 17, 25.

On this day, while the Priest is communicating himself this Communion is to be sung.

This is my body which is given for you: this cup is the new testament in my blood, saith the Lord: do this, as oft as ye shall drink it, in remembrance of me.[1]

Postcommunion.

Be present with us, we beseech thee, O Lord our God, and defend with thy continual help those whom thou hast refreshed with thy mysteries. Through etc.

MONDAY AFTER FIFTH SUNDAY IN LENT.[2]

At Mass.   *Office.*

Be merciful unto me, O Lord, for man goeth about to devour me: he is daily fighting and troubling me.[3]

Ps. Mine enemies are daily in hand to swallow me up: for they be many that fight against me.[4]

Gloria Patri *is not said.*

Let us kneel. Rise.

Collect.

Sanctify, we beseech thee, O Lord, our fasts, and mercifully bestow upon us the pardon of all our sins. Through etc.

Lesson. Jonah iii.

And the word of the Lord . . . did it not.

Gradual.

Hear my prayer, O God: and hearken unto the words of my mouth.[5]

℣. Save me, O God, for thy name's sake: and avenge me in thy strength.[6]

[1] Adapted from St. Luke xxii. 19, 20. See i. Cor. xi. 24, 25.
[2] Called "Judica," from the opening word of the Office for Passion Sunday.
[3] Ps. lvi. 1.   [4] *Ib.* 2.   [5] Ps. liv. 2.   [6] *Ib.* 1.

Tract.

O Lord, deal not with us etc.[1]

Gospel. St. John vii. 32—39.

And the Pharisees . . . should receive.

Offertory.

Turn thee, O Lord, and deliver my soul : O save me for thy
mercy's sake.[2]

℣. O Lord, rebuke me not in thine indignation : neither
chasten me in thy displeasure.[3]

Secret.

Receiving thy safe conduct we offer to thee, O Lord,
the sacrifice of praise, beseeching thee that we may more
safely and truly receive the same. Through etc.

Preface.

Who by the fasting of the body etc.[4]

Communion.

The Lord of Hosts, he is the king of glory.[5]

Postcommunion.

We beseech thee, O Lord, that the partaking of the
sacrament of salvation may both cleanse and heal us.
Through etc.

Over the people.

Bow down your heads before God.

Collect.

Grant, we beseech thee, O Lord, unto thy people the
spirit of truth and peace, that they may know thee with
all their mind, and work with pious devotion the things
which are well-pleasing unto thee. Through etc.

TUESDAY AFTER FIFTH SUNDAY IN LENT.

At Mass. *Office.*

O tarry thou the Lord's leisure : be strong and he
shall comfort thine heart ; and put thou thy trust in the
Lord.[6]

---

[1] As on Ash Wednesday, p. 149. [2] Ps. vi. 4. [3] *Ib.* 1.
[4] P. 35. [5] Ps. xxiv. 10. [6] Ps. xxvii. 16.

Ps. The Lord is my light and my salvation; whom then shall I fear?[1]

Gloria Patri *is not said.*

Let us kneel.   Rise.

Collect.

We beseech thee, O Lord, that our fast may be acceptable unto thee; and that by purifying us, it may make us worthy of thy grace, and lead to eternal recovery. Through etc.

Lesson.   Bel and the Dragon 29—42.

So they came . . . den of lions.[2]

Gradual.

Defend my cause, O Lord: O deliver me from the deceitful and wicked man.[3]

℣. O send out thy light and thy truth that they may lead me, and bring me unto thy holy hill.[4]

Gospel.   St. John vii. 1—13.

After these things Jesus . . . fear of the Jews.

Offertory.

And they that know thy name will put their trust in thee: for thou, Lord, hast never failed them that seek thee.   O praise the Lord, which dwelleth in Sion; for he forgetteth not the complaint of the poor.[5]

℣. Thou art set in the throne that judgest right.   Thou hast rebuked the heathen, and destroyed the ungodly.   Minister true judgment unto thy people, and be a defence for the oppressed.[6]

Secret.

We present this sacrifice to be offered to thee, O Lord; that it may obtain for us temporal consolation, and that we may with more certainty hope for thy eternal promises. Through etc.

Preface.

Who by the fasting of the body etc.[7]

---

[1] Ps. xxvii. 1.   [2] See Dan. xiv. (Vulgate).
[3] Ps. xliii. 1.   [4] *Ib.* 3.   [5] Ps. ix. 10, 11, 12.
[6] *Ib.* 4, 5, 8, 9.   [7] P. 35.

Communion.

Deliver me, O God of Israel, out of all my troubles.[1]

Postcommunion.

Grant, we beseech thee, almighty God, that we being continually occupied in divine things, may be made worthy to draw nigh to thy heavenly gifts.　Through etc.

Over the people.

Bow down your heads before God.

Collect.

Grant to us, Lord, we beseech thee, as a company of servants to persevere in doing thy will, that in our days thy people that serveth thee may be increased both in worth and number.　Through etc.

WEDNESDAY AFTER FIFTH SUNDAY IN LENT.

At Mass.　　　　　　　*Office.*

It is he that delivereth me from my cruel enemies, and setteth me up above mine adversaries, thou shalt rid me from the wicked man, O Lord.[2]

Ps.　I will love thee, O Lord, my strength: the Lord is my stony rock and my defence.[3]

Nothing further is said.[4]

Let us kneel.　Rise.

Collect.

Enlighten, O merciful God, the hearts of thy faithful people by this holy fast, and graciously give ear unto their supplications, unto whom thou hast given an hearty desire to pray.　Through etc.

Lesson.　Levit. xix. 11—19.

Ye shall not steal . . . keep my statutes.

---

[1] From Ps. xxv. 21.　　　[2] Ps. xviii. 49.　　　[3] *Ib.* 1.
[4] *I.e..* "Gloria Patri" is omitted.

Gradual.

I will magnify thee, O Lord, for thou hast set me up : and not made my foes to triumph over me.[1]

℣. O Lord my God, I cried unto thee, and thou hast healed me. Thou, Lord, hast brought my soul out of hell : thou hast kept my life from them that go down into the pit.[2]

Tract.

Bring thou me out of my troubles etc.[3]

Gospel. St. John x. 22—38.

And it was at Jerusalem . . . I in him.

Offertory.

Deliver me from mine enemies, O God : defend me, O Lord, from them that rise up against me.[4]

℣. For, lo, they lie waiting for my soul : and the mighty men are gathered against me.[5]

Secret.

Grant, we beseech thee, merciful God, that we may offer unto thee, with unfeigned obedience, the sacrifice of propitiation and praise. Through etc.

Preface.

Who by the fasting of the body etc.[6]

Communion.

I will wash my hands in innocency, O Lord, and so will I go to thine altar; that I may shew the voice of thanksgiving, and tell of all thy wondrous works.[7]

Postcommunion.

Having received the blessing of the heavenly gift, we humbly beseech thee, almighty God, that the same may produce in us the effect of the sacrament, and procure our salvation. Through etc.

Over the people.

Bow down your heads before God.

---

[1] Ps. xxx. 1.   [2] Ib. 2, 3.   [3] P. 162.   [4] Ps. lix. 1.
[5] Ib. 2.   [6] P. 35.   [7] Ps. xxvi. 6, 7.

Collect.

Lord, we beseech thee, that thy hoped for mercy may come to thy people which prayeth ; and of thy heavenly bounty grant unto them both to ask such things as be rightful, and also to obtain their petitions.   Through etc.

THURSDAY AFTER FIFTH SUNDAY IN LENT.

At Mass.   *Office.*

According to true judgment hast thou done all things that thou hast done unto us, O Lord, for we have sinned against thee, and have not obeyed thy commandments; but give glory unto thy name, and deal with us according to the multitude of thy mercies.[1]

Ps.   Great is the Lord, and worthy to be praised : in the city of our God, even upon his holy hill.[2]

Gloria Patri *is not said.*

Let us pray.   Let us kneel.   Rise.

Collect.

Grant, we beseech thee, almighty God, that the dignity of human nature, which hath been wounded by excess, may be cured by the process of healing moderation. Through etc.

Lesson.   Song of the Three Children 12—22.
And cause not . . . the whole world.

Gradual.

Bring presents, and come into his courts : O worship the Lord in the beauty of holiness.[3]

℣.   The Lord discovereth the thick bushes : in his temple doth every man speak of his honour.[4]

---

[1] Adapted from the Song of the Three Children, 5—7, 19, 20.
[2] Ps. xlviii. 1.   [3] Ps. xcvi. 8, 9.   [4] Ps. xxix. 8.

Gospel. St. John vii. 40—53.

Many of the people . . . his own house.

Offertory.

By the waters of Babylon we sat down and wept : when we remembered thee, O Sion.[1]

℣. Remember the children of Edom, O Lord, in the day of Jerusalem.[2]

Secret.

O Lord our God, who of these creatures which thou hast formed for the support of our weakness, has been pleased to command gifts to be dedicated to thy name ; grant, we beseech thee, that they may be unto us a help in this present life, and a sacrament unto life eternal. Through etc.

Preface.

Who by the fasting of the body etc.[3]

Communion.

O think upon thy servant as concerning thy word : wherein thou hast caused me to put my trust. The same is my comfort in my trouble.[4]

Postcommunion.

Grant, O Lord, that what we have received in our mouths we may take with pure minds, and that the temporal gift may become to us an eternal remedy. Through etc.

Over the people.

Bow down your heads before God.

Collect.

Be favourable, we beseech thee, O Lord, to thy people, that forsaking what displeaseth thee, they may the rather be filled with delight in thy commandments. Through etc.

[1] Ps. cxxxvii. 1. [2] *Ib.* 7.
[3] P. 35. [4] Ps. cxix. 49, 50.

Friday after Fifth Sunday in Lent.

At Mass.   *Office.*

Have mercy upon me, O Lord, for I am in trouble:
deliver me from the hand of mine enemies, and from
them that trouble me.   Let me not be confounded,
O Lord, for I have called upon thee.[1]

Ps. In thee, O Lord, have I put my trust : let me never be
put to confusion, deliver me in thy righteousness.[2]

Gloria Patri *is not said.*

Let us kneel.   Rise.

Collect.

O Lord, we beseech thee, graciously pour into our
hearts the help of thy grace : that we subduing our sins
by voluntary discipline, may rather mortify ourselves in
this life, than be consigned to eternal punishment.
Through etc.

Lesson. Jer. xvii. 13—18.

O Lord, all that forsake . . . double destruction.

Gradual.

Mine enemies speak peacefully to me, and in wrath they were
grievous to me.[3]

℣.   This thou hast seen, O Lord, my God : hold not thy
tongue then, go not far from me, O Lord.[4]

Tract.

O Lord, deal not with us etc.[5]

Gospel.   St. John xi. 47—54.

Then gathered . . . with his disciples.

Offertory.

Blessed art thou, O Lord ; O teach me thy statutes, and give
me not over to my proud oppressors.   So shall I make answer
unto my blasphemers.[6]

℣.   It grieveth me when I see the transgressors : O Lord,
when wilt thou be avenged of them that persecute me ? [7]

[1] Ps. xxxi. 10, 17, 19.   [2] *Ib.* 1.   [3] Ps. xxxv. 20 (Vulg.).
[4] *Ib.* 22.   [5] As on Ash Wednesday, p. 149.
[6] Ps. cxix. 12, 121, 42.   [7] *Ib.* 158, 84.

Secret.

Grant unto us, O merciful God, that we may always worthily serve at thy altar, and be saved by continual communion thereat. Through etc.

Preface.

Who by the fasting of the body etc.[1]

Communion.

Deliver me not over into the will of mine adversaries: for there are false witnesses risen up against me, and such as speak wrong.[2]

Postcommunion.

May the perpetual protection of the sacrifice which we have received never forsake us, O Lord, and ward off from us all things that are hurtful. Through etc.

Over the people.

Bow down your heads before God.

Collect.

Grant to us, Lord, we beseech thee, the pardon of our sins, and the increase of our religion; and that thou mayest multiply thy gifts upon us, make us more ready to obey thy commandments. Through etc.

SATURDAY AFTER FIFTH SUNDAY IN LENT.

At Mass.   *Office.*

Have mercy upon me, O Lord, for I am in trouble: deliver me from the hand of mine enemies; and from them that persecute me. Let me not be confounded, O Lord, for I have called upon thee.[3]

Ps. In thee, O Lord, have I put my trust: let me never be put to confusion, deliver me in thy righteousness.[4]

---

[1] P. 35.   [2] Ps. xxvii. 14.   [3] Ps. xxxi. 10, 17, 19.   [4] *Ib.* 1.

Gloria Patri *is not said.*

Let us kneel.   Rise.

Collect.

We beseech thee, O Lord, that thy people consecrated to thee may increase in the spirit of pious devotion ; that being exercised in holy actions they may be the more plenteously fulfilled with thy gifts, as they become more acceptable to thy majesty.   Through etc.

Lesson. Jer. xviii. 18—23.

Then they said . . . time of thine anger.

Gradual.

Mine enemies speak peacefully to me, and in wrath they were grievous to me.[1]

℣. This thou hast seen, O Lord my God : hold not thy tongue then, go not far from me, O Lord.[2]

Gospel. St. John vi. 53—71.

Then Jesus said . . . one of the twelve.

Offertory.

Remember that I stood before thee, that I might speak good in their behalf, and that I might turn away thine indignation from them.[3]

℣. Hear, O thou shepherd of Israel ; thou that leadest Joseph like a sheep.[4]

Secret.

Receive, O almighty Creator, the offering which we with fasting present unto thee, out of the largess of thine own bounty to us ; and graciously turn to our eternal welfare that which thou hast provided for our temporal support.   Through etc.

Preface.

Who by the fasting of the body etc.[5]

Communion.

Deliver me not into the will of mine enemies : for there are false witnesses risen up against me, and such as speak wrong.[6]

---

[1] Ps. xxxv. 20 (Vulg.).   [2] *Ib.* 22.   [3] Source unknown.
[4] Ps. lxxx. 1.   [5] P. 35.   [6] Ps. xxvii. 14.

Postcommunion.

We beseech thee, O Lord our God, that having been filled with the abundance of the divine gifts we may ever live by the participation thereof. Through etc.

Over the people.

Bow down your heads before God.

Collect.

May thy right hand, O Lord, we beseech thee, protect thy people that prayeth ; and worthily purify and teach them, so that they may both find present comfort, and make advance towards the good things to come hereafter. Through etc.

PALM SUNDAY.

After the sprinkling of holy water, this lesson shall be read with its title, at the altar step, on the south side, by an acolyte vested in an alb, over the flowers and leaves.

Lesson. Exod. xv. 27 ; xvi. 1—10.

And they came to Elim . . . in the cloud.

And the Gospel shall follow immediately ; and it shall be read where the gospels are read on ferial days, by a deacon turning to the east, in the manner of a simple feast, after receiving the blessing.

St. John xii. 12—19.

On the next day much people . . . gone after him.

The Gospel ended the blessing of flowers and leaves shall follow by a priest, vested in a red silk cope, standing on the third step of the altar, turning towards the south ; palms with flowers for the clergy having first been placed on the altar, but for others on the step of the altar on the south side.

I exorcise thee, O creature of flowers and leaves, in the name of God the Father almighty, and in the name of Jesus Christ his Son our Lord, and in the power of the

Holy Ghost. Henceforth all power of the adversary, all the host of the devil, all the strength of the enemy, all assaults of demons, be uprooted and transplanted from this creature of flowers and leaves, that thou pursue not by subtlety the footsteps of those who hasten to the grace of God. Through him who shall come to judge the quick and dead, and the world by fire. ℟. Amen.

Then shall be said these Collects without The Lord be with you, *but only with* Let us pray.

Collect.

Almighty everlasting God, who in the effusion of the deluge didst announce to Noe thy servant the restoration of peace to the earth by a dove bearing an olive branch in her mouth, we humbly beseech thee, that thy truth may sanctify this creature of flowers and leaves, and branches of palms, or leaves of trees, which we offer before the presence of thy glory, so that thy devout people taking them in their hands may be worthy to obtain the grace of thy benediction. Through etc.

All these Collects are said under the tone of a lesson, and with Let us pray.

O God, whose Son descended from heaven to earth for the salvation of the human race, and who when the hour of his passion was approaching willed to come to Jerusalem sitting on an ass, and to be called a king, and to be praised by the people, increase the faith of those that hope in thee, and mercifully hear the prayers of thy suppliants. We beseech thee, O Lord, let thy benediction come upon us, and vouchsafe to bless these branches of palms and of other trees, that all who shall bear them may be fulfilled with the gift of thy blessing. Grant, therefore, Lord, that as the children of the Hebrews met the same thy Son our Lord Jesus Christ with branches of palms and crying Hosanna in the highest ; so we, bearing branches of trees, may go to meet Christ with good works, and may attain to everlasting joy. Through etc.

Collect.

O God, who gatherest together that which is scattered, and preservest that which is gathered together ; who didst bless the people carrying branches of palms to meet Christ Jesus, bl + ess also these branches of palms and other trees, which thy servants bear faithfully for the blessing of thy name ; that into whatsoever place they shall be brought, all the inhabitants of that place may obtain thy blessing ; so that every adverse power having been put to flight, thy right hand may protect those whom it hath redeemed. Through etc.

Here shall the flowers and leaves be sprinkled with holy water and censed. Then is said

The Lord be with you, *and* Let us pray.

Collect.

O Lord Jesus Christ, Son of the living God, maker and redeemer of the world, who for the sake of our deliverance and salvation, didst deign to come down from the highest heaven, to take our flesh, and to endure thy passion ; and who of thine own free-will, when approaching the place of that same passion, didst will to be blessed and praised by the crowds coming to meet thee with branches of palms, and to be called in a clear voice the blessed king coming in the name of the Lord ; do thou now deign to accept our confession of praise, and to bl + ess and sancti + fy these branches of palms and of other trees and flowers ; so that whosoever shall bear anything hence in obedience to thy power, being hallowed with thy heavenly benediction, may be found worthy to receive remission of his sins, and the reward of everlasting life ; through thee, O Jesu Christ, our Saviour, who livest etc.

This done, the palms shall be distributed forthwith ; and meanwhile the following Anthems shall be sung, the Precentor beginning the Anthem.

The children of the Hebrews, carrying olive branches, went to meet our Lord, crying out and saying, Hosanna in the highest.

Another Anthem.

The children of the Hebrews spread their garments in the way, and cried saying, Hosanna to the Son of David; Blessed is he that cometh in the name of the Lord.

While the palm-branches are being distributed a shrine with relics is to be prepared, in which the Body of Christ[1] should hang in a pyx. It is to be borne by two clerks of the second rank, who shall advance to meet the procession at the place of the first station, instead of following the procession to that point. There should be no change of vestments. A lantern light, with an unveiled cross, and two banners should precede it. Then the procession shall advance to the place of the first station. The ministers in the procession shall be vested in girt albs, without tunicles or chasubles. The priest is to wear a red silk cope, the quire following him without any change of vestment. As they proceed the two following Anthems are to be sung.

Anthem.

Now[2] on the first day of unleavened bread the disciples came to Jesus saying unto him, Where wilt thou that we prepare for thee to eat the passover? But Jesus said unto them, Go into the city to such a man, and say unto him, The Master saith, My time is at hand; I will keep the passover at thy house with my disciples. And the disciples did as the Lord appointed them, and they made ready the passover.[3]

Anthem.

And when the Lord came nigh to Jerusalem, he sendeth forth two of his disciples, and saith unto them,

---

[1] *I.e.*, the Blessed Sacrament, reserved in one kind only, that òf the consecrated Wafer or Host.

[2] Only the catchwords of this and the following Anthems are given in the Missal. We have supplied the full texts from the "Sarum Processional," edit. W. G. Henderson : Leeds, 1882, p. 48.

[3] St. Mat. xxvi. 17—19.

Go your way unto the village over against you, and ye shall find a colt tied whereon never man sat ; loose him and bring him to me. If any man ask you, say ye, The Lord hath need of him. Loosing him, they brought the colt to Jesus, and cast their garments on him ; and he sat upon him. And some spread their garments in the way, and some strawed branches in the way. And they that followed cried, Hosanna, blessed is he that cometh in the name of the Lord. Blessed be the kingdom of our father David. Hosanna in the highest. Have mercy upon us, O Son of David.[1]

If these two Anthems are not sufficient to fill up the time occupied in reaching the first station, then the following anthems shall be used.

When the people had heard that Jesus was come to Jerusalem, they took branches of palm, and went out to meet him, and the children cried, saying, This is he who was to come for the salvation of the world ; this is our salvation, the redemption of Israel. How great is he whom thrones and dominions go forth to meet ! Fear not, daughter of Sion, behold thy king cometh unto thee riding upon a colt, the foal of an ass, as it is written, Hail, king, maker of the world, who art come to redeem us.[2]

Anthem.

Six days before the feast of the Passover, when the Lord came to the city of Jerusalem, children met him, both carrying in their hands branches of palms, and crying with a loud voice saying, Hosanna in the highest.

Anthem.

Six days before the passion the Lord came to the city of Jerusalem, and children met him, and they carried in their hands branches of palms, and they cried with a loud voice, saying, Hosanna in the highest. Blessed art thou who art come in the multitude of thy mercy. Hosanna in the highest.

[1] Adapted from St. Luke xix. 28—38.
[2] Partly from St. Mat. xxi. 5 or St. John xii. 15.

*Here the first station shall be made, that is to say, in the
extreme east of the north side of the church, and this Gospel
shall be read:*

Gospel. St. Mat. xxi. 1—9.

And when Jesus drew nigh . . . Hosanna in the highest.[1]

*This Gospel is to be read by the deacon, vested for the pro-
cession, standing not close to the cross, but before the priest, a
little apart from him, his position being somewhat altered according to the station. The deacon is to face to the north, and the
Gospel is to be read as on a simple feast of nine lessons, the benediction having been previously received in the usual manner.[2]*

*The Gospel being ended, three clerks of the second rank,
without changing their vestments, shall turn to the people, and
standing in front of and on the west side of the great cross,
shall together chant the following anthem or verse:*

Anthem.

Behold, thy king cometh unto thee, O Sion, mystical
daughter, sitting on beasts, of whose coming the prophetic
lesson hath now foretold.

*After each verse the Officiant, turning to the relics, shall
begin the Anthem:*

Hail, thou whom the people of the Hebrews bear
witness to as Jesus, coming to meet thee with palms,
shouting words of salvation.

*The quire shall take it up, kneeling and kissing the ground;
the Officiant himself kneeling first, with the quire. Then the
clerks standing before the relics shall sing the anthem:*

Behold thy king etc.

After which the senior [clerk] shall say the anthem, Hail,

---

[1] As on First Sunday in Advent, p. 75.

[2] At the close of the Gospel, some Service books (*i.e.*, the 1508 and
1517 editions of the "Sarum Processional") direct a boy vested like a
prophet to stand in some conspicuous place and to chaunt the following prophetic Lesson: "O Jerusalem, look to the East and see; lift
up thine eyes, O Jerusalem, and see the power of thy King." Compare
Baruch iv. 36; v. 5.

thou to whom, etc., *the quire rising and taking it up at the words* bear witness to.

Then shall the clerks, standing before the relics, without change of position, say the Verse :

This is he that cometh from Edom, with dyed garments from Bozrah ; this that is glorious in his apparel, travelling in the greatness of his strength ; not on war horses, nor in lofty turrets.[1]

Then the senior clerk, without change of position, shall say the verse :

Hail, light of the world, king of kings, glory of heaven, with whom abideth dominion, praise and honour, now and for ever.

The quire rising, and taking it up at the point king of kings. *The Clerks also, in front of the relics, without changing their position, shall say the Verse :*

This is he that cometh etc.

Also the senior Clerk, without changing his position, shall say the Anthem :

Hail, our salvation, our true peace, our redemption, our strength, who of thine own free will didst submit to the dominion of death on our behalf.

The quire rising and taking it up at the point our true peace.

Then shall the procession advance to the place of the second station ; the shrine, with the receptacle for relics, together with a light in a lantern, being carried between the subdeacon and the thurifer, with the banners on either side of them, the precentor beginning the Anthem :

Thou art worthy, O Lord our God, to receive glory and honour.

And also this Anthem :

The multitudes come to meet the Redeemer with flowers and palms, and give meet reverence to the triumphant conqueror. The Gentiles proclaim with

---

[1] Partly from Is. lxiii. 1.

their mouths the Son of God, and their voices praising Christ resound through the skies with Hosanna.

If these two anthems do not suffice to bring the procession to the place of the second station, then shall one or both of the following Responsories be sung.

Responsory.

The Lord Jesus six days before the Passover came to Bethany, where Lazarus had died, whom Jesus raised from the dead.[1]

℣. But there assembled there many of the Jews, that they might see Lazarus, whom Jesus raised from the dead.[2]

Responsory.

But the chief priests consulted that they might put Lazarus also to death, because that by reason of him many came, and believed on Jesus.[3]

℣. Therefore the people which was with him, when he called Lazarus out of the grave, and raised him from the dead, bare record.[4]

Here the second station shall take place, that is to say, on the south side of the church, where seven boys, from a very elevated position, shall sing :

℣. All glory, laud, and honour
    To thee, Redeemer, King,
  To whom the lips of children
    Made sweet Hosannas ring.

The quire is to repeat this stanza after each verse :

℣. Thou art the King of Israel,
    Thou David's royal Son,
  Who in the Lord's name comest,
    The King and blessed One.

℣. The company of angels
    Are praising thee on high ;
  And mortal men and all things
    Created make reply.

---

[1] St. John xii. 1.   [2] *Ib.* 9.   [3] *Ib.* 10, 11.   [4] *Ib.* 17.

℣. The people of the Hebrews
  With palms before thee went;
  Our praise and prayer and anthems
  Before thee we present.[1]

This station ended, the procession is to go through the middle of the cloister on the right hand as far as the west door of the church singing the

Responsory.

Then gathered the chief priests and the Pharisees a council and said, What do we? for this man doeth many miracles. If we let him thus alone, all men will believe on him, and the Romans shall come and take away both our place and nation.[2]

Here the third station shall take place, in front of the aforesaid door, where three clerks of the upper rank, standing in the doorway itself, without changing their vestments, shall turn to the people, and chant this verse :

℣. But one of them, named Caiaphas, being the high priest that same year, prophesied, saying, It is expedient for you that one man should die for the people, and that the whole nation perish not ; lest the Romans shall come and take away both our place and nation.[3]

This done, they shall enter the church by the same door, passing under the shrine and the receptacle for relics, held transversely, for them to pass under, while they sing

Responsory.

As the Lord was entering into the holy city the children of the Hebrews proclaimed the resurrection of life, and with branches of palms, cried out: Hosanna in the highest.

Here the fourth station is to be made, namely, before the cross [rood] in the church. At the station itself, after the cross has been now unveiled, the Officiant should begin the Anthem :

---

[1] "Hymns A. and M.," 2nd Edit., No. 98.   [2] St. John xi. 47, 48.
[3] *Ib.* 49, 50.

Anthem.

Hail, our King, Son of David, Redeemer of the world, whom the prophets have proclaimed to be the Saviour of the house of Israel that is to come. For thee the Father sent into the world to be the saving victim, whom all the saints expected from the beginning of the world, and now expect. Hosanna to the Son of David. Blessed is he that cometh in the name of the Lord. Hosanna in the highest.

The Officiant is to commence the above anthem, by repeating the word Hail *thrice, saying it louder each time. Then the quire takes it up at the words* our King, *both the Officiant and the quire genuflecting, and kissing the earth, after which the rest of the anthem is sung standing. This done, they shall enter the quire. At the entry into the quire they shall sing:*

Responsory.

Lying men compassed me about; they scourged me without a cause. But do thou, O Lord, my defender, avenge me.

℣. Deliver me from mine enemies, O Lord : defend me from them that rise up against me.[1]

Collect.

Almighty and everlasting God etc.[2]

All being now finished in connection with the procession, Mass shall begin :

At Mass.   *Office.*

Be not thou far from me O Lord : thou art my succour, haste thee to help me. Save me from the lion's mouth : thou hast heard me also from among the horns of the unicorn.[3]

Ps. My God, my God, look upon me : why hast thou forsaken me ?[4]

Gloria Patri *is omitted.*

---

[1] Ps. lix. 1.   [2] *I.e.*, the Palm Sunday Mass Collect.
[3] Ps. xxii. 19, 21.   [4] *Ib.* 1.

Collect.

Almighty and everlasting God, who hast sent our
Saviour to take upon him our flesh, and to suffer death
upon the cross, that mankind should follow the example
of his humility ; mercifully grant, that we may both follow
the example of his patience, and also be made partakers
of his resurrection. Through etc.

Epistle. Phil. ii. 5—11.
Let this mind . . . God the Father.

Gradual.

Thou hast holden me by my right hand : thou shalt guide me
with thy counsel ; and after that receive me with glory.[1]

Truly God is loving unto Israel, even unto such as are of a
clean heart. Nevertheless my feet were almost gone, my tread-
ings had well-nigh slipped. And why ? I was grieved at the
wicked ; I do also see the ungodly in such prosperity.[2]

Tract.

To be sung by the Quire in alternate verses.

My God, my God, look upon me : why hast thou
forsaken me.

℣. And art so far from my health, and from the
words of my complaint?

℣. O my God, I cry in the day-time, but thou
hearest not : and in the night season also I take no rest.

℣. And thou continuest holy, O thou worship of
Israel. Our fathers hoped in thee : they trusted in thee ;
and thou didst deliver them.

℣. They called upon thee, and were holpen : they
put their trust in thee, and were not confounded.

℣. But as for me, I am a worm and no man : a very
scorn of men and the outcast of the people.

℣. All they that see me laugh me to scorn : they
shoot out their lips, and shake their heads, saying,

℣. He trusted in God, that he would deliver him :
let him deliver him, if he will have him.

℣. They stand staring and looking upon me. They

---

[1] Ps. lxxiii. 22, 23.　　　[2] *Ib.* 1—3.

Ps 22¹⁸

part my garments among them, and cast lots upon my vesture.

V.   Save me from the lion's mouth : thou hast heard me also from among the horns of the unicorns.

V.   O praise the Lord, ye that fear him : magnify him, all ye of the seed of Jacob.

V.   They shall be counted unto the Lord for a generation. They shall come, and the heaven shall declare his righteousness.

V.   Unto a people that shall be born, whom the Lord hath made.[1]

Then followeth the Passion. And it is to be noticed that it is to be sung or recited in three tones—high, low, and middle. Because all the contents of the Passion are either the words of the Jews, or the disciples, or the words of Christ ; or the words of the Evangelist who tells the story. Therefore know that where you find the letter (a) prefixed, the words following are the words either of the Jews or the disciples which are to be recited in a high [alto] tone. Where you find the letter (b) prefixed, the words following are the words of Christ, which are to be recited in a low [bass] tone. Where you find the letter (m) prefixed, the words following are the words of the evangelist, which are to be read or sung by a middle [tenor] voice. This rule is to be observed in all the recitations of the Passion.

m. *V.* The Lord be with you.
    R. And with thy spirit.

The Passion of our Lord Jesus Christ according to Matthew.

Glory be to thee, O Lord, *is not said.*

St. Mat. xxvi. and xxvii. 1—61.

And it came to pass . . . against the sepulchre.

After the words yielded up the ghost, *the deacon is to incline, or prostrate himself, towards the East, and say privately,*

---

[1] Ps. xxii. 1—8, 17, 18, 21, 23, 31, 32.

[2] "Alta, bassa et media" ; *i.e.,* alto, bass, and tenor

Our Father, Hail Mary, *and* Into thy hands, O Lord, I commend my spirit; thou hast redeemed me, O Lord, thou God of truth.[1] *Then he shall rise and afterwards read the rest of the Passion. The Gospels at the end of all the Passions, including Good Friday, are to be said in a high [alto] voice, after the manner of a double feast. All the Passions are to be said in the manner aforesaid, according to the use of Sarum. But on Good Friday* The Lord *be with you is omitted, and the Gospel should be begun without any title.*

Gospel.

St. Mat. xxvi. 62—66.
Now the next day . . . setting a watch.

Offertory.

Thy rebuke hath broken my heart; I am full of heaviness; I looked for some to have pity on me, but there was no man, neither found I any to comfort me. They gave me gall to eat, and when I was thirsty, they gave me vinegar to drink.[2]

Secret.

We offer unto thee, O God, Father almighty, the whole burnt offering of the spotless Paschal Lamb; by whose blood, we beseech thee, save us from the ravages of the destroyer, and lead us into thy newly-promised land. Through etc.

Ferial Preface.

Communion.

Father, if this cup may not pass away from me, except I drink it, thy will be done.[3]

Postcommunion.

We beseech thee, O Lord, look graciously upon thy faithful people, that they calling to mind again the beginning of their redemption, may profit more and more through those things by the gift of which thou hast refreshed them. Through etc.

---

[1] Ps. xxxi. 6. [2] Ps. lxix. 21, 22.
[3] St. Mat. xxvi. 42.

MONDAY IN HOLY WEEK.[1]

At Mass.   *Office.*

Plead thou my cause, O Lord, with them that strive
with me : and fight thou against them that fight against
me.   Lay hand upon the shield and buckler, and stand
up to help me, O Lord, thou strength of my salvation.[2]

Ps.   Bring forth the spear, and stop the way against them that
persecute me.[3]

Gloria Patri *is not said.*

Collect.

Grant, we beseech thee, Almighty God, that we who by
reason of our weakness, faint under so many adversities,
may recover by pleading the passion of thy only-begotten
Son.   Through etc.

Lesson.   Is. l. 5—10.
The Lord God hath opened . . . upon his God.

Gradual.

Awake, O Lord, and stand up to judge my quarrel : avenge
thou my cause my God and my Lord.[4]

℣.   Bring forth the spear, and stop the way against them that
persecute me.[5]

Tract.

O Lord, deal not with us etc.[6]

Gospel.   St. John xii. 1—36.
Then Jesus six days . . . himself from them.

Offertory.

Deliver me, O Lord, from mine enemies; for I flee unto thee
to hide me.   Teach me to do the thing that pleaseth thee, for
thou art my God.[7]

℣.   Hearken unto me for thy truth and righteousness sake.
And enter not into judgment with thy servant, O Lord.[8]

---

[1] " Feria secunda post Dominicam in Ramis Palmarum."
[2] Ps. xxxv. 1, 2.   [3] *Ib.* 3.   [4] *Ib.* 23.
[5] *Ib.* 3.   [6] As on Ash Wednesday, p. 149.-50
[7] Ps. cxliii. 9, 10.   [8] *Ib.* 1, 2.

Ps. 103 [10]
      79 [8-9]

Secret.

May this oblation itself commend thy faithful people to thy majesty, O Lord ; which through thy Son our Lord Jesus Christ hath reconciled them that were at enmity. Who etc.

Preface.

Who by the fasting of the body etc.[1]

Communion.

Let them be put to confusion and shame together, that rejoice at my trouble : let them be clothed with rebuke and dishonour, that boast themselves against me.[2]

Postcommunion.

Having been filled with thy saving gift we beseech thy mercy, O Lord, that by this same sacrament, by which thou makest us to grow in this life, thou wouldest make us partakers of the life eternal. Through etc.

Over the people.

Bow down your heads before God.

Collect.

Help us, O God of our salvation, and grant that we may come with joy to the commemoration of those benefits by which thou hast deigned to restore us. Through etc.

TUESDAY IN HOLY WEEK.

At Mass.   *Office.*

But we ought to glory in the cross of our Lord Jesus Christ, in whom is our salvation, life, and resurrection, through whom we are saved and freed.[3]

Ps. God be merciful unto us and bless us : and shew us the light of his countenance, and be merciful unto us.[4]

---

[1] P. 35.
[2] Ps. xxxv. 26.
[3] Partly from Gal. vi. 14.
[4] Ps. lxvii. 1.

Let us kneel.   Rise.

Collect.

Almighty everlasting God, grant us so to celebrate the sacrament of the Lord's passion, that we may be found worthy to obtain pardon.   Through etc.

Lesson.   Jer. xi. 18—20.

The Lord hath given . . . revealed my cause.

Gradual.

Nevertheless, when they were sick, I put on sackcloth, and humbled my soul with fasting : and my prayer shall turn into mine own bosom.[1]

Plead thou my cause, O Lord, with them that strive with me : and fight thou against them that fight against me. Lay hand upon the shield and buckler : and stand up to help me.[2]

Then shall the Passion follow thus.

℣. The Lord be with you.

℟. And with thy spirit.

The Passion of our Lord Jesus Christ according to Mark.

m. St. Mark xiv. and xv. 1—41.

After two days . . . unto Jerusalem.

After the words gave up the ghost, *a genuflexion shall be made* [*by the Deacon*] *while he says* Our Father etc., Hail Mary etc., Into thy hands etc.[3]

Gospel.   St. Mark xv. 42—46.

And now when the even . . . the sepulchre.

Offertory.

Keep me, O Lord, from the hands of the ungodly : and preserve me from the wicked men, O Lord.[4]

℣. Who are purposed to overthrow my goings. The proud have laid a snare for me.[5]

Secret.

Sanctify, we beseech thee, O Lord, the oblations of a

---

[1] Ps. xxxv. 13.   [2] *Ib.* 1, 2.   [3] See rubric on p. 228.
[4] Ps. cxl. 4.   [5] *Ib.* 4, 5.

people devoted to thee ; that cleansed from the earthly conversation of the old man, we may be renewed by progress in a heavenly life.   Through etc.

Preface.

Who by the fasting of the body etc.[1]

Communion.

They that sit in the gate speak against me : and the drunkards make songs upon me.   But, Lord, I make my prayer unto thee : in an acceptable time.   Hear me, O God, in the multitude of thy mercy.[2]

Postcommunion.

Having been filled with the grace of thy holy gift, we humbly beseech thee, O Lord, that what in adoration we have thought sweet to our bodily taste, we may perceive to be more exceeding sweet to our souls.   Through etc.

Over the people.

Bow down your hearts before God.

Collect.

May thy pity, O God, protect us from all gradual surrender to the old man, and make us capable of a new and holy life.   Through etc.

WEDNESDAY IN HOLY WEEK.

At Mass.   *Office.*

At the name of the Lord every knee should bow, of things in heaven, and things in earth, and things under the earth ; because the Lord became obedient unto death even the death of the cross : therefore Jesus Christ is Lord, to the glory of God the Father.[3]

---

[1] See p. 35.   [2] Ps. lxix. 12—14.   [3] Phil. ii. 10, 8, 11.

Ps. Lord hear my prayer, and let my crying come unto thee.[1]

The Collect is to follow without The Lord be with you, *and only with* Let us pray, *and* Let us kneel. Rise.

Collect.

Grant, we beseech thee, almighty God, that we who are continually punished for our offences, may be delivered by the passion of thy Only-begotten one. Who etc.

Lesson. Is. lxii. 11 ; lxiii. 1—7.
Say ye to . . . bestowed on us.

Gradual.

Hide not thy face from thy servant, for I am in trouble : O haste thee, and hear me.[2]

℣. Save me, O God : for the waters are come in, even unto my soul. I stick fast in the deep mire, where no ground is.[3]

Then shall follow The Lord be with you. Let us pray. Let us kneel. Rise.

Collect.

O God, who hast willed that thy Son should suffer death upon the cross for us, that thou mightest drive away from us the power of the enemy, grant unto us thy servants that we may obtain the grace of his resurrection. Through etc.

Here the accustomed memories are said.

Lesson. Is. liii. 1—10, 12.
Who hath believed . . . for the transgressors.

The quire shall say the following Tract in alternate verses, in such way that the quire should be standing on the side where the Verse is sung, while the opposite side is seated. In this way the whole Tract is to be sung through by the quire in the stalls, from Septuagesima to Easter.

Tract.

Hear my prayer, O Lord : and let my cry come unto thee.

---

[1] Ps. cii. 1.   [2] Ps. lxix. 18.   [3] *Ib.* 1, 2.

℣. Hide not thy face from me in the time of my trouble : incline thine ear unto me.

℣. When I call : O hear me and that right soon.

℣. For my days are consumed away like smoke : and my bones are burnt up, as it were a fire-brand.

℣. My heart is smitten down, and withered like grass : so that I forget to eat my bread.

℣. Thou, O Lord, shalt arise, and have mercy upon Sion : for it is time that thou have mercy upon her.[1]

Then shall the Passion follow thus.

m. ℣. The Lord be with you.

℟. And with thy spirit.

The Passion of our Lord Jesus Christ according to Luke.

St. Luke xxii and xxiii. 1—49.

Now the feast . . . beholding these things.

When the deacon has said the words the veil of the temple was rent in the midst *the veil is to be let fall before the altar.*

After the words gave up the ghost *the deacon shall genuflect and say :* Our Father etc., Hail Mary etc., Into thy hands etc.[2]

Gospel. St. Luke xxiii. 50—53.

And behold . . . before was laid.

Offertory.

Hear my prayer, O Lord : and let my crying come unto thee.[3]

℣. Hide not thy face from me : hide not thy face from me.[4]

Secret.

Receive, we beseech thee, O Lord, the gift we offer, and so work in us, that we may apprehend with pious affections that which by the mystery of the passion of thy Son our Lord we do set forth. Through etc.

Preface.

Who by the fasting of the body etc.[5]

---

[1] Ps. cii. 1—4, 13.   [2] As on p. 228.   [3] Ps. cii. 1.
[4] *Ib.* 2.   [5] P. 35.

Communion.

I mingled my drink with weeping; for thou hast taken me up and cast me down: and I am withered like grass. But thou, O Lord, shalt endure for ever. Thou shalt arise and have mercy upon Sion: for it is time that thou have mercy upon her.[1]

Postcommunion.

Quicken our understanding, almighty God, that through the death in this world of thy Son, to which these adorable mysteries do testify, we may surely trust that thou hast given to us eternal life. Through etc.

Over the people.

Bow down your heads before God.

Collect.

We beseech thee, O Lord, to behold this thy family, for which our Lord Jesus Christ was contented to be betrayed, and given up into the hands of wicked men, and to suffer death upon the cross. Who now etc.

MAUNDY THURSDAY.[2]

In the first place, the reconciliation of penitents shall take place in the following manner. When None has been sung, the priest of the highest rank shall go to the west door of the church, having put on his priestly vestments and a red silk cope, attended by two deacons in albs and amices, but without the sub-deacon, and without the cross. A sackcloth banner is to precede him through the midst of the quire. The penitents, who are to be reconciled should be placed in the vestibule of the church. If the bishop be present, the principal archdeacon vested in a silk cope, and standing outside the door of the church is to read the following lesson on behalf of the penitents.

The accepted time is come, O venerable prelate, the day of divine propitiation and salvation of men; when

---

[1] Ps. cii. 9, 10, 11, 12, 13.
[2] The Latin title is "Feria V. in Cena Domini."

death was abolished, and eternal life begun; when a plant-
ing of new vines is so to be made in the vineyard of the
Lord of Sabaoth, that the blindness of the old man may
be purged away. For, albeit no time is devoid of the
riches of the goodness of God, yet now forgiveness of sins
is more ample by reason of his indulgence, and the admis-
sion of those who are beginning a new life is more
numerous by reason of his grace. By those to be re-
generated we are increased in numbers, by those who
return [to the unity of the church] we are increased in
strength. Waters wash; tears wash; hence there is joy
over the receiving of those that are called, and there is joy
over the absolution of penitents. Hence it is, that thy
suppliants, after that by neglect of the divine commandments, and by transgression of approved morals, they
have fallen into divers kinds of sin, humble and prostrate
cry unto God, in the words of the prophet, saying, We
have sinned with our fathers; we have dealt wickedly; we
have committed iniquity; have mercy, O Lord, upon us,
who turn not a deaf ear to the gospel words, Blessed are
they that mourn, for they shall be comforted. They have
eaten, as it is written, the bread of affliction; they have
watered their couch with tears; they have afflicted their
soul with grief, and their body with fasting, that they
might recover the health of their souls which they had
lost. Accordingly, it is the singular privilege of penitence
that it is both profitable to the individual and conduceth
to the common welfare of all. Renew, therefore, in them,
O apostolic prelate, whatsoever hath been decayed by the
suggestion, or rage, or ravage of the devil; by the merits
and patronage of thy prayers on their behalf, make these
men near to God, through the grace of divine reconciliation; so that they who were before displeasing in their
perverse ways, may now get the victory over the author
of their death, and rejoice that they please the Lord in the
land of the living.

This Lesson should not be read in the absence of the bishop.

R

The Lesson being finished, the bishop shall begin the anthem, Come ye, come ye, *inside the aforesaid door, turning to the north, and making the sign of the cross with his hand, as it were beckoning: Then the deacon, on the part of the penitents outside the door shall say,* Let us kneel. *Another deacon, on the part of the bishop, shall say,* Rise, *and this shall be done thrice, in such way, however, that after the third repetition of the Anthem, '* Let us kneel ' *is not said, but the quire follows up the whole Anthem, the precentor beginning,* Come, ye children, hearken unto me, I will teach you etc. *Then shall follow the Psalm:* I will alway,[1] *the whole Psalm being said with* Glory be to the Father etc. *and the Anthem is to be repeated after each Verse. While the Psalm and its anthem are being sung by the quire, the penitents are to be continually handed, one by one, by some priest of the quire, without any change of vestment, to the officiating priest, and by him they are to be restored to the bosom of the Church. This done, the procession shall return in the usual way to the quire. Then shall they all prostrate themselves, and the clerks in the quire shall say the seven penitential psalms, with* Glory be to the Father etc. *and* As it was etc., *and the Anthem* Remember not *with* Lord have mercy upon us, Christ have mercy upon us, Lord have mercy upon us. Our Father. *All this in front of the altar, as has been previously laid down for Ash Wednesday. Then shall the priest rise, and standing on right side of the altar, and facing south, say, without any inflection of voice:*

And lead us not into temptation.

℟. But deliver us from evil.

℣. My God, save thy servants and thy handmaidens,

℟. Which put their trust in thee.

℣. Turn thee again, O Lord, at the last,

℟. And be gracious unto thy servants.

℣. Send unto them, O Lord, help from thy holy place.

℟. And defend them out of Sion.

[1] Ps. xxxiv.

℣. Help us, O God, our Saviour.

℟. And for the glory of thy name deliver us; and be merciful unto our sins, for thy name's sake.

℣. Lord, hear my prayer.

℟. And let my cry come unto thee.

℣. The Lord be with you.

℟. And with thy spirit.

Let us pray.

Collect.

Be favourable, O Lord, to our supplications, and graciously listen unto me, who first of all stand in need of thy mercy; and grant unto me, whom, not by election of merit, but by the gift of thy grace, thou hast appointed unto this ministry, confidence in fulfilling the duty which thou hast laid upon me, and do thou of thy loving kindness work in our ministration. Through etc.

All these Collects are to be intoned as Lessons. Let us pray *is to be said before each, but* The Lord be with you *before the first Collect only.*

Collect.

O God, most gracious creator, and most compassionate restorer of mankind, who by the blood of thine Only Son hast redeemed mankind, cast down by the envy of the devil from immortality, quicken these thy servants, whom thou desirest in no wise to die unto thee, and do thou who dost not leave them to stray, receive them back after correction. Let the sorrowful sighings of these thy servants, O Lord, we beseech thee, move thy loving kindness. Do thou heal their wounds, and stretch out thy saving hand to them as they lie before thee. Let not thy church be robbed of any part of her body. Let not thy flock suffer loss. Let not the enemy rejoice over the injury to thy family. Let not a second death get possession of those who have been born again in the laver of salvation. To thee, therefore, O Lord, we humbly offer our prayers; to thee we pour out the sorrows of our heart. Spare thou them that confess; that by thy aid they may so weep over their sins in this mortal life, that in the tremendous day of judgment they may escape the sentence of eternal damnation, and may never know, most loving Father, the terrors of darkness, and the gnashing of teeth in flames; but that returning from the errors of their way into the path of righteousness, they may be wounded no more; but let that which thy grace hath bestowed, and thy pity hath reformed, be made whole and entire, and abide with them for ever. Through etc.

Collect.

O Lord, holy Father, almighty everlasting God, who hast deigned to heal our wounds, we thy humble priests desire and beseech thee mercifully to incline thine ears to our prayers, and by our confession to be moved to repent thee; and that thou wouldest forgive all our sins, and pardon all our offences; and that thou wouldest give to these thy servants, O Lord, pardon for punishment, joy for sorrow, life for death: so that they who trusting in thy mercy have arrived at so great a hope of the heights of heaven, may be accounted worthy to attain unto the blessings of the reward of thy peace, and unto thy heavenly gifts. Through etc.

Then without saying Let us pray, *the Priest shall turn to the people, and, with extended hand, say the Absolution in monotone.*

We absolve you in the place of blessed Peter, prince of the apostles, on whom the power of binding and loosing was conferred by the Lord, and so far as accusation pertaineth to you, and remission to us, may almighty God be unto you life and health, and the gracious pardoner of all your sins, Who liveth etc.

When the Priest says the words Who liveth etc. *all shall rise from their prostration, kissing the benches or the ground. And if a bishop be present, he shall pronounce the benediction.*

Then solemn Mass shall be begun, without ruling of the quire.

At Mass.   *Office.*

But we ought to glory in the cross of our Lord Jesus Christ, in whom is our salvation, life, and resurrection, through whom we have been saved and freed.[1]

Ps. God be merciful unto us, and bless us: and shew the light of his countenance upon us, and be merciful unto us.[2]

If a bishop be celebrant, Glory be to the Father etc. *is said. Whether a bishop be celebrant or not, the chant of* O Lord, maker of all creatures[3] *is used without its verses.* Glory be to God on high etc. *is to be said whether a bishop be celebrant or not. Then shall follow* Let us pray *without* Let us kneel *and* Rise.

Collect.

O God, from whom both the traitor Judas received the punishment of his crime, and the robber the reward of his confession, grant unto us the full effect of thy propitiation, that as in his passion our Lord Jesus Christ rendered unto each according to their different deservings, so having destroyed the old man in us, he may grant unto us the grace of his resurrection. Who with thee etc.

Epistle. 1 Cor. xi. 20—32.

When ye come together . . . with the world.

This Epistle aforesaid is to be read in the pulpit, and the Gradual is to be sung in the same place by two boys in surplices.

Gradual.

Christ became obedient for us unto death, even the death of the cross.[4]

℣. Wherefore God also hath highly exalted him, and given him a name which is above every name.[5]

---

[1] Partly from Gal. vi. 14.   [2] Ps. lxvii. 1.
[3] Kyrie eleyson, No. 8.
[4] Phil. ii. 8.   [5] *Ib.* 9.

The Gradual is to be repeated unless a bishop be celebrant.
The Gospel is to be read in the pulpit, as on Sundays.

Gospel.　St. John, xiii. 1—15.

Now before the feast . . . I have done to you.

This Gospel is to be read in the pulpit, as on Sunday, with-
out the Creed, unless a bishop shall be celebrating.　In the
latter case the Gospel is to be read after the manner of a
double feast, and the Creed is said.

Offertory.

The right hand of the Lord hath the pre-eminence: the right
hand of the Lord bringeth mighty things to pass.　I shall not die
but live, and declare the works of the Lord.[1]

Three hosts should be placed by the sub-deacon for consecra-
tion; of which two should be reserved for the following day,
one to be received by the priest, the other to be deposited with
the cross in the sepulchre.

Secret.

We beseech thee, O Lord, holy Father, almighty
eternal God, that he himself may make this sacrifice
acceptable to thee, who, according to to-day's tradition
set forth this to be done by his disciples, in remembrance
of him, Jesus Christ our Lord.　Who with thee etc.

Ferial Preface.

On this day the Sanctus *is to be solemnly sung, although*
there be no bishop present.　Within the Canon In communion
with *and* This oblation therefore *and* Who the day before
are said in the same way by a priest as by a bishop.　Before
the consecration, three boys, in surplices, shall together sing this
hymn O Redeemer etc.,[2] *the quire repeating the first two lines*
after each verse.　On this day 'O Lamb of God etc.' *is not*
said, nor should the Pax be given, unless a bishop should be

---

[1] Ps. cxviii. 16, 17.
[2] The text of this hymn is given in the "Sarum Processional," edit.
W. G. Henderson, Leeds, 1882, p. 58.

*celebrating; in that case 'O Lamb of God' is said solemnly,
as on a double feast, and the vessel containing the holy chrism
is to be kissed instead of the Pax.*

Communion.

The Lord Jesus, after he had supped with his disciples, washed
their feet and saith unto them, Know ye what I have done unto
you? I your Lord and master have given you an example, that ye
too should do as I have done.[1]

*When the Communion has been sung, festal Vespers shall be
begun at once, without ruling of the quire, and without O God
make speed etc. The Anthem shall be commenced by one of
superior rank.*

Anthem.

I will receive the cup of salvation: and call upon the
name of the Lord.[2]

Psalm.

I believed and therefore . . . O Jerusalem.[3]

Ps 116 10-16

*Glory be to the Father etc. is not said, but the Anthem is
to be repeated at the end of the Psalm. The same rule is to
be observed for all the following Psalms.*

Anthem.

I laboured for peace among them that were enemies
unto peace : when I spake unto them thereof, they made
them ready to battle.[4]

Psalm.

When I was in trouble . . . ready to battle.[5]

Anthem.

Keep me, O Lord, from the hands of the ungodly.[6]

---

[1] Partly from St. John, xiii. 12, 15.   [2] Ps. cxvi. 12.
[3] Ps. cxvi. 10—16.   [4] Ps. cxx. 5, 6 (Vulg. cxix. 7).
[5] Ps. cxx.   [6] Ps. cxl. 4.

Psalm.

Deliver me, O Lord, . . . continue in thy sight.[1]

Anthem.

Keep me from the snare that they have laid for me, and from the traps of the wicked doers.[2]

Psalm.

Lord, I call upon thee . . . escape them.[3]

Anthem.

I looked also on my right hand and saw there was no man that would know me.[4]

Psalm.

I cried unto the Lord . . . to my company.[5]
After the fifth Anthem, the Anthem As they were eating *etc. is to be begun at once.*

Anthem.

As they were eating, Jesus took bread, and blessed it, and brake it, and gave it to his disciples.[6]

Song of Blessed Mary.

My soul doth magnify . . . for ever.[7]

After the repetition of the Anthem the priest shall say the Postcommunion in the usual manner, with The Lord be with you *and* Let us pray.

Postcommunion.

We beseech thee, O Lord our God, that having been refreshed with life-giving food, we may, through thy gift of immortality, obtain that which we follow after in this time of our mortal life.   Through etc.

---

[1] Ps. cxl.   [2] Ps. cxli. 10.   [3] Ps. cxli.
[4] Ps. cxlii. 4.   [5] Ps. cxlii.   [6] St. Matt. xxvi. 26.
[7] St. Luke, i. 46—55.

Thus Mass and Vespers are to be finished together; the deacon pronouncing the words Depart, the Mass is ended *if a Bishop be celebrating: if not, Mass and Vespers are alike to be finished with* Let us bless the Lord. *On account of the solemnity of the day, both deacon and sub-deacon are to be vested in dalmatic and tunicle, even if a bishop be not celebrating.*

After refection the clergy shall assemble at the church, to wash the altars, to perform the Maundy, and to say Compline.

First, let water be blessed in the usual way, outside the quire, privately. Then, *let two priests of higher rank be ready, with deacon and sub-deacon of the second rank, and a candle-bearer of the first rank, all vested in albs and amices, and two clerks bearing wine and water; and let them begin at the high altar and wash it, pouring over it wine and water. Mean-while, let the Responsory* On the Mount of Olives etc. *be sung by the whole quire before the altar, with its Verse, but without* Glory be to the Father etc.

1 *Responsory.*

On the mount of Olives I prayed unto the Father: Father, if it be possible, let this cup pass from me; the spirit indeed is willing, but the flesh is weak. Thy will be done.[1]

℣. Nevertheless, not as I will, but as thou wilt. Thy will be done.[2]

2 *Responsory.*

Lying men compassed me about; they scourged me without a cause. But thou, O Lord, my defender, avenge me.[3]

℣. For trouble is hard at hand, and there is none to help.[4] But thou, O Lord, etc.

3 *Responsory.*

My soul is sorrowful even unto death; tarry ye here, and watch with me. Now shall ye see the multitude

[1] St. Matt. xxvi. 39, 41. [2] *Ib.* 39.
[3] Adapted from Pss. cix. 2, and iii. 3. [4] Ps. xxii. 11.

which shall compass me about. Ye shall take to flight,
and I will go to be sacrificed for you.[1]

℣. Behold, the hour is at hand, and the Son of Man
shall be delivered into the hands of sinners. Ye shall
take to flight etc.[2]

4 *Responsory.*

Lo, we have seen him, that he hath no form or comeli-
ness; there is no beauty in him: he hath borne our sins,
and he sorroweth for us; but he was wounded for our
iniquities. By whose stripes we are healed.[3]

℣. Surely he hath borne our griefs and carried our
sorrows.[4] By whose stripes etc.

5 *Responsory.*

To-day one of my disciples shall betray me. Woe to
that man by whom I shall be betrayed. Good were it for
that man if he had never been born.[5]

℣. He that dippeth his hand with me in the dish, he
it is that shall betray me into the hands of sinners.[6] Good
were it etc.

6 *Responsory.*

Judas, the wickedest trafficker, sought the Lord with a
kiss; he as an innocent lamb refuseth not the kiss of
Judas. For a sum of money he betrayed Christ to the
Jews.[7]

℣. Drunken with the poison of covetousness, while
he seeks for gain, he finds a noose.[8] For a sum of
money etc.

7 *Responsory.*

Could ye not watch with me one hour, ye who en-
couraged [each other] to die for me? See ye not even

---

[1] Adapted from St. Matt. xxvi. 36, etc. [2] *Ib.* 45.
[3] Adapted from Is. liii. 2, etc. [4] *Ib.* 4.
[5] Adapted from St. Matt. xxvi. 21, 24, etc. [6] *Ib.* 23.
[7] Adapted from St. Matt. xxvi. 48—50, 15.
[8] Based on St. Matt. xxvii. 5.

Judas how he sleepeth not, but hasteneth to betray me to the Jews? [1]

℣. Sleep on now, and take your rest; behold, he is at hand that will betray me. [2] See ye not etc.

8 *Responsory.*

The elders of the people took counsel that they might take Jesus by subtlety, and kill him. They came out as against a thief, with swords and staves. [3]

℣. They imagined wickedness with themselves, and went out. [4] They came out etc.

9 *Responsory.*

O Judas, who hast cast away the counsel of peace and hast covenanted with the Jews for thirty pieces of silver, thou hast sold the blood of the just one, and bestowedst the kiss of peace, which thou hadst not in thy breast. [5]

℣. Thy mouth was full of malice, and thy tongue did set forth deceit. [6] And thou bestowedst etc.

10 *Responsory.*

The heavens shall discover the iniquity of Judas, and the earth shall rise up against him, and his sin shall be manifest in the day of the Lord's anger. With them that said to the Lord God, Depart from us, we desire not the knowledge of thy ways. [7]

℣. He shall be reserved for the day of destruction, and at the day of vengeance he shall be led out. [8] With them that said etc.

When this is finished, a priest of higher rank shall say in a moderately loud voice, without note, a Verse and Collect of the Saint in whose honour the altar is consecrated. The Collect is to terminate with the formula Through Christ etc. *without*

---

[1] Based on St. Matt. xxvi. 40.
[2] *Ib.* 45, 46.
[3] Based on St. Matt. xxvi. 3, 4.
[4] Compare Ps. cxl. 2.
[5] Based on St. Matt. xxvii.
[6] Compare Ps. l. 19.
[7] Job, xxi. 14.
[8] Compare Jude 6.

being preceded or followed by The Lord be with you, *and only* ' Let us pray' *being said before it. In the same way all the altars in the church are to be washed, with the Responsories and Verses as already set forth, beginning with the Responsory* On the mount of Olives etc. *with a Verse and Collect of the Saint, as already laid down. No Responsory is to be begun except in front of an altar, and it is to be sung through there in the way described. The Responsory sung at the last ablution shall always be* Lying men compassed me etc. *If there be more altars in the church than there be Responsories in the preceding group,*[1] *the group shall be recommenced in the same order, provided that the Responsory* Lying men compassed me etc. *be always sung last.*[2]

After the washing of the altars they shall enter the Chapter-house, and the deacon shall read the Gospel, as it was read at Mass.

Gospel.   St. John, xiii. 1—15.

Now before the feast . . . I have done to you.

Then shall follow the Sermon. Which being done, the two priests aforesaid shall rise up, and beginning with those of highest rank shall wash the feet of all, one on one side of the quire, and the other on the other; and lastly they shall wash each others' feet. Meanwhile, the following Anthems with their Psalms shall be sung by the whole quire sitting.

Anthem.

A new commandment I give unto you, that ye love one another, as I have loved you, saith the Lord.[3]

Ps. lxvii.

God be merciful unto us and bless us, etc

---

[1] *historia.*

[2] These Responsories, etc., are printed from the Sarum Gradual as given in the "Sarum Missal," edit. 1861, coll. 309-310. For fuller forms *see* "Sarum Processional," edit. 1882, pp. 60-63.

[3] St. John, xiii. 34.

The whole Psalm is to be said without Glory be to the Father etc., *and the Anthem is to be repeated after each verse. All the Anthems and Psalms which follow are to be repeated in the same way.*

Anthem.

Let us love one another, for love is of God; and he that loveth his brother is born of God, and seeth God.[1]

Ps. cxxxiii.

Behold, how good and joyful a thing it is, etc.

Anthem.

In those days a woman in the city which was a sinner, when she knew that Jesus sat at meat in the house of Simon the leper, brought an alabaster box of ointment, and stood behind at the feet of the Lord Jesus weeping, and began to wash his feet with her tears, and did wipe them with the hairs of her head, and kissed his feet, and anointed them with ointment.[2]

Ps. li.

Have mercy upon me, O God, after thy great goodness, etc.

Anthem.

Mary, therefore, anointed the feet of Jesus, and wiped them with her hair.[3]

Ps. cxix.

Blessed are those that are undefiled in the way etc.

Anthem.

After the Lord rose from supper, he poured water into a basin, and began to wash his disciples' feet. This example left he them.[4]

Ps. xlix.

O hear ye this, all ye people etc.

[1] 1 St. John, iv. 7.   [2] From St. Luke, vii. 37, 38.
[3] *Ib.*   [4] From St. John, xiii. 4, 5.

The following Anthems may be sung, if necessary; otherwise, they may be altogether omitted.

Anthem.

Ye call me Master and Lord, and ye say well, for so I am. If I then, your Lord and Master, have washed your feet, ye ought also to wash one another's feet.[1]

Anthem.

If I, your Lord and Master, have washed your feet, how much more ought ye to wash one another's feet.[2]

Anthem.

Before the feast of the passover, when Jesus knew that his hour was come that he should depart out of this world, supper being ended, he rose, and girded himself with a towel, and poured water into a basin, and began to wash the disciples' feet.[3]

Anthem.

He cometh to Peter. Peter saith unto him, Thou shalt never wash my feet. Jesus answered him, If I wash thee not, thou hast no part with me. Lord, not my feet only, but also my hands and my head.[4]

After the washing of feet, and after a sermon, they shall partake of the loving-cup.[5] And when all has been duly performed, one priest shall say the following prayers thus.

℟. We wait for thy loving-kindness, O God,
℣. In the midst of thy temple.[6]
℟. Thou hast charged,
℣. That we should diligently keep thy commandments.[7]

---

[1] From St. John, xiii. 13, 14. [2] *Ib.*
[3] From *Ib.* 1, 2, 4, 5.   [4] From *Ib.* 6, 8, 9.   [5] *potus charitatis.*
[6] Ps. xlviii. 8.   [7] Ps. cxix. 4.

℟. Behold, how good and joyful a thing it is,

℣. Brethren, to dwell together in unity.[1]

℟. O Lord, hear my prayer ;

℣. And let my crying come unto thee.[2]

℟. The Lord be with you.

℣. And with thy spirit..

Let us pray.

Be present, we beseech thee, O Lord, at the performance of our bounden duty; and because thou didst deign to wash thy disciples' feet, despise not thou the work of thy hands, which thou hast commanded unto us to be retained; but as the outward impurities of our bodies are here washed away, so may the inward sins of us all be cleansed by thee, which do thou thyself deign to grant. Who livest etc.

If there be no clerk present to preach a sermon, all the rest having been first performed, the prayers aforesaid follow the washing of the feet. Then shall the following Gospel be read, without title, by some deacon of the second rank, vested in a surplice; the blessing having been first asked of the Officiant. It should be read after the manner of a Lesson, while the brethren partake of the loving-cup. At the final words Arise, let us go hence, *all present will retire.*[3]

Gospel. St. John, xiii, 16—38 : xiv. 1—31.

Verily, verily, I say unto you . . . let us go hence.

GOOD FRIDAY.[4]

When None has been said, the priest shall go to the altar, vested in his sacerdotal vestments, in a red chasuble, accom-

---

[1] Ps. cxxxiii. 1.   [2] Ps. lxi. 1.

[3] "into the church and there say Compline privately." "Processional," edit. W. G. Henderson, Leeds, 1882, p. 69.

[4] The Latin title is *Feria sexta in die Parasceues,* *i.e.,* the Day of Preparation.

panied by deacon and sub-deacon, and by the other ministers of the altar, all to be vested in albs and amices. Forthwith an acolyte, vested in alb, shall go to the step of the quire, to read the following lesson, without title, thus:

Lesson.   Hosea, vi. 1—6.

Come and let us return . . . burnt offerings.

The quire shall then say the following Tract, alternately.

Tract.

O Lord, I have heard thy speech and was afraid; I considered thy works, and was astonished.

℣. In the midst of two living creatures thou shalt be made known; when the years shall have approached thou shalt be recognised, when the time shall have come thou shalt show thyself.

℣. While my mind shall have been troubled at it, in wrath thou wilt remember mercy.

℣. God came from Lebanon, and the Holy One from the shady and thick mountain.

℣. His glory covered the heavens, and the earth was full of his praise.[1]

Then shall follow the Collect without The Lord be with you *and with* Let us kneel *only.*   Rise.

Collect.

O God, from whom both the traitor Judas received the punishment of his crime, etc.[2]

The sub-deacon shall read the following lesson, without title, at the step of the quire, thus:

Lesson.   Exod. xii. 1—11.

And the Lord spake . . . the Lord's passover.

---

[1] Based on Habakkuk, iii. 2, 3.
[2] As on Maundy Thursday, p. 241.

Then shall the quire say the following Tract, alternately.

Tract.

Deliver me, O Lord, from the evil man; and preserve me from the wicked man.

℣. Who imagine mischief in their hearts; and stir up strife all the day long.

℣. They have sharpened their tongue like a serpent: adder's poison is under their lips.

℣. Keep me, O Lord, from the hands of the ungodly: preserve me from the wicked men,

℣. Who are purposed to overthrow my goings. The proud have laid a snare for me,

℣. And spread a net abroad with cords: yea, and set traps in my way.

℣. I said unto the Lord, Thou art my God: hear the voice of my prayer, O Lord.

℣. O Lord God, thou strength of my health: thou hast covered my head in the day of battle.

℣. Let not the ungodly have his desire, O Lord: let not his mischievous imagination prosper, lest they be too proud.

℣. Let the mischief of their own lips fall upon the head of them: that compass me about.

℣. The righteous also shall give thanks unto thy name, and the just shall continue in thy sight.[1]

The Passion shall follow without The Lord be with you, *and without title, thus:*

Passion. St. John, xviii. and xix. 1—37.

At the words They parted my raiment among them, *two acolytes shall approach, one at the right, the other at the left side of the altar, and shall remove from it two linen cloths, which were placed upon the altar for that purpose.*

[1] Ps. cxl. 1—9, 13.

S

After the words He bowed his head and gave up the ghost, *there shall follow* Our Father, etc., Hail Mary etc., Into thy hands etc.

Gospel. St. John, xix. 38—42.

And after this Joseph . . . nigh at hand.

Solemn Prayers follow. Let us kneel *is said before each of them, except before that in which prayer is made on behalf of the Jews.*

Collect.

Let us pray, most dearly beloved unto us, first of all for the holy Church of God, that our God and Lord would vouchsafe to preserve it in peace throughout the whole world, subjecting to it principalities and powers; and that he would grant unto us, that we leading a quiet and peaceable life may glorify God the Father almighty.

Then shall the priest say, Let us pray, *and the deacon shall then say,* Let us kneel. Rise.

Collect.

Almighty everlasting God, who hast revealed thy glory to all nations in Christ, preserve, we beseech thee, the works of thine own mercy, that thy Church which is spread throughout the whole world may persevere with steadfast faith in the confession of thy name. Through etc.

The quire shall answer Amen, *and all Collects shall be finished in the aforesaid tone.*

Collect.

Let us pray also for our most blessed Pope *N.*, that our God and Lord who hath chosen him into the order of the Episcopate may preserve him in health and safety for his holy Church, to rule the holy people of God.

Let us pray.　　　　Let us kneel.　　　　Rise.

Collect.

Almighty everlasting God, by whose counsel all things are established, mercifully regard our prayers, and of thy goodness preserve the Prelate[1] chosen for us, that the Christian people which is governed by such authority may increase in meritorious faith under so great a Pontiff. Through etc.

Collect.

Let us pray also for all bishops, presbyters,[2] deacons, sub-deacons, acolytes, exorcists, readers, doorkeepers, confessors, virgins, widows, and for all the holy people of God.

Let us pray.   Let us kneel.   Rise.

Collect.

Almighty everlasting God, by whose Spirit the whole body of the Church is governed and sanctified, hearken unto our supplication for all orders of men; that by the gift of thy grace every member of the same may faithfully serve thee.   Through etc.

Collect.

Let us pray for our most Christian King *N.*, that our Lord and God may make all barbarous nations subject to him, for our perpetual peace.

Let us pray.   Let us kneel.   Rise.

Collect.

Almighty everlasting God, in whose hand are the powers of all and the rights of all kingdoms, graciously behold the empire of Christendom, that the nations which trust in their own fierceness may be repressed by the right hand of thy power.   Through etc.

---

[1] *Antistitem.*   [2] *Presbyteris.*

Collect.

Let us pray also for our Catechumens, that our Lord and God may open the ears of their hearts, and the door of his mercy; that, having received the remission of all their sins through the laver of regeneration, they may themselves also be found worthy in Christ Jesus our Lord.

Let us pray.　　Let us kneel.　　Rise.

Collect.

Almighty everlasting God, who continually enrichest thy Church with new offspring, increase the faith and understanding of our Catechumens; that, having been born again in the Font of Baptism, they may be joined to thy adopted children.　Through etc.

Collect.

Let us pray, most dearly beloved unto us, to God the Father almighty, that he would purge the world of all errors, remove diseases, drive away famine, open prisons, loose chains, grant a safe return to travellers, health to the sick, and a haven of safety to such as are at sea.

Let us pray.　　Let us kneel.　　Rise.

Collect.

Almighty everlasting God, the consolation of the sorrowful, the strength of those that travail, let the prayers of such as call upon thee in any manner of tribulation come unto thee; that all may rejoice that thy mercy hath been present with them in all their necessities.　Through etc.

Collect.

Let us pray also for Heretics and Schismatics, that our God and Lord Jesus Christ would deliver them from all errors, and would vouchsafe to recall them to their holy mother, the Catholic and Apostolic Church.

Let us pray.　　Let us kneel.　　Rise.

Collect.

Almighty everlasting God, who savest all men, and wouldest not that any should perish, look on those souls which have been deceived by the fraud of the devil; that, laying aside all malice and heresy, the hearts of the erring may learn wisdom, and return to the unity of thy truth. Through etc.

Collect.

Let us pray also for the perfidious Jews, that our God and Lord would take away the veil from their hearts, that they themselves also may acknowledge Jesus Christ our Lord.

Let us pray, Let us kneel, *and* Rise *are not said here.*

Collect.

Almighty everlasting God, who dost not reject from thy mercy even the perfidious Jews, hear our prayers which we offer unto thee for the blindness of that people, that, acknowledging the light of thy truth which is Christ, they may be brought out of their darkness. Through etc.

Collect.

Let us pray also for Pagans, that almighty God would remove iniquity from their hearts; that, leaving their idols they may be converted to the living and true God, and his only Son, Jesus Christ our God and Lord, with whom and with the Holy Ghost God liveth and reigneth, world without end.

Let us pray.   Let us kneel.   Rise.

Collect.

Almighty everlasting God, who wouldest not the death of sinners, but ever seekest their life, mercifully receive our prayer, and deliver them from the worship of idols, and gather them into thy holy Church, to the praise and glory of thy name. Through etc.

The Collects being ended, the priest shall put off his chasuble, and seat himself in his own seat by the altar, with the deacon and sub-deacon. Meanwhile, two other priests of higher rank, barefoot, and vested in albs, without apparels, solemnly holding aloft between them in their arms the veiled cross, shall take up their position behind the high altar, on the right side, and chant these verses:

O my people, what have I done unto thee, or wherein have I wearied thee? testify against me. Because I brought thee up out of the land of Egypt, thou hast prepared a cross for thy Saviour.

Two deacons of the second rank, in their black copes, standing at the step of the quire, and turning to the altar shall say:

Agyos O Theos, Agyos Iskyros, Agyos Athanatos, Eleyson ymas.[1]

The quire, genuflecting, and kissing the benches thrice at each response, and each time rising again, shall respond:

Holy God, Holy and Strong, Holy and Immortal, have mercy upon us.

Priests. Because I led thee through the wilderness forty years, and I fed thee with manna, and brought thee into a land sufficiently good, thou hast prepared a cross for thy Saviour.

Deacons. Agyos O Theos, etc.

Quire. Holy God, Holy etc.

Priests. What could I have done more unto thee that I have not done? I planted thee indeed, O my vineyard, with fair fruit, and thou art become very bitter unto me; for thou gavest me to drink in my thirst vinegar mingled with gall, and piercedst thy Saviour's side with a spear.

Deacons. Agyos O Theos, etc.

Quire. Holy God, Holy etc.

---

[1] These are Greek words, the translation of which is contained in the following response of the quire. They form the Trisagion.

Then the priests shall uncover the cross by the altar on the right side, and sing this Anthem:

Behold the wood of the cross, on which hung the salvation of the world. O come, let us adore.

The quire genuflecting, and kissing the benches, shall respond with the Anthem:

We adore thy cross, O Lord, and we praise and glorify thy holy resurrection; for, lo, by the cross joy hath come to the whole world.

Ps. lxvii.

God be merciful unto us and bless us; etc.

The whole Psalm is to be said by the whole quire, without Glory be to the Father etc., *and after each verse the anthem shall be repeated in the same way by the whole quire, genuflecting. Meanwhile the cross shall be solemnly placed on the third step of the altar, two priests being seated close to it, one on the right hand, the other on the left.*

Then shall the clerks proceed barefooted to adore the cross, beginning with those of highest rank.

When the psalm, with its anthem, is finished, the following hymn is to be sung by two priests, seated in the meantime close to the cross in the manner above mentioned. The first verse of the hymn is to be repeated after each verse of the hymn by the quire, who are to be in the meantime seated.

Hymn.

Crux Fidelis
Venantius Fortunatus

Faithful cross, above all other
One and only noble tree,
None in foliage, none in blossom,
None in fruit thy peer may be;
Sweetest wood, and sweetest iron,
Sweetest weight is hung on thee.

Faithful cross etc.

Sing, my tongue, the glorious battle;
  Sing the last, the dread affray;
O'er the cross, the Victor's trophy,
  Sound the high triumphal lay,
How, the pains of death enduring,
  Earth's Redeemer won the day.

                    Faithful cross etc.

He, our Maker, deeply grieving
  That the first-made Adam fell,
When he ate the fruit forbidden,
  Whose reward was death and hell,
Marked e'en then this tree, the ruin
  Of the first tree to dispel.

                    Faithful cross etc.

Thus the work for our salvation
  He ordainèd to be done;
To the traitor's art opposing
  Art yet deeper than his own;
Thence the remedy procuring
  Whence the fatal wound begun.

                    Faithful cross etc.

Therefore, when at length the fulness
  Of the appointed time was come,
He was sent, the world's Creator,
  From the Father's heavenly home,
And was found in human fashion,
  Offspring of the Virgin's womb.

                    Faithful cross etc.

Now the thirty years accomplished
  Which on earth he willed to see,
Born for this, he meets his passion,
  Gives himself an offering free;
On the cross the Lamb is lifted,
  There the sacrifice to be.

                    Faithful cross etc.

There the nails and spear he suffers,
    Vinegar, and gall, and reed;
From the sacred body piercèd
    Blood and water both proceed;
Precious flood, which all creation
    From the stain of sin hath freed.

                Faithful cross etc.

Praise and honour to the Father,
    Praise and honour to the Son,
Praise and honour to the Spirit,
    Ever Three and ever One;
One in might, and One in glory,
    While eternal ages run.[1]

                Faithful cross etc.

When the hymn is finished, the cross shall be carried through the midst of the quire by the two priests aforesaid to a spot where it may be adored by the people before some altar; and in the mean time this Anthem following, with its verse, shall be sung in the quire by the whole quire, seated, the precentor beginning it:

Anthem.

Whilst the maker of the world suffered the punishment of death upon the cross, and crying with a loud voice gave up the ghost, lo! the veil of the temple was rent, and the graves were opened, for there was a great earthquake, because the world cried aloud that it could not endure the death of the Son of God.

℣. Therefore, the side of the crucified Lord being pierced by a soldier's spear, there came forth blood and water, for our redemption and salvation.

℣. O admirable price! by the weighing of which the captivity of the world hath been redeemed, the infernal

---

[1] Hymns A. and M., 2nd edit. No. 97. "Sarum Processional," edit. W. G. Henderson, Leeds, 1882, p. 71.

gates of hell have been broken asunder, and the door of
the kingdom [of heaven] hath been opened unto us.

℣. Therefore the side of the crucified etc.[1]

*When the cross has been adored, and the aforesaid Anthem
and its verses are finished, the priests shall carry the cross back
again to the high altar, through the midst of the quire, with
the same reverence with which they carried it forth.*

*Then shall all the clerks come together from the quire to the
altar, and the priest shall again put on the chasuble, which he
had previously put off, and approach to the step of the altar
with deacon and subdeacon, and say the* Confession, Almighty
God have mercy etc., *and the* Absolution *with the Suffrages,
and the Collect,* Take away from us, we beseech thee etc.,
but the kiss of peace is not to be given here.

*Then after the sacrifice has been placed upon the altar in the
accustomed way and censed, together with an infusion of water
and wine in the chalice, after washing his hands, he shall say
with reverence in front of the altar,* In the spirit of humility
etc., *kissing the altar, and blessing the sacrifice. Then he
shall turn himself and say,* Brethren pray etc., *in the accustomed way.*

*Immediately afterwards he shall say in a low voice without
note,* Let us pray. Admonished by saving precepts etc.,
with the Lord's prayer, Our Father etc. *The quire shall
respond,* But deliver us from evil. *Then shall the priest say,*
Deliver us, we beseech thee, O Lord, etc., *and* Graciously
give peace etc. *In this prayer while the words are said,*
Through the same etc., *he shall break the body of the Lord,
as is accustomed to be done on other days. Then shall he say
in a low voice without note,* World without end, *the quire
responding,* Amen.

*Afterwards he shall lower a particle of the host into the
chalice as is usual.*

The peace of God etc. *and* O Lamb of God etc. *are not
said, nor should the pax be given; but the priest should
immediately communicate himself, saying,* The body of our Lord

---

[1] "Sarum Processional," edit. W. G. Henderson, Leeds, 1882, p. 72.

etc., *and at the reception of the body and blood*, The body and blood of our Lord Jesus Christ protect us to everlasting life. Amen. *with no previous prayer.*

Then after washing of hands they shall say vespers, not chanting them, but saying them two by two privately before the altar, thus:

Anthem. I will receive the cup of salvation etc.[1]

Psalm cxvi, 10. I believed, and therefore etc.[2] *and the other Anthems, with their Psalms, as on Maundy Thursday.*

Anthem. And as they were eating etc.[3]

Psalm. My soul doth magnify etc.[4]

Then Our Father etc. *is said standing, together with the Psalm* Have mercy upon me, O God, etc,[5] *at the conclusion of which the priest shall say the Postcommunion audibly, but without note, and without* The Lord be with you *and* Let us pray.

Postcommunion.

We beseech thee, O Lord, to behold this thy family, for which our Lord Jesus Christ was contented to be betrayed into the hands of wicked men, and to suffer death upon the cross. Who now etc.

Thus shall Mass and Vespers be finished together. Neither The Lord be with you *nor* Let us bless the Lord, *nor* Depart, the mass is finished, *are to be said.*

After Vespers are finished the priest shall put off his chasuble, and taking with him one of superior rank,[6] both being in surplices and barefoot, shall replace the cross in the sepulchre, along with the Lord's Body in the pyx, himself alone commencing the Responsory:

I am counted as one of them that go down into the pit: and I have been even as a man that hath no strength, free among the dead.[7]

---

[1] Ps. cxvi. 12.

[2] Ps. cxvi. 10, forming first verse of Ps. cxv. in the Vulgate.

[3] St. Matt. xxvi. 26.　　　[4] St. Luke, i. 46-55.　　　[5] Ps. li.

　　[6] *unum de prœlatis.*　　　　　[7] Ps. lxxxviii. 3, 4.

℣. Thou hast laid me in the lowest pit, in a place of darkness, and in the deep.[1]
I have been even etc.

Both shall genuflect at the beginning, and then rise, and similarly in the next Responsory; the quire taking it up with its verse, and kneeling continuously to the end of the service.

Then when the sepulchre has been censed, and the door shut, the same priest shall begin the Responsory:

The Lord being buried, the sepulchre was sealed: rolling a stone to the door of the sepulchre: setting soldiers to watch it.
Lest peradventure his disciples should come and steal him away, and say unto the people, He is risen from the dead.
Setting soldiers etc.[2]

At each of these three following Anthems the two aforesaid priests shall kneel continuously. Then shall the priest begin the Anthem:

I will lay me down in peace and take my rest: for it is thou, Lord, only that makest me dwell in safety.[3]

Also the following Anthem:
At Salem is his tabernacle, and his dwelling in Sion.[4]

Also the following Anthem:
My flesh also shall rest in hope.[5]

When these Anthems are finished, and prayers have been said at pleasure by all, secretly, with genuflection, all others shall go back, as they please, in no fixed order; but the priest shall put on his chasuble again, and depart in the same order

---

[1] Ps. lxxxviii. 5.   [2] Adapted from S. Matt. xxvii. 60, 64, 66.
[3] Ps. iv. 9, 10.   [4] Ps. lxvi. 2.   [5] Ps. xvi. 10.

with which he went up at the beginning of the service, attended by deacon and subdeacon, and the other ministers of the altar.

From that time one wax candle at least shall burn continually before the sepulchre, until the procession of the Lord's Resurrection on Easter Day, only to be extinguished when the Psalm, Blessed be the Lord God of Israel etc., *and the rest which follows it, is sung on the next night. In the same way it is to be extinguished on the vigil of Easter, when the new fire is blessed, until the Paschal candle, thirty-six feet in height, is lighted.*

Easter Even.[1]

First of all, the blessing of the fire shall be performed, by the officiant, vested in his sacerdotal vestments, with a silk cope, the deacon being vested in a dalmatic, the sub-deacon in a tunicle, and the other ministers of the altar in albs and amices. They are to have neither light, nor candles, nor cross, nor fire in the censer. Also some one of the first rank, vested in a surplice, bearing an extinguished wax taper upon a spear, preceding the procession, walking after the bearer of holy water, shall advance processionally through the midst of the quire for the blessing of the new fire, the members of the quire following him without change of habit. They shall proceed to a pillar on the south side of the church, close to the font, where the officiating priest shall bless the fire which is there to be kindled, in the midst between two columns. On the way thither the Psalm, The Lord is my light and my salvation etc.,[2] *is to be said, without note, and without* Glory be to the Father etc.

The station at the fire is to be arranged thus. The priest is to stand close to the fire, facing eastwards, with the deacon on his left, and the subdeacon on the left of the deacon. One candle-bearer is to stand opposite the priest, and at the right of the candle-bearer, nearer to the priest, shall stand a boy,

[1] The S. title is *Sabbatum Sanctum*, or Holy Saturday.
[2] Ps. xxvii.

holding a book.   Another candle-bearer shall stand behind the priest.   The water-bearer shall stand at the right of the same candle-bearer, closer to the priest; and in the hindmost place of all, on the west, shall stand the bearer of the spear, with the wax taper.   The thurifer shall stand at the south side of the fire, for the purpose of receiving fire in the censer after the blessing thereof; all these ministers facing the priest, while the quire is congregated together on the north side.

Then shall follow the solemn blessing of the fire by the priest thus:

The Lord be with you.

Let us pray.

O Lord our God, Father almighty, unfailing light, maker of all lights, hear us, thy servants, and ble + ss this fire which is consecrated by thy sanctifying benediction; do thou, who lightest every man that cometh into this world, enlighten the consciences of our hearts with the fire of thy love; that we being inflamed by thy fire, and illuminated by thy light, and having the darkness of sin expelled from our hearts, may by thy guiding light be deemed worthy to come to light eternal; and as thou madest fire to shine for thy servant Moses by the pillar of fire advancing through the red sea, so enkindle our light, and let the candle which shall be lit thereat, ever remain blessed in honour of thy majesty; and whosoever shall bear light from it, let him be illuminated by the light of spiritual grace.   Through etc.

All these Collects are said with Let us pray *in the tone of a Lesson.   At this point holy water shall be sprinkled over the fire.   Then shall be said:*

The Lord be with you.

Let us pray.

Collect.

O Lord, holy Father, almighty ever-living God, vouchsafe to ble + ss and sanctify this fire, which we unworthy presume to ble + ss, through the invocation of thy only-begotten Son, our Lord Jesus Christ. Do thou, most merciful Father, hallow it with thy bless + ing, and grant that it may conduce to the profit of the human race. Through etc.

Collect.

Prevent us, O Lord, we beseech thee always, here and everywhere, with thy heavenly light, that we may both discern with clear vision and receive with worthy effect the mystery whereof thou hast willed us to be partakers. Through etc.

Then shall follow the blessing of the incense[1] in this form:

I exorcise thee, most unclean spirit, and every illusion of the enemy, in the name of God the Father-almighty, and in the name of Jesus Christ his Son, and in the power of the Holy Ghost, that thou shouldest depart and withdraw from this creature of frankincense or incense with all thy deceitfulness and guile ; that this creature may be sancti + fied in the name of our Lord Jesus Christ, that all who taste, or touch, or smell it, may receive the virtue and aid of the Holy Ghost, that wheresoever this incense or frankincense shall be, there thou shalt in no wise dare to approach, nor presume to raise opposition ; but whosoever thou art, O thou unclean spirit, thou shalt flee far hence and depart, adjured by the name and power of God the Father almighty, and of his Son, our Lord Jesus Christ, who shall come in the Holy Spirit to judge the quick and the dead, and thee, the false accuser, and the world, by fire. ℟. Amen.

Collect.

We beseech thy everlasting and most righteous loving-kindness, O Lord, holy Father, almighty everlasting God,

---

[1] *Thymiamatis sive incensi.*

that thou wouldest vouchsafe to ble + ss and sancti + fy this species of frankincense or incense, that it may be an incense acceptable to thy divine majesty for a sweet savour; let this species be bless + ed by thee; let it be sancti + fied by the invocation of thy holy name, so that wheresoever the fumes thereof shall reach, every kind of evil spirit may be cast out and put to flight; even as with the incense of the fish's liver, which the archangel Raphael shewed thy servant Tobias, when he went to set Sara free.[1] Through etc.

Collect.

May thy bless + ing, O Lord, descend upon this species of incense or frankincense, as on that of which thy prophet David sang, saying, Let my prayer be set forth in thy sight as the incense[2]; let it be unto us an odour of comfort, sweetness, and grace; that by its fumes every illusion of the enemy, of mind and body, may be put to flight; that we may be, in the words of the apostle Paul, a sweet savour unto God.[3] Before the face of this incense or frankincense let every assault of devils flee away, as dust before the face of the wind, and as smoke before the face of the fire. And grant, most holy Father, that this incense of sweet savour may abide for ever for the aid of thy Church, and for the cause of religion, that by mystic signification the fragrant odour may shew forth to us the sweetness of spiritual virtues. Therefore, we beseech thee, almighty God, by the illimitable right hand of thy majesty, that thou wouldst deign to ble + ss this creature compounded of a mixture of various things, that wherever the smoke of its sweet scent shall spread abroad, it may miraculously prevail, in virtue of thy holy name, to put to flight all phantastic assaults of unclean spirits, and to drive away all diseases, and to restore health, and with most fragrant odour to diffuse its sweet smell before thee for evermore. Through etc.

[1] Tobit, vi. 7.   [2] Ps. cxli. 2.   [3] Eph. v. 2.

After the blessing of the incense a censer shall be filled with coals together with incense, and the new fire shall be censed. Then shall the taper on the spear alone be lit from the new fire, the other lights in the church having been first extinguished. Then the procession shall return to the quire in the accustomed order. While returning, two clerks of the second rank in surplices shall sing this Hymn, Thou leader kind, *etc. The first verse is to be repeated by the quire after each verse. While the aforesaid clerks sing their verse they are to be standing still, while the quire moves on; and while the quire is singing the first verse the clerks are to be moving forward. The same rule is to be observed when* Thou, the holy angels' king *is sung with its verses.*

℣. Thou leader kind, whose word called forth the
    radiant light,
  Who by set bounds dividest night and day,
When the sun set, in gloom rose chaos on our sight:
  Give back, O Christ, Thy light, Thy servants pray.

℣. Although, with countless stars and with the silvery
    tint
  Of lunar lamp, thou dost the heavens dye,
Yet dost thou teach us how, by sudden stroke of flint,
  The rock-born seed of light to vivify.

Quire. Thou leader kind, etc.

℣. Lest man forget the hope for man of heavenly light,
    That in Christ's body lies a hidden thing;
Who willèd to be called the steadfast Rock of might,
  Whence by our little sparks our race should spring.

Quire. Thou leader kind, etc.

℣. So in that room, O Lord, Thou didst thy gifts
    display—
  To wit, the flickering tongues that flame-like fall;
Till then obscur'd and lost, new light brings back the day,
  And vanquished night withdraws her riven pall.

Quire. Thou leader kind, etc.

T

℣. Through whom thy honour, praise, and wisdom all
    divine,
  Majesty, goodness, mercy, shine and blend:
And to maintain thy realm in threefold might combine,
  Knitting time now with time that cannot end.

Quire. Thou leader kind, etc.[1]

*Then shall follow the Blessing of the Paschal Candle by the
deacon, vested as for a procession, facing north, and standing
at the step of the quire,[2] accompanied by two candle-bearers,
one on his right hand, one on his left, both turning towards
him, and holding unlighted candles. The sub-deacon shall
stand opposite to him, and close to the subdeacon the bearer of
the spear, turning towards him in the same way. The thurifer
shall stand behind the deacon, while the deacon chants as
follows:*

Now let the angelic host of heaven exult, let the divine
mysteries be celebrated with exultation, and let the
trumpet of salvation sound for the victory of so great a
King.

Let the earth rejoice, irradiated with so great brilliancy,
and illuminated by the splendour of the eternal King, let
it perceive the darkness of the universe to have been done
away.

Let mother church also be joyful, adorned with the
brilliancy of so great a light, and let this court resound
with the mighty voices of peoples.

Wherefore, most dearly beloved brethren, as ye stand
before the so wonderful brilliance of this holy light, I
beseech you invoke along with me the tender mercy of
almighty God;

That he who hath deigned to enrol me, not for mine own
merits, within the number of the Levites, pouring forth

---

[1] *Inventor rutili dux bone luminis,* etc. The text is given in the
"Sarum Processional," edit. W. G. Henderson, Leeds, 1882, p. 79.

[2] *ad gradum presbyterii, i.e.,* the eastern end of the quire, between the
quire and the altar.

upon me the grace of his light, may cause me to declare fully the praise of this taper.

Through our Lord Jesus Christ his Son, who with him liveth and reigneth God in the unity of the Holy Ghost.

℣. World without end.

℟. Amen.

℣. The Lord be with you.

℟. And with thy spirit.

℣. Lift up your hearts.

℟. We lift them up unto the Lord.

℣. Let us give thanks unto our Lord God.

℟. It is meet and right so to do.

Because it is very meet and right to proclaim with full desire of heart and mind, and through the instrumentality of the voice, the invisible God almighty, the Father, and his only-begotten Son, our Lord Jesus Christ, together with the Holy Ghost.

Who paid for us the debt of Adam to the eternal Father, and blotted out the bond of the old sin by his holy blood.

For this is the Paschal feast, in which that true Lamb is slain, and the door-posts are consecrated by his blood.

This is the night in which thou first madest our fathers, the children of Israel, whom thou leddest up out of Egypt, to pass through the Red Sea dry-shod.

This, therefore, is the night in which he cleared away the shades of sin by the pillar of light.

This is the night which, as at this day, sets apart from the vices of this world and from the darkness of sin, and restores to grace, and unites in sanctity the believers in Christ throughout the whole world.

This is the night in which Christ burst the bonds of death, and rose a conqueror from the grave.

For it had advantaged us nothing to be born except we had the advantage of redemption.

O marvellous condescension of thy loving-kindness concerning us!

O inestimable tenderness of love! thou gavest up thy Son to redeem thy servant.

O truly necessary sin of Adam and of ourselves, which was blotted out by the death of Christ!

O happy guilt, the desert of which was to gain such and so great a Redeemer!

O truly blessed night, to the desert of which alone was granted to know the time and the hour in which Christ rose from the grave!

This is the night of which it was written, And the night is as clear as the day,[1] and, Then shall my night be turned to day.[2]

Therefore, the hallowing of this night putteth wickedness to flight, washeth away sins, and restoreth innocency to the fallen, and joy to the sorrowful; it banisheth hatred, and prepareth peace, and maketh sovereignties to yield.

Therefore, in favour of this night, receive, O holy Father,

Here the deacon shall put incense into the candle or into the candlestick in the form of a cross; and in the same way into the small candle, the bearer thereof approaching with it.

the evening sacrifice of this incense,

Which the holy church offereth to thee by the hands of her ministers in this solemn oblation of wax, the work of the bee.

But now we know the praise of this pillar, which the glowing fire kindleth to the honour of God.

At this point the candle shall be lit from the new fire, and not be extinguished till after Compline on the day following. And the Paschal candle shall burn continuously throughout Easter week at Matins, and at Mass, and at Vespers; and likewise on the Octave of Easter. But on all Sundays from the Octave of Easter until Ascension Day it shall be lit at

---

[1] Ps. cxxxix. 11.   [2] *Ib.* 10.

Mass only, as well as on the feasts of St. Mark the Evangelist, and of SS. Philip and James the Apostles. On the Annunciation of the Blessed Mary, and on the Invention of the Holy Cross it shall be lighted as on the Octave of Easter.

Then shall the candle-bearers light their candles throughout the church.

Which although it be divided into parts of borrowed light, knoweth not loss. It is fed by the liquid wax which the queen bee produced for the composition of this precious taper.[1]

O blessed night, which spoiled the Egyptians, and enriched the Hebrews! Night in which heavenly things are united to earthly.

We beseech thee, O Lord, that this candle, consecrated to the honour of thy name, may last unfailing for dispelling the darkness of this night.

Being accepted for its sweet odour, let it be mingled with the lights above.

May the Morning Star find it burning,

That Morning Star, I say, who knoweth no setting;

He who returned from the grave and shone serene upon mankind.

We, therefore, pray thee, O Lord, that thou wouldest grant unto us thy servants, all the clergy, and the most devout people, together with our father pope *N*, and our king *N*, and also our bishop *N*, that in quietness of time we may keep our paschal joy,

Who ever livest, reignest, rulest, and also art glorified, God alone, alone the most highest, O Jesus Christ, with the Holy Spirit in the glory of God the Father.

When the blessing of the Paschal candle has been finished, the priest who is going to conclude the Office, vested in his chasuble, shall go to the high altar with his ministers, without saying the confession, but only Our Father, *etc. Then having*

---

[1] A longer and a wonderful account of the bee occurs at this point in older pre-Sarum Missals. *See* "Leofric Missal," Oxford, 1883, p. 97.

kissed the altar, he shall proceed, with his ministers, to sit down. The candle on the spear shall depart; but a minister shall bring another candle to the left side of the altar, and shall stand on the step, facing south, until the Seven-fold Litany is finished.

The candle-stick, with the Paschal candle, should be taken away on the Friday after Ascension Day.

Afterwards the lessons shall be read, without titles, by persons of higher rank, on the step of the quire.

First Lesson. Gen. i.—ii. 2.

In the beginning . . . which he had made.

All Collects are said without The Lord *be with you and without* Let us kneel. Rise *is said, but only with* Let us pray.

Collect.

God, who hast wonderfully created man, and hast yet more wonderfully redeemed him, grant unto us, we beseech thee, to resist with strength of mind the allurements of sin, so that we may be found worthy to attain unto joys eternal. Through etc.

Second Lesson. Exod. xiv. 24—xv. 1.

And it came to pass . . . and spake, saying.

All Tracts are said by the quire alternately, except the last Tract, namely, O praise the Lord, all ye heathen, *etc.*

Tract.

I will sing unto the Lord, for he hath triumphed gloriously; the horse and his rider hath he thrown into the sea. The Lord is my strength and my song, and he is become my salvation.[1]

℣. He is my God, and I will prepare him an habitation; my father's God, and I will exalt him.[2]

℣. The Lord is a man of war; the Lord is his name.[3]

---

[1] Exod. xv. 1, 2.   [2] *Ib.* 2.   [3] *Ib.* 3.

Let us pray.

Collect.

God, whose ancient miracles we perceive to cast their beams even on our age; because while thou didst stretch out the right hand of thy power to deliver one people from Egyptian persecution, thou dost turn it to the working out of the salvation of the gentiles through the water of regeneration; grant, we beseech thee, that the fulness of the whole world may become the sons of Abraham, and succeed to the dignity of Israel. Through etc.

Third Lesson. Is. iv.
And in that day . . . and from rain.

Tract.

My well-beloved hath a vineyard in a very fruitful hill.[1]

℣. And he fenced it, and gathered out the stones thereof, and planted it with the choicest vine, and built a tower in the midst of it.[2]

℣. And also made a winepress therein; for the vineyard of the Lord of Hosts is the house of Israel.[3]

Let us pray.

Collect.

God, who in the pages of both testaments hast instructed us in the celebration of the Paschal sacrament, give unto us such a sense of thy mercies, that out of our reception of thy present gifts there may arise a firm expectation of gifts to come. Through etc.

Fourth Lesson. Deut. xxxi. 22-30.
Moses therefore wrote . . . they were ended.

---

[1] Is. v. 1.   [2] *Ib.* 2.   [3] *Ib.* 2, 7.

Tract.

Give ear, O ye heavens, and I will speak; and hear, O earth, the words of my mouth.[1]

℣. My doctrine shall drop as the rain, my speech shall distil as the dew, as the small rain upon the tender herbs,[2]

℣. And as snow upon the hay: because I will publish the name of the Lord.[3]

℣. Ascribe ye greatness unto our God. His work is perfect; for all his ways are judgment.[4]

℣. A God of truth, and without iniquity; just and holy is the Lord.[5]

Collect.

God, who dost ever multiply thy Church by the calling of the gentiles, mercifully grant that those who are washed by thee in the water of baptism may be defended by thy continual protection. Through etc.

This Collect is not followed by a Lesson, but by a Tract.

Tract.

Like as the hart desireth the water-brooks, so longeth my soul after thee, O God.[6]

℣. My soul is athirst for God, yea, even for the living God: when shall I come to appear before the presence of God?[7]

℣. My tears have been my meat day and night; while they daily say unto me, Where is now thy God?[8]

Then shall follow two Collects, united under one Let us pray.[9]

---

[1] Deut. xxxii. 1.　　　[2] *Ib.* 2.　　　[3] *Ib.* 2 (with difference), 3.
[4] *Ib.* 3, 4 (partly).　　　　　　[5] *Ib.* 4.
[6] Ps. xlii. 1.　　　　　[7] *Ib.* 2.　　　　　　[8] *Ib.* 3.
[9] The Rubric adds "sub uno Per Dominum," which we have omitted, as it does not seem to be the case.

Collect.

Grant, we beseech thee, almighty God, that we who keep this Paschal feast may be kindled with heavenly desires, and may thirst after the fount of life, Jesus Christ, thy Son, our Lord. Who liveth etc.

Almighty everlasting God, look graciously upon the devotion of thy people, as they are born again, and as, like the hart, they seek the fountain of waters; and mercifully grant that the thirst of their faith may sanctify their souls and bodies in the mystery of baptism. Through etc.

Then shall follow the Sevenfold Litany,[1] which is said in the midst of the quire by seven boys in surplices; meanwhile, the priest shall put off his chasuble, and put on a red silk cope, still standing before the altar, until the Litany has been sung through.

Litany.

Lord, have mercy upon us.
Christ, have mercy upon us.
Christ, hear us.
Holy Mary, pray for us.
Holy mother of God, pray for us.
Holy Virgin of virgins, pray for us.
Holy Michael, pray for us.
Holy Gabriel, pray for us.
Holy Raphael, pray for us.
All ye holy Angels and Archangels of God, pray for us.
Holy John Baptist, pray for us.
All holy Patriarchs and Prophets, pray for us.
Holy Peter, pray for us.
Holy Andrew, pray for us.
Holy John, pray for us.
Holy James, pray for us.
Holy Philip, pray for us.
Holy Bartholomew, pray for us.

[1] *Septiformis Letania.*

Holy Matthew, pray for us.
All holy apostles and evangelists, pray for us.
Holy Stephen, pray for us.
Holy Linus, pray for us.
Holy Cletus, pray for us.
Holy Laurence, pray for us.
Holy Vincent, pray for us.
Holy Sixtus, pray for us.
Holy Denys, with thy companions, pray for us.
All holy martyrs, pray for us.
Holy Sylvester, pray for us.
Holy Gregory, pray for us.
Holy Hilary, pray for us.
Holy Martin, pray for us.
Holy Remi,[1] pray for us.
Holy Ouen,[2] pray for us.
Holy Augustine, pray for us.
All holy confessors, pray for us.
Holy Mary Magdalene, pray for us.
Holy Felicitas, pray for us.
Holy Perpetua, pray for us.
Holy Agatha, pray for us.
Holy Agnes, pray for us.
Holy Cecilia,[3] pray for us.
Holy Scholastica, pray for us.
All holy virgins, pray for us.
All ye saints, pray for us.

If the bishop be present, he shall stand at his seat, vested in a silk cope, while the above Litany is sung.

When this Litany is finished, the Fivefold[4] Litany shall be forthwith begun, which should be said by five deacons of the second rank, in surplices, in the midst of the quire, and should be finished in the same tone. When the clause, Holy Mary, *etc., is reached, the procession should immediately go to bless*

---

[1] Remigius.   [2] Audoenus.   [3] Cæcilia.
[4] *Quintapartita Letania.*

the fonts in this order. First, an acolyte, carrying the cross,
vested in alb and tunicle; after him, two candle-bearers in
albs and amices; then a thurifer, similarly vested; after him,
two boys in surplices, walking side by side, one carrying a book,
the other, on the right, carrying a candle for blessing the fonts;
then two deacons of the second rank, in albs and amices,
walking side by side, one carrying the oil, the other, on his
right, carrying the chrism; then the sub-deacon in a tunicle;
then the deacon¹ in dalmatic; then the priest in a red silk
cope; the rest of the clerks following without any change of
habit. Proceeding down the south side of the church they shall
come to the font, the aforesaid deacons singing the Litany,
invoking fire out of each order of Saints, walking in the midst
of the clerks of the second rank, after the officiant, thus:

Litany.

Lord, have mercy upon us.
Christ, have mercy upon us.
O Christ, hear us.
Holy Mary, pray for us.
Holy mother of God, pray for us.
Holy Virgin of virgins, pray for us.
Holy Michael, pray for us.
Holy Gabriel, pray for us.
Holy Raphael, pray for us.
All holy Angels and Archangels of God, pray for us.
Holy John Baptist, pray for us.
All holy Patriarchs and Prophets, pray for us.
Holy Paul, pray for us.
Holy James, pray for us.
Holy Thomas, pray for us.
Holy Symon, pray for us.
Holy Thaddæus, pray for us.
All holy apostles and evangelists, pray for us.
Holy Clement, pray for us.
Holy Cornelius, pray for us.

---

¹ *subdiaconus* by error for *diaconus*.

Holy Cyprian, pray for us.
Holy Sebastian, pray for us.
Holy Maurice, with thy companions, pray for us.
All holy martyrs, pray for us.
Holy Benedict, pray for us.
Holy Nicholas, pray for us.
Holy Germanus, pray for us.
Holy Romanus, pray for us.
Holy Aldhelm, pray for us.
Holy Augustine, pray for us.
All holy confessors, pray for us.
Holy Lucy, pray for us.
Holy Petronilla, pray for us.
Holy Katherine, pray for us.
Holy Christina, pray for us.
Holy Bridget, pray for us.
All holy virgins, pray for us.

In these two Litanies, neither Father of heaven, nor Son, Redeemer of the world, nor Holy Ghost, God, nor Holy Trinity, one God, are said.

Pope Gelasius assigns as a reason for these omissions that Christ lay in the grave until the third day.[1]

The station at the font on the west side is to be made in this order until the Litany is sung through. The priest is to stand at the step of the font, on the west. Behind him are to stand five deacons singing the Litany. Then on another step of the font, on the east, will stand the boy carrying the book; then the deacon, then the subdeacon, then the oil and the chrism,

---

[1] This rubric has been abbreviated from the corrupt Latin text, which runs thus :

Item Gelasius Papa ostendit dicens; Quia ipse qui Pater et Filius et Spiritus Sanctus, una persona in Trinitate et tres personæ in Unitate, et in sepulchro se custodiri mittitur, omnino dicit adhuc surrexerat a mortuis qui voluit prophetiam implere, sed jacuit in sepulchro usque ad tertium diem, quod bene istæ predictæ quatuor clausulæ in his Letaniis possent prætermitti.

*then the bearer of the font candle, then the thurifer, then[1] the
oil,[1] then the candle-bearer, then two acolytes carrying the cross,
all alike facing east.*

*The position of the assistant ministers with reference to the
celebrant, who is to face eastward in blessing the font, will be
as follows. The deacon shall stand next to the priest on the
right, the subdeacon on the left. The attendant bearing the
chrism shall stand next the deacon, and the cross-bearer opposite
the priest, but facing him. Next to him in the same way shall
stand two candle-bearers, behind the candle-bearer[2] and the
thurifer. He who carries the candle [for the font] shall stand
between the deacon and the chrism; and the boy who carries
the book, between the sub-deacon and the oil. The bishop, if
he be present, shall stand behind those who sing the Litany,
occupying, as in other processions, the last place.*

Then the officiant at the font shall begin as follows:

℣. The Lord be with you.
℟. And with thy spirit.

Let us pray.

Almighty everlasting God, be present at the mysteries
of thy great goodness, be present at thy sacraments, and
send forth the spirit of adoption, for the re-creation of the
new people, whom the font of baptism brings forth for
thee; that whatsoever is to be done by our humble
ministry may be fulfilled by the effectual working of thy
power.

He shall proceed as follows:

Through our Lord Jesus Christ, thy Son, who liveth and
reigneth with thee in the unity of the Holy Ghost, God,
℣. World without end.
℟. Amen.

[1-1] These words seem to be superfluous. The reading is probably
corrupt.

[2] *ceroferarium*, apparently an error for 'cross-bearer.'

℣. The Lord be with you.

℟. And with thy spirit.

℣. Lift up your hearts.

℟. We lift them up unto the Lord.

℣. Let us give thanks unto our Lord God.

℟. It is meet and right so to do.

It is very meet, right, and our bounden duty,[1] that we should at all times and in all places, give thanks unto thee, O Lord, holy Father, almighty everlasting God, who by thy invisible power dost wonderfully work out the effect of thy sacraments.

And although we be unworthy to perform so great mysteries, yet do not thou leave us desolate of thy gifts of grace, but incline thy merciful ear[2] to our prayers.

O God, whose Spirit moved upon the face of the waters at the very beginning of the world, so that even then nature conceived the power of the sanctification of water:

O God, who by washing away the crimes of a guilty world through water didst signify a kind of regeneration in the downpour of the deluge, so that by the mystery of one and the same element, there should be both an end of vice and a source of virtue:

Look down, we beseech thee, O Lord, upon the face of thy Church, and multiply thy acts of regeneration in her. Thou who by the power of thy grace outpoured dost gladden thy city, and openest the font of baptism for the calling in of the gentiles throughout the whole world, that at the command of thy majesty it may receive the grace of thy Only-begotten of the Holy Spirit:

Here he shall divide the water with his hand in the form of a cross.

May he fertilize this water prepared for the regeneration of man by the secret admixture of his light, that by a holy conception a heavenly offspring may come forth from the spotless womb of the divine font as a new

---

[1] *Vere dignum et justum est, æquum et salutare.*   [2] *aures.*

creature, and may all who differ in sex or age be begotten by parent grace into one and the same infancy. Wherefore, at thy command, O Lord, let every unclean spirit depart far hence, let the whole malice and fraud of the devil stand afar off. Let the intermixture of the power of the enemy have no place here, nor creep in surreptitiously, nor corrupt and poison.

Let this creature be holy and innocent, free from all assault of the adversary, and justified by the departure of all wickedness. Let it be a living + font, a regenerating + water, a purifying + stream; so that all who are to be washed in this laver of salvation may obtain the favour of perfect purification, through the operation in them of the Holy Spirit.

Wherefore, I bless thee, O creature of water, by the living + God, by the true + God, by the holy + God, by the God who in the beginning did divide thee by his word from the dry land, whose Spirit moved upon thee, who made thee to flow out of paradise, and commanded thee to water the whole earth in four rivers:

Here shall the priest cast water with his hand out of the font into the four quarters.

Who, when thou wast bitter in the wilderness, infused sweetness into thee, and made thee meet to drink, and brought thee forth from the rock for the thirsty people.

I ble + ss thee through Jesus Christ, his only Son, our Lord, who in Cana of Galilee by a wonderful miracle through his own power changed thee into wine.

Who did walk upon thee with his feet, and was baptized in thee by John in the river Jordan. Who did bring thee forth out of his side together with blood, and commanded his disciples that believers should be baptized in thee, saying, Go ye, teach all nations, baptizing them in the name of the Father, and of the Son, and of the Holy Ghost. *Here he shall change his tone, as it were, reading.* Do thou, almighty and merciful God, be present with us as we keep these precepts; do thou graciously breathe upon us. *Here he shall breathe upon the font thrice in the form of a cross.* Do thou with thy mouth bless these clear waters, that beside their natural cleansing power over the bodies which may be washed therein, they may also be effectual to the purifying of souls. *Here he shall cause drops from the candle to fall into the font in the form of a cross, and then say:* Let the power of the Holy Ghost descend into this font, and into the fulness thereof, and make the whole substance of this water fruitful in regenerating power. *Here he shall dip the candle into the midst of the font, making the sign of the cross, and then proceed:* Here let the stains of all sins be blotted out; here let nature, formed after thine own image, and reformed to the honour of its author, be cleansed from all the filthiness of the old man, *here the candle shall be taken out of the font with these words:* that every man that approacheth this sacrament of regeneration may be born again into a new infancy of true innocence. Through our Lord Jesus Christ, thy Son. Who liveth and reigneth with thee, in the unity of the Holy Ghost, God for ever and ever. Amen.

At the consecration of the font, no oil or chrism is to be poured in, unless there is someone to be baptized. The blessing of the font being ended, three clerks of the higher rank, vested in silk copes, shall chant this Litany, and the quire shall repeat the first two lines after each verse.

> Thou, the holy angels' king,
> Succour to the whole world bring.

Of the Branch thou virgin mother, thee for us we first
  bid pray,
Thee and those high angel orders, who the Father's hest
  obey.

Quire. Thou, the holy angels' king, etc.

O ye armies apostolick, plead with Christ the royal Lord,
Plead ye suppliant, mighty martyrs, plead ye by your
  blood outpoured.

Quire. Thou, the holy angels' king, etc.

Make entreaty, meek confessors, and ye virgins swell the
 sound,
That for us by God's free mercy, times of pardon may
 abound.

Quire. Thou, the holy angels' king, etc.

All ye holy men and righteous, we with prayers before
 you fall,
That the guilt by your imploring may be purged of one
 and all.

Quire. Thou, the holy angels' king, etc.

Christ, kind shepherd, hear thy people's craving, thou who
 didst create,
Primal germ, in things created leaving power to generate.

Quire. Thou, the holy angels' king, etc.

Holy Spirit, thou co-equal with the Father and the Son,
Make us love thee only ever while unending ages run.

Quire. Thou, the holy angels' king, etc.

When the Litany Thou, the holy angels' king, etc. *is
finished, Mass shall be begun, solemnly, by the precentor, without
rulers of the quire, with* Lord have mercy etc. *in the chant*
O light, source of the highest light, etc.,[1] *without the
verses. Meanwhile, having put on his chasuble, the priest
shall say, at the altar, the Confession,* May almighty God
have mercy, *and the Absolution, with the Suffrages, and the
Collect,* Take away from us, we beseech thee, O Lord,
etc.,[2] *in the usual way, but without the kiss of peace. Then
he shall cense the altar, and afterwards begin,* Glory be to
God on high, etc. *Then shall all take off their black copes,
and genuflect, and all the bells shall be rung together in a clash,
while the quire sings the words,* and in earth peace, etc.
Then shall follow The Lord be with you *and* Let us pray.

[1] Kyrie eleyson, No. 6. [2] Page 23.

U

Collect.[1]

O God, who dost enlighten this most holy night with the glory of the Lord's resurrection, preserve in the children of thy new family the spirit of adoption which thou hast given, that being renewed both in body and mind they may offer unto thee a pure service. Through etc.

The following Epistle is to be read in the pulpit:

Epistle. Col. iii. 1—4.

If ye then be risen . . . in glory.

After the Epistle has been read, two clerks of the second rank, in silk copes, shall sing the Alleluya *in the pulpit. The quire shall repeat after them the* Alleluya, *and the clerks shall sing the verse,*

℣. O give thanks unto the Lord, for he is gracious: because his mercy endureth for ever.[2]

The quire shall end it with the cadence.[3] Then the clerks shall repeat the Alleluya *without a cadence. Then shall follow the Tract, which shall be sung, whole and entire, by two clerks of the second rank, in black copes, at the step of the quire, the quire meanwhile remaining seated.*

Tract.

O praise the Lord, all ye heathen: praise him, all ye nations.

℣. For his merciful kindness is ever more and more towards us: and the truth of the Lord endureth for ever.[4]

Meanwhile the deacon shall proceed with the sub-deacon, through the midst of the quire, after the accustomed manner,

---

[1] The title on the top margin, *In Sabbato sancto,* 'On Holy Saturday,' is now changed to *In Vigilia Paschæ,* 'On the Vigil of Easter.' It was originally a midnight mass, there being no consecration of the Eucharist on Good Friday or Easter Even.

[2] Ps. cxviii. 1.   [3] *neuma.*   [4] Ps. cxvii.

without the cross, to read the Gospel, two candle-bearers preceding him with extinguished lights. And the Gospel shall be read in the pulpit, as on Sundays.

Gospel. St. Matt. xxviii. 1—7.

In the end of the sabbath . . . I have told you.

The Creed is not said, but after the Gospel there follow: The Lord be with you *and* Let us pray. *No Offertory is said.*

Secret.

Receive, we beseech thee, O Lord, the prayers of thy people with the oblation of these sacrifices, that being consecrated in the Paschal mysteries, they may by thy help avail to thy eternal welfare. Through etc.

Preface.

And thee indeed at all seasons, but most chiefly on this night,[1] etc.

[Within the Canon.]

In communion with and celebrating the most holy night, etc. *and* This oblation therefore, etc.

This Preface is said through the whole of Easter week,[2] and on all Sundays up to Ascension Day, when the Mass is of the Resurrection. But the In communion with etc. *and* This oblation therefore, etc. *are only said throughout Easter week, and on the Octave of Easter Day. On this day the* Sanctus *is said solemnly, the priest saying,* The peace of the Lord be with you always, *and the quire responding* And with thy spirit. *The* Agnus Dei *is not said, nor is the* Pax *given; but after an interval festal Vespers shall be begun without rulers of the quire, without ringing of bells, and without* O God, make speed to save us. *One of the higher rank shall commence thus, on behalf of the quire:*

Alleluya.

---

[1] Page 36.
[2] But with 'day' (*die*) substituted for 'night' (*nocte*).

Psalm.

O praise the Lord, all ye heathen: praise him, all ye nations.

For his merciful kindness is ever more and more towards us: and the truth of the Lord endureth for ever.[1]

Glory be to the Father, etc.

As it was in the beginning etc.

Anthem, in full.

Alleluya. Alleluya. Alleluya. Alleluya.

After this, the Anthem to Magnificat shall be begun at once by one of the upper grade next in rank after the celebrant; but it is not to be chanted through by the quire before the Psalm is intoned. Neither the altar nor the quire is to be censed.

Anthem.

In the end of the sabbath, as it began to dawn toward the first day of the week, came Mary Magdalene and the other Mary to see the sepulchre.[2] Alleluya.

Psalm. Magnificat.[3]

After the Anthem has been repeated the priest shall say, The Lord be with you *and* Let us pray.

Collect:

Pour upon us, O Lord, the spirit of thy love, that they whom thou hast satisfied with the Paschal sacrament, may through thy goodness be made to be of one mind. Through etc.

Thus mass and vespers shall be finished together, the deacon saying, Depart, the mass is finished, *with the tone of the* Alleluya.

EASTER DAY.[4]

On Easter Day before mass and the ringing of the bells the clerks shall assemble at the church, and all the lights shall be

---

[1] Ps. cxvii.   [2] St. Matt. xxviii. 1.   [3] St. Luke, i. 46-55.
[4] "Sarum Processional," edit. W. G. Henderson, Leeds, 1882, p. 91.

lit throughout the church. Two clerks of higher rank, with candle-bearers, thurifers, and the clergy around them, shall go to the sepulchre, and after first censing the sepulchre with great veneration, that is to say, with genuflection, they shall speedily and with privacy place the body of the Lord upon the altar. Then they shall take again the cross out of the sepulchre, and some person of superior rank shall begin the anthem, Christ being raised, *etc. Therewith the procession shall advance by the south door of the presbytery through the middle of the quire. The cross which has been raised from the sepulchre is to be reverently borne on their arms by the two priests aforesaid, with thurifers and candle-bearers preceding them, through the north door of the presbytery to an altar on the north-side of the church, those of higher rank advancing first, and the quire not changing their dress. The Lord's body, which has been placed in a pyx on the altar, shall be left in the custody of the sub-treasurer, who shall suspend it in the aforesaid pyx within the tabernacle. Then all the bells shall be rung in a clash, and this anthem shall be sung.*

Anthem.

Christ being raised from the dead dieth no more; death hath no more dominion over him; for in that he liveth, he liveth unto God.[1] Alleluia. Alleluia.

℣. Now let the Jews declare how the soldiers who guarded the sepulchre lost the king when the stone was placed, wherefore they kept not the rock of righteousness; let them either produce him buried, or adore him rising, saying with us, (*the quire shall answer thus*) Alleluia, alleluia.

When the anthem with its verse has been finished by the whole quire, the person of highest rank, at the station, shall turn to the altar, and begin this verse:

℣. The Lord is risen from the grave.
℞. Who hung for us upon the tree.

---

[1] Rom. vi. 9, 10.

Let us pray.

O God, who didst will thy Son to suffer death upon the cross for us, that thou mightest cast out of us the power of the enemy, grant unto us thy servants that we may ever live in the joy of his resurrection.　Through etc.

The Lord be with you *is neither to precede nor follow this collect.*

When the collect is finished all shall genuflect with joy in the same place, and adore the cross, especially those of higher rank, and then they shall return quietly, without procession, to the quire.　After this all the crosses and all the images shall be uncovered throughout the church, and the bells shall be rung for matins, in the usual way.　On this day there shall be no procession to the cross at matins, as on other days.

On Easter Day, and on all Sundays from now until the Feast of Trinity, this anthem shall be sung at the sprinkling of water, namely:

Anthem.

I saw waters issuing out of the temple on the right hand.　Alleluia.

And all those unto whom that water shall come shall live.　And they shall say, Alleluia, Alleluia.

Psalm.

O give thanks unto the Lord, for he is gracious: because his mercy endureth for ever.[1]

I saw water etc.

Glory be to the Father, etc.

And all those etc.

On this day, after sext has been sung, and holy water sprinkled, a procession shall be ordered to the step of the quire, as on Christmas Day, with a water-bearer, three crosses, two candle-bearers, and two thurifers, and sub-deacon and deacon, each carrying a gospel-book; and the procession shall advance

---

[1] Psalm cxviii. 1.

*through the midst of the quire and the church, going round both
the church and the cloisters. First of all, three clerks of higher
rank shall begin the prose in the quire, in the following way:*

Tune 53

Hail, festal day, whose glory never ends,
Now hell is vanquished, Christ to heaven ascends.

*The quire shall repeat these two lines after each verse, the
precentor commencing with* Hail, festal day. *Whenever* Hail,
festal day *is said, the first verse should be sung through by the
clerks aforesaid in the midst of the quire, before the procession
sets forward.*

All nature, with new births of beauty gay,
Acknowledges her Lord's return to-day.
                                    Hail, festal day, etc.

The Crucified is King; creation's prayer
To its Creator rises everywhere.
                                    Hail, festal day, etc.

Let what thou promisedst, fair Power, be done;
The third day shines; arise, O buried One.
                                    Hail, festal day, etc.

It cannot be that Joseph's sepulchre
Should keep the whole world's Ransom, prisoner.
                                    Hail, festal day, etc.

No rock of stone his passage can withstand,
Who gathers all the world within his hand.
                                    Hail, festal day, etc.

Leave to the grave thy grave-clothes; let them fall:
Without thee we have naught, and with thee all.
                                    Hail, festal day, etc.

Bring back the day—thy dying made it night—
That ages in thy face may see the light.
                                    Hail, festal day, etc.

Thy rescued are like sand beside the sea,
And where their Saviour goes, they follow free.

> Hail, festal day, etc.

The law of death has ceased the world to blight,
And darkness quails before the face of light.

> Hail, festal day, etc.[1]

In returning as far as the cross in the church, by the same door by which the procession set forth, this anthem shall be said, the precentor commencing, in this manner:

An angel stood at the sepulchre of the Lord, clad in shining raiment: the women beholding him, filled with exceeding great terror, stood afar off. Then the angel spake, and said unto them, Fear not, I say unto you, for he whom ye seek among the dead now liveth, and the life of mankind hath risen with him. Alleluia.

Three clerks of higher rank, vested in silk copes, standing in the pulpit, and turning to the people, shall say this verse, in the following manner:

℣. Praise him who was crucified in the flesh; and glorify him who was buried on our behalf, and adore him who rose from the dead.

Fear not, etc.

At the entrance to the quire the precentor shall begin the anthem, Christ being raised etc., *and it shall be sung through with its verse, by the whole quire, as above.*[2]

℣. The Lord is risen from the grave.
℟. Who hung for us upon the tree.

Collect.

God, who through thy only-begotten One[3] etc.

---

[1] Hymns A. and M., New edition, No. 144.   [2] Page 289.
[3] See below in the Mass for Easter Day.

At Mass.

At Mass.   *Office.*

When I wake up I am present with thee, alleluya;
thou hast laid thine hand upon me, alleluya; such know-
is too wonderful for me, alleluya, alleluya.[1]

Ps.   O Lord, thou hast searched me out and known me: thou
knowest my down sitting and mine uprising.[2]

Glory be to the Father, etc.

Glory be to God on high, etc.

Collect.

God, who through thine only-begotten One, hast on
this day overcome death, and opened unto us the gate of
everlasting life; as by prevention thou dost put into our
minds good desires, so by thy help bring the same to
good effect.[3]   Through etc.

Epistle.   1 Cor. v. 7, 8.

Purge out therefore . . . sincerity and truth.

Gradual.

This is the day which the Lord hath made: we will rejoice
and be glad in it.[4]

℣.   O give thanks unto the Lord, for he is gracious; because
his mercy endureth for ever.[5]   Alleluya.

℣.   Christ our Passover is sacrificed.[6]

*This Alleluya is said in place of the Gradual on the Octave
of Easter, and on all Sundays from this time up to Ascension
Day, at the Mass of the Resurrection.*

---

[1] Ps. cxxxix. 18, 4, 5.   [2] *Ib.* 1.

[3] We have kept as closely as possible to the Prayer Book translation of
difficult words; but the following better rendering by Mr. James Rhoades
was given in the "Guardian" of April 11th, 1906, p. 620: "May the
holy aspirations, which thou breathest going before us, by thy heavenly
succour be followed and fulfilled."

[4] Ps. cxviii. 24.   [5] *Ib.* 1.   [6] 1 Cor. v. 7.

Sequence.

This day the dawn glows bright above the sun,
Telling how Christ hath fought and glorious victory won.
Jesus hath triumphed o'er the haughty foe
In majesty, and his foul camp laid low.
　　　　Unhappy sin of Eve,
　　　　　　Of which all death do reap:
　　　　　O happy Mary's child,
　　　　　　With whom now feast we keep.
　Blest be the Queen, exalted high,
　Bearing the King who puissantly
　Despoiled hell and reigneth in the sky.
　O King for ever, graciously
　Accept our heralding of thee,
　To thee at God's right hand on high,
　Crying aloud incessantly.
　Death's power in all lands o'erthrown,
　Thou in triumph high art gone
　To joys of heaven which are thine own.
　O vast, O lovely clemency,
　Light-giving boon of Christ on high,
　Breathing on us benignantly.
　Honour to thee and praise,
　Who didst the load upraise
　Which burdened our old days.
　Brightly gleam the courts of God,
　Purchased by the crimson flood
　Of the Lamb's most precious blood.
　By his mighty virtue he
　Cleansèd all our misery,
　Granting gifts benign and free.
　Awestruck, within myself I gaze
　Upon the wonders of these days,
　That before our unworthy eyes
　Such mighty sacraments should rise.
　From the root of David springing,
　Of Judah's tribe the Lion, thou

Hast arisen, glory bringing,
Who didst seem a Lamb but now.
Thou who laidst the earth's foundations,
Seekest now the realms on high,
To eternal generations
Recompensing righteously.
Prince of evil, wicked fiend,
What avails thy impious lie?
In fiery chains thou art confined
By Christ's glorious victory.
Ye peoples! marvel at the tale!
Whoe'er such miracles hath heard?
That death o'er death should so prevail,
Such grace on sinners be conferr'd!
Judea, unbelieving land,
Look forth, and on the Christians gaze.
See how in joyous crowds they stand,
And chant the blest Redeemer's praise!
Wherefore, O Christ, our holy King,
Loose us from guilt, and pardon bring.
Grant that thy chosen bands with thee
May rise in blest felicity,
And of thy grace rewarded be.
The Holy Paraclete's blest comfort, Lord,
We look for, trusting to thy gracious word,
Soon as Ascension's holy day
In solemn joy hath passed away;
When thou, returning to the skies,
O'ershadow'd by a cloud, to endless praise dost rise.

Gospel. St. Mark, xvi. 1—7.

Mary Magdalene and . . . as he said unto you.

Creed.

Offertory.

The earth trembled and was still, when God arose to judgment.[1] Alleluya.

---

[1] From Ps. lxxvi. 8, 9.

Secret.

Receive, we beseech thee, O Lord, the prayers of thy people, together with the offerings of the sacrifice, that being consecrated in these Paschal mysteries, they may, by thy assistance, avail to our eternal healing.   Through etc.

Preface.

And thee indeed at all seasons,[1] etc.

Within the Canon.

In communion with etc. *and* This oblation, therefore, etc.

Communion.

Christ our passover is sacrificed, alleluya : therefore let us keep the feast with the unleavened bread of sincerity and truth,[2] alleluya, alleluya, alleluya.

Postcommunion.

Pour into us, O Lord, the spirit of thy love; that those whom thou hast fed with the Paschal sacrament, may by thy goodness be made of one mind.   Through etc.

MONDAY AFTER EASTER.

At Mass.   *Office.*

The Lord hath brought you into a land flowing with milk and honey, alleluya : and that the law of the Lord may always be in your mouth.[3]   Alleluya, alleluya.

Ps. O give thanks unto the Lord, for he is gracious : because his mercy endureth for ever.[4]

Lord, have mercy. etc.
Glory be to God on high, etc.

[1] Page 36.
[3] From Exod. xiii. 5, 9.
[2] From 1 Cor. v. 7, 8.
[4] Ps. cxviii. 1.

Collect.

O God, who in the Paschal feast hast conferred restoration upon the world, continue, we beseech thee, unto thy people this heavenly gift, that they may both be found worthy to attain unto perfect freedom, and also to advance unto life eternal.   Through etc.

Lesson.   Acts, x. 37—43.

That word I say . . . remission of sins.

Gradual.

This is the day which the Lord hath made: we will rejoice and be glad in it.[1]

℣. Let Israel now confess that he is gracious, and that his mercy endureth for ever.[2]

Alleluya. ℣. Did not our hearts burn within us, while he talked with us by the way, concerning Jesus?[3]

Sequence.

Purge the old leaven out, that we
May welcome with sincerity
　　The resurrection new;
This is our hope's expected hour;
Behold this day of mighty power,
　　By the Law's witness true:
This day hath spoiled th' Egyptian foe,
And let the Hebrew captives go
　　From iron bondage free,
Who, toiling for deliverance, pined
'Midst clay and bricks and straw, confined
　　In cruel slavery.
Now let the praise of God most high,
And voices shouting victory,
　　Break forth in triumph free;
This is the day the Lord hath made,
This day hath all our grief repaid,
　　The day of jubile.

[1] Ps. cxviii. 24.　　　[2] Ib. 2.　　　[3] From St. Luke, xxiv. 32.

The Law foreshadow'd things to come,
Christ, of all promises the sum,
   Doth all things consummate;
The precious blood of Christ outpour'd
Hath wholly quenched the flaming sword,
   Unguarded is the gate.
Jesus, who made us laugh for joy,
By Isaac is foreshown, the boy
   For whom the ram was slain:
Forth from the pit doth Joseph rise,
So, breaking through death's iron ties,
   Jesus comes back again.
Free from the serpent's deadly power,
He Pharaoh's serpents doth devour,
   Like Moses' rod of yore;
To those by fiery serpent's bite
Wounded, the brazen serpent's sight
   Doth life and health restore.
Piercing his jaw with mystic hook,
Leviathan Christ captive took;
   In cockatrice's den
He, the weaned child, puts in his hand,
Forthwith dismayed he quits the land,
   Erst the world's denizen.
To Bethel when Elisha went,
The mocking tribe, by she-bears rent,
   Soon felt the bald-head's wrath;
David escapes in subtilty,
The scape-goat swiftly speeds away,
   The living bird flies forth.
With jaw-bone armed hath Samson slain
A thousand men, and doth not deign
   In his own tribe to wed:
From Gaza's gates he burst the bar,
And bearing posts and doors afar,
   To the hill-top he sped;
So from the portals of the grave
The tribe of Judah's Lion brave,
   On the third day doth rise.

When roared the Father's voice on high,
He to our mother in the sky
   Bare back the precious prize.
The whale doth Jonah fugitive—
Of Jonah true figurative—
After the third day forth alive
   Out of his belly throw:
The clustered grape of Cyprus' vine
Doth swell and bring forth generous wine,
The synagogue's pale blossoms pine,
   The Church doth bloom and grow.
'Twixt death and life the fight is done,
The Lord is risen, the victory won,
Witnesses with th' Anointed One,
   Rise many saints beneath;
Let the new morning's joyous ray
Clear yester-even's tears away,
It is the time of holy-day,
   For life hath vanquished death.
O Jesu! victor, life, we pray,
Jesu, of life the well-trod way,
Whose death hath death abolishèd,
Deign us with faith assured to lead
   Unto the Paschal board.
O living bread! O welling spring!
True fruitful vine! to thee we sing,
Deign us to feed, to cleanse us deign;
From second death and bitter pain
   Deliver us, O Lord.   Amen.

Gospel.   St. Luke, xxiv. 13—35.

And, behold, two . . . breaking of bread.

Creed.

I believe etc.

Offertory.

The angel of the Lord descended from heaven, and said unto the women, Whom seek ye? He is risen, as he said.[1] Alleluya.

Secret.

We beseech thee, O Lord, as we offer this Paschal sacrifice, that what we celebrate with outward act, we may comprehend with inward effect, through him who rose from the dead, our Lord Jesus Christ, thy Son, Who etc.

Communion.

The Lord is risen, and hath appeared unto Peter.[2]

Postcommunion.

We beseech thee, O Lord, that the devout partaking of the Paschal sacrament may have its perfect working in us, and may win our thoughts from earthly affections to the heavenly ordinance. Through etc.

TUESDAY AFTER EASTER.

At Mass. *Office.*

She shall give him the water of wisdom to drink. Alleluya. He shall be stayed upon her, and shall not be moved. Alleluya. She shall exalt him for ever.[3] Alleluya. Alleluya.

Ps. O give thanks unto the Lord, for he is gracious: because his mercy endureth for ever.[4]

Collect.

O God, who dost continually multiply thy church with new offspring, grant unto thy servants that they may hold fast in their lives the sacrament which they have received by faith. Through etc.

---

[1] From St. Matt. xxviii. 2, 5, 6.
[2] St. Luke, xxiv. 34.
[3] Ecclus. xv. 3, 4, 5.
[4] Ps. cxviii. 1.

Lesson. Acts, xiii. 26—33.

Men and brethren . . . Jesus again.

Gradual.

This is the day which the Lord hath made : we will rejoice and be glad in it.[1]

℣. Let them give thanks whom the Lord hath redeemed, and delivered them from the hand of the enemy, and gathered them out of the lands.[2]

Alleluya. Jesus our Lord rose, and stood in the midst of his disciples, and said, Peace be unto you.[3]

Sequence.

Pour forth, chaste band, your holy canticles,
With deep-toned organ-peal accompanied ;
Unto the King who burst the gates of hell,
Our God, repeat your joyful melodies.
When death he had o'ercome, he rose again,
Bearing perpetual joy to all the world.
Lost souls, that haunt Cocytus' dismal brink,
Unwonted brightness wondering descry
As he doth enter, blessed Lord of life.
  The mighty demon multitude,
Smitten with fear and trembling, quake ;
  Deeply they sigh and wail aloud,
And much they marvel, who so bold
  To break the iron prison-bars.
Meanwhile into the courts above,
  Begirt with glittering bands he comes,
And comforts the disciples' fainting hearts.
Let us awe-struck his trophies contemplate,
And with low voice our supplication make,
That we amidst the honour'd virgin band
May celebrate our Easter Festival,
And on the hallow'd Galilæan day
Gaze on the glorious beams of dawning light.

[1] Ps. cxviii. 24. [2] Ps. cvii. 2, 3.
[3] Partly from St. Luke, xxiv. 36.

Gospel.　St. Luke, xxiv. 36—47.

Jesus himself stood . . . among all nations.

Creed.

Offertory.

The Lord thundered out of heaven, and the Highest gave his thunder.　The springs of the waters were seen.[1]　Alleluya.

Secret.

Receive, O Lord, the prayers of thy church, which rejoiceth in the grace of its redemption, that it may be sustained by confidence in these present gifts, and by faith in thy resurrection.　Who livest, etc.

Communion.

If ye be risen with Christ, seek those things which are above, alleluya, where Christ sitteth on the right hand of God.　Set your affection on things above.[2]　Alleluya.

Postcommunion.

We beseech thee, O Lord, that the mysteries of which we have partaken may sanctify us, and enable us duly to observe the Paschal feast.　Through etc.

WEDNESDAY AFTER EASTER.

At Mass.　　　　　　*Office.*

Come ye blessed of my Father, receive the kingdom, alleluya, which is prepared for you from the beginning of the world.[3]　Alleluya, alleluya, alleluya.

Ps.　Sing unto the Lord a new song: for he hath done marvellous things.[4]

Collect.

O God, who makest us glad by the yearly solemnity of the resurrection of our Lord, mercifully grant, that

---

[1] Ps. xviii. 13, 15.　　　　　　[2] Col. iii. 1, 2.
[3] St. Matt. xxv. 34.　　　　　　[4] Ps. xcviii. 1.

through the feasts which we keep in this world, we may
be made worthy to attain unto the joys of the world to
come.   Through etc.

Lesson.   Acts, iii. 12, 13—15, 17—19.
And when Peter . . . blotted out.

Gradual.

This is the day which the Lord hath made: we will rejoice and
be glad in it.[1]
℣. The right hand of the Lord hath the pre-eminence: the
right hand of the Lord bringeth mighty things to pass.[2]
℟ Alleluya.   The Lord arose, and meeting the women, said, All
hail.   Then they came and held him by his feet.[3]

Sequence.

Let all the world with prayer and praise
Their yearly alleluias raise
 Easter to celebrate;
Let infants, by baptismal spell
Washed and made white, renouncing hell,
 With them in concert wait.
Let us adapt our slackened strings,
While modulated cadence rings,
 Attuned to proses fit.
For Christ is the meek victim made,
Who on the cross, our loss to aid,
 Bare vileness infinite.
He, life abiding evermore,
The pains of death all meekly bore,
 And drank the cup of gall;
Sharp words refused not to abide,
Nail-piercèd hands and riven side;
 Unmurmuring suffered all.
He, our sins bearing, after death
Descended into hell beneath
 And spoiled the ancient foe;

---

[1] Ps. cxviii. 24.   [2] *Ib.* 16.
[3] Adapted from St. Matt. xxviii. 9.

Then of the captured arms he bare
Triumphant to the upper air
   He made an open show.
Lo! he, resuming flesh, doth deign
On the third day to rise again,
   Bursting death's prison gate;
Haste we to him, our praise to pay,
By whom shines life's eternal ray,
To heavenly courts the very way;
   On him our blessings wait.

Gospel. St. John, xxi. 1—14.
After these things . . . risen from the dead.

Creed.

Offertory.

The Lord opened the doors of heaven. He rained down manna also upon them for to eat, and gave them food from heaven. So man did eat angel's food.[1] Alleluya.

Secret.

May the sacrifices, O Lord, offered in the Paschal rejoicings obtain for us the gift of thy gracious favour, by which thy church is wonderfully fed and nourished. Through etc.

Communion.

Christ being raised from the dead dieth no more, alleluya. Death hath no more dominion over him,[2] alleluya, alleluya.

Postcommunion.

We beseech thee, O Lord, that the reception of thy adorable sacrament may both cleanse us from the old man, and change us into a new creature. Through etc.

THURSDAY AFTER EASTER.

At Mass.   *Office.*

They magnified with one accord thine hand that fought for them, alleluya: for wisdom opened the mouth of the

[1] Ps. lxxviii. 24-26.   [2] Rom. vi. 9.

dumb, and made the tongues of them that cannot speak eloquent,[1] alleluya, alleluya.

Ps. O give thanks unto the Lord, for he is gracious: because his mercy endureth for ever.[2]

Collect.

O God, who hast united divers nations in the confession of thy name, grant that those who have been born again in the baptismal font may be one both in inward faith and in outward devotion. Through etc.

Lesson. Acts, viii. 26—40.

And the angel . . . to Cæsarea.

Gradual.

This is the day which the Lord hath made: we will rejoice and be glad in it.[3]

℣. The same stone which the builders refused is become the head-stone in the corner. This is the Lord's doing: and it is marvellous in our eyes.[4]

The Gradual is not to be repeated after its verse on this day or on the next.

Alleluya. On the day of my resurrection, saith the Lord, I will go before you into Galilee.[5]

Sequence.

Say, our home revisiting,
From what region dost thou spring,
To the world new joys to bring?
With clear voice and placid eyes,
"Alleluia!" she replies,
"I declare high mysteries;
I have heard an angel cry,
Christ, the Lord of stars on high,
Hath arisen gloriously."

---

[1] Wisdom, x. 20, 21.
[2] Ps. cxviii. 1.
[3] Ps. cxviii. 24.
[4] *Ib.* 22, 23.
[5] Adapted from St. Matt. xxviii. 7.

Forthwith like a bird that flies,
Winging joyous through the skies,
Back she to her fellows hies;
Tells them that the old law's sway
Is made void and passed away,
And new grace doth reign to-day.
Wherefore your loud voice of praise,
Fellow-servants, now upraise,
Christ this day our ransom pays.
God the Father did ordain
That the Son by hands profane
For our safety should be slain.
To the bitter cross and grave
Willingly himself he gave,
Us from death for aye to save.
Wherefore now each troubled breast
May in safety take its rest,
Winning life for ever blest.
Join we now, O friends, to greet
Easter-tide with homage meet:
Peace in Christ is made complete.

Gospel.   St. John, xx. 11—18.
But Mary stood . . . these things unto her.

Offertory.

On the day of your feast, saith the Lord, I will bring you into a land flowing with milk and honey.[1]

Secret.

Graciously accept, we beseech thee, O Lord, the gifts of thy people, that having been renewed by the confession of thy name in baptism, they may obtain everlasting felicity.   Through etc.

Communion.

Ye, his peculiar people, shew forth the praises of him, alleluya, who hath called you out of darkness into his marvellous light.[2] Alleluya.

[1] Partly from Ex. iii. 8.   [2] 1 Pet. ii. 9.

Postcommunion.

Hear our prayers, O Lord, that the reception of the sacred mysteries of our redemption may obtain for us help in this life present, and win for us the joys of the life everlasting. Through etc.

FRIDAY AFTER EASTER.

At Mass. *Office.*

The Lord brought them out safely, alleluya, and over-whelmed their enemies with the sea.[1] Alleluya, alleluya, alleluya.

Ps. Hear my law, O my people: incline your ears unto the words of my mouth.[2]

Collect.

Almighty everlasting God, who hast given unto us the Paschal sacrament in the covenant of the reconciliation of mankind, grant that what we profess in our minds we may practise in our lives. Through etc.

Epistle. 1 St. Peter, iii. 18—22.

For Christ also hath once . . . right hand of God.

Gradual.

This is the day which the Lord hath made: we will rejoice and be glad in it.[3]

℣. Blessed be he that cometh in the name of the Lord. God is the Lord who hath showed us light.[4]

The Gradual is not to be repeated.

Alleluya. ℣. Tell it out among the heathen that the Lord hath reigned from the tree.[5]

Sequence.

Unto the Paschal Victim bring,
Christians, your thankful offering—

[1] Ps. lxxviii. 54.
[2] Ps. lxxviii. 1.
[3] Ps. cxviii. 24.
[4] *Ib.* 26, 27.
[5] Ps. xcvi. 10.

The Lamb redeemed the flock,
So sinners Christ, who knew no guile,
Did to the Father reconcile.
  Meeting in wondrous shock
Lo! death and life in combat strive,
The Lord of life, who died, doth reign alive.
  Declare unto us, Mary, say,
  What thou sawest on the way?
I saw the grave that could not Christ retain;
I saw his glory when he rose again;
I saw the angelic witnesses around;
The napkin and the linen clothes I found.
  Christ our hope hath risen, and he
  Will go before to Galilee.
Believe we Mary's word alone; refuse
To heed the sayings of the lying Jews.
Christ from the dead we know is risen indeed;
Victorious King, have pity in our need.

Gospel.   St. Matt. xxviii. 16—20.

Then the eleven disciples . . . end of the world.

Creed.

Offertory.

This shall be a day to be remembered by you, alleluya, and ye
shall keep it for a solemn feast-day for the Lord in your generations, a day for a statute for ever,[1] alleluya, alleluya, alleluya.

Secret.

We beseech thee, O Lord, graciously receive the
offerings which we present for an atonement for the sins
of those who have been born again, and for the hastening
of thy heavenly succour.   Through etc.

---

[1] Adapted from Levit. xxiii. 21.

Communion.

All power is given unto me in heaven and in earth, alleluya. Go ye, teach all nations, baptizing them in the name of the Father, and of the Son, and of the Holy Ghost,[1] alleluya, alleluya.

Postcommunion.

O God, who by the remission of sins hast begotten the children of thy adoption, grant that all thy faithful may truly apprehend that which they have received in this present sacrament. Through etc.

SATURDAY AFTER EASTER.

Office.

He brought forth his people with joy, alleluya, and his chosen with gladness,[2] alleluya, alleluya.

Ps. O give thanks unto the Lord, and call upon his name: tell the people what things he hath done.[3]

Lord, have mercy.

Collect.

Grant, we beseech thee, almighty God, that we who have celebrated with reverence this Paschal feast, may through it be found worthy to arrive at everlasting joys. Through etc.

Lesson. 1 St. Pet. ii. 1—10.

Wherefore laying aside . . . obtained mercy.

Two boys in surplices in the pulpit shall then say:

Alleluya. ℣. This is the day which the Lord hath made: we will rejoice and be glad in it.[4]

Alleluya *is not to be repeated. The first* Alleluya *is never to be repeated after its verse when there are two* Alleluyas:

---

[1] St. Matt. xxviii. 18, 19.

[2] Ps. cv. 42.   [3] *Ib.* 1.   [4] Ps. cxviii. 24.

but the second Alleluya *is to be repeated after its verse. In the same way when there is only one* Alleluya, *that* Alleluya *is to be repeated. Then two other boys in surplices standing at the step of the quire shall sing the following* Alleluya.

Alleluya. ℣. Praise the Lord, ye servants: O praise the name of the Lord.[1]

To be finished by the quire.

℣. Blessed be the name of the Lord: from this time forth for evermore.[2]

In the same way to be finished by the quire. The Alleluya *shall be repeated without the cadence.*

Sequence.

Upon the week's first dawning gray,
The Son of God that blessed day
   Our hope and glory rose;
The king of evil and his crew
Vanquished, hell's portals open threw,
   And triumphed o'er his foes.
He by his resurrection blest,
Throughout the world with joy confest,
   Doth consolation shed.
Harbinger of his rising then,
Right quickly Mary Magdalen
   With her glad tidings sped.
She to Christ's brethren, grieving sore
That their dear Lord should be no more,
   Did joy long-looked-for bring;
O blessed eyes! which first did see
Set free from death's captivity
   The world's almighty King!
This is indeed that woman wailing
At Jesus' feet, whose grace availing
   Did wash her sins away;

---

[1] Ps. cxiii. 1.   [2] *Ib.* 2.

While silent she doth pray and weep
For Christ her Lord, affection deep
   Her actions all display,
Not ignorant whom she worships there,
Nor yet for what should be her prayer,
   Her guilty soul is healed.
O Mary! mother of devotion!
Star thou art callèd of the ocean
   By merit of thy deed!
Made equal to Christ's mother, when
That name thou didst receive from men,
   Far lower is thy meed;
She, the world's mistress glorified;
The sinner, thou, beatified;
The church doth each one welcome in
Of happiness the origin.
The portal, she, through which the light
Upon our darkness dawnèd bright:
Thou, herald of thy risen Lord,
Mad'st the world glad in full accord.
O Mary Magdalen! we pray,
Hear thou our joyful vows to-day:
To merit grace, before Christ's face,
   This company commend;
That so the fount of mercy great,
Which washed thee in thy lost estate,
May cleanse us too, his servants true,
   And gracious pardon send.

Gospel. St. John, xx. 1—9.

The first day of the week . . . from the dead.

Creed.

Offertory.

Blessed be he that cometh in the name of the Lord: we have wished you good luck, ye that are of the house of the Lord. God is the Lord, who hath shewed us light.[1] Alleluya, alleluya.

[1] Ps. cxviii. 26, 27.

Secret.

Grant, we beseech thee, O Lord, that we may always shew forth our gratitude by these Paschal mysteries; that the work of restoration being continually carried on in us, may be unto us a cause of perpetual gladness. Through etc.

Communion.

As many of you as have been baptized into Christ have put on Christ.[1] Alleluya.

Postcommunion.

We beseech thee, O Lord, that we may be quickened by the gift of our redemption, and that through this help to eternal salvation, a true faith may ever be increased in us. Through etc.

SUNDAY IN THE OCTAVE OF EASTER.

At Mass.[2]   *Office as on Easter Day.*

              Collect as on Easter Day.

              Epistle as on Easter Day.

Gradual.

Alleluya.   Christ our Passover is sacrificed for us.[3]
Alleluya.   The angel of the Lord descended from heaven, and came and rolled back the stone from the door, and sat upon it.[4]

Sequence.

Let us with lowly tone
    The Saviour's praises sing;
Messiah on his heavenly throne
    Devoutly worshipping;
Who deigned in flesh to shade
    His glorious deity;

[1] Gal. iii. 27.   [2] This mass is not in R.
[3] 1 Cor. v. 7.   [4] St. Matt. xxviii. 2.

Himself of no repute he made
  Us lost ones to set free.
He in a manger lies,
  Wrapp'd in his swaddling band,
Grieving o'er their lost Paradise,
  Who brake God's high command.
He was to Simeon's sight
  By Mary's arms conveyed;
And circumcision's holy rite
  Unmurmuringly obeyed.
Cleansing he doth receive
  By legal offering pure,
Who sinners doth himself reprieve
  And of release assure;
Permits his servant's hands
  His Master to baptize,
The glozing tempter's wiles withstands,
  Stones cast in hatred flies;
God-man, most meek, most high,
  Sleeps weary, hath no meat,
Pours forth sad tears in charity,
  Washes his servants' feet.
Yet through these lowly signs
  Of poor humanity,
Brightly by works and doctrine shines
  His present deity.
To grace the nuptial board
  Water he turned to wine,
To blinded eyes he light restored,
  Clad with a light divine.
Touch'd by his finger fled
  The leper's foul disease;
He from corruption raised the dead,
  And gave the palsied, ease.
He with five loaves of bread
  Five thousand satisfied,
On water, as on land, did tread,
  The wild winds pacified.

The stammering tongue he freed,
　　The fevers drove away;
Ears, taught once more the voice to hear,
　　Attest his mighty sway.
When 'midst such wondrous signs
　　His days were gliding by,
He to vile hands himself resigns,
　　Condemned unrighteously.
Upon the cross to die
　　He patiently did brook,
But on his death with darkened eye
　　The sun refused to look.
The day the Lord hath made
　　Scarce on the world had shone,
When he to loving hearts conveyed
　　Tidings of victory won.
His voice first Mary hears,
　　Next, to th' apostles' hearts,
His word the opened scripture clears,
　　And hidden truths imparts.
Therefore with one accord
　　Creation doth rejoice,
And welcome back the risen Lord
　　With gratulating voice.
The flowers, the fruitful fields,
　　With new-born freshness spring,
Touched by new warmth, the keen frost yields,
　　And birds their pæans sing.
O'ercast with sudden shade
　　Of gloom at Jesus' death,
The sun and moon, now glorious made,
　　Illumine all beneath.
Fair earth from hill and dell
　　Doth Christ with joy accost,
Which trembled, threatening ruin fell,
　　When he gave up the ghost.
Exult we on that day
　　When Jesus rose again,

And opened wide the living way
By which our life we gain.
Let stars, earth, heaven, rejoice,
And all the quires on high
Upraise their glorifying voice,
To praise the Trinity.

Gospel as on Easter Day.

Offertory as on Easter Day.

Secret as on Easter Day.

Preface, etc., as on Easter Day.

Communion as on Easter Day.

Postcommunion as on Easter Day.

Sunday Mass for the Week.[1]

At Mass.   *Office.*

As new-born babes, alleluya, as reasonable beings desire
the sincere milk of the word.[2]   Alleluya, alleluya.

Ps. Sing we merrily unto God our strength : make a cheerful
noise unto the God of Jacob.[3]

Neither Glory be to God on high etc. *nor* Depart, the
Mass is finished *are to be said on ferial days throughout the
year when the Mass is of the feria.*[4]

Collect.

Grant, we beseech thee, almighty God, that we who
have fulfilled the Paschal feast, may by thy bounty hold
it fast in our life and actions.   Through etc.

---

[1] =R. Mass for Low Sunday, so called from being a reflection of the
glories of Easter Day. The R. name is *Dominica in albis*, i.e., *in albis
depositis*, it being the last day on which the white dresses of the newly-
baptized were anciently worn.

[2] 1 Pet. ii. 2.   [3] Ps. lxxxi. 1.   [4] A curiously-placed rubric.

On all ferial days in the Paschal season, and on all feasts of three lessons without ruling of the quire, three Collects are said, as has been previously laid down under the first Sunday in Advent.[1]

Epistle.   1 St. John, v. 4—10.

Whatsoever is born . . . witness in himself.

In the place of a Gradual shall be said the following:

Alleluya. ♯. After eight days Jesus came, the doors being shut, and stood in the midst of his disciples, and said, Peace be unto you.[2]

Alleluya. ♯. The angel of the Lord descended from heaven, and came and rolled back the stone, and sat upon it.[3]

Another ♯.

The angel answered, and said unto the women, Whom seek ye? But they said, Jesus of Nazareth.[4]

These two verses are said alternately throughout the week, provided that the verse The angel answered etc. *is said first at a ferial mass. If there should be no vacancy for a ferial mass throughout the week, then the last verse should be omitted altogether in that year.*

And be it noted that throughout the same time two Alleluyas *are said every day at mass, whatsoever the service may be, except on the Vigils of Easter, Ascension, and Pentecost, and except at masses which are said with a procession.*

Gospel.   St. John, xx. 19—31.

The same day . . . through his name.

Offertory.

The angel of the Lord descended from heaven, and said unto the women, Whom seek ye? He is risen, as he said.[5] Alleluya.

---

[1] Page 70.
[3] St. Matt. xxviii. 2.
[5] Adapted from St. Matt. xxviii. 2, 6.

[2] St. John, xx. 26.
[4] Partly from *Ib.* 5.

Secret.

Receive, we beseech thee, O Lord, the gifts of thy glad Church; and as thou hast given her cause for so great joy, grant her also the fruition of everlasting felicity. Through etc.

Communion.

Reach hither thy hand, and behold the place of the nails, alleluya; and be not faithless, but believing,[1] alleluya, alleluya.

Postcommunion.

We beseech thee, O Lord our God, that thou wouldest make those holy mysteries, which thou hast bestowed upon us for the protection of our renewed life, to be unto us a healing remedy, both now and evermore. Through etc.

WEDNESDAY.

Epistle. 1 Cor. xv. 12—23.

Now if Christ . . . in his own order.

Gospel. St. Mark, xvi. 9—13.

Now when Jesus . . . believed they them.

FRIDAY.

Epistle. Heb. xiii. 17—21.

Obey them . . . and ever. Amen.

Gospel. St. Matt. xxviii. 8—15.

And they departed . . . until this day.

It is to be observed that on all feasts with rulers of the quire from the Octave of Easter until Ascension Day, the second Alleluya *shall be one of the following: after which those for Easter week shall be recommenced, viz., those for the third, fourth, and fifth days of the week in order. When these have*

---

[1] Adapted from St. John, xx. 27.

Y

been said, then the following shall be recommenced, being nine in number:

Alleluya. ℣. Abide with us, O Lord, for it is toward evening, and the day is far spent.[1]

Alleluya. ℣. It was fitting that Christ should suffer, and rise from the dead, and thus enter into his glory.[2]

Alleluya. ℣. Christ being raised from the dead dieth no more; death hath no more dominion over him.[3]

Alleluya. ℣. The most high hath risen from the grave, who hung for us upon the tree.[4]

Alleluya. ℣. Christ hath risen, and hath shined on his people, whom he himself hath redeemed with his blood.[4]

Alleluya. ℣. Christ died for our sins, and rose again for our justification.[5]

Alleluya. ℣. Jesus our Lord rose, and stood in the midst of his disciples, and said, Peace be unto you.[6]

Alleluya. ℣. The Lord rose, and meeting the women, said, All hail: then they came and held him by the feet.[7]

Alleluya. ℣. On the day of my resurrection, saith the Lord, I will go before you into Galilee.[8]

If the service of any feast with rulers of the quire be held on this Sunday, or on any following Sunday [in Eastertide] then the second Alleluya at mass will not be that of the Sunday, but one of the nine aforesaid Alleluyas taken in order.

Second Sunday after Easter.

On this day, and on all Sundays up to Ascension Day, if it be not a feast with ruling of the quire, the mass of the Resurrection is to be said, as on Easter Day, with the exception of the Gradual, and of In communion with *etc., and of* This oblation, therefore, *etc., but there is to be no memory of the Sunday at the mass of the Resurrection. The Sequence,* Unto the Paschal Victim bring,[9] *is to be always said. If a feast of any saint with ruling of the quire occur on a Sunday, then*

---

[1] St. Luke. xxiv. 29.   [2] *Ib.* 26.   [3] Rom. vi. 9.
[4] Source unknown.   [5] Rom. iv. 25.   [6] St. Luke, xxiv. 36.
[7] St. Matt. xxviii. 9.   [8] From St. Mark, xvi. 7.   [9] Page 307.

the saint's day mass is to be said, with a memory of the resurrection, but not of the Sunday.

Be it noted, that on all Sundays from Easter Day to Ascension Day, Alleluya. ℣. Christ our Passover *will be said first, and secondly, the* Alleluya *of the Sunday, because it makes more mention of the resurrection, in the last place. Within the period aforesaid, whatever the mass may be, there shall be a memory of the resurrection with the prayer,* O God, who through thy only-begotten Son, etc.,[1] *except on the Invention of the holy Cross. But the Sunday mass is to be said throughout the week with the ferial Preface, and if there be no ferial day throughout the week unoccupied by a festival, then the mass is said on Sunday in chapter.*

Sunday mass for the second week after Easter:

At Mass. . Office.

The earth is full of the goodness of the Lord, alleluya: by the word of the Lord were the heavens made,[2] alleluya, alleluya.

Ps. Rejoice in the Lord, O ye righteous: for it becometh well the just to be thankful.[3]

Collect.

O God, who by the humiliation of thy Son hast raised a prostrate world, grant unto thy faithful people perpetual joy, and cause them whom thou hast rescued from the calamity of everlasting death, to have the fruition of joys eternal. Through etc.

Epistle. 1 St. Pet. ii. 21—25.

Christ also suffered . . . of your souls.

Alleluya. ℣. I am the good shepherd, and know my sheep, and am known of mine.[4]

Alleluya. ℣. The good shepherd hath risen: who hath given his life for his flock.[5]

---

[1] In the Easter-tide mass, among the common memories.
[2] Ps. xxxiii. 5, 6.   [3] *Ib.* 1.
[4] St. John, x. 14.   [5] Partly from *Ib.* 11.

Gospel. St. John, x. 11—16.

I am the good . . . and one shepherd.

Offertory.

O God, thou art my God, early will I seek thee: I will lift up my hands in thy name,[1] alleluya.

Secret.

May this sacred oblation ever win for us a saving blessing, and effectually work in us that which in mystery it sheweth forth. Through etc.

Communion.

I am the good shepherd, alleluya: and I know my sheep, and am known of mine,[2] alleluya, alleluya.

Postcommunion.

Grant, we beseech thee, almighty and merciful God, that we who receive thy quickening grace may ever glory in thy gift. Through etc.

WEDNESDAY.

Epistle. 1 Pet. i. 18—25.

Forasmuch as ye know . . . endureth for ever.

Gospel. St. Luke, xxiv. 1—12.

Upon the first day . . . come to pass.

FRIDAY.

Epistle. Rom. v. 18—21.

As by the offence . . . Christ our Lord.

Gospel. St. Matt. ix. 14—17.

Then came to him . . . both are preserved.

---

[1] Ps. lxiii. 1, 5. [2] St. John, x. 14.

THIRD SUNDAY AFTER EASTER.

At Mass.   *Office.*

O be joyful in the Lord, all ye lands, alleluya; sing praises unto the honour of his name, alleluya: make his praise to be glorious.[1]   Alleluya, alleluya, alleluya.

Ps. Say unto God, O how wonderful art thou in thy works; through the greatness of thy power.[2]

Collect.

O God, who shewest to them that be in error the light of thy truth, to the intent they may return into the way of righteousness, grant unto all them that are admitted into the fellowship of Christ's religion, that they may eschew those things that are contrary to their profession, and follow all such things as are agreeable to the same. Through etc.

Epistle. 1 Pet. ii. 11—19.

Dearly beloved . . . is thankworthy.

Alleluya. ℣. A little while and ye shall not see me, saith the Lord: and again, A little while and ye shall see me, because I go to the Father.[3]

Alleluya. ℣. But I will see you again, and your heart shall rejoice, and your joys no man taketh from you.[4]

Alleluya. ℣. Christ is risen who created all things, and who pitied mankind.[5]

Throughout this week at mass on ferial days, the first of the above Alleluyas, viz., A little while and ye shall not etc. is said in place of a Gradual; and the other two Alleluyas are said alternately on ferial days, and on feasts of three lessons. The same rule is also to be observed in the following week.

Gospel. St. John, xvi. 16—22.

A little while . . . taketh from you.

---

[1] Ps. lxvi. 1.   [2] *Ib.* 2.   [3] St. John, xvi. 16.   [4] *Ib.* xvi. 22.
[5] Source unknown.

Offertory.

Praise the Lord, O my soul; while I live will I praise the Lord : yea, as long as I have any being, I will sing praises unto my God.[1]

Secret.

We beseech thee, O Lord, that through these mysteries it may be granted unto us to bridle earthly desires, and to learn to love things heavenly. Through etc.

Communion.

A little while and ye shall not see me, alleluya; and again, A little while and ye shall see me, because I go to the Father,[2] alleluya, alleluya.

Postcommunion.

Regard thy people, we beseech thee, O Lord, and graciously absolve from the sins of this world, those whom thou hast vouchsafed to renew by eternal mysteries. Through etc.

Wednesday.

Epistle. 1 St. John, ii. 1—8.
These things write I . . . now shineth.

Gospel. St. John, iii. 25—36.
Then there arose . . . abideth on him.

Friday.

Epistle. 1 Thess. v. 5—11.
Ye are all the children . . . edify one another.

Gospel. St. John, xii. 46—50.
I am come a light . . . so I speak.

---

[1] Ps. cxlvi. 1.　　　　　　　[2] St. John, xvi. 16.

FOURTH SUNDAY AFTER EASTER.

At Mass.   *Office.*

O sing unto the Lord a new song, alleluya; for he hath done marvellous things, alleluya; his righteousness hath he openly shewed in the sight of the heathen,[1] alleluya, alleluya.

Ps. With his own right hand, and with his holy arm, hath he gotten himself the victory.[2]

Collect.

O God, who makest the faithful to be of one mind, grant unto thy people that they may love the thing which thou commandest, and desire that which thou dost promise, that so among the sundry and manifold changes of the world our hearts may surely there be fixed where true joys are to be found. Through etc.

Epistle. St. James, i. 17—21.

Every good gift . . . save your souls.

Alleluya. ℣. I go my way to him that sent me: but because I have said these things unto you, sorrow hath filled your heart.[3]

Alleluya. ℣. I tell you the truth: it is expedient for you that I go away.[4]

Alleluya. ℣. The Lord hath risen indeed, and hath appeared unto Peter.[5]

These ℣℣. are to be used in accordance with the directions previously laid down.[6]

Gospel. St. John, xvi. 5—15.

I go my way . . . shew it unto you.

Offertory.

O be joyful in the Lord, all ye lands, be joyful in the Lord, all ye lands: sing praises unto the honour of his name. O come hither and hearken, all ye that fear God, and I will tell you what God hath done for my soul,[7] alleluya.

---

[1] Ps. xcviii. 1-3.   [2] *Ib.* 2.   [3] St. John, xvi. 5.   [4] *Ib.* 7.
[5] St. Luke, xxiv. 34.   [6] Page 317.   [7] Ps. lxvi. 1, 14.

Secret.

O God, who, when thou hadst risen from the dead, after thy passion, didst return again in greater power unto thy disciples, mercifully grant that this Paschal sacrifice may both reconcile us to thy majesty and make us more prompt to obtain thy grace by good works. Who livest etc.

Communion.

When the Comforter is come, even the Spirit of truth, he shall reprove the world of sin, and of righteousness, and of judgment,[1] alleluya, alleluya.

Postcommunion.

Help us, O Lord our God, that through those gifts which we have received with faith, we may both be cleansed from sin and delivered from all dangers. Through etc.

WEDNESDAY.

Epistle.   St. James, ii. 1—13.
My brethren, have not . . . against judgment.

Gospel.   St. John, xvii. 11—15.
Holy Father, keep . . . them from the evil.

FRIDAY.

Epistle.   St. James, ii. 24—26.
Ye see then how . . . is dead also.

Gospel.   St. John, xiii. 33—36.
Little children, yet . . . follow me afterwards.

FIFTH SUNDAY AFTER EASTER.

At Mass.   *Office.*

With a voice of singing declare ye, and let alleluya be heard: utter it even to the end of the earth; the Lord hath redeemed his people,[2] alleluya, alleluya.

---

[1] St. John, xvi. 8.   [2] From Is. xlviii. 20.

Ps.   O be joyful in the Lord, all ye lands : sing praises unto the honour of his name, make his praise to be glorious.[1]

Collect.

O God, from whom all good things do come, grant to us thy humble servants, that by thy inspiration we may think those things that be good, and by thy guiding may perform the same.   Through etc.

Epistle.   St. James, i. 22—27.

Be ye doers . . . unspotted from the world.

Alleluya.   *V.*   Hitherto have ye asked nothing in my name : ask and ye shall receive.[2]

Alleluya.   *V.*   Christ being raised from the dead dieth no more : death hath no more dominion over him.[3]

Gospel.   St. John, xvi. 23—30.

Verily, verily, I say . . . forth from God.

Offertory.

O praise our Lord God, ye people ; and make the voice of his praise to be heard ; who holdeth our soul in life, and suffereth not our feet to slip.   Praised be God, who hath not cast out my prayer, nor turned his mercy from me.[4]   Alleluya.

Secret.

Receive, we beseech thee, O Lord, the prayers of thy faithful people, together with these oblations, that through these duties of pious devotion we may pass to our eternal glory.   Through etc.

Communion.

O sing unto the Lord, alleluya : sing unto the Lord and praise his name ; be telling of his salvation from day to day,[5] alleluya, alleluya.

---

[1] Ps. lxvi. 1.   [2] St. John, xvi. 24.   [3] Rom. vi. 9.
          [4] Ps. lxvi. 7, 8, 18.   [5] Ps. xcvi. 2.

Postcommunion.

Grant to us, Lord, we beseech thee, that being satisfied with the fulness of the heavenly table, we may both desire those things that be right, and also may obtain our desire.   Through etc.

Rogation Monday.

If it be not a feast with ruling of the quire, the mass for the fifth Sunday after Easter is to be said, after sext, as high mass; and the following mass is said in procession.

Office.

So shall he hear my voice out of his holy temple, alleluya; and my complaint shall come before him; it shall enter even into his ears,[1] alleluya, alleluya.

Ps. I will love thee, O Lord my strength; the Lord is my stony rock, and my defence, my Saviour.[2]

Collect.

Grant, we beseech thee, almighty God, that we who in our affliction put our trust in thy goodness, may ever be defended against adversity by thy protection.   Through etc.

The second Collect shall be that of the patron saint of the church, the third Collect that of All Saints.

Epistle.   St. James, v. 16—20.

Confess your faults . . . multitude of sins.

Alleluya.   ℣. O give thanks unto the Lord, for he is gracious; because his mercy endureth for ever.[3]

Gospel.   St. Luke, xi. 5—13.

Which of you . . . them that ask him.

---

[1] Ps. xviii. 6.   [2] *Ib.* 1.   [3] Ps. cxviii. 1.

Offertory.

I will give great thanks unto the Lord with my mouth, and praise him among the multitude; for he shall stand at the right hand of the poor, to save his soul from unrighteous judges,[1] alleluya.

Here there shall be a sermon to the people, if it be desired.

Secret.

May these gifts, O Lord, we beseech thee, both loose the bonds of our wickedness, and win for us the gift of thy mercy. Through etc.

Communion.

Ask and ye shall receive; seek and ye shall find; knock and it shall be opened unto you. For every one that asketh receiveth, and he that seeketh findeth, and to him that knocketh it shall be opened,[2] alleluya.

Postcommunion.

Further our prayers, we beseech thee, O Lord, with thy gracious favour; that we who have received thy gifts in time of trouble, may by reason of our comfort grow in love to thee. Through etc.

ROGATION TUESDAY.

High mass of St. Mary is to be said unless some feast with ruling of the quire occur on the same day; and the mass, I am the salvation etc.,[3] is to be said in procession, where a station takes place. Only one Alleluya is said at this mass. On the vigil of the Ascension the mass 'of Peace'[4] is said in procession; nevertheless, if a feast of some saint with ruling of the quire occur on Rogation Monday, then the Sunday mass is to be said on the Tuesday, or on the vigil of the Ascension, in procession, where the station takes place. In the same way when a feast with ruling of the quire occurs on the vigil of the

---

[1] Ps. cix. 29, 30.
[2] St. Luke, xi. 9, 10.
[3] Votive mass for Tuesdays.
[4] Among the votive masses.

Ascension, then the mass of the vigil is said in procession, where the station takes place. On these three days, high mass is always said in quire after sext, and after this mass None is said at once; and then the procession shall start forth.

VIGIL OF THE ASCENSION.

At Mass.   *Office.*

O clap your hands together, all ye people: O sing unto God with the voice of melody,[1] alleluya, alleluya.

Ps. He shall subdue the people under us; and the nations under our feet.[2]

Collect.

Grant, we beseech thee, almighty Father, that our minds may ever be intent upon that place whither thy only-begotten Son, our Lord, the glorious author of the approaching festival, hath entered in before; and that we may in our conversation attain to that to which by our faith we reach forward. Through etc.

Memories of St. Mary and of All Saints.

Lesson. Acts, iv. 32—35.

And the multitude . . . as he had need.

Alleluya. ℣. O clap your hands together, all ye people: O sing unto God with the voice of melody.[3]

Gospel. St. John, xvii. 1—11.

Offertory.

Ye men of Galilee, why stand ye gazing up into heaven? This same Jesus, which is taken up from you into heaven, shall so come in like manner as ye have seen him go into heaven,[4] alleluya.

Secret.

We humbly present, O Lord, this sacrifice in honour of the adorable ascension of thy Son, for which we are

---

[1] Ps. xlvii. 1.   [2] *Ib.* 3.   [3] *Ib.* 1.   [4] Acts, i. 11.

preparing ; grant, we beseech thee, that by means of this
most holy communion, we may rise through him and
with him into heavenly places. Who liveth etc.

Ferial Preface.

Communion.

Father, while I was with them, I kept them whom thou gavest
me; alleluya. But now I come to thee. I pray not that thou
shouldest take them out of the world, but that thou shouldest keep
them from the evil;[1] alleluya, alleluya.

Postcommunion.

Grant, we beseech thee, O Lord, that through this
sacrament which we have received, our devout affections
may thither ascend where Jesus Christ, our Lord, is with
thee in the substance of our nature. Who liveth etc.

ASCENSION DAY.[2]

At Mass.   *Office.*

Ye men of Galilee, why stand ye gazing up into
heaven? alleluya. He shall so come in like manner as
ye have seen him go into heaven,[3] alleluya, alleluya,
alleluya.

Ps. And while they looked steadfastly toward heaven, as he
went up, behold, two men stood by them in white apparel, which
also said:[4]

> Lord have mercy etc.

> Glory be to God on high etc.

Collect.

Grant, we beseech thee, almighty God, that like as we
do believe thy only-begotten Son, our redeemer, to have
ascended unto the heavens, so we may also in mind dwell
in heavenly places. Through etc.

---

[1] St. John, xvii. 12, 13, 15.   [2] *In die Ascensionis Domini.*
[3] Acts, i. 11.   [4] *Ib.* i. 10, 11.

Lesson. Acts, i. 1—11.

The former treatise . . . go into heaven.

Alleluya. *V.* God is gone up with a merry noise; and the Lord with the sound of the trump.[1]

On this day, and on the octave, even if a double feast occur thereon, is said:

Alleluya. Christ, when he ascended up on high, led captivity captive, and received gifts for men.[2]

Daily throughout the octave, except on Sunday and on the octave, whether the service be of the Ascension or of any feast with ruling of the quire, with the exception of the feasts of Philip and James, and of the Invention of the Holy Cross, the second Alleluya *and V. will be:*

Alleluya. *V.* The Lord in the holy place of Sinai, when he ascended up on high, led captivity captive.[3]

Sequence.

The almighty King, victorious, on this day,
Having redeemed the world with puissant might,
Ascended to the skies from whence he came.
After his resurrection he confirmed
The apostles' hearts for forty holy days,
Leaving his pledge of love, the kiss of peace,
And gave them power of remitting sins,
And sent them to baptize in all the world,
In grace of Father, Son, and Holy Ghost;
Commanding, as he sat with them at meat,
They should not from Jerusalem depart,
But wait for gifts which had been promisèd.
"After not many days, the Paraclete,
The Spirit, I will send to you on earth;
Ye shall bear witness to me in Judæa,
And in Jerusalem, or in Samaria."

---

[1] Ps. xlvii. 5.   [2] Eph. iv. 8.   [3] Ps. lxviii. 17, 18.

And when he had said this, it came to pass
While they beheld, lo! he was taken up,
And a bright cloud out of their sight received him,
As towards heaven steadfastly they looked.
And lo! two men, in white apparel clad,
Stood by them, saying, "Wherefore gaze ye so
Into the height of heaven? for this Jesus,
Who now from you to God's right hand is taken,
Shall so come, in like manner as he goeth,
The intrusted talents' usury to require."

God of heaven, of earth, of sea!
Thou dost man—thy creature erst—
Whom by fraud and subtilty
Satan drave, like him accurst,
Out of Eden's garden fair
Down to regions of despair:
Whom thou didst redeem again
By thy blood and bitter pain—
Bear to paradise once more,
Whence by sin he fell of yore.
Lord, when thou as judge shalt come,
All the universe to doom,
Grant us, we devoutly pray,
Thy beatitude for aye,
In that land of saints, where we
May alleluias sing to thee.

Gospel.   St. Mark, xvi. 14—20.

Afterwards he appeared . . . signs following.

Creed.

Offertory.

God is gone up with a merry noise; and the Lord with the
sound of the trump,[1] alleluya.

---

[1] Ps. xlvii. 5.

Secret.

Receive, O Lord, the gifts which we offer for the glorious ascension of thy Son ; and mercifully grant that we may be delivered from present dangers and may attain unto eternal life. Through etc.

Preface.

Who, after his resurrection etc.[1]

In communion with etc.[1]

These are said throughout the whole Octave, and even on Sunday, when the mass is of the Ascension.

Communion.

Sing unto the Lord, who sitteth in the heavens over all from the beginning.[2]

Postcommunion.

Grant to us, we beseech thee, almighty and merciful God, that what we perceive to have been received in visible mysteries we may obtain in their invisible efficacy. Through etc.

This same mass is said throughout the whole Octave, except when a feast with ruling of the quire occurs, and except on Sunday, but without either Sequence or Creed.

SUNDAY AFTER ASCENSION DAY.[3]

At Mass.   *Office.*

Hearken unto my voice, O Lord, when I cry unto thee, alleluya. My heart hath talked of thee. I have sought thy face. Thy face, Lord, will I seek. O hide not thou thy face from me,[4] alleluya, alleluya.

Ps. The Lord is my light and my salvation : whom then shall I fear ?[5]

---

[1] Page 37.   [2] Ps. lxviii. 32, 33.   [3] *Dominica infra Octavas Ascensionis.*
[4] Ps. xxvii. 8, 9, 10.   [5] *Ib.* 1.

Lord, have mercy etc. *is then said, from the fourth day within the Octave, with ruling of the quire, although some feast with ruling of the quire shall have been celebrated on the Friday or Saturday preceding.*

Collect.

Almighty everlasting God, make us ever both to entertain a devout will towards thee, and to serve thy majesty with sincere hearts. Through etc.

Memory of the Ascension.

Epistle. 1 St. Peter, iv. 7—11.

Be ye therefore sober . . . through Jesus Christ.

Alleluya. ℣. God reigneth over the heathen; God sitteth upon his holy seat.[1]

Alleluya. ℣. I will not leave you comfortless: I go away and come again unto you, and your heart shall rejoice.[2]

No Sequence is said.

Gospel. St. John, xv. 26—xvi. 4.

When the Comforter . . . told you of them.

Offertory.

Praise the Lord, O my soul; while I live will I praise the Lord: yea, as long as I have any being, I will sing praises unto my God,[3] alleluya.

Secret.

Grant, we beseech thee, almighty God, that we may acceptably offer this sacrifice, to become the body and blood of him, whom sitting at the right hand of thy power we assuredly believe to be interceding for us, our Lord Jesus Christ, thy Son. Who with thee etc.

---

[1] Ps. xlvii. 8.   [2] St. John, xiv. 18; xvi. 22.   [3] Ps. cxlvi. 1.

Communion.

Father, when I was with them I kept those that thou gavest me, alleluya. But now I come to thee. I pray not that thou wouldest take them out of the world, but that thou wouldest keep them from the evil,[1] alleluya, alleluya.

Postcommunion.

Grant, we beseech thee, almighty God, that through this most holy communion we may confidently believe that to be accomplished in the body of the whole Church, which has already been accomplished in her head. Through etc.

If any feast with ruling of the quire occur on this sunday, the whole service shall be of the feast, and the sunday mass shall be said in chapter with the chant for Kyrie eleyson, Gloria in excelsis, Sanctus, *and* Agnus, *as on a feast of three lessons without ruling of the quire, with one* Alleluya. ℣. God reigneth etc. *The second* Alleluya. ℣. I will not leave you etc. *will then be used at the mass of the feast, except on the feast of the holy cross. The second* Alleluya *will also be used on the morrow of the Octave of the Ascension, although the full service of St. Mary be taking place.*

On the Octave of Ascension Day, everything shall be done at mass as on Ascension Day, after the manner of a simple feast, with the exception of the Sequence and the Creed.

On Friday, the whole service shall be of St. Mary, if no feast with ruling of the quire occur.

VIGIL OF PENTECOST.

The priest shall go to the altar, with deacon and sub-deacon, and the other ministers of the altar, solemnly apparelled, as on Easter Even, without the confession being said, but only Our Father etc. ; *and then the lessons following shall be read by persons of higher rank, vested in surplices, at the step of the quire, without titles.*

[1] St. John, xvii. 12, 13, 15.

First Lesson. Gen. xxii. 1—19.

God did tempt . . . at Beer-sheba.

Then shall follow a Collect without The Lord be with you *and only with* Let us pray.

Collect.

God, who by the works of thy servant Abraham hast given examples of obedience unto mankind, grant to us both to break down the depravity of our wills, and to fulfil thy righteous precepts in all things. Through etc.

Second Lesson. Deut. xxxi. 22—30.

Moses therefore wrote . . . they were ended.[1]

All Tracts, except the last, are to be sung by the quire alternately; and all Collects, except the last, are to be said without The Lord be with you, *and only with* Let us pray.

Collect.

O God, who art the glory of the faithful, and the life of the just, who by thy servant Moses hast instructed us also in the measure of sacred song; grant the gift of thy mercy to all nations, by bestowing happiness and removing terror far away; that warnings of punishment may become the instruments of eternal happiness. Through etc.

Third Lesson. Is. iv.

And in that day . . . and from rain.[2]

Tract.

My well-beloved hath a vineyard,[2] etc.

Collect.

O God, who instructedst us in the pages of both testaments for the celebration of the present festival, give us

---

[1] This was the fourth Lesson on Easter Even; p. 275.
[2] As on Easter Even; p. 275.

such a sense of thy mercies, that from our experience of present gifts our hope of future gifts may be confirmed. Through etc.

Fourth Lesson. Baruch, iii. 9—37.
Hear, Israel . . . conversed with men.

Collect.

O God, who by the mouth of thy prophets hast taught us to forsake the things of this world, and to press towards things eternal; grant unto thy servants that by thy heavenly inspiration we may be able to fulfil that which we know thee to have commanded. Through etc.

Tract.

Like as the hart desireth the water-brooks: so longeth my soul after thee, O God.[1]

℣. My soul is athirst for God, yea, even for the living God: when shall I come to appear before the presence of God?

℣. My tears have been my meat day and night; while they daily say unto me, Where is now thy God?[2]

Then the two Collects following are said, under one ending, and under one Let us pray.

Collect.

Grant, we beseech thee, almighty God, that we who celebrate the feast of the gift of the Holy Spirit, being kindled with heavenly desires, may thirst for the fountain of life, our Lord Jesus Christ, thy Son.

Another Collect.

Almighty everlasting God, who hast willed the Paschal sacrament to be contained in the mystery of fifty days,[3]

---

[1] As on Easter Even; p. 276.   [2] Ps. xlii. 1-3.
[3] *qui Paschale sacramentum quinquaginta dierum voluisti mysterio contineri.* This phrase seems to suggest that Easter-tide extended up to Whitsunday (inclusive). Quinquagesima was sometimes used as a name for Easter-tide.

grant, we beseech thee, that the nations scattered abroad by the confusion of tongues may by thy heavenly gift be gathered together into one confession of thy name. Through etc.

Then shall follow the Litanies and the benediction of the font, as on Easter Even, that is to say, in the same manner and order both in going, and in returning, and in the station. In returning Thou the holy angels' king etc.[1] *is said. Afterwards mass is begun with* Kyrie eleyson, *while in the meantime the priest is to say the confession etc. in the usual way. Then shall follow* Gloria in excelsis. *Then all shall put off their black copes, and genuflect, and all the bells shall be rung. Then shall be said :*

The Lord be with you.

Collect.

Grant, we beseech thee, almighty God, that the rays of thy brightness may shine forth upon us, and that the light of thy light may by the illumination of the Holy Spirit strengthen the hearts of those who have been born again through thy grace. Through etc.

Lesson. Acts, xix. 1—8.

And it came to pass . . . kingdom of God.

After the Epistle has been read, two clerks of the second rank, vested in silk copes, shall chant this Alleluya *in the pulpit, the quire taking it up.*

Clerks. ℣. O give thanks unto the Lord, for he is gracious : because his mercy endureth for ever.[2]

The quire shall finish with the cadence. Then the clerks shall recommence the Alleluya *without the cadence. Then shall follow the Tract, which is to be sung, whole and entire, by two clerks of the second rank in black copes, at the step of the quire, the quire meanwhile remaining seated.*

---

[1] Page 284.   [2] Ps. cxviii. 1.

Tract.

O praise the Lord all ye heathen : praise him all ye nations.

℣. For his merciful kindness is ever more and more towards us : and the truth of the Lord endureth for ever.[1]

Meanwhile the deacon shall proceed with the sub-deacon through the midst of the quire, after the accustomed manner, without the cross, to read the Gospel, two candle-bearers preceding him with extinguished lights. And the Gospel shall be read in the pulpit as on Sundays.

Gospel. St. John, xiv. 15—21.
If ye love me . . . myself to him.

The Creed is not said.

Offertory.

When thou lettest thy breath go forth they shall be made, and thou shalt renew the face of the earth : the glorious majesty of the Lord shall endure for ever.[2]   Alleluya.

Secret.

We beseech thee, O Lord, mercifully to give heed to the offerings of thy people ; and that they may be rendered acceptable unto thee, may the saving advent of the Holy Spirit purge our consciences.   Through etc.

The Ferial Preface.   On this day the Sanctus and Agnus are said solemnly.

Communion.

In the last day of the feast Jesus stood, and cried, saying, He that believeth in me, as the scripture hath said, out of his belly shall flow rivers of living water.   But this spake he of the Spirit, which they that believe on him should receive,[3] alleluya, alleluya.

---

[1] Ps. cxvii., as on Easter Even, p. 286.
[2] Ps. civ. 30.   [3] St. John, vii. 37, 38, 39.

Postcommunion.

Grant, we beseech thee, almighty God, that the Holy Spirit may come, and clearly make manifest to us the majesty of thy Son. Through etc.

WHITSUNDAY.[1]

At Mass.   *Office.*

The Spirit of the Lord filleth the world, alleluya: and that which containeth all things hath knowledge of the voice,[2] alleluya, alleluya, alleluya.

Ps. Let God arise, and let his enemies be scattered: let them also that hate him flee before him.[3]

Collect.

God, who as at this time didst teach the hearts of thy faithful people by the sending to them the light of thy Holy Spirit, grant us by the same Spirit to have a right judgment in all things, and evermore to rejoice in his comfort. Through etc.

Lesson.   Acts, ii. 1—11

When the day of Pentecost . . . works of God.

Alleluya. ℣. When thou lettest thy breath go forth they shall be made: and thou shalt renew the face of the earth.[4]

Alleluya. ℣. The Holy Spirit proceeding from the throne illuminated the hearts of the apostles this day with invisible power.[5]

Sequence.

Now may the Holy Spirit's grace
Make us his own abiding place,
Our inmost souls to dispossess
Of spiritual wickedness.
Most gracious Spirit, light of all,
Our minds from darkness disenthral:

---

[1] *In die sancto Pentecostes.*   [2] Wisdom, i. 7.
[3] Ps. lxviii. 1.   [4] Ps. civ. 30.   [5] Source unknown.

O thou, who holy thoughts dost love,
Pour down thine unction from above.
Thou who all ill dost purify,
From blindness purge our inner eye,
To see the Father on his throne
On whom pure hearts shall gaze alone.
To speak of Christ thou didst inspire
The seers with prophetic fire;
Didst teach apostles without fear
Christ's banner through the world to rear.
When God did by his word create
Heaven, earth, and sky, that fabric great,
Thou, brooding o'er the waters' face,
Didst shed abroad thy mystic grace.
Thou quickenest with fostering breath
Water to ransom souls from death;
Thou dost revive the hearts of men
With spiritual life again.
The world by variance rent, O Lord,
Thou hast to unity restored;
Idolaters thou dost recall,
Best Master, to the God of all.
Thou, Holy Spirit, graciously
Hear us who lift our prayer to thee,
Without whom prayers are all in vain,
Nor can the ear of God attain;
Thou, who enfold'st in thy embrace
The saints of every age and race,
And dost their energies inflame
By virtue of thy holy name;
A gift unwonted pouring out
On the apostles' band devout,
Throughout all ages yet unknown,
Hast made this day of high renown.

Gospel.   St. John, xiv. 23—31.

If a man love me . . . so I do.

Creed.

Offertory.

Stablish the thing, O God, that thou hast wrought in us. For thy temple's sake at Jerusalem, so shall kings bring presents unto thee,[1] alleluya.

Secret.

Sanctify, we beseech thee, O Lord, the gifts we offer, and cleanse our hearts by the light of thy Holy Spirit. Through etc.

Preface.

Who, ascending above,[2] etc.

This Preface is to be said daily throughout this week, and in all masses of the Holy Ghost throughout the year, except that the words 'as on this day,' *which occur in the Preface, are not to be used outside this week. The* In communion with *etc. and* This oblation, therefore, *etc. are said only up to Trinity Sunday.*

Communion.

Suddenly there came a sound from heaven, as of a rushing mighty wind, where they were sitting, alleluya: and they were all filled with the Holy Ghost, and spake of the wonderful works of God,[3] alleluya, alleluya.

Postcommunion.

May the outpouring of the Holy Spirit cleanse our hearts, O Lord, and render them fruitful by the inward dew of his grace. Through etc.

MONDAY IN WHITSUN WEEK.

At Mass. *Office.*

He should have fed them with the finest wheat flour, alleluya: and with honey out of the stony rock should I have satisfied thee,[4] alleluya, alleluya, alleluya.

[1] Ps. lxviii. 28, 29.
[2] Page 37.
[3] Mainly from Acts, ii. 2, 4, 11.
[4] Ps. lxxxi. 17.

Ps. Sing we merrily unto God our strength : make a cheerful noise unto the God of Jacob.[1]

Collect.

O God, who didst give the Holy Ghost unto thine apostles, grant unto thy people an effectual answer to their devout petition, that they to whom thou hast vouchsafed faith may also enjoy thy gift of peace. Through etc.

Lesson. Acts, x. 42—48.

And he commanded . . . name of the Lord.

Alleluya. 𝖵. When thou lettest thy breath go forth, they shall be made : and thou shalt renew the face of the earth.[2]

Alleluya. 𝖵. The Comforter, which is the Holy Ghost, whom the Father will send in my name, he will teach you all truth.[3]

Sequence.

Now let the sacred quire,
With holy symphony,
The promised joys sound forth
In fulness sent from heaven.
Assembled in one place,
The apostolic band
Awaits the glorious gifts.
Forthwith a voice divine,
Filling their hearts with power,
Attests the Comforter.
In every tongue they speak
Some mighty mystery
And wondrous works of God.
In canticles divine
His praises to rehearse
The assembly ceases not.
O God of all the earth,
Thee sun and moon do praise;

[1] Ps. lxxxi. 1.   [2] Ps. civ. 30.   [3] From St. John, xiv. 26.

The universal host
Of heaven in concert join
Their voice with waters deep.
Thee sings the genial earth;
Thee all the glittering stars;
Thee ransom'd souls adore,
Rejoicing in thy love.
The Jews amazed declare, that cursed band
Is of new wine's inebriation full;
Counting those filled with grace as full of wine.
These holy mysteries receiving, Peter
Doth conquer and subdue those hardened hearts,
Affirming this to be foretold by Joel.
Now triumphing our soul
Doth utter songs devout,
That for the heavenly visitant
A place she may prepare.
Let every string proclaim
Thy holy praise abroad,
That we may entertain
Those hallow'd gifts of grace.
All this pure offering
Of melody accept,
That so we may attain
Thine heavenly seat on high,
Whence light for ever flows.
Thou who didst consecrate
Those hallowed feasts of old,
Fulfil us now with light:
Or in thy heavenly realms
Grant us perpetual joys.
O Holy Ghost, thanksgiving meet,
And glory in thy starry seat
Is ever due to thee.
Deign thou in stately happiness
Our souls and bodies to possess,
O Christ, eternally.

Gospel. St. John, iii. 16—21.

God so loved . . . wrought in God.

Creed.

Offertory.

The Lord thundered out of heaven, and the highest gave his thunder: and the springs of the waters were seen.[1]

Secret.

Grant, we beseech thee, O Lord, that according to the promise of thy Son, our Lord Jesus Christ, the Holy Ghost may both more abundantly reveal to us the hidden mystery of this sacrifice, and may graciously disclose to us all truth. Through etc.

Preface.

Who ascending above etc. *and* In communion with etc. *and* This oblation therefore etc.[2]

Communion.

The Holy Ghost shall teach you, alleluya, whatsoever I have said unto you,[3] alleluya, alleluya.

Postcommunion.

We beseech thee, O Lord, to work fully in us the healing virtue of our redemption, that we may be found worthy to become the dwelling-place of the Holy Ghost. Through etc.

TUESDAY IN WHITSUN WEEK.

At Mass.   *Office.*

Receive the gift that is given you, and be glad, giving thanks unto God, alleluya, who hath called you to the heavenly kingdom,[4] alleluya, alleluya, alleluya.

Ps. Hear my law, O my people: incline your ears unto the words of my mouth.[5]

[1] Ps. xviii. 13, 15.   [2] Page 37.   [3] From St. John, xiv. 26.
[4] 2 Esdras, ii. 37.   [5] Ps. lxxviii. 1.

Collect.

We beseech thee, O Lord, that the power of the Holy
Ghost may come upon us, and that he may both merci-
fully cleanse our hearts, and defend us from all adversity.
Through etc.

Epistle.   Acts, viii. 14—17.

Now when the apostles . . . the Holy Ghost.

Alleluya.   ℣.   When thou lettest thy breath go forth, they shall
be made : and thou shalt renew the face of the earth.[1]

Alleluya.   ℣.   Come, Holy Ghost, fill the hearts of thy faithful
people, and kindle in them the fire of thy love.[2]

Sequence.

Now prompt, O muse, the fitting strain,
And let the organ lend its tempered might;
Swell, pipe and string, the joyous note of praise;
Whilst we, with lifted heart and voice,
Devoutly sing the honour of this day;
For on this day descends the Paraclyte
Upon Christ's faithful ones, filling their souls with grace.
A sudden sound is heard, and tongues of fire are seen,
And lo! with accents not their own,
Untaught of man, they speak the wondrous works of God.
Yet carnal unbelief cries scornfully,
" Full of new wine are these : " misdeeming them
Whose hearts the blessed Spirit with love inflames.
　　　　It is the fiftieth day
　　　　From the great resurrection morn;
Into their heart of hearts down glides the mystic fire;
While to the city a clear sign is given.
Then forth they go, a light amid the gloom,
Dropping the word's good seed in every land
　　　　With many a sign of power,
　　　　While the supernal dew
Blesses the thirsty new-sown field.

[1] Ps. civ. 30.　　　　　　[2] Source unknown.

And now, O Christ, thy servants waiting on thee
Here in thine house, would fain their voice attune
To that new song which saints in glory sing.
To him be endless glory, honour, power,
Who to all men that serve him faithfully,
In every clime, the Spirit's aid vouchsafes—
Meekly, with one accord, the wondrous gift we seek,
That he, the Holy Ghost, our inmost hearts
First cleansing, with all wisdom may enlighten.   Alleluya.

Gospel.   St. John, x. 1—10.
Verily, verily, I say . . . more abundantly.

Creed.

Offertory.
The Lord opened the doors of heaven.   He rained down manna
also upon them for to eat, and gave them food from heaven.   So
man did eat angels' food,[1] alleluya.

Secret.
We beseech thee, O Lord, that the Holy Ghost may
descend upon the altar, and that he may both sanctify the
gifts of thy people, and mercifully cleanse the hearts of
them that receive the same.   Through etc.

Communion.
The Spirit which proceedeth from the Father, alleluya, he shall
glorify me,[2] alleluya, alleluya.

Postcommunion.
We beseech thee, O Lord, that the Holy Ghost may
renew our souls, since he himself is the remission of all
sins.   Through etc.

EMBER WEDNESDAY.[3]

*No other high mass than that of the fast is said, according to
the use of the Sarum either on this day or on Friday or Saturday
in Ember Week.*

---

[1] Ps. lxxviii. 24, 25, 26.   [2] From St. John, xv. 26, and xvi. 14.
[3] *Feria quarta Quatuor temporum.*

At Mass.   *Office.*

O God, when thou wentest before thy people, alleluya, making a way for them, alleluya, dwelling among them,[1] alleluya, alleluya.

Ps.   Let God arise, and let his enemies be scattered; let them also that hate him flee before him.[2]

Kyrie eleyson, *with its verses, is then said. Then shall immediately follow* Glory be to God on high etc. The Lord be with you *is not to be said, but only* Let us pray.

Collect.

Grant, we beseech thee, almighty God, that the Holy Ghost may remove all carnal desires from our minds, and mightily pour into us spiritual gifts.   Through etc.

Lesson.   Wisdom, i. 1—7.

Love righteousness . . . of the voice.

The above is to be read in the pulpit by an acolyte vested in a surplice. Then three clerks of the second rank, in silk copes, shall say in the same place:

Alleluya.   ℣. When thou lettest thy breath go forth, they shall be made: and thou shalt renew the face of the earth.[3]

Alleluya *is not to be repeated, but there shall follow* The Lord be with you *and* Let us pray.

Collect.

We beseech thee, O Lord, that the Holy Ghost the Comforter, which proceedeth from thee, may illumine our minds, and lead us into all truth, as thy Son hath promised.   Who liveth etc.

Lesson.   Acts. ii. 14—21.

But Peter standing . . . shall be saved.

---

[1] Partly from Ps. lxviii. 7.   [2] *Ib.* 1.   [3] Ps. civ. 30.

Alleluya. ℣. The apostles began to speak with other tongues the wonderful works of God.[1]

The Alleluya *is to be repeated without the cadence.*

Sequence.

Th' illustrious day, when from the throne
the fire of God came rushing down
    on Christ's assembled band;
To enrich their tongues, their hearts to fill;
to kindred praise invites us still
    of heart, and tongue, and hand.
Christ on this pentecostal day
revisiting without delay
    the bride, his promise sent;
After the honey's treasured worth,
the rock a store of oil gave forth,
    the rock now permanent.
From Sinai's mount proclaimed the law
graven on stone the people saw,
    not sent in tongues of fire:
Newness of heart, and quickened mind,
with unity of tongue combined,
    The chosen few inspire.
O happy, O most festive day!
whereon the early founders lay
    the Church's pediment;
The rising Church's first-fruits born
to life anew this holy morn
    three thousand souls present.
The two loaves by the law ordained,
two people represent, retained
    By faith's adoptive tie;
The head-stone of the corner, set
between the two, together met,
    hath wrought out unity.

[1] From Acts, ii. 11.

New bottles, not the worn and old,
new wine are suitable to hold;
    with oil Elisha fills
The widow's vessels not a few;
so on fit hearts his holy dew
    God graciously distils.
We are not worthy of this wine,
nor oil, nor of this dew divine,
    if discord reigns within:
His consolation cannot find
a place in a divided mind,
    or heart obscured by sin.
Come, holy Comforter benign,
our tongues control, our hearts incline;
if on us thy blest presence shine,
    no poison harms, no gall;
There is no joy, no pure content,
no health, no calm stabiliment,
sweetness hath no constituent,
    except thy grace do all.
Thou art the light, the oil to cure,
thou, working in the water pure,
mysterious virtue dost assure
    to bless thy chosen race.
By new creation born again,
to praise thee now our hearts are fain;
by nature sons of wrath, we gain
    the privilege of grace,
Thou art the gift, the giver, too,
all good on earth to thee is due;
with gratitude our hearts endue,
to praise thy name with accents true
    do thou our lips ordain;
Cleanse us, we pray, from all our sin,
of purity thou origin;
that we, renewed in Christ, may win
perfect life, and bring us in
    where joys in fulness reign.

Gospel. St. John, vi. 44—51.

No man cometh . . . life of the world.

Creed.

Offertory.

My delight shall be in thy commandments which I have loved. My hands also will I lift up unto thy commandments which I have loved,[1] alleluya.

Secret.

We beseech thee, O Lord, that the Holy Ghost may sanctify the gifts now offered unto thee, and that our partaking of them may guard us from the contagion of all sin. Through etc.

Communion.

My peace I give unto you, alleluya; my peace I leave with you,[2] alleluya, alleluya.

Postcommunion.

May the perpetual splendour of thy brightness, O Lord, shine upon us by virtue of this mystery; and may the grace of the Holy Spirit, together with the consubstantial Son, illuminate us. Through etc.

THURSDAY IN WHITSUN WEEK.

Office.

As on Whitsunday,[3] without the verses.[4]

Collect.

Grant, we beseech thee, almighty and merciful God, that thy Holy Spirit may come unto us, and dwell in us, and make us to be a temple worthy of his glory. Through etc.

---

[1] Ps. cxix. 47, 48.
[2] St. John, xiv. 27.
[3] Page 339.
[4] *i.e.* of the Kyrie eleyson, as farsed [No. 1].

Lesson. Acts, viii. 5—8.

Then Philip went down . . . in that city.

Alleluya. *V.* When thou lettest thy breath go forth, they shall be made: and thou shalt renew the face of the earth.[1]

Alleluya. *V.* Suddenly there came a sound from heaven, as of a rushing, mighty wind.[2]

Sequence.

Now let the sacred band the Lord's high names expand,
Messiah, Saviour, Lord of Hosts, Emmanuel,
Only-Begotten, Way, Life, Hand, Homoousion,
Beginning, the First-Born, Wisdom, and Power,
The Head, and End, Alpha and Omega,
Fountain of Good, Advocate, Mediator,
Lamb, Sheep, Calf, Dragon, Lion, Ram, and Worm,
Mouth, Word, Sun, Brightness, Glory, Light, and Image,
Bread, Blossom, Vine, Mount, Door, Rock, Corner-Stone,
Messenger, Bridegroom, Shepherd, Prophet, Priest,
The Lord, Immortal, God, Almighty, Jesus,
May he our Saviour be, to whom be glory ever.[3]

Gospel. St. Luke, ix. 1—6.

Then he called . . . healing everywhere.

Creed.

Offertory.

Stablish the thing, O God, that thou hast wrought in us, for thy temple's sake at Jerusalem: so shall kings bring presents unto thee.[4]

---

[1] Ps. civ. 30.   [2] Acts, ii. 2.

[3] The following Hebrew and Greek words (in Latin dress) occur in this Sequence: Messias, Sother, Emmanuel, Sabaoth, Adonay, Homoousyon, Alpha, oo (=Omega), Paraclitus, Athanatos, Kyrios, Theos, Panton craton, Ysus. Apart from first words of lines, only eight of the titles commence with a capital letter in the original Latin.

[4] Ps. lxviii. 28, 29.

Secret.

Endue our gifts, O Lord, with the virtue of the Holy Ghost, that he may make discernible to us now and for evermore that which in the present solemnity we hallow to thy name. Through etc.

Communion.

Suddenly there was a sound from heaven as of a rushing, mighty wind, where they were sitting, alleluya: and they were all filled with the Holy Ghost, and spake the wonderful works of God,[1] alleluya, alleluya.

Postcommunion.

We beseech thee, O Lord, that through the operation of the Holy Ghost our vices may be purged away by this heavenly sacrifice, that we may ever be made meet for thy gifts. Through etc.

EMBER FRIDAY.

At Mass.   *Office.*

O let my mouth be filled with thy praise, alleluya, that I may sing, alleluya: my lips will be fain when I sing unto thee,[2] alleluya, alleluya.

Ps. In thee, O Lord, have I put my trust, let me never be put to confusion: but rid me, and deliver me in thy righteousness.[3]

Collect.

Grant, we beseech thee, merciful Lord, unto thy Church, that when it is gathered together by thy Holy Spirit, it may in no way be disturbed by any assault of the enemy. Through etc.

Lesson. Acts, ii. 22—28.

Ye men of Israel . . . thy countenance.

---

[1] From Acts, ii. 2, 4, 11.   [2] From Ps. lxxi. 7, 21.   [3] *Ib.* 1.

Alleluya. ℣. When thou lettest thy breath go forth, they shall be made: and thou shalt renew the face of the earth.[1]

Alleluya. ℣. The Spirit of the Lord hath filled the world: and that which containeth all things hath knowledge of the voice.[2]

Sequence.

Now let all the Church uniting,
Praises meet to God reciting,
Tune aloud their grateful songs;
On this day the Spirit Holy
Deigned upon the apostles lowly
Grace to pour in fiery tongues.
May the Comforter indwelling,
From our hearts all sin expelling,
Take us for his own abode;
Gifts and graces high outpouring,
In our breasts devotion storing,
So our life shall please our God.
May we Alleluias singing,
Through all ages ceaseless ringing,
Raise our acclamations high,
Praise ascribe and exaltation,
Honour, might, and adoration,
Unto God eternally.

Gospel.   St. Luke, v. 17—26.

And it came to pass . . . strange things to-day.

Creed.

Offertory.

Praise the Lord, O my soul: while I live will I praise the Lord: yea, as long as I have any being, I will sing praises unto my God,[3] alleluya.

Secret.

May the sacrifice offered in thy presence, O Lord, be consumed by the same divine fire, by which the Holy

[1] Ps. civ. 30.   [2] Wisdom, i. 7.   [3] Ps. cxlvi. 1.

Ghost influenced the hearts of the disciples of thy Christ.
Through etc.

Communion.

The wind bloweth where it listeth, and thou hearest the sound
thereof, but canst not tell whence it cometh, and whither it
goeth.[1]　Alleluya, alleluya.

Postcommunion.

Grant, we beseech thee, almighty God, that by the
receiving of this sacrament the vices of our weak nature
may be so purged away that we may perceive in ourselves
the gift of thy grace promised anew through the Holy
Ghost.　Through etc.

EMBER SATURDAY.

At Mass.　　　　　　　　*Office.*

The love of God is shed abroad in your hearts,
alleluya: by his Spirit which dwelleth in you,[2] alleluya,
alleluya.

Ps.　O Lord, God of my salvation, I have cried day and night
before thee.[3]

Kyrie eleyson *is sung solemnly without verses.*　Gloria in
excelsis *is to follow as within the Octave, with ruling of the
quire.　All Collects are to be said without* The Lord be with
you, *and only with* Let us pray, *except the last Collect, before
the Epistle.　And all Lessons are to be read with their titles,
at the step of the quire, the readers being in surplices.　The
first lesson shall be read by an acolyte, the other lessons by
clerks of the second rank, and the fifth lesson by some person
of the higher rank.　Each* Alleluya *is to be sung by two boys
in surplices in the same place without any repetition of* alleluya
after its verse.

---

[1] St. John, iii. 8.　　　[2] From Rom. v. 5.　　　[3] Ps. lxxxviii. 1.

Collect.

We beseech thee, O Lord, graciously pour the Holy
Spirit into our hearts, by whose wisdom we were created,
and by whose providence we are governed. Through etc.

Lesson. Joel, ii. 28—32.

I will pour . . . shall be delivered.

Alleluya. ℣. When thou lettest thy breath go forth, they shall
be made : and thou shalt renew the face of the earth.[1]

Alleluya *is not repeated after the verse, but* Let us pray *is
forthwith said.*

Collect.

Let thy Holy Spirit, O Lord, we beseech thee, inflame
us with that fire which our Lord Jesus Christ sent on
earth, and earnestly desired that it should be kindled.
Who liveth etc.

Lesson. Levit. xxiii. 9—11, 15—17, 21.

When ye be come into . . . your generations.

Alleluya. ℣. Come, Holy Ghost, fill the hearts of thy faithful people, and kindle in them the fire of thy love.[2]

Collect.

O God, who for the healing of our souls hast ordered
our bodies to be mortified by devout fasting, mercifully
grant that we may ever faithfully serve thee both in soul
and body. Through etc.

Lesson. Deut. xxvi. 1—3, 7—11.

When thou art come in . . . given unto thee.

Alleluya. The apostles spake with other tongues the wonderful
works of God.[3]

---

[1] Ps. civ. 30.   [2] Not from H. S.   [3] Partly from Acts, ii. 11.

Collect.

Grant, we beseech thee, almighty God, that being taught by this wholesome fast, we may abstain from all vices and more readily obtain thy favour.   Through etc.

Lesson.   Levit. xxvi. 3—13.
If ye walk in . . . be my people.

Alleluya.   ℣.   Suddenly there came a sound from heaven as of a mighty, rushing wind.[1]

Collect.

Grant, we beseech thee, almighty God, that we may so abstain from carnal feasting, that we may fast in like manner from the assaults of vice.   Through etc.

Lesson.   Song of the Three Children, 26—66.[2]
The angel of the Lord . . . for ever.

The whole Lesson should be read on the vigil of the Holy Trinity, and in the month of September.[3]

Two clerks of the second rank, vested in surplices, and standing at the step of the quire, shall say as follows:

Alleluya.   Blessed art thou, O Lord God of our fathers, and to be praised for evermore.[4]

Alleluya *is not to be repeated.*   The Lord be with you *and* Let us pray *shall follow.*

---

[1] Acts, ii. 2.

[2] This Lesson, which is given in a somewhat compressed form, represents the following verses in Vulg., viz., Dan. iii. 49, 50, 47, 48, 50, 51-54, then an inserted verse, 55, then an inserted verse, 56-58, 61-66, 71, 67, 68, 75, 74, 75, 76, 79-87. The Latin readings differ widely from the Vulgate *textus receptus*, following the old-Latin, but this is a subject which cannot be entered upon in detail here.

[3] Referring to those two Ember Saturdays.   Some editions had rubrics shortening this Lesson in Advent and Lent.

[4] Song of the Three Children, v. 29.

Collect.

O God, who for thy three children didst assuage the flames of fire, mercifully grant that through the coming of thy Holy Spirit we thy servants may not be set on fire by the flames of vice. Through etc.

Lesson. Acts, xiii. 44—52.

The whole city . . . the Holy Ghost.

The Lesson is to be read in the pulpit: after which two clerks of the upper rank, in silk copes, shall say in the same place:

Alleluya. ℣. O praise the Lord, all ye heathen : praise him, all ye nations.[1]

The Alleluya *is to be repeated without the cadence.*

Sequence.

Now let the sacred band etc.[2]

Gospel. St. Luke, iv. 38—43.

And he arose . . . other cities also.

Creed.

Offertory.

O Lord, God of my salvation, I have cried day and night before thee : let my prayer enter into thy presence, O Lord,[3] alleluya.

Secret.

Send, we beseech thee, O Lord, the Holy Spirit, that he may both make these present gifts thy sacrament to us, and purify our hearts for the receiving of the same. Through etc.

Communion.

I will not leave you comfortless : I will come again to you, alleluya, and your heart shall rejoice,[4] alleluya, alleluya.

---

[1] Ps. cxvii. 1.   [2] Page 351.   [3] Ps. lxxxviii. 1.
[4] St. John, xiv. 18 ; xvi. 22.

Postcommunion.

May thy holy mysteries, O Lord, supply in us a divine
fervour, that we may find delight both in their celebration
and in their effect.   Through etc.

TRINITY SUNDAY.

At Mass.   *Office.*

Blessed be the Holy Trinity, and the undivided Unity;
we will praise him because he hath dealt mercifully with
us.[1]

Ps. Let us bless the Father and the Son with the Holy
Ghost.[2]

Nothing is to be said further.

Collect.

Almighty and everlasting God, who hast given unto us
thy servants grace, by the confession of a true faith, to
acknowledge the glory of the eternal Trinity, and in the
power of thy majesty to worship the Unity; we beseech
thee that thou wouldest keep us steadfast in this faith,
and evermore defend us from all adversities.   Who
livest etc.

Lesson.   Rev. iv. 1—10.

After this I looked . . . for ever and ever.

Gradual.

Blessed art thou, O Lord, who beholdest the depths, and sittest
upon the cherubim.[3]

℣. O ye heavens, bless ye God, for he hath dealt mercifully
with us.[4]

Alleluya.   ℣. Blessed art thou, O Lord God of our fathers,
and to be praised for ever.[5]

---

[1] From Tobit, xii. 6.   [2] Not in H. S.
[3] Song of the Three Children, 32.   [4] *Ib.* 36 (partly).   [5] *Ib.* 29.

Sequence.

Blest be the holy Trinity,
  eternal Godhead Thou;
Father, Son, Holy Ghost, one God
  To whom all creatures bow.
Three Persons in one Godhead dwell,
  One will have all the three
in perfect harmony combined,
  nor ever disagree:
Godhead in Unity consists,
  three Gods there cannot be;
So the right faith by Christ set forth
  confesses stedfastly.
This is the faith which souls enthralled
  doth from their sins release,
And leads them to the cloudless land
  of purity and peace.
There in one dulcet symphony
  the hosts of heaven unite;
The steps of Christ enthroned on high
  they follow clad in white.
There, while this life's vicissitudes
  pass by and quickly fade,
In the changed raiment, which they yearn
  to win, they stand arrayed.
We likewise, as in duty bound,
  would pay our debts to heaven,
Contracted in this lower world,
  as grace to us is given;
That after death we with the blest
  may full communion gain,
And when the righteous doom is fixed
  may heaven's high courts attain;
Where God in glory manifest
  pours forth undying light,
Where is the Saviour's face for aye,
  that beatific sight;

That sight doth o'er the angel's breasts
　　irradiating shine,
While their adoring gaze they fix
　　on Christ the Lord divine.
Like thirst to theirs the holy saints
　　in heart and flesh will feel,
When for their righteous deeds the judge
　　a recompence shall deal.

Gospel. St. John, iii. 1—15.

There was a man . . . eternal life.

Offertory.

Blessed be God the Father, and the Only-begotten Son of God: also the Holy Ghost, because he hath dealt mercifully with us.[1]

Secret.

Sanctify, we beseech thee, O Lord God, holy Trinity, through the invocation of thy holy name, the offering of this oblation; and through it perfect us ourselves to be an eternal gift unto thee. Who livest etc.

Preface.

Who with thy only-begotten Son etc.[2]

Communion.

We bless the God of heaven, and we will give thanks unto him in the sight of all that live, because he hath dealt mercifully with us.[3]

Postcommunion.

May the reception of this sacrament, O Lord our God, and the confession of the everlasting holy Trinity, and of the undivided Unity of the same, be profitable to our salvation both in body and soul. In which thou livest etc.

---

[1] Partly from Tobit, xii. 6 (Vulg.).
[2] Page 38.　　　　　　　　　　　　　　[3] Tobit, xii. 6.

A Memory of the Trinity is to be made at Mass daily throughout the whole week, except on the feast of Corpus Christi; and the Trinity mass is to be said, when the service is of the Trinity, unless the mass I am the salvation of the people etc.[1] *is to be said, throughout the week.*

Corpus Christi.

At Mass.   *Office.*

He should have fed them also with the finest wheat-flour, alleluya, and with honey out of the stony rock should I have satisfied thee,[2] alleluya, alleluya, alleluya.

Ps. Sing we merrily unto God our strength: make a cheerful noise unto the God of Jacob.[3]

Kyrie. O Lord, fountain of goodness etc.[4]

Collect.

O God, who in a wonderful sacrament hast left us a memory of thy passion, grant us, we beseech thee, so to venerate the sacred mysteries of thy body and blood, that we may ever perceive in ourselves the fruit of thy redemption. Who livest etc.

Epistle. 1 Cor. xi. 23—29.

For I have received . . . the Lord's body.

Gradual.

The eyes of all wait upon thee, O Lord: and thou givest them their meat in due season.[5]

V. Thou openest thine hand: and fillest all things living with plenteousness.[6]

Alleluya. *V.* My flesh is meat indeed, and my blood is drink indeed: he that eateth my flesh and drinketh my blood dwelleth in me, and I in him.[7]

---

[1] *Salus populi.* Third Votive Mass.
[2] Ps. lxxxi. 17. [3] *Ib.* 1. [4] No. [3].
[5] Ps. cxlv. 15. [6] *Ib.* 16. [7] St. John, vi. 55, 56.

Sequence.

Sion, lift thy voice and sing,
praise thy Saviour and thy king,
   praise with hymns thy shepherd true;
Strive thy best to praise him well,
yet doth he all praise excel,
   none can ever reach his due.

See to-day before us laid
the living and life-giving bread,
   theme for praise and joy profound;
The same which at the sacred board
was by our incarnate Lord
   given to his apostles round.

Let the praise be loud and high,
sweet and tranquil be the joy
   felt to-day in every breast.
On this festival divine
which records the origin
   of the solemn eucharist.

On this table of the king,
our new Paschal offering
   brings to end the olden rite.
Here for empty shadows fled
is reality instead;
   here, instead of darkness, light.

His own act, at supper seated,
Christ ordained to be repeated
   In his memory divine;
Wherefore now with adoration
we the host of our salvation
   consecrate from bread and wine.

Hear what holy church maintaineth
that the bread its substance changeth
   into flesh, the wine to blood;
Doth it pass thy comprehending?
faith, the law of sight transcending,
   leaps to things not understood.

Here beneath these signs are hidden
priceless things, to sense forbidden;
   signs, not things, are what we see;
Flesh from bread, and blood from wine,
yet is Christ in either sign
   all entire confessed to be.

They, too, who of him partake,
sever not, nor rend, nor break,
   but entire their Lord receive;
Whether one or thousands eat,
all receive the self-same meat,
   Nor the less for others leave.

Both the wicked and the good
eat of this celestial food,
   but with ends how opposite!
Here 'tis life, and there 'tis death,
the same, yet issuing to each
   in a difference infinite.

Not a single doubt retain,
when they break the host in twain,
that in each part there doth remain
   what was in the whole before;
Since the simple sign alone
suffers change in state or form,
   the signified remaining one
   and the same for evermore.

Lo! upon the altar lies,
hidden deep from mortal eyes,
bread of angels from the skies
    made the food of mortal man.
Children's meat to dogs denied,
in old types fore-signified,
in the manna heaven-supplied,
    Isaac and the Paschal lamb.

Jesu, shepherd of the sheep,
thou thy flock in safety keep;
living bread, thy life supply,
strengthen us, or else we die;
fill us with celestial grace.
Thou who feedest us below,
source of all we have or know,
grant that with thy saints above,
sitting at the feast of love
we may see thee face to face.

Gospel. St. John, vi. 55—58.
My flesh is meat . . . live for ever.

Offertory.

The priests of the Lord offer the offerings made by fire and the bread of their God : therefore they shall be holy unto their God, and they shall not profane his name,[1] alleluya.

Secret.

We beseech thee, O Lord, mercifully to grant unto thy church the gifts of unity and peace, which are mystically represented in the gifts which we offer. Through etc.

Preface.

Because by the mystery etc.[2]

---

[1] Levit. xxi. 6.   [2] Page 34.

This Preface is said throughout the whole Octave, when the service is of the Octave, and in every commemoration of the same throughout the whole year.

Communion.

As often as ye eat this bread and drink this cup, ye do shew the Lord's death till he come. Wherefore, whosoever shall eat this bread and drink this cup of the Lord unworthily shall be guilty of the body and blood of the Lord,[1] alleluya.

Postcommunion.

Grant, we beseech thee, O Lord, that we may be fulfilled with the eternal fruition of thy godhead, which in this life the partaking of thy precious body and blood doth prefigure. Who livest etc.

This mass is said throughout the whole week, when the service is of the Octave, but without the Sequence and the Creed. When the Octave is kept with ruling of the quire, the Sequence Lo! upon the altar[2] *is said daily throughout the Octave, when the mass is of the Octave.*

FIRST SUNDAY AFTER TRINITY.

At Mass.   *Office.*

My trust is in thy mercy, O Lord, and my heart is joyful in thy salvation. I will sing of the Lord, because he hath dealt so lovingly with me.[3]

Ps. How long wilt thou forget me, O Lord, for ever: how long wilt thou hide thy face from me?[4]

Collect.

O God, the strength of them that put their trust in thee, mercifully accept our prayers; and because the

---

[1] 1 Cor. xi. 26, 27.   [2] Page 364.
[3] Ps. xiii. 5, 6.   [4] *Ib.* 1.

2 B

weakness of our mortal nature can do nothing without thee, grant us the help of thy grace, that in keeping of thy commandments we may please thee both in will and deed. Through etc.

A memory of the Trinity shall be made on all Sundays up to Advent, except when any Sunday is entirely transferred.

Note, that throughout the summer when a double feast occurs on a Sunday, there shall be no memory of the Sunday at Mass, although sometimes a memory shall have been necessarily made at Vespers or at Matins in silence, as has been elsewhere laid down. But when any feast of nine lessons occurs on a Sunday, there shall always be a memory of the Sunday and of the Trinity at mass, when a memory shall have been made at Vespers and at Matins, unless the Sunday mass ought to be sung on the Sunday itself in chapter.

Lesson. 1 St. John, iv. 8—21.

God is love . . . his brother also.

Gradual.

I said, Lord, be merciful unto me: heal my soul, for I have sinned against thee.[1]

℣. Blessed is he that considereth the poor and needy: the Lord shall deliver him in the time of trouble.[2]

Alleluya. ℣. Ponder my words, O Lord: consider my meditation.[3]

No Sequence is said when the service is of the Sunday, until Advent.

Gospel. St. Luke, xvi. 19—31.

There was a certain rich . . . rose from the dead.

Offertory.

O hearken unto the voice of my calling, my king and my God: for unto thee will I make my prayer, O Lord.[4]

---

[1] Ps. xli. 4.   [2] *Ib.* 1.   [3] Ps. v. 1.   [4] *Ib.* 2.

Secret.

O God, who renewest us, who are created after thine own image, both by sacraments and by precepts, mercifully accept the prayers and gifts of thy suppliants, that what trust in their own merits cannot secure, these propitiatory offerings may obtain for them. Through etc.

Communion.

I will speak of all thy marvellous works: I will rejoice and be glad in thee: yea, my songs will I make of thy name, O most highest.[1]

Postcommunion.

Grant, we beseech thee, O Lord, that we, who have been filled with so great bounties, may both receive the gift of salvation and never cease from praising thee. Through etc.

WEDNESDAY.

Epistle. 2 Peter, i. 16—19.

We made known . . . in your hearts.

Gospel. St. Matt. v. 17—19.

Think not that . . . kingdom of heaven.

SECOND SUNDAY AFTER TRINITY.

At Mass.   *Office.*

The Lord was my upholder. He brought me forth also into a place of liberty: he brought me forth, even because he had a favour unto me.[2]

Ps. I will love thee, O Lord my strength; the Lord is my stony rock, and my defence, and my Saviour.[3]

---

[1] Ps. ix. 1, 2.   [2] Ps. xviii. 18, 19.   [3] *Ib.* 1.

Collect.

O Lord, who never failest to help and govern them whom thou dost bring up in thy steadfast love, make us to have a perpetual fear and love of thy holy name. Through etc.

Epistle. 1 St. John, iii. 13—18.

Marvel not, my brethren . . . and in truth.

Gradual.

When I was in trouble I called upon the Lord: and he heard me.[1]

℣. Deliver my soul, O Lord, from lying lips, and from a deceitful tongue.[2]

Alleluya. ℣. God is a righteous judge, strong and patient: and God is provoked every day.[3]

Gospel. St. Luke, xiv. 16—24.

A certain man . . . taste of my supper.

Offertory.

Turn thee, O Lord, and deliver my soul: O save me for thy mercy's sake.[4]

Secret.

May the oblation to be offered to thy name purify us, O Lord, and make us day by day to live a more heavenly life. Through etc.

Communion.

I will sing of the Lord, because he hath dealt so lovingly with me: yea, I will praise the name of the Lord most highest.[5]

Postcommunion.

Having received these holy gifts, we beseech thee, O Lord, to grant that the more frequently we approach these mysteries, the more effectually we may work out our salvation. Through etc.

[1] Ps. cxx. 1.   [2] Ib. 2.   [3] Ps. vii. 12.
[4] Ps. vi. 4.   [5] Ps. xiii. 6.

Wednesday.

Epistle. Eph. iv. 17—24.

This I say, therefore, . . . true holiness.

Gospel. St. Matt. xxi. 23—27.

And when he was come . . . do these things.

Third Sunday after Trinity.

At Mass.   *Office.*

Turn thee unto me, and have mercy upon me, O Lord, for I am desolate, and in misery. Look upon my adversity and misery: and forgive me all my sin, O my God.[1]

Ps. Unto thee, O Lord, will I lift up my soul; my God, I have put my trust in thee: O let me not be confounded.[2]

Collect.

O Lord, we beseech thee, mercifully to hear our supplications; and grant that we, to whom thou hast given an hearty desire to pray, may by thy aid be defended. Through etc.

Epistle. 1 St. Peter, v. 6—11.

Humble yourselves, therefore, . . . ever and ever.

Gradual.

O cast thy burden upon the Lord: and he shall nourish thee.[3]

℣. When I cried unto the Lord, he heard my voice from the battle that was against me.[4]

Alleluya. ℣. I will love thee, O Lord my strength: the Lord is my stony rock, and my defence, and my Saviour.[5]

Gospel. St. Luke, xv. 1—10.

Then drew near . . . that repenteth.

---

[1] Ps. xxv. 15, 17.   [2] *Ib.* 1.   [3] Ps. lv. 23.
[4] Partly from Ps. lv. 18, 19.   [5] Ps. xviii. 1.

Offertory.

They that know thy name will put their trust in thee: for thou, Lord, hast never failed them that seek thee. O praise the Lord which dwelleth in Sion; for he forgetteth not the complaint of the poor.[1]

Secret.

We beseech thee, O Lord, to sanctify the gifts now offered unto thee, that they may become the body and blood of thy Only-begotten One, for our healing. Who liveth etc.

Communion.

I have called upon thee, O God, for thou shalt hear me: incline thine ear unto me, and hearken unto my words.[2]

Postcommunion.

Having received the holy gifts, we beseech thee, O Lord, that by their virtue thou wouldest purify us from all vices, and fill us abundantly with the gifts of thy grace. Through etc.

WEDNESDAY.

Epistle. 2 Tim. iv. 17, 18.
The Lord stood by me . . . Amen.

Gospel. St. Matt. v. 25—30.
Agree with thine adversary . . . into hell.

FOURTH SUNDAY AFTER TRINITY.

At Mass.   *Office.*

The Lord is my light and my salvation; whom shall then I fear? the Lord is the strength of my life; of whom then shall I be afraid? When mine enemies and my foes came upon me, they stumbled and fell.[3]

---

[1] Ps. ix. 10, 11, 12.   [2] Ps. xvii. 6.   [3] Ps. xxvii. 1, 2.

Ps. Though an host of men were laid against me, yet shall not my heart be afraid.[1]

Collect.

O God, the protector of all that trust in thee, without whom nothing is strong, nothing is holy, multiply upon us thy mercy; that, thou being our ruler and guide, we may so pass through things temporal, that we lose not the things eternal. Through etc.

Epistle. Rom. viii. 18—23.

For I reckon . . . of our body.

Gradual.

Be merciful to our sins, O Lord. Wherefore do the heathen say, Where is now their God?[2]

℣. Help us, O God of our salvation, and for the glory of thy name, O Lord, deliver us.[3]

Alleluya. The king shall rejoice in thy strength, O Lord: exceeding glad shall he be of thy salvation.[4]

Gospel. St. Luke, vi. 36—42.

Be ye therefore merciful . . . brother's eye.

Offertory.

Lighten mine eyes that I sleep not in death, lest mine enemies say, I have prevailed against him.[5]

Secret.

Regard, we beseech thee, O Lord, the offerings of thy suppliant Church; and grant that they may be ever consecrated and received for the salvation of thy faithful people. Through etc.

Communion.

The Lord is my stony rock and my defence, my Saviour, my God, and my might.[6]

---

[1] Ps. xxvii. 3. [2] Ps. lxxix. 9, 10. [3] *Ib.* 9.
[4] Ps. xxi. 1. [5] Ps. xiii. 3, 4. [6] Ps. xviii. 1.

Postcommunion.

May thy holy gifts, O Lord, which we have received, quicken us; and having cleansed us from our sins, prepare us for thine everlasting mercy. Through etc.

WEDNESDAY.

Epistle. 1 St. John, ii. 3—6.

Hereby we do know . . . as he walked.

Gospel. St. Matt. xvii. 10—18.

His disciples asked him . . . that very hour.

FIFTH SUNDAY AFTER TRINITY.

At Mass.   *Office.*

Hearken unto my voice, O Lord, when I cry unto thee. Thou hast been my succour, leave me not, neither forsake me, O God of my salvation.[1]

Ps. The Lord is my light and my salvation : whom then shall I fear?[2]

Kyrie eleyson etc.

Collect.

Grant, we beseech thee, O Lord, that the course of this world may be so peaceably ordered by thy governance, that thy Church may joyfully serve thee in godly quietness. Through etc.

Epistle. 1 St. Peter, iii. 8—15.

Be ye all . . . in your hearts.

Gradual.

Behold, O God, our defender, and look upon thy servants.[3]

℣. O Lord God of hosts, hear the prayers of thy servants.[4]

---

[1] Ps. xxvii. 8, 11.   [2] Ps. xxvii. 1.
[3] From Ps. lxxxiv. 8.   [4] From *Ib.* 9.

Alleluya. ℣. In thee, O Lord have I put my trust; let me never be put to confusion; rid me and deliver me in thy righteousness; incline thine ear unto me: make haste to deliver me.[1]

Gospel. St. Luke, v. 1—11.

As the people pressed . . . followed him.

Offertory.

I will thank the Lord for giving me warning: I have set God always before me; for he is on my right hand, therefore shall I not fall.[2]

Secret.

Let our humble prayers, we beseech thee, O Lord, ascend into thy merciful presence; and let thy divine power, which thou bestowest upon us abundantly for the purification of our minds, descend upon these oblations. Through etc.

Communion.

One thing have I desired of the Lord, which I will require; even that I may dwell in the house of the Lord all the days of my life.[3]

Postcommunion.

We beseech thee, O Lord, that these holy mysteries may purify us, and protect us by their efficacy. Through etc.

WEDNESDAY.

Epistle. 1 Tim. ii. 1—7.

I exhort . . . in faith and verity.

Gospel. St. Luke, viii. 22—25.

Now it came to pass . . . obey him.

---

[1] Ps. xxxi. 1, 2.　　[2] Ps. xvi. 8, 9.　　[3] Ps. xxvii. 4.

SIXTH SUNDAY AFTER TRINITY.

At Mass.   *Office.*

The Lord is my strength and he is the wholesome
defence of his Anointed. Save thy people, O Lord, and
give thy blessing unto thine inheritance: feed them for
ever.[1]

Ps. Unto thee will I cry, O Lord my strength: think no
scorn of me, lest if thou make as though thou hearest not, I become
like them that go down into the pit.[2]

Collect.

O God, who hast prepared for them that love thee
good things as yet unseen, pour into our hearts such love
towards thee, that we loving thee in all things and above
all things, may obtain thy promises, which exceed all that
we can desire. Through etc.

Epistle. Rom. vi. 3—11.

Know ye not . . . Jesus Christ our Lord.

Gradual.

Turn thee, O Lord, at the last, and be gracious unto thy
servants.[3]

℣. Lord, thou hast been our refuge from one generation.[4]

Alleluya. ℣. Deliver me from mine enemies, O God; defend
me from them that rise up against me.[5]

Gospel. St. Matt. v. 20—24.

For I say unto you . . . offer thy gift.

Offertory.

O hold thou up my goings in thy paths, that my footsteps slip
not. Incline thine ear to me, and hearken unto my words. Shew
thy marvellous loving-kindness, thou that art the saviour of them
that put their trust in thee, O Lord.[6]

---

[1] Ps. xxviii. 9, 10.   [2] *Ib.* 1.   [3] Ps. xc. 13.
[4] Ps. xc. 1.   [5] Ps. lix. 1.   [6] Ps. xvii. 5-7.

Secret.

Favourably hear our supplications, O Lord, and graciously receive the offerings of thy servants; that what each hath offered to the honour of thy name, may be profitable to the salvation of all men.   Through etc.

Communion.

Therefore will I offer in his dwelling an oblation with great gladness: I will sing and speak praises unto the Lord.[1]

Postcommunion.

Grant, we beseech thee, O Lord, that we, who have been fed with this heavenly gift, may be cleansed from our secret sins, and delivered from the snares of our enemies.   Through etc.

WEDNESDAY.

Epistle.   1 St. John, ii. 21—25.

I have not written . . . eternal life.

Gospel.   St. Mark, x. 17—21.

When he was gone . . . follow me.

SEVENTH SUNDAY AFTER TRINITY.

At Mass.   *Office.*

O clap your hands together, all ye people: O sing unto God with the voice of melody.[2]

Ps.   He shall subdue the people under us: and the nations under our feet.[3]

Collect.

God of all power, who art the author of all good things, graft in our hearts the love of thy name, increase in us

---

[1] Ps. xxvii. 7.   [2] Ps. xlvii. 1.   [3] *Ib.* 3.

true religion, nourish us with all goodness, and of thy great mercy keep us in the same.   Through etc.

Epistle. Rom. vi. 19—23.

I speak after . . . Christ our Lord.

Gradual.

Come ye children, and hearken unto me: I will teach you the fear of the Lord.[1]

℣. They had an eye unto him and were lightened: and their faces were not ashamed.[2]

Alleluya.   Thou, O God, art praised in Sion: and unto thee shall the vow be performed in Jerusalem.[3]

Gospel. St. Mark, viii. 1—9.

In those days . . . sent them away.

Offertory.

Like as in burnt offerings of rams and bullocks, and like as in ten thousands of fat lambs, so let our sacrifice be in thy sight this day, and grant that we may wholly go after thee; for they shall not be confounded that put their trust in thee, O Lord.[4]

Secret.

Favourably hear our supplications, O Lord, and mercifully receive these offerings of thy people, and that the vow of none may be of no effect, and that the request of none may be sent empty away, grant that the things which we ask faithfully, we may obtain effectually.   Through etc.

Communion.

Bow down thine ear to me: make haste to deliver me.[5]

Postcommunion.

We beseech thee, O Lord, to grant that having been replenished with thy gifts, we may both be cleansed by their efficacy and strengthened by their aid.   Through etc.

---

[1] Ps. xxxiv. 11.   [2] Ib. 5.   [3] Ps. lxv. 1.
[4] Song of the Three Children, 17.   [5] Ps. xxxi. 2.

Epistle.   Rom. viii. 1—6.

There is therefore now . . . life and peace.

Gospel.   St. Matt. xii. 1—7.

At that time Jesus . . . the guiltless.

EIGHTH SUNDAY AFTER TRINITY.

At Mass.   *Office.*

We wait for thy loving-kindness, O God, in the midst of thy temple.   O God, according to thy name, so is thy praise unto the world's end : thy right hand is full of righteousness.[1]

Ps.   Great is the Lord, and highly to be praised : in the city of our God, even upon his holy hill.[2]

Collect.

O God, whose providence ordereth all things, we humbly beseech thee to put away from us all hurtful things, and to give us those things which be profitable for us.   Through etc.

Epistle.   Rom. viii. 12—17.

Therefore, brethren, we . . . joint-heirs with Christ.

Gradual.

And be thou my strong rock, and house of defence, that thou mayest save me.[3]

℣.   In thee, O Lord God, have I put my trust : let me never be put to confusion.[4]

Alleluya.   ℣.   Hear my law, O my people.[5]

Gospel.   St. Matt. vii. 15—21.

Beware of false . . . which is in heaven.

---

[1] Ps. xlviii. 8, 9.   [2] *Ib.* 1.

[3] Ps. xxxi. 3.   [4] *Ib.* 1.   [5] Ps. lxxviii. 1.

Offertory.

For thou shalt save the people that are in adversity: and shalt bring down the high looks of the proud. For who is God, beside thee, O Lord?[1]

Secret.

O God, who by one perfect sacrifice hast confirmed the various offerings under the law, accept this sacrifice offered unto thee by thy devout servants, and sanctify it by a like blessing to that wherewith thou didst sanctify the offering of righteous[2] Abel, that what each hath offered in honour of thy majesty may be profitable for the salvation of all. Through.

Communion.

O taste and see how gracious the Lord is: blessed is the man that trusteth in him.[3]

Postcommunion.

May thy wholesome working, O Lord, both mercifully set us free from our perverse ways, and lead us unto those things which be rightful. Through etc.

WEDNESDAY.

Epistle. Rom. v. 8—11.
God commendeth . . . Lord Jesus Christ.

Gospel. St. Mark, ix. 38—48.
Master, we saw . . . is not quenched.

NINTH SUNDAY AFTER TRINITY.

At Mass. *Office.*

Behold, God is my helper: the Lord is with them that uphold my soul. He shall reward evil unto mine

---

[1] Ps. xviii. 27, 31.

[2] *justi.* The translation 'righteous' is copied from the A. V. in St. Matt. xxiii. 35. The *justi* as a class are enumerated among departed saints, liturgically. See Harl. MS. 7653 in Antiphonary of Bangor, part ii. p. 86. The title is no doubt borrowed from Heb. xii. 23.

[3] Ps. xxxiv. 8.

enemies: destroy thou them in thy truth, O God, my defender.[1]

Ps. Save me, O God, for thy name's sake: and avenge me in thy strength.[2]

Collect.

Grant to us, Lord, we beseech thee, the spirit to think and do always such things as be rightful; that we, who cannot exist without thee, may be enabled to live according to thy will.   Through etc.

Epistle.   1 Cor. x. 6—13.

Let us not lust . . . able to bear it.

Gradual.

O Lord, our Governor, how excellent is thy name in all the world.[3]

V. Thou that hast set thy glory above the heavens.[4]

Alleluya.   *V.* Sing we merrily unto God our strength: make a cheerful noise unto the God of Jacob.   Take the psalm: the merry harp with the lute.[5]

Gospel.   St. Luke, xvi. 1—9.

There was a certain rich . . . habitation.

Offertory.

The statutes of the Lord are right and rejoice the heart: sweeter also than honey and the honey-comb, and thy servant keepeth them.[6]

Secret.

Receive, we beseech thee, O Lord, the gifts which of thine own bounty we present unto thee, that these most holy mysteries may, by the powerful working of thy grace, make us holy in conversation in this present life, and bring us to the joys everlasting.   Through etc.

---

[1] Ps. liv. 4, 5.   [2] *Ib.* 1.   [3] Ps. viii. 1.   [4] *Ib.*
[5] Ps. lxxxi. 1, 2.   [6] Ps. xix. 8, 10, 11.

Communion.

Seek ye first the kingdom of God, and all things shall be added unto you, saith the Lord.[1]

Postcommunion.

We beseech thee, O Lord, that this heavenly mystery may renew us both in soul and body, that we may inwardly perceive the virtue of that which we outwardly perform. Through etc.

WEDNESDAY.

Epistle. Rom. vi. 16—18.

Know ye not . . . of righteousness.

Gospel. St. Luke, xvi. 10—15.

He that is faithful . . . sight of God.

TENTH SUNDAY AFTER TRINITY.

At Mass.   *Office.*

When I called upon the Lord, he heard my voice from the battle that was against me, and brought them down, even God that endureth for ever. O cast thy burden upon the Lord, and he shall nourish thee.[2]

Ps. Hear my prayer, O God: and hide not thyself from my petition. Take heed unto me, and hear me.[3]

Collect.

Let thy merciful ears, O Lord, be open to the prayers of thy humble servants; and that they may obtain their petitions make them to ask such things as shall please thee. Through etc.

Epistle. 1 Cor. xii. 2—11.

Ye know that ye . . . as he will.

---

[1] St. Matt. vi. 33.   [2] From Ps. lv. 17-20, 23.   [3] *Ib.* 1, 2.

Gradual.

Keep me, O Lord, as the apple of an eye: hide me under the shadow of thy wings.[1]

℣. Let my sentence come forth from thy presence: and let thine eyes look upon the thing that is equal.[2]

Alleluya. ℣. O Lord God of my salvation, I have cried day and night before thee.[3]

Gospel. St. Luke, xix. 41—47.

And when he was come . . . in the temple.

Offertory.

Unto thee, O God, will I lift up my soul: my God, I have put my trust in thee: O let me not be confounded, neither let mine enemies triumph over me. For all they that hope in thee shall not be ashamed.[4]

Secret.

Grant us, O Lord, we beseech thee, frequently and worthily to approach these mysteries, because, as often as this commemorative sacrifice is celebrated, the work of our redemption is carried out. Through etc.

Communion.

Thou shalt be pleased with the sacrifice of righteousness, with the burnt offerings and oblations upon thine altar, O Lord.[5]

Postcommunion.

May communion in thy sacrament, O Lord, both bestow upon us purity and contribute to our unity. Through etc.

Wednesday.

Epistle. 1 Cor. xv. 39—46.

All flesh is not . . . which is spiritual.

Gospel. St. Luke, xxi. 34—36.

Take heed to yourselves . . . Son of man.

---

[1] Ps. xvii. 8.   [2] Ib. 2.   [3] Ps. lxxxviii. 1.
[4] Ps. xxv. 1, 2.   [5] Ps. li. 19.

2 C

Eleventh Sunday after Trinity.

At Mass.   *Office.*

God in his holy habitation, God that maketh men to be of one mind in an house: he will give strength and power unto his people.[1]

Ps. Let God arise, and let his enemies be scattered: let them also that hate him flee before him.[2]

Collect.

O God, who declarest thy almighty power most chiefly in shewing mercy and pity, mercifully grant unto us thy grace, that we, running the way of thy promises, may be made partakers of thy heavenly treasure. Through etc.

Epistle. 1 Cor. xv. 1—10.

Moreover, brethren, . . . not in vain.

Gradual.

My heart hath trusted in God and I am helped: therefore my heart danceth for joy, and in my song will I praise him.[3]

V. Unto thee will I cry, O Lord: my God, think no scorn of me.[4]

Alleluya. *V.* Lord, thou hast been our refuge: from one generation to another.[5]

Gospel. St. Luke, xviii. 9—14.

And he spake . . . shall be exalted.

Offertory.

I will magnify thee, O Lord, for thou hast set me up, and not made my foes to triumph over me. O Lord my God, I cried unto thee, and thou hast healed me.[6]

Secret.

May this consecrated oblation be presented before thee, O Lord, which thou hast in such wise appointed to be

---

[1] Ps. lxviii. 5, 6, 35.   [2] *Ib.* 1.   [3] Ps. xxviii. 8.   [4] *Ib.* 1.
[5] Ps. xc. 1.   [6] Ps. xxx. 1, 2.

offered in honour of thy name, that it may at the same time be made to work our healing. Through etc.

Communion.

Honour the Lord with thy substance, and with the first fruits of all thine increase: so shall thy barns be filled with plenty, and thy presses shall burst out with new wine.[1]

Postcommunion.

We beseech thee, O Lord our God, that thou wouldest mercifully never leave those destitute of thy aid whom thou ceasest not to restore by divine sacraments. Through etc.

WEDNESDAY.

Epistle. 1 Cor. vi. 15—20.

Know ye not . . . in your body.

Gospel. St. Luke, xviii. 1—8.

And he spake . . . avenge them speedily.

TWELFTH SUNDAY AFTER TRINITY.

At Mass.   *Office.*

Haste thee, O God, to deliver me: make haste to help me, O God. Let them be ashamed and confounded that seek after my soul.[2]

Ps. Let them be turned backward and put to confusion that wish me evil.[3]

Collect.

Almighty and everlasting God, who in the abundance of thy mercy art wont to give more than either we desire or deserve, pour down upon us thy mercy, forgiving us those things whereof our conscience is afraid, and giving us those things which we are not worthy to ask. Through etc.

---

[1] Prov. iii. 9, 10.   [2] Ps. lxx. 1, 2.   [3] *Ib.* 2.

Epistle. 2 Cor. iii. 4—9.

Such trust have we . . . in glory.

Gradual.

I will alway give thanks unto the Lord: his praise shall ever be in my mouth.[1]

℣. My soul shall make her boast in the Lord: the humble shall hear thereof and be glad.[2]

Alleluya. ℣. O come, let us sing unto the Lord: let us heartily rejoice in the strength of our salvation.[3]

Another Verse.

℣. Let us come before his presence with thanksgiving: and shew ourselves glad in him with psalms.[4]

Gospel. St. Mark, vii. 31—37.

And again departing . . . dumb to speak.

Offertory.

Moses besought the Lord his God, and said, Lord, why doth thy wrath wax hot against thy people? Spare the wrath of thy soul. Remember Abraham, Isaac, and Jacob, to whom thou swarest to give a land flowing with milk and honey. And the Lord repented of the evil which he said he would do unto his people.[5]

Secret.

Look down, we beseech thee, O Lord, mercifully on this our bounden service; that the gift which we offer may be acceptable to thee, and may be a succour to our frailty. Through etc.

Communion.

The earth is filled with the fruit of thy works, O Lord: that he may bring food out of the earth, and wine that maketh glad the heart of man, and oil to make him a cheerful countenance, and bread to strengthen man's heart.[6]

---

[1] Ps. xxxiv. 1.   [2] Ib. 2.   [3] Ps. xcv. 1.   [4] Ib. 2.
[5] Adapted from Exod. xxxii. 11-14.   [6] Ps. civ. 13, 15.

Postcommunion.

Grant, we beseech thee, O Lord, that in partaking of thy sacrament we may have a sense of support both in mind and body, and being saved in both we may glory in the fulness of the heavenly healing. Through etc.

WEDNESDAY.

Epistle. 2 Cor. iv. 5—11.

We preach not ourselves . . . mortal flesh.

Gospel. St. Matt. xi. 20—24.

Then began he to upbraid . . . than for thee.

THIRTEENTH SUNDAY AFTER TRINITY.

At Mass. *Office.*

Look upon the covenant, O Lord, and forget not the congregation of the poor for ever. Arise, O God, maintain thine own cause: forget not the voice of thine enemies.[1]

Ps. O God, wherefore art thou absent from us so long? Why is thy wrath so hot against the sheep of thy pasture?[2]

Collect.

Almighty and merciful God, of whose only gift it cometh that thy faithful people do unto thee true and laudable service, grant, we beseech thee, that we may without stumbling run the way of thy promises. Through etc.

Epistle. Gal. iii. 16—22.

Now to Abraham . . . them that believe.

---

[1] From Ps. lxxiv. 21, 20, 23, 24.   [2] *Ib.* 1.

Gradual.

Look upon thy covenant, O Lord, and forget not the congregation of the poor for ever.[1]

℣. Arise, O God, maintain thine own cause: and forget not the voice of thine enemies.[2]

Alleluya. ℣. For the Lord is a great God: and a great king above all the earth.[3]

Gospel. St. Luke, x. 23—37.

Blessed are the eyes . . . do thou likewise.

Offertory.

My hope hath been in thee, O Lord: I have said, Thou art my God. My time is in thy hand.[4]

Secret.

Mercifully look down, O Lord, we beseech thee, on the offerings which we present on thy holy altar; that by obtaining abundant pardon for us, they may redound to the honour of thy name. Through etc.

Communion.

Thou didst send us from heaven bread, O Lord, able to content every man's delight, and agreeing to every taste.[5]

Postcommunion.

We beseech thee, O Lord, that participation in this holy mystery may quicken us; and procure for us both pardon and protection. Through etc.

WEDNESDAY.

Epistle. 1 Thess. ii. 9—13.

Ye remember, brethren, . . . you that believe.

Gospel. St. Matt. xii. 14—21.

Then the Pharisees . . . Gentiles trust.

---

[1] Ps. lxxiv. 21, 20. [2] *Ib.* 23, 24. [3] Ps. xcv. 3.
[4] Ps. xxxi. 16-17. [5] Wisdom, xvi. 20.

FOURTEENTH SUNDAY AFTER TRINITY.

At Mass.   *Office.*

Behold, O God our defender, and look upon the face
of thine anointed.   For one day in thy courts : is better
than a thousand.[1]

Ps. O how amiable are thy dwellings, thou Lord of hosts.
My soul hath a desire and longing to enter into the courts of the
Lord.[2]

Collect.

Almighty and everlasting God, give unto us the
increase of faith, hope, and charity ; and that we may
obtain that which thou dost promise, make us to love that
which thou dost command.   Through etc.

Epistle. Gal. v. 16—24.

Walk in the Spirit . . . affections and lusts.

Gradual.

It is a good thing to give thanks unto the Lord : and to sing
praises unto thy name, O most highest.[3]

℣. To tell of thy loving kindness early in the morning, and of
thy truth in the night season.[4]

Alleluya. ℣. O give thanks unto the Lord, and call upon his
name : tell the people what things he hath done.[5]

Gospel. St. Luke, xvii. 11—19.

And it came to pass . . . made thee whole.

Offertory.

The angel of the Lord tarrieth round about them that fear him,
and delivereth them.   O taste and see how gracious the Lord is.[6]

Secret.

Be favourable, O Lord, to thy people ; be favourable
to their gifts ; that being appeased by this oblation, thou

---

[1] Ps. lxxxiv. 9, 10.   [2] *Ib.* 1.   [3] Ps. xcii. 1.   [4] *Ib.* 2.
[5] Ps. cv. 1.   [6] Ps. xxxiv. 7, 8.

mayest bestow upon us pardon, and grant our requests.
Through etc.

Communion.

The bread that I will give is my flesh, which I will give for the
life of the world.[1]

Postcommunion.

May thy sacraments, O God, continually purify and
strengthen us, and lead us to the attainment of everlasting
salvation.   Through etc.

WEDNESDAY.

Epistle.   1 Tim. i. 8—14.

We know that the law . . . in Christ Jesus.

Gospel.   St. Luke, xx. 1—8.

And it came to pass . . . do these things.

FIFTEENTH SUNDAY AFTER TRINITY.

At Mass.   *Office.*

Bow down thine ear, O Lord, and hear me : my God,
save thy servant that putteth his trust in thee.   Be
merciful unto me, O Lord, for I will call daily upon thee.[2]

Ps.   Comfort the soul of thy servant : for unto thee, O Lord,
do I lift up my soul.[3]

Collect.

Keep, we beseech thee, O Lord, thy Church with thy
perpetual mercy, and because the frailty of man without
thee cannot but fall, keep us ever by thy help from all
things hurtful, and lead us to all things profitable to our
salvation.   Through etc.

Epistle.   Gal. v. 25, 26 ; vi. 1—10.

If we live . . . household of faith.

---

[1] St. John, vi. 51.   [2] Ps. lxxxvi. 1-3.   [3] *Ib.* 4.

Gradual.

It is better to trust in the Lord : than to put any confidence in man.[1]

℣. It is better to trust in the Lord : than to put any confidence in princes.[2]

Alleluya. ℣. O God, my heart is ready, my heart is ready : I will sing and give praise with the best member that I have.[3]

Gospel. St. Matt. vi. 24—33.

No man can . . . added unto you.

Offertory.

I waited patiently for the Lord : and he inclined unto me and heard my calling. And he hath put a new song in my mouth : even a thanksgiving unto our God.[4]

Secret.

Grant, O Lord, we beseech thee, that this saving offering may be to us both the cleansing away of our sins, and the reconciliation of us to thy loving kindness. Through etc.

Communion.

He that eateth my flesh, and drinketh my blood, dwelleth in me, and I in him, saith the Lord.[5]

Postcommunion.

May thy sacraments, O God, ever purify and strengthen us, and lead us to the attainment of everlasting salvation. Through etc.

WEDNESDAY.

Epistle. 1 Tim. i. 8—14.

But we know . . . in Christ Jesus.

Gospel. St. Luke, xx. 1—8.

And it came to pass . . . I do these things.

---

[1] Ps. cxviii. 8. [2] Ib. 9. [3] Ps. cviii. 1.
[4] Ps. xl. 1, 3. [5] St. John, vi. 56.

Sixteenth Sunday after Trinity.

At Mass.   *Office.*

Be merciful unto me, O Lord: for I will call daily upon thee. For thou, Lord, art good and gracious, and of great mercy unto all them that call upon thee.[1]

Ps. Bow down thine ear, O Lord, and hear me: for I am poor and in misery.[2]

Collect.

O Lord, we beseech thee, let thy continual pity cleanse and defend thy Church, and because it cannot continue in safety without thy succour, let it be governed evermore by thy favour. Through etc.

Epistle. Eph. iii. 13—21.

I desire that . . . without end. Amen.

Gradual.

The heathen shall fear thy name, O Lord: and all the kings of the earth thy majesty.[3]

℣. When the Lord shall build up Sion: and when his glory shall appear.[4]

Alleluya. ℣. Ye that fear the Lord, put your trust in the Lord: he is their helper and defender.[5]

Gospel. St. Luke, vii. 11—16.

And it came to pass . . . visited his people.

Offertory.

Make haste, O Lord, to help me. Let them be ashamed and confounded together, that seek after my soul to destroy it.[6]

Secret.

We beseech thee, O Lord, that thy sacrament may keep us in safety; and ever defend us against the assaults of the devil. Through etc.

---

[1] Ps. lxxxvi. 3, 5.   [2] *Ib.* 1.   [3] Ps. cii. 15.   [4] *Ib.* 16.
[5] Ps. cxv. 11.   [6] Ps. xl. 16, 17.

Communion.

Lord, I will make mention of thy righteousness only. Thou, O God, hast taught me from my youth up until now : forsake me not, O God, in mine old age, when I am grey headed.[1]

Postcommunion.

We beseech thee, O Lord, that the working of this heavenly gift may take possession both of our souls and bodies ; that what it alloweth, and not that which our own mind deviseth, may continually prevent us. Through etc.

WEDNESDAY.

Epistle. Col. ii. 8—13.

Beware lest any man . . . all trespasses.

Gospel. St. Mark, viii. 22—26.

And he cometh . . . any in the town.

SEVENTEENTH SUNDAY AFTER TRINITY.

At Mass.   *Office.*

Righteous art thou, O Lord : and true is thy judgment. O deal with thy servant according unto thy loving mercy.[2]

Ps. Blessed are those that are undefiled in the way : and walk in the law of the Lord.[3]

Collect.

Lord, we pray thee that thy grace may always prevent and follow us, and make us continually to be given to good works. Through etc.

Epistle. Eph. iv. 1—6.

I, therefore, the prisoner . . . in you all.

---

[1] Ps. lxxi. 14-16.   [2] Ps. cxix. 137, 124.   [3] *Ib.* 1.

Gradual.

Blessed are the people whose God is the Lord Jehovah: and blessed are the folk that the Lord hath chosen to him to be his inheritance.[1]

℣. By the word of the Lord were the heavens made: and all the hosts of them by the breath of his mouth.[2]

Alleluya. ℣. The right hand of the Lord bringeth mighty things to pass: the right hand of the Lord hath the pre-eminence.[3]

Gospel. St. Luke, xiv. 1—11.

And it came to pass . . . be exalted.

Offertory.

I Daniel prayed unto my God, and said: Hear, O Lord, the prayers of thy servant: cause thy face to shine upon thy sanctuary; and mercifully look down upon this thy people, which is called by thy name, O God.[4]

Secret.

Cleanse us, O Lord, we beseech thee, by the effectual working of this present sacrifice; and by thy mercy make us meet to be partakers thereof. Through etc.

Communion.

Promise unto the Lord your God, and keep it, all ye that are round about him: bring presents unto him that ought to be feared. He shall refrain the spirit of princes: and is wonderful among the kings of the earth.[5]

Postcommunion.

We beseech thee, O Lord, mercifully to purify our souls, that we may receive consequently help for our bodies both now and hereafter. Through etc.

WEDNESDAY.

The Epistle and Gospel are the same as those appointed for the Wednesday after the twenty-third Sunday after Trinity.

[1] Ps. xxxiii. 12. [2] Ib. 6. [3] Ps. cxviii. 16.
[4] From Dan. ix. 4, 17, 18. [5] Ps. lxxvi. 11, 12.

EIGHTEENTH SUNDAY AFTER TRINITY.

At Mass.   *Office.*

Give peace, O Lord, to them that wait for thee, and let thy prophets be found faithful. Hear the prayers of thy servant, and of thy people Israel.[1]

Ps. I was glad when they said unto me: We will go into the house of the Lord.[2]

Collect.

Lord, we beseech thee, grant thy people grace to withstand the temptations of the devil, and with pure minds to follow thee the only God. Through etc.

Epistle. 1 Cor. i. 4—8.

I thank my God . . . our Lord Jesus Christ.

Gradual.

I was glad when they said unto me: We will go into the house of the Lord.[3]

℣. Peace be within thy walls: and plenteousness within thy palaces.[4]

Alleluya. ℣. I was glad when they said unto me: We will go into the house of the Lord.[5]

[Alleluya.] ℣. Our feet shall stand in thy gates: O Jerusalem.[6]

These last two Verses are said alternately throughout the week, but in such wise that Our feet shall stand etc. *is said first, when the service is ferial. If there be no ferial day throughout the week vacant for this purpose, then in that year the last Verse shall be omitted altogether.*

Gospel. St. Matt. xxii. 35—46.

Then one of them . . . any more questions.

Offertory.

Moses consecrated an altar unto the Lord, offering burnt-offerings thereon, and sacrificing a peace offering: he made an evening

---

[1] Adapted from Ecclus. xxxvi. 16, 17.   [2] Ps. cxxii. 1.   [3] *Ib.*
[4] Ps. cxxii. 7.   [5] *Ib.* 1.   [6] *Ib.* 2.

sacrifice for a sweet odour to the Lord God in the sight of the children of Israel.[1]

Secret.

We humbly beseech thy majesty, O Lord, that these holy things which we present, may set us free both from past and from future transgressions. Through etc.

Communion.

Bring presents, and come into his courts. O worship the Lord in the beauty of holiness.[2]

Postcommunion.

Almighty God, we beseech thee, that by thy sanctifying ordinances both our vices may be cured, and eternal healing may spring up for us. Through etc.

WEDNESDAY.

Epistle. Rom. xv. 30—33.

Now I beseech you . . . with you all. Amen.

Gospel. St. Matt. xiii. 31—35.

The kingdom of heaven . . . of the world.

NINETEENTH SUNDAY AFTER TRINITY.

At Mass. *Office.*

I am the salvation of the people, saith the Lord: in whatsoever distress they shall call upon me, I will hear them; and I will be their Lord for ever.[3]

Ps. Hear my law, O ye people: incline your ears unto the words of my mouth.[4]

Collect.

O Lord, forasmuch as without thee we are not able to please thee, we beseech thee that thy pity may work in us and direct our hearts. Through etc.

---

[1] Based upon Exod. xxiv. 4, 5.   [2] Ps. xcvi. 8, 9.
[3] Source unknown. Compare ii. Chron. xx. 9.   [4] Ps. lxxviii. 1.

Epistle. Eph. iv. 23—28.

Be renewed . . . to him that needeth.

Gradual.

Let my prayer be set forth in thy sight as the incense, O Lord.[1]

℣. Let the lifting up of my hands be an evening sacrifice.[2]

Alleluya. ℣. They that put their trust in the Lord shall be even as the mount Sion : which may not be removed, but standeth fast for ever, in Jerusalem.[3]

Gospel. St. Matt. ix. 1—8.

And he entered into . . . unto men.

Offertory.

Though I walk in the midst of trouble, yet shalt thou refresh me, O Lord : thou shalt stretch forth thy hand upon the furiousness of mine enemies, and thy right hand shall save me.[4]

Secret.

O God, who by our communion in this sacred sacrifice makest us to be partakers of the one supreme divine nature, grant, we beseech thee, that as we know thy truth, so we may attain unto it by a worthy understanding and conversation. Through etc.

Communion.

Thou hast charged : that we shall diligently keep thy commandments. O that my ways were made so direct : that I might keep thy statutes![5]

Postcommunion.

We give thee thanks, O Lord, who hast fed us with this holy gift, beseeching thee of thy mercy that thou wouldest make us worthy partakers of it. Through etc.

---

[1] Ps. cxli. 2. [2] *Ib.* [3] Ps. xxv. 1.
[4] Ps. cxxxviii. 7. [5] Ps. cxix. 4, 5.

WEDNESDAY.

Epistle. 2 Thess. ii. 15—17; iii. 1—5.
Therefore, brethren, stand . . . waiting for Christ.

Gospel. St. Matt. xiii. 36—43.
His disciples came . . . let him hear.

TWENTIETH SUNDAY AFTER TRINITY.

At Mass.   *Office.*

In all things that thou hast brought upon us, O Lord,
thou hast executed true judgment: we have trespassed,
and not obeyed thy commandments, but give glory to thy
name, and deal with us according to the multitude of thy
mercy.[1]

Ps. Great is the Lord and highly to be praised: in the city of
our God, even upon his holy hill.[2]

Collect.

O almighty and merciful God, of thy bountiful goodness keep us, we beseech thee, from all things that may
hurt us, that we, being ready both in body and soul, may
cheerfully accomplish those things that thou wouldest
have done. Through etc.

Epistle. Ephes. v. 15—21.

See then that . . . fear of Christ.

Gradual.

The eyes of all wait upon thee, O Lord: and thou givest them
their meat in due season.[3]

℣. Thou openest thine hand: and fillest all things living with
plenteousness.[4]

Alleluya. ℣. Out of the deep have I called unto thee, O
Lord: Lord, hear my voice.[5]

---

[1] Partly from Song of the Three Children, 5-7, 19, 20.
[2] Ps. xlviii. 1.   [3] Ps. cxlv. 15.   [4] *Ib.* 16.   [5] Ps. cxxx. 1.

Gospel.   St. Matt. xxii. 1—14.

And Jesus answered . . . few are chosen.

Offertory.

By the waters of Babylon we sat down and wept: when we remembered thee, O Sion.[1]

Secret.

Grant, we beseech thee, O Lord, that these gifts which we offer in the sight of thy majesty may be profitable for our salvation.   Through etc.

Communion.

O think upon thy servant, O Lord, as concerning thy word: wherein thou hast caused me to put my trust.   The same is my comfort in my trouble.[2]

Postcommunion.

May thy healing virtue, O Lord, both mercifully free us from our frowardness, and make us ever hold fast to thy commandments.   Through etc.

WEDNESDAY.

Epistle.   2 Tim. ii. 1—7.

Thou, therefore, my son, . . . in all things.

Gospel.   St. Luke, xiv. 12—15.

When thou makest . . . kingdom of God.

TWENTY-FIRST SUNDAY AFTER TRINITY.

At Mass.　　　　　　　*Office.*

O Lord, the whole world is in thy power, and there is no man that can gainsay thee; for thou hast made all things, heaven, and earth, and all the wondrous things under heaven.   Thou art lord of all things.[3]

---

[1] Ps. cxxxvii. 1.　　[2] Ps. cxix. 49, 50.　　[3] Esther, xiii. 9, 10, 11.

2 D

Ps. Blessed are those that are undefiled in the way: and walk in the law of the Lord.[1]

Collect.

Grant, we beseech thee, merciful Lord, to thy faithful people pardon and peace; that they may be cleansed from all their sins, and serve thee with a quiet mind. Through etc.

Epistle. Ephes. vi. 10—17.

Finally, my brethren, be strong . . . word of God.

Gradual.

Lord, thou hast been our refuge: from one generation to another.[2]

V. Before the mountains were brought forth, or ever the earth and the world were made: thou art God from everlasting, and world without end.[3]

Alleluya. *V.* Praise the Lord, O my soul; while I live will I praise the Lord: yea, as long as I have any being, I will sing praises unto my God.[4]

Gospel. St. John, iv. 46—53.

There was a certain . . . his whole house.

Offertory.

There was a man in the land whose name was Job, perfect and upright, and one that feared God: and Satan asked that he might tempt him; and power was given him by the Lord over his possessions, and over his flesh, and he destroyed all his substance, and his sons; he smote his flesh also with a grievous boil.[5]

Secret.

Let these mysteries, O Lord, we beseech thee, provide for us a heavenly medicine, and cleanse away the vices of our hearts. Through etc.

---

[1] Ps. cxix. 1.   [2] Ps. xc. 1.   [3] *Ib.* 2.
[4] Ps. cxlvi. 1.   [5] Adapted from Job, i. 1 etc.

Communion.

My soul hath longed for thy salvation; and I have a good hope because of thy word. When wilt thou be avenged of them that persecute me? They persecute me falsely: be thou my help, O Lord my God.[1]

Postcommunion.

Make us, we beseech thee, O Lord, always to obey thy commandments, that we may be rendered worthy of thy sacred gifts. Through etc.

WEDNESDAY.

Epistle. 1 Thess. i. 4—10.

Knowing, brethren beloved . . . even Jesus.

Gospel. St. Luke, vi. 6—11.

And it came to pass . . . do to Jesus.

TWENTY-SECOND SUNDAY AFTER TRINITY.

At Mass.   *Office.*

If thou, Lord, wilt be extreme to mark what is done amiss: O Lord, who may abide it? For there is mercy with thee, O God of Israel.[2]

Ps. Out of the deep have I called unto thee, O Lord: Lord hear my voice.[3]

Collect.

Lord, we beseech thee to keep thy household [the Church] in continual godliness; that through thy protection it may be free from all adversities, and devoutly given to serve thee in good works, to the glory of thy name. Through etc.

Epistle. Phil. i. 6—11.

We are confident . . . praise of God.

[1] Ps. cxix. 81, 84, 86.   [2] Ps. cxxx. 3, 4.   [3] *Ib.* 1.

Gradual.

Behold how good and joyful a thing it is: brethren, to dwell together in unity! [1]

℣. It is like the precious ointment upon the head, that ran down unto the beard: even unto Aaron's beard. [2]

Alleluya. ℣. He healeth those that are broken in heart: and giveth medicine to heal their sickness. [3]

Another verse.

[Alleluya.] The Lord promised his blessing: and life for ever-more. [4]

These last two Verses are said alternately throughout the week, when the service is ferial. If there be no ferial day throughout the week vacant for this purpose, then the second Verse shall be omitted altogether.

Gospel. St. Matt. xviii. 23—35.

The kingdom of heaven . . . their trespasses.

Offertory.

Remember me, O Lord, who art above all power; give me proper and eloquent speech in my mouth, that my words may be pleasing in the presence of princes. [5]

Secret.

Mercifully receive, O Lord, the sacrifice by which thou hast willed that both thou thyself shouldest be propitiated, and that salvation should be restored to us in the might of thy loving-kindness. Through etc.

Communion.

I say unto you, there is joy in the presence of the angels of God over one sinner that repenteth. [6]

Postcommunion.

Having partaken of the food of immortality, we beseech thee, O Lord, that that which we have received

---

[1] Ps. cxxxiii. 1.   [2] *Ib.* 2.   [3] Ps. cxlvii. 3.   [4] Ps. cxxxiii. 4.
[5] Based upon Esther, xiv. 12, 13.   [6] St. Luke, xv. 10.

with our mouths may bring forth in us the fruit of pure minds. Through etc.

WEDNESDAY.

Epistle. Rom. iii. 19—26.

Now we know that . . . believeth in Jesus.

Gospel. St. Mark, xi. 23—26.

Verily I say . . . forgive your trespasses.

TWENTY-THIRD SUNDAY AFTER TRINITY.

At Mass.   *Office.*

I know the thoughts that I think toward you, saith the Lord, thoughts of peace and not of evil. Then shall ye call upon me, and I will hearken unto you, and I will turn away your captivity from all places.[1]

Ps. Lord, thou hast become gracious unto thy land: thou hast turned away the captivity of Jacob.[2]

Collect.

O God, our refuge and strength, who art the author of all godliness, be ready to hear the devout prayers of thy Church; and grant that those things which we ask faithfully we may obtain effectually. Through etc.

Epistle. Phil. iii. 17—21.

Brethren, be followers . . . unto himself.

Gradual.

It is thou, O Lord, that savest us from our enemies: and puttest them to confusion that hate us.[3]

℣. We make our boast of God all day long: and will praise thy name for ever.[4]

Alleluya. ℣. He maketh peace in thy borders: and filleth thee with the flour of wheat.[5]

---

[1] From Jer. xxix. 11, 12, 14.   [2] Ps. lxxxv. 1.
[3] Ps. xliv. 8.   [4] *Ib.* 9.   [5] Ps. cxlvii. 14.

Gospel. St. Matt. xxii. 15—21.

Then went the Pharisees . . . that are God's.

Offertory.

Out of the deep have I called unto thee, O Lord: Lord, hear my voice.[1]

Secret.

We beseech thee, O Lord, to make us attentive unto thy sacred service; and that we may serve thee without any stain of offence, do thou thyself make us such as thou commandest us to be. Through etc.

Communion.

Verily, I say unto you, what things soever ye desire, when ye pray, believe that ye receive them, and ye shall have them.[2]

Postcommunion.

Having received, O Lord, the gifts of the holy mystery, we humbly beseech thee, that what thou hast commanded us to do in remembrance of thee, may be an effectual help to our weakness. Through etc.

WEDNESDAY.

Epistle. Rom. v. 17—21.

For if by one . . . Jesus Christ our Lord.

Gospel. St. Matt. xvii. 24—27.

When they were come . . . for me and thee.

TWENTY-FOURTH SUNDAY AFTER TRINITY.

At Mass.   *Office.*

I know the thoughts that I think toward you, saith the Lord, thoughts of peace and not of evil. Then shall ye call upon me, and I will hearken unto you, and I will turn away your captivity from all places.[3]

---

[1] Ps. cxxx. 1.   [2] St. Mark, xi. 24.   [3] From Jer. xxix. 11, 12, 14.

Ps. Lord, thou art become gracious unto thy land; thou hast turned away the captivity of Jacob.[1]

Collect.

O Lord, we beseech thee, absolve thy people from their offences; that through thy bountiful goodness we may be delivered from the bonds of those sins which by our frailty we have committed. Through etc.

Epistle. Col. i. 9—11.

For this cause . . . with joyfulness.

Gradual.

But it is thou, O Lord, that savest us from our enemies: and puttest them to confusion that hate us.[2]

℣. We make our boast of God all day long: and will praise thy name for ever.[3]

Alleluya. ℣. O Lord my God, in thee have I put my trust: save me from all them that persecute me, and deliver me.[4]

Gospel. St. Matt. ix. 18—22.

While he spake . . . from that hour.

Offertory.

Out of the deep have I called unto thee, O Lord: Lord, hear my voice.[5]

Secret.

We beseech thee, O Lord, that the offering of this present gift may cleanse us, and make us wholly worthy of the sacred things which we have received. Through etc.

Communion.

Verily, I say unto you, what things soever ye desire, when ye pray, believe that ye receive them, and ye shall have them.[6]

Postcommunion.

Receiving thy heavenly gift, we beseech thee, O Lord, that thou wilt not suffer that which thou hast ordained

[1] Ps. lxxxv. 1.   [2] Ps. xliv. 8.   [3] *Ib.* 9.
[4] Ps. vii. 1.   [5] Ps. cxxx. 1.   [6] St. Mark, xi. 24.

for the healing of thy faithful people to turn to our condemnation. Through etc.

WEDNESDAY.

Epistle. 1 Cor. x. 20—31.
I would not that . . . the glory of God.

Gospel. St. Matt. xxi. 28—32.
A certain man . . . might believe him.

SUNDAY NEXT BEFORE ADVENT.

At Mass. *Office.*

I know the thoughts that I think toward you, saith the Lord, thoughts of peace, and not of evil. Then shall ye call upon me, and I will hearken unto you, and I will turn away your captivity from all places.[1]

Ps. Lord, thou art become gracious unto thy land: thou hast turned away the captivity of Jacob.[2]

Collect.

Stir up, we beseech thee, O Lord, the wills of thy faithful people; that they more plenteously bringing forth the fruit of good works, may of thy loving-kindness be more plenteously rewarded. Through etc.

Lesson. Jer. xxiii. 5—8.
Behold the days . . . their own land.

Gradual.

It is thou that savest us from our enemies: and puttest them to confusion that hate us.[3]

℣. We make our boast of God all day long: and will praise thy name for ever.[4]

---

[1] From Jer. xxix. 11, 12, 14.   [2] Ps. lxxxv. 1.
[3] Ps. xliv. 8.   [4] Ps. xliv. 9.

Alleluya. ℣. The heathen shall fear thy name, O Lord: and all the kings of the earth thy majesty.[1]

Throughout the week, when the service is ferial, the following Verse is said:

Alleluya. ℣. When Israel came out of Egypt: and the house of Jacob from among the strange people.[2]

Or this Verse:

Alleluya. ℣. I will give thanks unto thee with my whole heart: even before the gods will I sing praise unto thee.[3]

Gospel. St. John, vi. 5—14.

When Jesus then lifted . . . into the world.

Offertory.

Out of the deep have I called unto thee, O Lord: Lord, hear my voice.[4]

Secret.

Favourably regard, O Lord, the sacrifice which is about to be offered unto thee, that it may both cleanse us from the corruptions of our present state and make us acceptable unto thy name. Through etc.

Communion.

Verily, I say unto you, what things soever ye desire, when ye pray, believe that ye receive them, and ye shall have them.[5]

Postcommunion.

Grant, we beseech thee, almighty God, that our souls having been satisfied with the divine gift, may be filled with a longing desire to be kindled by the flame of thy Spirit, and to shine as bright lights in the presence of Christ thy Son at his coming. Through etc.

---

[1] Ps. cii. 15.　　[2] Ps. cxiv. 1.　　[3] Ps. cxxxviii. 1.
[4] Ps. cxxx. 1.　　[5] St. Mark, xi. 24.

When the period between the first Sunday after Trinity[1] *and Advent Sunday is prolonged, the Office* I know the thoughts *etc. is to be sung on three Sundays, as has been previously laid down. When the period is short, then on the Sunday next before Advent shall always be sung the Mass with the Office* I know the thoughts etc. *Collect,* Stir up, we beseech thee, etc. *Epistle,* Behold the days come, etc. *Gospel,* When Jesus then lifted, etc. *But if there should not be a Sunday vacant, then it should have the first place to be sung on ferial days throughout the week. Other Sunday masses which shall have remained over should be sung on ferial days.*

EMBER WEDNESDAY IN SEPTEMBER.[2]

At Mass.   *Office.*

Sing we merrily unto God our strength : make a cheerful noise unto the God of Jacob. Take the psalm : the merry harp with the lute. Blow up the trumpet in the new moon : for this was made a statute for Israel, and a law of the God of Jacob.[3]

Ps. This he ordained in Joseph for a testimony : when he came out of the land of Egypt.[4]

No more is said. The Collect follows without The Lord be with you *and only with* Let us pray.

Collect.

We beseech thee, O Lord, that the frailty of our nature may be sustained by the support of thy mercy; that as in itself it continually decayeth, so by thy merciful goodness it may be renewed. Through etc.

---

[1] Referred to as *Deus omnium,* which are the opening words of the Respond to the first Lesson at Nocturns on the first Sunday after Trinity in the S. Breviary.

[2] The three September Ember Masses are printed in R. between the seventeenth and eighteenth Sundays after Pentecost.

[3] From Ps. lxxxi. 1-4.   [4] *Ib.* 5.

Lesson. Amos, ix. 13—15.

Behold the days come . . . the Lord thy God.

Gradual.

Come, ye children, and hearken unto me: I will teach you the fear of the Lord.[1]

℣. They had an eye unto him and were lightened: and their faces were not ashamed.[2]

The Gradual is not to be repeated. Both The Lord be with you *and* Let us pray *are said here.*

Collect.

Grant, we beseech thee, O Lord, the supplication of thy servants; that while they abstain from bodily food, their souls may also fast from sin. Through etc.

The usual Memories are to be said here.

Lesson. Nehem. viii. 1—10.[3]

And all the people . . . is your strength.

Gradual.

Who is like unto the Lord our God, that hath his dwelling so high: and yet humbleth himself to behold the things that are in heaven and earth?[4]

℣. He taketh up the simple out of the dust: and lifteth the poor out of the mire.[5]

Gospel. St. Mark, ix. 17—29.

And one of the multitude . . . and fasting.

Offertory.

And my delight shall be in thy commandments: which I have loved. My hands also will I lift up unto thy commandments, which I have loved.[6]

---

[1] Ps. xxxiv. 11. [2] *Ib.* 5. [3] Omitting part of verse 4.
[4] Ps. cxiii. 5. [5] *Ib.* 6. [6] Ps. cxix. 47, 48.

Secret.

O God, who hast willed to constitute thy sacrament of
these fruits of the earth, vouchsafe, we beseech thee,
through it to bestow upon us help both in this present
life and in the life eternal.   Through etc.

Communion.

Eat the fat, and drink the sweet, and send portions unto them
for whom nothing is prepared: for this day is holy unto the Lord
our God; neither be ye sorry, for the joy of the Lord is your
strength.[1]

Postcommunion.

Partaking, O Lord, of these heavenly gifts, we humbly
beseech thee that what by thy special grace we celebrate
with careful service, we may also by thy gift be worthily
disposed to receive.   Through etc.

EMBER FRIDAY.

At Mass.   *Office.*

Let the heart of them rejoice that seek the Lord.
Seek the Lord, and his strength: seek his face evermore.[2]

Ps.   O give thanks unto the Lord, and call upon his name:
tell the people what things he hath done.[3]

Collect.

Grant, we beseech thee, almighty God, that we who
observe these appointed holy times with yearly worship,
may please thee both in body and soul.   Through etc.

Lesson.   Hosea, xiv. 1—9.[4]

O Israel, return . . . walk in them.

Gradual.

Turn thee again, O Lord, at the last: and be gracious unto thy
servants.[5]

℣. Lord, thou hast been our refuge: from one generation to
another.[6]

---

[1] Nehem. viii. 10.   [2] Ps. cv. 3, 4.   [3] *Ib.* 1.
[4] Omitting part of verses 9 and 10 (Vulg.)   [5] Ps. xc. 13.   [6] *Ib.* 1.

Gospel. St. Luke, vii. 36—50.
And one of the Pharisees . . . go in peace.

Offertory.

Praise the Lord, O my soul: and forget not all his benefits; making thee young and lusty as an eagle.[1]

Secret.

We beseech thee, O Lord, that the offering of our fast may be acceptable unto thee, and by atoning for sin make us worthy of thy grace, and bring us to the things eternal which thou hast promised. Through etc.

Communion.

O turn from me shame and rebuke: for I have kept thy commandments, O Lord; for thy testimonies are my delight.[2]

Postcommunion.

We beseech thee, almighty God, that rendering thanks unto thee for the bounties which we have received, we may be partakers of still greater blessings. Through etc.

EMBER SATURDAY.

At Mass.   *Office.*

O come, let us worship and fall down: and kneel before the Lord our maker. For he is the Lord our God.[3]

Ps. O come, let us sing unto the Lord: let us heartily rejoice in the strength of our salvation.[4]

All Collects, except the last, are said without The Lord be with you, *and with* Let us pray *only.*

Collect.

Almighty and everlasting God, who by a wholesome abstinence healest both our bodies and souls, we humbly

---

[1] Ps. ciii. 2, 5.   [2] Ps. cxix. 22, 24.
[3] Ps. xcv. 6, 7.   [4] Ps. xcv. 1.

beseech thy majesty that thou wouldest graciously accept our devout prayers and fast, and grant us thy help both now and hereafter. Through etc.

All Lessons are to be read with their titles. The Lessons and Graduals are to be arranged from this point in the order laid down in the Advent Ember season.

Lesson. Levit. xxiii. 26—32.

And the Lord spake . . . your sabbath.

Gradual.

Be merciful, O Lord, to our sins, for thy name's sake. Wherefore do the heathen say: Where is now their God?[1]

℣. Help us, O God of our salvation: and for the glory of thy name, O Lord, deliver us.[2]

The Gradual is not to be repeated.

Collect.

Grant unto us, we beseech thee, almighty God, that by fasting we may be filled with thy grace, and that by abstinence we may be made stronger than all our enemies. Through etc.

Lesson. Levit. xxiii. 39—43.

In the fifteenth day . . . Lord your God.

Gradual.

Behold, O God our defender: and look upon thy servants.[3]

℣. O Lord God of hosts, hear the prayer of thy servants.[4]

Collect.

Grant, we beseech thee, O Lord, that thy faithful people may rejoice in the benefits which have been humbly implored; and that they who reverence thee by their outward fasting may be fulfilled with the abundance of thy good things. Through etc.

[1] Ps. lxxix. 9, 10.
[2] Ib. 9.
[3] From Ps. lxxxiv. 9.
[4] Ib. 8.

Lesson. Micah, vii. 14, 16, 18—20.

Feed thy people . . . days of old.

Gradual.

Let my prayer be set forth in thy sight as the incense, O Lord.[1]

℣. Let the lifting up of my hands be an evening sacrifice.[2]

Let us pray.

Collect.

Grant, we beseech thee, O Lord, that we may so abstain from carnal feastings, as to fast in like manner from the vices that assault us. Through etc.

Lesson. Zech. viii. 14—20.

Thus saith the Lord . . . the Lord of hosts.

Gradual.

Save thy people, O Lord, and give thy blessing unto thine inheritance.[3]

℣. Unto thee, O Lord, will I cry: think no scorn of me, O my God, lest I become like them that go down into the pit.[4]

Let us pray.

Collect.

As thou grantest unto us, O Lord, to offer unto thee this solemn fast, so bestow upon us, we beseech thee, the aid of thy pardoning mercy. Through etc.

Lesson. Song of the Three Children, 26—66.

The angel of the Lord . . . for ever.

The fifth Lesson The angel of the Lord etc. *is to be read in its entirety, as on the Ember Saturday in Whitsun-week.*[5]

---

[1] Ps. cxli. 2.   [2] *Ib.*
[3] Ps. xxviii. 10.   4 *Ib.* 1.   5 Page 356.

Then two clerks of the second rank, vested in surplices, and standing at the step of the quire, shall sing the following Tract together:

Tract.

Ever adore the Almighty,
And bless him for ever and ever.

The quire shall repeat the same lines.

Clerks. ℣. The stars of heaven, the whole race of men, both the sun and its sister, and the lights of the sky,

Quire. Ever adore etc.

Clerks. ℣. So, too, all the waters above, the dew and the rain, and every breeze,

Quire. And bless him etc.

Clerks. ℣. Fire and heat, burning and freezing, cold and warmth, and hoar-frost,

Quire. Ever adore etc.

Clerks. ℣. Snow and ice, both night and day, light and darkness, lightnings, clouds,

Quire. And bless him etc.

Clerks. ℣. Deserts, mountains, green herbs, hills, rivers, fountains, sea, and waters,

Quire. Ever adore etc.

Clerks. ℣. All things living which the sea beareth, the air quickeneth, and the earth nourisheth,

Quire. And bless him etc.

Clerks. ℣. Every race of men, Israel himself, and all the servants and worshippers of Christ,

Quire. Ever adore etc.

Clerks. ℣. Holy and humble men of kindly heart, and the three children that overcame,

Quire. And bless him etc.

Clerks. ℣. Ready duly to despise the flames of the fiery furnace, and the commands of the tyrant,

Quire. Ever adore etc.

Clerks. ℣. Praise be to the Begetter and to the Begotten; and praise be to the blessed holy Spirit,

Quire. And bless him etc.

Then shall the clerks recommence the Tract, Ever adore etc., *and it shall be sung through by the quire. And then shall follow* The Lord be with you *and* Let us pray.

Collect.

O God, who for the three children didst quench the flames of fire, grant, we beseech thee, that we thy servants may not be consumed by the flames of our sins. Through etc.

Epistle. Heb. ix. 2—12.

There was a tabernacle . . . redemption for us.

Two clerks of the second rank, vested in their black copes, and standing at the step of the quire, shall say together the following Tract, whole and entire:

Tract.

O praise the Lord, all ye heathen: praise him all ye nations.[1]

℣. For his merciful kindness is ever more and more towards us: and the truth of the Lord endureth for ever.[2]

Gospel. St. Luke, xiii. 6—17.

He spake also . . . done by him.

Offertory.

O Lord God of my salvation, I have cried day and night before thee: let my prayer enter into thy presence, O Lord.[3]

Secret.

We beseech thee, O Lord, to look favourably upon our gifts and fasts, for thou appointest the same that thou mayest be appeased thereby. Through etc.

---

[1] Ps. cxvii. 1.   [2] *Ib.* 2.

[3] Ps. lxxxviii. 1.

Communion.

In the seventh month ye shall keep a feast, because I made the children of Israel dwell in booths, when I brought them out of the land of Egypt.   I am the Lord your God.[1]

Postcommunion.

We beseech thee, O Lord, that thy sacrament may perfect in us that which it containeth; that we may receive in truth and reality what we now offer under a figure.   Through etc.

ANNIVERSARY OF DEDICATION OF A CHURCH.

At Mass.   *Office.*

How dreadful is this place! this is the house of God; and this is the gate of heaven; and it shall be called the court of God.[2]

In Easter-tide there shall be added Alleluya.

Ps.   The Lord is king, and hath put on glorious apparel: the Lord hath put on his apparel, and girded himself with strength.[3]

Collect.

O God, who restorest to us, year by year, the day of the consecration of this thy holy temple, and ever presentest us again in safety at thy holy mysteries; hearken unto the prayers of thy people, and grant that whosoever shall enter into this temple to ask any blessing, may rejoice to have obtained all his petitions.   Through etc.

Lesson.   Rev. xxi. 2—5.

And I John saw . . . all things new.

Gradual.

This place hath been made by God an inestimable mystery: it is without reproach.[4]

---

[1] Adapted from Levit. xxiii. 41-43.
[2] Partly from Gen. xxviii. 17.   [3] Ps. xciii. 1.   [4] Source unknown.

℣. O God, on whom the quire of angels attendeth, hear the prayers of thy servants.[1]

℟. Alleluya. ℣. I will worship toward thy holy temple, and praise thy name.[2]

The two following Alleluyas *are said alternately throughout the Octave, except on Sunday and on the Octave itself.*

Alleluya. ℣. How dreadful and adorable is this place: truly this is none other than the house of God, and the gate of heaven.[3]

Alleluya. ℣. The house of the Lord hath been established upon the top of the mountains, and hath been exalted above all hills.[4]

The following Sequence is said, even though the feast fall in Lent.

Sequence.

Jerusalem and Sion's daughters fair,
assembled band, who in the faith have share,
with joyful voice unceasingly declare
           Alleluya.

For on this day Christ for his spouse doth take
our mother for his faith and justice' sake,
whom he brought out of misery's deep lake,
           the holy Church.

She in the Holy Spirit's clemency,
bride in the bridegroom's grace rejoicing high,
in glorious place by queens exaltingly
           is callèd blessed.

Midst plaudits loud forthwith is given her dower,
a dower most wonderful! a threefold power
reaching to heaven, to earth, and to the lower
           dungeons of hell.

[1] Source unknown.   [2] Ps. cxxxviii. 2.
[3] Gen. xxviii. 17.   [4] Is. ii. 2 (Vulg.)

Doubt not my words, though marvellous they be,
her from his side, endowed thus wealthily,
As the God-man, a mighty mystery,
    himself brought forth.

That in such wise should be the Church's birth—
the woman showed in figure upon earth,
when she from Adam's side first issued forth,
    ill-omened Eve.

Eve was but step-mother to all her seed;
to the elect this mother is indeed
the port of life, and unto those in need
    a hiding-place.

Fair, wonderful in off-spring, great in might,
as moon, as sun, she shines in beauty bright,
more terrible than army for the fight
    set in array.

One and alone she is, yet manifold;
receiving all, yet one unbroken fold;
to multitudes, herself one, young and old
    she doth give birth.

This was by Jordan's parted waters shown,
this she who came from distant lands makes known,
attracted by the marvellous renown
    of Solomon's lore.

By divers types prefigured, this is she,
in bridal vesture clad resplendently,
above the heavenly hosts upraised to be
    with Christ conjoined.

O solemn festival of high delight!
which doth with Christ himself the Church unite,
wherein our own salvation's marriage rite
    we celebrate.

O entertainment sweet, assembly blest!
which to the fallen gives consoling rest;
to them that have lost hope, the sore distressed,
        a breathing time.

There are rewards unto the righteous given,
there joy anew God's angels in the heaven,
there hearts are gladdened with the gracious leaven
        of charity.

The source of wisdom from eternity,
by gracious, all-disposing scrutiny,
in the due course of things did this foresee
        should come to pass.

Therefore, when Christ his marriage-feast shall make,
may we with joy of true delights partake,
and never the blest company forsake
        of his elect.   Amen.

*Between Septuagesima and Ash Wednesday the following
Tract is said on the Octave only of this feast.*

Tract.

O how amiable are thy dwellings: thou Lord of hosts!
my soul hath a desire and longing to enter into the courts
of the Lord.[1]

℣. My heart and my flesh rejoice in the living God.[2]

℣. Yea, the sparrow hath found her an house, and
the swallow a nest where she may lay her young.[3]

℣. Even thy altars, O Lord of hosts, my king and
my God.[4]

℣. Blessed are they that dwell in thy house: they
will be alway praising thee.[5]

In Easter-tide the second Alleluya *of the Resurrection shall
be said daily throughout the Octave, and on the eighth and
also on the first day.*

[1] Ps. lxxxiv. 1, 2.   [2] *Ib.* 2.   [3] *Ib.* 3.   [4] *Ib.*   [5] *Ib.* 4.

Gospel. St. Luke xix. 1—10.

And Jesus entered . . . that which was lost.

Offertory.

O Lord God, in the uprightness of mine heart I have willingly offered all these things : and now have I seen with joy thy people which are present here : O God of Israel, keep the imagination of the heart of thy people.[1]

In Easter-tide shall be said Alleluya.

Secret.

Favourably answer our prayers, we beseech thee, O Lord ; that whosoever of us are met together within the circuit of these temple walls, in which we celebrate the anniversary of their dedication, may please thee with full and perfect devotion both of body and soul ; so that while we pay these our present vows, we may by thy help be made worthy to attain unto the reward everlasting. Through etc.

Ferial Preface.[2]

Communion.

My house shall be called the house of prayer, saith the Lord : in it whosoever asketh receiveth ; and he that seeketh findeth ; and unto him that knocketh it shall be opened.[3]

In Easter-tide there shall be added Alleluya, alleluya.

Postcommunion.

O God, who hast deigned to call the Church thy spouse, that she who obtained grace through her devout faith should also obtain dignity from that name ; grant that all this people, who serve thy name, may be found worthy to have a share in that title. Through etc.

If this feast fall between Septuagesima and Easter, there shall be said at the end of mass, Let us bless the Lord.

---

[1] From 1 Chron. xxix. 17, 18.   [2] Page 40.
[3] From St. Matt. xxi. 13, and vii. 8.

*But if it fall at any other time of the year, mass shall be con-
cluded with,* Depart, the mass is ended.   *This same mass of
the Dedication shall be said throughout the whole Octave,
whenever this feast shall fall (that is to say, from the Octave
of the Epiphany up to Septuagesima, and from the Octave of
Easter up to Ascension Day, and from the Feast of the Holy
Trinity up to the Advent of our Lord), unless a feast of nine
lessons shall intervene; but without Sequence and Creed; except
that on Sunday the following Sequence is said:*

Sequence.

Now let the faithful quire their serenade
   to high heaven sing;
The chamber of the queen is ready made
   for glory's king.
The lowly burr doth thus with lily wed,
   with sun a star;
To God the soul, in mystic union led,
   a shrine doth rear.
Christ and the Church, in chaste espousal knit,
   this day we praise;
Thus man to God his spirit doth unite
   in yoke of grace;
Flesh to the Son of God in marriage high
   hath thus attained;
The peerless Son to deep humility
   did condescend.
The mightiest one of low estate did seek,
and by his Word the bride, so dark and meek,
   made clean and white.
What he ordainèd he hath so fulfilled
who the impure could make, if so he willed,
   all pure as light.
O handmaid, haste thy liberty to gain,
that sceptred with thy husband thou may'st reign;
Thy spouse consider; him whom types disguise
true faith discerneth with unclouded eyes.

Octave of the Dedication of a Church.

Gospel. St. Luke, vi. 47, 48.
Whosoever cometh . . . upon a rock.

Creed.

All shall be done as on the first day, with this Sequence:

Sequence.

The dwellings of the Lord of hosts how fair!
the master-builder's courts how sure they are!
Unharmed by winds, or floods, or rain,
for ever settled they remain.
How majestic their foundations!
shadowy prefigurations
    they in mystic type portray.
Formed from sleeping Adam's side,
Eve of the approaching bride
    doth a sign convey.
Framed of wood the ark doth save
Noah guided o'er the wave,
    when the world was drowned.
Sarah, stricken now in years,
laughs when she an infant bears;
    her joy doth ours expound.
Long widowed, veiled in robes unfitting,
Thamar, by the wayside sitting,
    to Judah twins doth bear.
The royal maiden doth deliver
the infant Moses from the river,
    in bulrush ark laid near.
This is the male lamb sacrificed,
with which all Israel was sufficed,
    and by its blood brought nigh;
Of Sheba's utmost parts the queen
in quest of wisdom here is seen,
    king Solomon to try:

Black, yet comely, see we her,
perfumed with frankincense and myrrh,
    with balmy odours fraught.
Thus things to come which types concealed,
the day of grace hath now revealed,
    and illustration brought.
Now let us take our rest and sing,
with the belovèd tarrying,
    the marriage hour is come;
The trumpets, as the guests go in,
with echoing tones the feast begin,
    the psaltery charms them home;
Ten thousand thousand voices raise
with one consent the Bridegroom's praise,
    and Alleluya! Alleluya! cry,
    in everlasting joy, unceasingly.

Gospel. St. John, x. 22—30.
And it was at Jerusalem . . . are one.

The Creed is not said unless it be a Sunday. If the feast fall between Ash Wednesday and Maundy Thursday, notice shall be taken of the feast on the first day only, with the exception of the memory within the Octave, and on the Octave.

CONSECRATION OF A CHURCH.

At Mass.   *Office.*

How dreadful is this place! this is the house of God; and this is the gate of heaven; and it shall be called the court of God.[1]

In Easter-tide there shall be added Alleluya.

Ps. The Lord is king, and hath put on glorious apparel: the Lord hath put on his apparel, and girded himself with strength.[2] Glory be to the Father, etc.

[1] Partly from Gen. xxviii. 17.   [2] Ps. xciii. 1.

Collect.

O God, who art thyself the author of the gifts to be consecrated unto thee, pour forth thy benediction upon this house of prayer; that the help of thy defence may be perceived by all who call upon thy name. Through etc.

Epistle. Rev. xxi. 2—5.

And I John saw . . . all things new.

Gradual.

This place hath been made by God an inestimable mystery; it is without reproach.[1]

V. O God, on whom the quire of angels attendeth, hear the prayers of thy servants.[1]

Alleluya. *V*. I will worship toward thy holy temple, and praise thy name.[2]

Sequence.

The dwellings etc., *as on the Octave of a Dedication.*[3]

Gospel. St. Luke, xix., 1—10.

And Jesus entered . . . that which was lost.

Offertory.

O Lord God, in the uprightness of mine heart I have willingly offered all these things; and now have I seen with joy thy people which are present here: O God of Israel, keep the imagination of the heart of thy people.[4]

On Easter-tide there shall be added Alleluya.

Secret.

O God, who in every place of thy dominion art wholly present, and workest wholly, graciously accept the sacrifice offered to thy name; and as thou art the founder of this house, be thou also its protector, that in the power of the Holy Ghost they who serve thee here may alway have free access for devotion unto thyself. Through etc.

---

[1] Source unknown.　　　　　　　　[2] Ps. cxxxviii. 2.
[3] See p. 420.　　　　　　　　　[4] From 1 Chron. xxix. 17, 18.

Communion.

My house shall be called the house of prayer, saith the Lord: in it whosoever asketh receiveth; and he that seeketh findeth; and unto him that knocketh it shall be opened.[1]

In Easter-tide shall be added Alleluya, alleluya.

Postcommunion.

Refreshed by the sacrament of salvation, we render thanks to thee; and beseech thee to fill this temple with the glory of thy majesty, that in honour of thy name it may become unto thy people a house of prayer. Through etc.

RECONCILIATION OF A CHURCH.

At Mass.   *Office.*

When I shall be sanctified in you, I will gather you out of all countries. Then will I sprinkle clean water upon you, and ye shall be clean from all your filthiness, and a new spirit will I give you.[2]

In Easter-tide there shall be added Alleluya.

Ps. I will always give thanks unto the Lord: his praise shall ever be in my mouth.[3]

Collect.

O God, who hast said, My house shall be called a house of prayer, vouchsafe to cleanse and hallow this house, which hath been polluted and defiled by the abominations of the heathen; so that thou mayest mercifully hear and graciously perform the prayers and vows of them that call upon thee in this place. Who livest etc.

[1] From St. Matt. xxi. 13 and vii. 8.
[2] From Ezek. xxxvi. 23-26.   [3] Ps. xxxiv. 1.

Epistle. Rev. xxi. 2—5.

And I John saw . . . all things new.

Gradual.

Bring presents and come into his courts: O worship the Lord in the beauty of holiness.[1]

℣. The Lord discovereth the thick bushes: in his temple doth every man speak of his honour.[2]

Alleluya. ℣. O give thanks unto the Lord, and call upon his name: tell the people what things he hath done.[3]

Gospel.　St. Luke, vi. 43—48.

A good tree bringeth . . . upon a rock.

Offertory.

I Daniel prayed unto my God, saying, Hear, Lord, the prayers of thy servant; cause thy face to shine upon thy sanctuary, and graciously behold this people upon whom thy name hath been invoked, O God.[4]

Here shall be added Alleluya, alleluya.[5]

Secret.

We beseech thee, O Lord, that this offering may both cleanse this place from the impurities of wicked men, [*or* from the offence which has been committed,] and may make our supplications both here and everywhere acceptable unto thee. Through etc.

Communion.

Then shalt thou be pleased with the sacrifice of righteousness, with the burnt offerings and oblations, upon thine altar, O Lord.[6]

In Easter-tide shall be added Alleluya, alleluya.

[1] Ps. xcvi. 8, 9.　　　　　[2] Ps. xxix. 8.
[3] Ps. cv. 1.　　　　　[4] Partly from Dan. ix. 4, 17, 18.
[5] The Latin text adds here *in Tractu præcedente.*
[6] From Ps. li. 19.

Postcommunion.

Partaking of the gifts of eternal salvation, we humbly entreat thee, O Lord, that this temple [*or* cemetery] being cleansed from the pollutions of the heathen [*or* the wicked] may abide under the sanctification of thy blessing; and that our hearts being freed from all defilements of sin, may ever devoutly serve thee. Through etc.

Here endeth the Proper of Seasons.[1]

[1] *Finit Temporale.*

*Printed by Alexander Moring Ltd.,
The De La More Press, 32 George
Street, Hanover Square, London, W.*